MODERN WARFARE

MODERN WARFARE
Armed Groups, Private Militaries, Humanitarian Organizations, and the Law

Edited by Benjamin Perrin

UBCPress · Vancouver · Toronto

20 19 18 17 16 15 14 13 12   5 4 3 2 1

Printed in Canada on FSC-certified ancient-forest-free paper
(100% post-consumer recycled) that is processed chlorine- and acid-free.

Library and Archives Canada Cataloguing in Publication

Modern warfare : armed groups, private militaries, humanitarian organizations, and the law / edited by Benjamin Perrin.

Includes bibliographical references and index.
Also issued in electronic format.
ISBN 978-0-7748-2232-9 (bound); 978-0-7748-2233-6 (pbk.)

1. Humanitarian law. 2. Insurgency. I. Perrin, Benjamin

KZ6471.M63 2012   341.6'7   C2011-908219-5

Canadä

UBC Press gratefully acknowledges the financial support for our publishing program of the Government of Canada (through the Canada Book Fund), the Canada Council for the Arts, and the British Columbia Arts Council.

This book has been published with the help of a grant from the Canadian Federation for the Humanities and Social Sciences, through the Aid to Scholarly Publications Program, using funds provided by the Social Sciences and Humanities Research Council of Canada.

UBC Press
The University of British Columbia
2029 West Mall
Vancouver, BC V6T 1Z2
www.ubcpress.ca

To my Grandfathers, both of whom inspired me.
One showed me the enduring value of diligent research.
The other served the cause of freedom in the Canadian
Armed Forces.

Contents

Preface

This book is the culmination of "The Edges of Conflict" project, which began in 2007 as a joint initiative between the University of British Columbia's Liu Institute for Global Issues and the Canadian Red Cross to engage in the debate regarding the changing nature of armed conflict and to improve respect for the rule of law in complex security environments. The specific goals of the endeavour were threefold:

- to examine and debate contemporary challenges of armed conflict
- to develop new conceptual approaches, policy recommendations, and areas for further research to address the challenge to international humanitarian law posed by the changing nature of armed conflict
- to raise awareness of contemporary conflict issues, build Canadian capacity, and ensure policy coherence by engaging a wide range of Canadian and international actors.

The project began in January 2008 with a consultation in the form of a "fast-talk" with several leading experts in order to narrow and identify areas for research. As a result of this consultation, five research papers were commissioned and published on the project website (http://www.edgesofconflict.com) in March 2008. From these initial papers, the path for future research became clear, with two main thematic areas emerging.

The first is the complex interaction in conflict and post-conflict settings between non-state actors (including humanitarian organizations, private military and security companies, and non-state armed groups) and state armed forces. The interplay between these diverse actors has given rise to concepts such as "humanitarian space" and counterinsurgency doctrine in order to manage the tensions between them. The coexistence of these actors in modern armed conflict thus became a central focus of the project from the very beginning. The second area of interest arising from the "fast-talk process" focused on violence that does not fall within the definition of an armed conflict but is detrimental and threatening to civilian populations, such as low-level insurgencies and endemic urban violence.

These two thematic areas are of particular relevance to Canadians due to the overseas missions of the Canadian Forces in areas such as Afghanistan and Haiti, as well as the plethora of humanitarian organizations that are based in Canada and that operate in conflict and post-conflict environments around the world.

Following the initial phase of research, the project advisory group decided to host an international conference in Vancouver, British Columbia, in 2009. Experts from Canada and around the world came to share their current research in the priority areas that were identified through the fast-talk process and commissioned research papers. The conference included a specialized panel on Afghanistan as a case study of a complex security and humanitarian environment. Thematic panels then discussed each topic in greater detail, identified gaps and challenges in the implementation and enforcement of applicable legal regimes, and made further recommendations to address the most immediate challenges. These panels included: the rise of non-state armed groups, shrinking humanitarian space, the expansion of private military and security companies, and the advent of endemic urban violence. A conference report summarized the proceedings and was widely distributed in print and on the project website.

Following the Vancouver conference, participants from diverse backgrounds along with other international experts were invited to submit papers for this edited volume as a lasting scholarly contribution to international humanitarian law, policy, and practice. A series of policy papers were also prepared and were presented in April 2010 in Ottawa to the community of humanitarian policy advisors in government and academia as well as practitioners.

We hope that you will find this book to be a thoughtful and timely critique of the current state of international humanitarian law and practice.

Professor Benjamin Perrin, University of British Columbia
Ilario Maiolo, Canadian Red Cross

Acknowledgments

This project has been a fascinating opportunity to engage with a broad range of scholars, practitioners, members of the uniformed military, representatives of non-governmental organizations, and students over the last three years. I want to thank Brian Job and Julie Wagemakers for inviting me to participate in this project at the University of British Columbia's Liu Institute for Global Issues and for placing their confidence in me to spearhead this edited volume. Coordinating so many contributors was made much easier because of the diligent work of Sally Reay. Our partners at the Canadian Red Cross, including Ilario Maiolo, Isabelle Daoust, George Chandler, and Michelle Hassen, were a pleasure to work with throughout this collaborative initiative. Randy Schmidt at UBC Press provided invaluable advice from the earliest phases of this project up to publication, and Ann Macklem's editorial work was first rate.

The Government of Canada, through the Department of Foreign Affairs and International Trade and the Department of National Defence, was very supportive of this project and provided much appreciated financial support for the research published in this book. The views expressed, of course, are only those of the authors in their personal capacities.

An excellent team of UBC students provided research assistance at various phases of this project. I would like to thank law students Jacky Sin and Laura Best for their enthusiasm and thoughtful contributions. Most of all, I am indebted to UBC doctoral student Brendan Naef, who assisted me in editing the entire manuscript of this edited volume. His diligence, hard work, and insightful comments made a notable positive impact.

I would also like to thank my colleagues at the UBC Faculty of Law for their support and advice at various stages, particularly Dean Mary Anne Bobinski, Natasha Affolder, Doug Harris, Janine Benedet, and Margot Young. Finally, I want to thank my wife and family for their encouragement and support in seeing this book to completion.

Abbreviations

AFRICOM	United States African Command
ANSA	armed non-state actor
ATT	Arms Trade Treaty
BAPSC	British Association of Private Security Companies
CIDA	Canadian International Development Agency
CNA	Chin National Army (Burma/Myanmar)
CNF	Chin National Front (Burma/Myanmar)
CPLA	Chinese People's Liberation Army
CPN-M	Communist Party of Nepal–Maoist
CVR	Community Violence Reduction program (Haiti)
DCAF	Geneva Centre for the Democratic Control of Armed Forces
DDR	Disarmament, Demobilization, and Reintegration
DFID	Department for International Development (United Kingdom)
DRC	Democratic Republic of the Congo
ECOWAS	Economic Community of West African States

ELN	Ejército de Liberación Nacional (National Liberation Army) (Colombia)
FARC	Fuerzas Armadas Revolucionarios de Colombia (Revolutionary Armed Forces of Colombia)
FLN	Front de Libération Nationale (National Liberation Front) (Algeria)
FMLN	Frente Farabundo Martí para la Liberación Nacional (Farabundo Martí National Liberation Front) (El Salvador)
GATT	General Agreement on Tariffs and Trade
GOA	Government of Afghanistan
HNP	Haitian National Police
HPG	Humanitarian Policy Group
HRL	human rights law
HSI	Haiti Stabilization Initiative
IACHR	Inter-American Commission on Human Rights
IACtHR	Inter-American Court of Human Rights
ICBL	International Campaign to Ban Landmines
ICoC	International Code of Conduct for Private Security Service Providers
ICRC	International Committee of the Red Cross
ICTY	International Criminal Tribunal for the former Yugoslavia
ICU	Islamic Courts Union (Somalia)
IDP	internally displaced person
IED	improvised explosive device
IFRC	International Federation of Red Cross and Red Crescent Societies
IHL	international humanitarian law
IHRL	international human rights law
IMTF	Integrated Mission Task Force
IOM	International Organization for Migration
ISAF	International Security Assistance Force
ISP	Inspektionen för Strategiska Produkter (Sweden)

LTTE	Liberation Tigers of Tamil Eelam (Sri Lanka)
MANPADS	Man Portable Air Defence Systems
MINUSTAH	United Nations Stabilization Mission in Haiti
MONUC	United Nations Organization Mission in the Democratic Republic of the Congo
MSF	Médecins Sans Frontières
NATO	North Atlantic Treaty Organization
NDFP	National Democratic Front of the Philippines
NGO	non-governmental organization
NSA	non-state actor
NSAG	non-state armed group
OCHA	Office for the Coordination of Humanitarian Affairs (United Nations)
ODA	official development assistance
OECD	Organisation for Economic Co-operation and Development
OECD-DAC	OECD Development Assistance Committee
OEF	Operation Enduring Freedom
ONUSAL	United Nations Observer Mission in El Salvador
OPAC	Optional Protocol to the Convention on the Rights of the Child on the Involvement of Children in Armed Conflict
PBC	Peacebuilding Commission (United Nations)
PKK	Kurdistan Workers' Party
PMC	private military company
PMSC	private military/private security company
PRT	Provincial Reconstruction Team (in Afghanistan)
PSC	private security company
QIP	quick impacts project
ROCK	Representative of Canada in Kandahar
RUF	Revolutionary United Front (Sierra Leone)
S/CRS	Office of the Coordinator for Reconstruction and Stabilization
SALW	small arms and light weapons

SIPRI	Stockholm International Peace Research Institute
SPLM/A	Sudan People's Liberation Movement/Army
SSR	security sector reform
START	Stabilization and Reconstruction Team (Canada)
TCN	third-country national
UNAMA	United Nations Assistance Mission in Afghanistan
UNAMIR	United Nations Assistance Mission for Rwanda
UNCT	United Nations Country Team
UNDP	United Nations Development Programme
UN-HABITAT	United Nations Human Settlements Programme
UNHCR	Office of the United Nations High Commissioner for Refugees
UNICEF	United Nations Children's Fund
UNOCHA	United Nations Office for the Coordination of Humanitarian Affairs
UNODC	United Nations Office on Drugs and Crime
UPC	Union des Patriotes Congolais (Democratic Republic of the Congo)
USAID	United States Agency for International Development
UXO	unexploded ordnances
WFP	World Food Programme (United Nations)

MODERN WARFARE

Introduction

BENJAMIN PERRIN

A great deal has changed since the birth of the modern humanitarian movement in 1859, when Henry Dunant, who would go on to create the Red
Cross, witnessed the heart-wrenching suffering of the Battle of Solferino.
One hundred fifty years later, the Edges of Conflict project was launched
with the aim of better understanding the changing nature of armed conflict
in order to improve respect for the rule of law in complex security environments. Like all anniversaries, this one prompted a mixture of celebration,
reflection, and assessment.

Since the terrorist attacks of 11 September 2001, international humanitarian law (IHL) scholarship, particularly in North America, has largely focused on issues related to the status of "unlawful combatants," the obligations
involved in transferring detainees, limitations on methods of interrogation,
and other topics tied to the War on Terror.[1] Another stream of scholarship
has focused on the *jus ad bellum* question of humanitarian intervention,
reacting to atrocities in Darfur, Rwanda, Sierra Leone, East Timor, and the
former Yugoslavia.[2] Although these are topical and important matters, the
singular focus upon them has come at the expense of other emergent trends
that also demand attention.

The proliferation of non-state actors in contemporary armed conflict and
post-conflict environments has shaken the foundations of IHL[3] so significantly that some legal scholars question its continued relevance.[4] These
non-state actors include numerous humanitarian organizations operating

with diverse mandates, private security and military contractors hired by a wide array of clients, and non-state armed groups that have expanded significantly since the end of the Cold War. The co-existence of these state and non-state actors in modern armed conflict environments is part of a "new culture of war"[5] that concepts like "humanitarian space" and counterinsurgency doctrines have attempted to confront.

Alongside these developments, there has been a growth in widespread forms of violence affecting civilians that may not fall within the definition of "armed conflict," which is necessary to engage IHL. In many instances, endemic urban violence and low-level insurgencies have claimed more lives and harmed more civilians than some armed conflicts. This expansion of non-state actors and forms of widespread violence pose a significant challenge to the classical underpinnings of IHL in its effort to prevent unnecessary suffering and mitigate the worst effects of armed conflict.

This edited volume engages experts from around the world in exploring and debating a series of specific challenges to the ongoing relevance and validity of IHL. Given that both the issues and proposed solutions reach across disciplines, these experts represent a diverse group, including legal scholars and other academics, humanitarian policy advisors, and representatives of private military organizations and internationally respected research and policy institutions.[6] Such an approach is critical to bridge the gap between theory and practice across complex and interrelated issues such as the four principal challenges addressed here. Each of the four major sections of this book begins with a longer chapter to provide context for the topic being addressed. The subsequent chapters delve further into specific subtopics and case studies, in order to advance the particular theme more fully than individual chapters would do in isolation.

Non-State Armed Groups: The Compliance Challenge

Non-state armed groups (NSAGs) pose a significant challenge to the ongoing relevance and validity of IHL. M. Cherif Bassiouni has gone so far as to point to a "crisis of compliance" due, in part, to the fact that NSAGs who are militarily outmatched in asymmetric non-international armed conflicts may have little interest in respecting a system of rules that restrains the means and methods that they can employ to achieve their objectives. Furthermore, these non-state actors often lack sufficient training, discipline, and oversight by their commanders, and have little expectation that they will be held accountable for serious violations of IHL.[7]

Some NSAGs are more deliberate in their violations of IHL as part of concerted strategies to terrorize local populations to submit to their *de facto* rule, or as part of a campaign of persecution or "ethnic cleansing." In these situations, no amount of training or oversight is likely to promote compliance – the very objective of such NSAGs is to violate IHL. Despite the passage of almost twenty years since the renaissance of international criminal prosecutions, beginning with the International Criminal Tribunal for the former Yugoslavia, only the smallest fraction of serious violators of IHL will ever face criminal sanctions before national or international courts and tribunals. Given this reality, the deterrent value of the remote threat of such prosecutions has been questioned.[8] More is clearly needed than merely enhancing criminal sanctions against members of NSAGs for serious violations of IHL.

For those NSAGs that can potentially be incentivized or otherwise encouraged to comply with IHL, little is offered from existing rights and obligations set out in conventional legal sources. If members of these NSAGs are apprehended, they may be afforded basic protections in Common Article 3 of the 1949 *Geneva Conventions* and in the 1977 Protocol II additional to the same, but they are also exposed to domestic criminal prosecution for taking part in hostilities, unlike lawful combatants in an international armed conflict. The threat of criminal sanction for violating IHL is thus likely to be a hollow one, given that participants in an NSAG have already exposed themselves to the most serious sanctions by choosing to take up arms against their state.

While the trend towards the "humanization" of the laws of war has progressed substantially, pragmatism and reciprocity have historically played a dominant role in the development of IHL. It should not come as a surprise, therefore, that efforts to enhance compliance by NSAGs go beyond legalistic or moral admonitions. The contemporary project to engage NSAGs has been called "as important as peace treaties in traditional wars and the *Geneva Conventions* with regard to humanitarian concerns."[9] Consequently, each chapter in this section explores various means to address the challenge of promoting compliance with IHL by NSAGs, drawing on the expertise of a diverse range of contributors.

René Provost explores the concept of reciprocity in Chapter 1, arguing that it does not depend on actual symmetry between the parties to the conflict in order to function, as some have previously asserted. The denial of prisoner-of-war status for rebel combatants, combined with the infrequency of criminal sanctions against members of NSAGs in domestic courts or international tribunals for violations of IHL, creates a situation where, according to Provost, "there is neither a reciprocal pull to compliance nor a credible threat of enforcement, leaving victims of war gravely underprotected." Provost proposes that legal pluralism offers a better way to persuade NSAGs to comply with IHL. For example, alternative forums such as Geneva Call involve NSAGs entering into "deeds of commitment" dealing with particular subject areas that mirror obligations set out in treaty law. Such commitments have the potential to encourage mutual acceptance of similar obligations, albeit in different form, between states and NSAGs. Provost argues that by creating these zones of "normative convergence," based on mutual expectations between states and NSAGs, greater acceptance of humanitarian norms is made possible.

In Chapter 2, Sophie Rondeau advocates increased reliance on the role of reciprocity, broadly understood, to generate enhanced respect for IHL by NSAGs. Although reciprocity has generally played an important role in public international law, and specifically in the historical development of humanitarian norms, the legitimacy of reciprocity as an IHL compliance mechanism has substantially eroded through treaty-based and customary IHL. Rondeau argues, however, that this trend should not diminish the pragmatic value of reciprocity in creating a "culture of compliance" between states and NSAGs in asymmetric non-international armed conflict. She addresses the controversial topics of reprisals and forms of so-called positive reciprocity, such as the recognition of belligerency status for NSAGs, amnesties, and the inclusion of these actors in future negotiations on the development of humanitarian law.

The Geneva Call case study is presented in Chapter 3 by three authors from the organization: Elisabeth Decrey Warner, Jonathan Somer, and Pascal Bongard. Over the last decade, Geneva Call has engaged approximately sixty NSAGs and successfully obtained written commitment from most of them to prohibit the use, production, and transfer of anti-personnel landmines. Overall, these signatories have complied with their commitments and also destroyed thousands of stockpiled anti-personnel mines. The authors observe that although commitments from NSAGs have had a positive influence on state policy in the relevant territories, there are numerous examples of conflicts where both states and NSAGs have made commitments related to anti-personnel landmines even when the opposing party has not entered into reciprocal undertakings. The authors posit that NSAG compliance with humanitarian norms is more likely when there is substantive equality in the obligations owed by states and NSAGs, a factor that is more important than the equal participation of NSAGs in the norm formation process itself. After such norms have been developed, however, securing the declaration of NSAGs to abide by them is an important aspect of ownership on which monitoring and accountability can be based.

In Chapter 4, Sandesh Sivakumaran discusses the role of NSAGs in the formation and enforcement of IHL, premised on the view that some form of participation is necessary to provide a sense of ownership that will enhance compliance. Concerns about conferring legitimacy on NSAGs by involving them in treaty negotiations, and the unsettled status of NSAG practice in deriving customary international law, are identified as obstacles, however. At the same time, these entities continue to issue unilateral declarations, enter into bilateral agreements with opposing states, issue codes of conduct, and sign deeds of commitment to respect humanitarian norms – despite the uncertain legal status of these statements. Sivakumaran also considers initiatives to engage NSAGs, including Geneva Call and the United Nations Security Council–mandated plans of action dealing with the recruitment and use of child soldiers. With respect to the enforcement of IHL norms, this chapter considers the practice of some NSAGs of creating courts to prosecute violations of IHL. It identifies the tension between support of such courts, contemplated by certain treaty provisions, and concerns over legitimizing the NSAG concerned.

In Chapter 5, Pablo Policzer and Valerie Yankey-Wayne explore the transfer of small arms and light weapons to NSAGs and the need for a more effective international response to the regulation of the arms trade. They point to research findings that most NSAGs obtain such weapons "from poorly controlled state stockpiles and through sophisticated criminal networks." Accordingly, this chapter argues that greater monitoring of state end use is needed, with both internal command-and-control mechanisms and external governmental and non-governmental monitoring bodies. It also discusses the importance of engaging NSAGs and other non-state actors, such as private military and security companies, in this process.

Private Military and Security Companies and Humanitarian Organizations: An Uneasy Combination

Private military and security companies are notable, often controversial, non-state actors in complex security environments and modern armed conflict. They provide a range of services for an array of clients, such as national militaries, government agencies, corporations, individuals, and even humanitarian organizations. Their legitimacy has been disputed, however, as a result of allegations of misconduct in Iraq and elsewhere, and unsuccessful efforts to ban foreign security firms outright in Afghanistan. Despite this, private military and security companies have a continuing presence in the world's major conflict and post-conflict areas due to the ongoing demand of a range of clients who claim to depend on them for the ability to operate.

In recent years, several significant initiatives have been launched to enhance private military and security companies' respect for IHL and human rights standards. These approaches have relied to varying degrees on the involvement of states as well as industry and civil society. They evidence a persistent concern among the international community about violations allegedly committed by contractors, and the perceived inadequacy of simply relying on the existing corpus of international law or models of self-regulation to oversee the conduct of these non-state actors.

In 2008, the *Montreux Document on Pertinent International Legal Obligations and Good Practices for States Related to Operations of Private Military and Security Companies during Armed Conflict*[10] was an attempt by a group of seventeen states to articulate their views on the current state of international legal obligations of home, territorial, contracting, and other states in a non-binding document. The following year, the more ambitious effort of proposing a UN *Draft International Convention on the Regulation, Oversight and Monitoring of Private Military and Security Companies*[11] was undertaken by the UN Working Group on the Use of Mercenaries as a Means of Violating Human Rights and Impeding the Exercise of the Right of Peoples to Self-Determination. Although seriously flawed,[12] the Draft Convention demonstrates a tendency towards tightening the reins on private military and security companies, recognizing that the risks they present as transnational non-state actors cannot be effectively addressed only by national governments acting on their own accord. Most recently, in late 2010, the Swiss government supported the creation of an International Code of Conduct for Private Security Service Providers that has been signed by fifty-eight companies.[13] This voluntary code that purports to be grounded in IHL and human rights standards also includes a grievance procedure for reviewing alleged violations. The robustness and effectiveness of this initiative remains to be tested, but the mere existence of the new code of conduct demonstrates an interest not only among states but also among private military and security companies themselves in clearer oversight of such companies' activities – and if these firms can participate in shaping the rules (as opposed to a formal treaty process, where they have no official status), all the better from their perspective.

In the context of this flurry of international activity, Part 2 of this book probes the interaction between private armed security contractors and humanitarian organizations from several perspectives. It also explores the obligations of various states regarding the activities of these contractors. In Chapter 6, I examine how complex issues in delivering humanitarian assistance have challenged the traditional consent-based model of securing the safe delivery of aid in contemporary armed conflict. Non-international armed conflicts, ethnically motivated attacks, insurgencies, and failing states present heightened risks to humanitarian organizations, and incidents of serious violence against humanitarian aid personnel are perceived to have occurred. As a result, some humanitarian organizations have turned to defensive armed protection, including the use of private security contractors, while other organizations are concerned that such practices undermine the impartiality, neutrality, and independence of humanitarian aid. After critically evaluating this debate, I address two threshold IHL issues: (1) Is the protected status of humanitarian personnel under IHL suspended or lost if they use armed private security contractors? (2) Is humanitarian access to provide relief affected by the decision to hire a private security company for armed protection of relief consignments?

After these basic questions about whether a humanitarian organization legally *could* hire a private security company are addressed, Andrew Bearpark and Jamie Williamson stake out opposing positions on whether humanitarian organizations *should* work with private security companies. In Chapter 7, Bearpark recognizes that a "convergence of interests" exists between humanitarian organizations and private security companies, beyond defensive armed protection, including a wide range of services, such as consultancy, training, and other behind-the-scenes services. He also believes that a dialogue between humanitarian organizations and private security companies would be beneficial in overcoming the current ad hoc approach to contracting that is exposing humanitarians to poor or even harmful services.

Conversely, Williamson argues in Chapter 8 that any advantages of using armed security that humanitarian organizations gain in the short term are outweighed in the long term by the erosion of the fundamental principles of neutrality and impartiality. Since the early 1990s, the International Red Cross and Red Crescent Movement has expressed such concerns and has articulated a general policy against the use of armed escorts for its humanitarian relief convoys. Williamson sets out the detailed minimal conditions that must be satisfied when any component of the movement is considering the exceptional use of armed escorts. He also highlights contracting standards in the *Montreux Document*, mentioned above. In his final analysis, however, Williamson argues that these conditions and standards alone may still be insufficient to ensure that beneficiaries and parties to the conflict will view the use of armed escorts by humanitarian organizations in a positive light.

Since IHL has developed prior to the proliferation of private military and security companies, there has been significant debate in recent years about the status, rights, and obligations of such companies' personnel in situations of armed conflict. In Chapter 9, Fred Schreier explores each of these critical questions and finds that the existing corpus of IHL already provides a response to them. He also synthesizes the current views of scholars and the group of states participating in the crafting of the *Montreux Document* concerning the obligations of contracting states, territorial states, home states, and all other states.

"Humanitarian Space": A Concept Worth Resuscitating?

Delivery of humanitarian assistance in conflict zones by impartial and neutral aid organizations has been a significant contribution of the international humanitarian movement. Although the definition of "humanitarian space" lacks consistency, it generally refers to the freedom of non-governmental humanitarian organizations to assess humanitarian needs and deliver aid and assistance independently – without interference from state actors or donors.

Increasingly, however, aid is being delivered by military actors and intergovernmental agencies with specific political and strategic objectives. There is also a continuum of activities, ranging from relief on the one hand to long-term reconstruction projects on the other, that are being carried out in broader integrated missions that seek to bring stability to troubled regions. Counterinsurgency doctrines have also adopted this approach to "win hearts and minds." Nowhere has this approach been more fully developed and implemented than in Afghanistan, where it has at times raised concerns among the approximately eight hundred international and local non-governmental organizations (NGOs) operating in the country alongside the US-led Operation Enduring Freedom (OEF) and the NATO-led International Security Assistance Force (ISAF).[14]

Given the expansion in the activities and actors delivering humanitarian aid, the concept of humanitarian space as developed by humanitarian activists is being challenged. To date, however, the debate surrounding the erosion or shrinking of humanitarian space has focused primarily on who is delivering the aid and under what constraints they are operating, rather than on the beneficiaries of the aid and their best interests.

In Chapter 10, Sylvain Beauchamp traces the historical origins of the humanitarian space debate as well as the tension between the various civilian and military actors engaged in delivering a range of supports to civilian populations during armed conflict, occupation, natural disasters, and development activities. Beauchamp reconceptualizes the concept of humanitarian space by analyzing relevant principles from IHL and international human rights law, as well as key sources from the UN and Red Cross systems. He argues that ultimately the debate should be refocused on meeting the needs of the beneficiaries of such aid in a non-discriminatory and impartial manner, rather than on which actor is delivering the aid or assistance.

The International Committee of the Red Cross (ICRC) approach of gaining humanitarian access through acceptance is discussed in Chapter 11 by Michael Khambatta. In his view, gaining long-term and sustainable humanitarian access is best pursued through adherence to the core principles of neutrality, impartiality, and independence. Because counterinsurgency doctrines and "stability operations" increasingly include humanitarian and development activities, however, challenges will continue to arise for organizations such as the ICRC that are also active in such theatres of operation.

In Chapter 12, Valerie Oosterveld offers a critique of the concept of humanitarian space from the perspective of women, who are disproportionately affected by gender-based and sexual violence during armed conflict. She explores how, even in the purported humanitarian space of refugee and internally displaced persons camps, women and girls have faced sexual exploitation and abuse from other camp members and those charged with providing them with assistance and protection. Some important changes have been made to address the problem, but more needs to be done. Oosterveld also argues that the targeting, and subsequent withdrawal, of humanitarian actors has a significant negative impact on female aid beneficiaries, particularly in terms of access to essential healthcare services. The chapter concludes with a discussion of concerns about the treatment of female victim-witnesses testifying about sexual violence before international criminal tribunals as a further limitation on their ability to be protected from such devastating harm perpetrated during armed conflict.

In Chapter 13, Emily Paddon and Taylor Owen consider the case study of
Afghanistan, and the challenges to the concept of humanitarian space posed
by the emerging model of "integrated peacebuilding." The concept of integrating the delivery of aid and development with political and strategic objectives has reached its zenith in the post-9/11 intervention in Afghanistan.
The authors explore the resulting tensions between the military and NGOs,
within the NGO community itself, and between NGOs and donor governments. They argue that "a completely neutral space for all humanitarian action [is now] an unrealistic goal" in Afghanistan, but that there are some
promising practices to better delineate the boundaries between humanitarian and instrumental delivery of support in such situations.

Endemic Urban Violence: Regulating Widespread Violence Short of Armed Conflict

In some areas of the world, widespread and pervasive urban violence has
caused harm to civilians comparable to that in some war zones. Gang violence, unlawful killings, kidnappings and forced disappearances, torture,
robbery, and other grave human rights violations have taken a terrible toll
on local populations. Shocking statistics demonstrate the scope of this human tragedy: "Latin America, with only 14% of the world's population accounts for 42% of firearms-related homicides in the world. Brazil has the
highest number of national gun-related deaths in the world, surpassing even
Iraq on a per capita basis in 2006. In Guatemala, less than 2% of homicides
result in criminal charges, with approximately 20,000 gang-related murders
in the past five years."[15] In some major cities, the sheer death toll from urban
violence exceeds that of some armed conflicts.

Despite the widespread suffering, violence, and death, there has not yet
been a determined international effort to confront endemic urban violence.
Many countries are increasingly faced with sustained and organized instances of violence that do not meet the definition of armed conflict necessary
to trigger the application of IHL. These unconventional forms of violence
are nevertheless of great significance because of their devastating impact on
civilians as well as the instability they foster, threatening to undermine local
governments and even regional peace and security.

Consequently, in 2007 the International Conference of the Red Cross
and Red Crescent identified urban violence as one of "four great challenges
facing the world today which affect the individual and specifically the most
vulnerable."[16] The humanitarian movement's concern for widespread violence in global cities raises several critical issues: Are there gaps in international law with respect to endemic urban violence? Should the principles

of IHL be applicable to these situations? Are other bodies of law more appropriate? What policy recommendations and enhanced implementation of existing legal principles can address the root causes of urban violence?

In Chapter 14, Carlos Iván Fuentes considers whether, and to what extent, IHL standards should govern situations of endemic urban violence that fall short of the current definition of an armed conflict necessary to trigger the application of IHL. He argues that although it may be tempting to apply various IHL principles to such situations, including the protected status of civilians, obligations to provide humanitarian assistance, prohibitions on the use of children in conflict, and the concept of protected objects, such application would ultimately be ill-suited to address endemic urban violence. He finds, however, some promise in the potential of international human rights law, as it has been applied within the Inter-American human rights system, to redress some of the root causes and accountability needed to confront widespread urban violence.

In Chapter 15, Robert Muggah and Oliver Jütersonke critically assess the mainstreaming of the concepts of fragility (situations where "governments cannot or will not deliver core functions to the majority of its people") and stabilization (the use of strategic multisector approaches to restore order). They argue that such concepts are not well suited to achieving long-term positive outcomes, including in urban areas where humanitarian actors are beginning to play a great role in attempting to alleviate suffering. Instead, the case study of the ICRC's recent efforts in Rio de Janeiro, Brazil, is presented as an alternative concept to promote the resilience of urban areas affected by widespread violence.

In Chapter 16, Robert Muggah examines the interplay between humanitarian actors and the various approaches to pursing "stabilization" in areas of endemic urban violence in Haiti, notably Cité Soleil and Bel Air. While many humanitarian organizations were initially reluctant to cooperate or to coordinate their activities with the UN Stabilization Mission in Haiti or efforts by other states in the country, a form of pragmatic collaboration eventually developed among some of them. The result appears to be progress in terms of declining rates of serious violence and the creation of spaces for socioeconomic development.

Finally, in Chapter 17, Gurvinder Singh and Judi Fairholm assess the relationship between violence against children in the private sphere and violence in increasingly urban public spaces. This analysis insists on a broader view of what is typically considered to be encompassed in the problem of urban violence, both to recognize the reality faced by children around the world and to identify root causes of public manifestations of violence. The authors recognize that violence against children is aggregated across a spectrum that flows from the individual to their family to their community, and finally to their society as a whole. Singh and Fairholm argue for comprehensive preventative programs to address the underlying causes of violence against children, inspired by the UN *Convention on the Rights of the Child*.

The potential – and limitations – of IHL to play a constructive role in addressing the needs of those affected by armed conflict and widespread violence is a common theme that runs throughout this book. This balanced approach is neither naïve (believing that more or better laws hold all the answers) nor cynical (believing the law to be wholly irrelevant). By adopting a wider lens than the simple consideration of settled standards of humanitarian law, the contributors consider first principles, related bodies of law, and humanitarian policy as well as the social science evidence on the prevention and mitigation of violence and conflict in order to tackle the various challenges raised in these pages. This common project harks back to the original inspiration of Henry Dunant and the powerful idea that unnecessary suffering can be mitigated through the enterprise and dedication of thoughtful, concerned citizens. It is thus a modest tribute to his inspiring vision, over 150 years later.

NOTES

1 See, *e.g.*, Clark Butler, ed., *Guantanamo Bay and the Judicial-Moral Treatment of the Other* (West Lafayette, IN: Purdue University Press, 2007); Michael N. Schmitt and Jelena Pejic, eds., *International Law and Armed Conflict: Exploring the Faultlines* (Leiden and Boston: Martinus Nijhoff, 2007); David Rodin, ed., *War, Torture, and Terrorism: Ethics and War in the 21st Century* (Malden, MA: Blackwell, 2007); Wolff Heintschel von Heinegg and Volker Epping, eds., *International Humanitarian Law Facing New Challenges: Symposium in Honour of Knut Ipsen* (Berlin and New York: Springer, 2007); Mirko Bagaric, *Future Directions in International Law and Human Rights* (Melbourne: Sandstone Academic Press, 2007).
2 See, *e.g.*, George P. Fletcher and Jens David Ohlin, *Defending Humanity: When Force Is Justified and Why* (Oxford and New York: Oxford University Press, 2008); Thomas E. Hill, *Kant and Humanitarian Intervention* (Toronto: Faculty of Law, University of Toronto, 2008); Mohamed Abdelsalam Babiker, *Application of International Humanitarian and Human Rights Law to the Armed Conflicts of the Sudan* (Antwerp: Intersentia, 2007).
3 The use of the term *IHL* is intended to encompass a broad corpus of international law applicable during armed conflict, including both customary and conventional sources. Most notable among the conventional IHL sources are the landmark four *Geneva Conventions* of 1949 and their two *Additional Protocols* of 1977.

4   M. Cherif Bassiouni, "The New Wars and the Crisis of Compliance with the Law of Armed Conflict by Non-State Actors" (2008) 98 J. Crim. L. & Criminology 711 at 714.

5   *Ibid.* at 717.

6   The usual disclaimer applies here, *i.e.*, that contributors to this book are expressing their own personal views and not necessarily those of the organizations with which they are affiliated or employed.

7   Bassiouni, *supra* note 4 at 715.

8   David Whippman, "Atrocities, Deterrence, and the Limits of International Justice" (1999-2000) 23 Fordham Int'l L.J. 473.

9   Claudia Hoffman, "Engaging Non-State Armed Groups in Humanitarian Action" (2006) 13 International Peacekeeping 396.

10 *The Montreux Document on Pertinent International Legal Obligations and Good Practices for States Related to Operations of Private Military and Security Companies during Armed Conflict* (Montreux: Government of Switzerland, 2008), online: ICRC <http://www.icrc.org/web/>.

11 United Nations Office of the High Commissioner for Human Rights (UNHCR), Working Group on the Use of Mercenaries as a Means of Violating Human Rights and Impeding the Exercise of the Right of Peoples to Self-Determination (UN Working Group), *Draft International Convention on the Regulation, Oversight and Monitoring of Private Military and Security Companies* (final draft for distribution, 13 July 2009).

12 For critical commentary on the Draft Convention, see Benjamin Perrin, "Searching for Accountability: The Draft UN International Convention on the Regulation, Oversight and Monitoring of Private Military and Security Companies" (2009) 47 Can. Y.B. Int'l Law 299-317.

13 Government of Switzerland, *International Code of Conduct for Private Security Service Providers* (9 November 2010), online: <http://www.icoc-psp.org>.

14 Lara Olson, "Fighting for Humanitarian Space: NGOs in Afghanistan" (2006) 9 Journal of Military and Strategic Studies 1-28.

15 Rebecca Comley *et al.*, *Urban Violence: The Silent War of the Americas* (Vancouver: Action Canada, 2008) at 4, online: Action Canada <http://www.actioncanada.ca/en/>.

16 ICRC, "Together for Humanity, 30th International Conference of the Red Cross and Red Crescent," 26-30 November 2007, Doc. 30IC/07/R1/Declaration, at 1, online: ICRC <http://www.icrc.org/>.

PART 1

NON-STATE ARMED GROUPS: THE COMPLIANCE CHALLENGE

Asymmetrical Reciprocity and Compliance with the Laws of War

RENÉ PROVOST

How does one get the Taliban in Afghanistan, the FARC[1] in Colombia, Russian troops in Georgia, and Blackwater contractors in Iraq to improve their dismal record of compliance with international humanitarian law (IHL)? The recipe, inasmuch as one can be surmised, will involve a complex mix of carrot and stick, normative and political, humanitarian and strategic. One basic question is the degree to which reciprocity is a toxic factor in the normative dynamics of international humanitarian law, importing conditionality and offering excuses to match any violation committed by the other side, or whether there lies in reciprocity a force that can be successfully marshalled to improve the protection of the victims of war. A second, related question is the extent to which an armed conflict has to involve symmetrical forces in order for reciprocity to operate at all. Several authors have suggested that reciprocity simply cannot operate in the context of asymmetrical wars.[2] What follows is an attempt to show that even in asymmetrical conflicts unreceptive to humanitarian ideals such as those listed above, reciprocity offers such potential that it should not be discounted as merely another hurdle to be overcome in the application of the laws of war; rather, it is one of the bases on which legitimate norms can be established to link participants variously positioned in a regime like international humanitarian law.

Reciprocity and Asymmetry

There is a lingering semantic debate regarding the most appropriate label to describe the legal regulation of the conduct of war and protection of its victims, from "laws of war" to "international humanitarian law," "humanitarian law of armed conflicts," or "law of armed conflict."[3] Beneath the semantics lurks a divergence regarding the central focus of this body of norms, whether it be the protection of fundamental individual interests or the reconciliation of effective waging of war with elementary considerations of humanity. Part of this discussion has taken the form of an argument that IHL has been undergoing a process of "humanization."[4] What is meant by this is that there is a greater emphasis on the protection of individual victims of armed conflicts as the raison d'être of this field, leading to a rebalancing of military necessity and the considerations of humanity said to be at the heart of IHL. The humanization of IHL thus seeks to place the individual, especially the individual victim in need of protection, at the core of the regime. At a systemic level, the humanization of the laws of war is a regional skirmish in a general penetration of human rights concepts into every aspect of public international law, including trade, labour standards, environmental protection, and so on. Because of the similarity between the fundamental objectives of human rights and those of IHL – that is, the protection of essential human needs and interests – a certain reading of the relationship between these two fields has promoted the view that IHL is, in reality, a subset of human rights. In this sense, IHL is seen as a *lex specialis* adjusted to the realities of war but still organically subsumed under the *lex generalis* of human rights. The discussion of the relationship between IHL and human rights is a far-ranging one, touching on the normative (for example, do protected persons hold individual rights under the *Geneva Conventions*?) and the institutional (for example, to what extent should universal and regional human rights implementation mechanisms rely upon and directly apply IHL?).[5]

A structural issue in the discussion of the relationship between human rights and IHL relates to the comparative significance of reciprocity in the two fields. Reciprocity is at once a legal, political, and sociological phenomenon, present to some degree in most legal regimes.[6] It reflects the fact that most agents will agree to be bound by a norm on the basis that they thereby obtain a benefit. In the context of public international law, states will indeed usually demand a *quid pro quo* in the exchange of rights and obligations created by a treaty or under customary law. Human rights stand as an exception to this practice, largely a reflection of the fact that human rights norms are not aimed primarily at protecting state interests but rather those of individuals and, to a lesser degree, groups. In this context, it makes little sense to demand that state obligations be synallagmatic, that is, reciprocally tied one to the other. One consequence of the non-reciprocal nature of human rights obligations, customary as well as conventional, is that a state can never justify its violations of human rights on the basis that other states are doing the same. IHL, on the other hand, arose in part from the belligerent practice of agreeing to cartels setting out the conditions under which a particular conflict was to be prosecuted. Even in the context of the early multilateral treaties on the laws of war, both the Hague and Geneva strands, it was clear that states were agreeing to be bound on the basis of reciprocity. This is evidenced by the inclusion of *si omnes* clauses, making the treaty inapplicable to an armed conflict if even one of the belligerent states involved was not a party to the treaty. Such an absolute insistence on reciprocity was abandoned by the Second World War, although the extent to which reciprocity was expunged from IHL remains the object of significant contention. In this context, and to be specified in the remainder of this chapter, I will particularly aim my remarks at the wisdom of rejecting the relevance of reciprocity in IHL in situations of asymmetrical wars, perhaps an unexpected area in which to question the assertion.

Traditional wars of the eighteenth, nineteenth, and early twentieth centuries are said to have followed a roughly symmetrical model.[7] This means that the newfound state monopoly on warfare reflected a Westphalian notion of the sovereign equality of states. Thus, states were increasingly seen as legally equal, despite the fact that they might never have been so from a political or military perspective. Other forms of what today might be considered to amount to an armed conflict persisted, but IHL was born and shaped by the symmetrical vision of warfare, with very limited space made for conflicts not following this model, including internal uprisings and their suppression.[8] Likewise, the expansion of European empires during the nineteenth century was carried out with significant use of armed force, but this practice was considered to fall outside the purview of what might feed into the emergence of a European international legal system, including the laws of war.[9] Quite the opposite, IHL may be seen as part of the tools used to further the *mission civilisatrice* invoked at the time as one of the justifications for colonial expansion.[10] So-called uncivilized peoples eventually joined the Western system, beginning with the Ottoman Empire and Japan, but adherence to the humanitarian regime as it stood was the price of admission to the concert of civilized nations. Both internal strife and colonial wars were seen as matters not suitable for regulation by international law whatsoever. The IHL regime we have today, global as it might be, has its roots firmly planted in the European experience of interstate warfare, taken as both symmetrical and reciprocal.

The practice and legal construction of war have evolved since the formative period of the laws of war between the second half of the nineteenth century to roughly the first half of the twentieth. Two changes have particular salience for a discussion of reciprocity: the inclusion of internal conflicts and the practice of proxy warfare. First, with the advent of civil wars on a scale similar to international armed conflicts, particularly the experience of the Spanish Civil War, came the desire to more formally regulate non-international armed conflicts within the IHL regime.[11] Once the concept of armed conflict as governed by IHL is enlarged to include internal wars, any notion of presumed symmetry among parties to a conflict must necessarily be abandoned. Relatively few conflicts since the Second World War have replicated the Spanish Civil War model of a rebel group and government of near-equal strength, each acting as a proto-state within the portion of territory it controls. More often, there is a radical asymmetry between a manifestly more powerful government force and a weaker insurgent group. At the other end of the spectrum, there have been a few instances of failed states in which civil wars have arisen among various non-state groups without the participation of government forces. Somalia provides perhaps the best example of this type of situation, in which symmetry of sorts may re-emerge among the various fighting forces.

As a second major point, the post–Second World War formation of two global political blocs and the threat of mutual nuclear annihilation resulted in fewer international armed conflicts between states of roughly equal size. When the Cold War degenerated into armed hostilities, they typically involved at least one proxy state, much weaker than its opponent. In such conflicts, the legal characterization of which caused innumerable disputes, belligerents could hardly be considered to be in a symmetrical power relationship. Finally, the recent appearance of new players, most significantly private military contractors, raises the question of the role they will play in the power relationships between belligerent parties. Through both their status and purpose, and by operating in a space that falls between previously acknowledged categories of IHL, private military contractors introduce a distinct form of asymmetry.[12] Their sheer numbers,[13] the strategic significance of their role, and the occurrence of serious incidents suggesting violations of the laws of war all combine to underscore the importance of including private military contractors in any analysis of the legal impact of asymmetrical warfare.[14]

To what extent, then, does IHL continue to be wedded to a construct of symmetrical belligerent relations? Some, like Toni Pfanner, have expressed skepticism as to whether the humanitarian legal regime is suitable for effectively regulating asymmetrical conflicts.[15] Underpinning such a view is an impression that reciprocity is unlikely to play a significant role in such conflicts.[16] I now focus on the extent to which contemporary IHL has challenged the above beliefs by making space for reciprocity in asymmetrical conflicts.[17]

The Place of Reciprocity in International Humanitarian Law

In any legal regime, reciprocity plays an important function in the creation, application, and sanction of norms.[18] As noted above, the laws of war did not escape this mould and were shaped in their initial phase through cartels and direct exchanges of interdependent promises to abide by certain rules during a given conflict. There was a marked similarity between the initial *Geneva* and *Hague Conventions* and such cartels.[19] The eventual abandonment of the *si omnes* clauses in these conventions marked only the first step in a process of questioning the extent to which IHL ought to be tributary to reciprocity in all respects. The inclusion in Common Article 1 of the four *Geneva Conventions* of 1949 of a general obligation for state parties not only to "respect" but also to "ensure respect" of the *Geneva Conventions* clearly required states to intervene to demand respect for these rules even when they had no direct interest in the matter, and hence when they were not likely to be acting in the defence of reciprocal interests.[20] This broad duty has attracted a fair amount of doctrinal attention suggesting that it corresponds, *inter alia*, to a state duty to intercede with belligerents towards cessation of violations of the laws of war, to vote against resolutions of international organizations that contravene the *Geneva Conventions* or their *Additional Protocols*, and to amend domestic legislation so that it is consistent with applicable IHL.[21] The fact that this non-reciprocal duty has generated precious little state practice, despite ample opportunities, should perhaps be cause for concern as to the comparative effectiveness of such obligations.[22]

Another sector of IHL that has witnessed a rolling back of the significance of reciprocity concerns belligerent reprisals. According to the laws of war, a party to an armed conflict is entitled to take normally prohibited measures in reaction to an earlier breach by the enemy, with a view to bringing to a halt such violation and the resumption of full compliance with IHL.[23] In addition to the risk that belligerents will answer tit-for-tat each violation under the guise of reprisals, which could spiral to potentially displace humanitarian law as a whole, the very possibility of authorizing any act that falls short of the requirements of humanity seems objectionable. Successive conventions have removed various categories of individuals and objects from the list of potential targets of reprisals, which are now limited to combatants and arguably some non-military objects.[24] This is amplified by the abstention of states, with a few notable exceptions, from engaging in any form of belligerent reprisals. The result is a considerably reduced role for an institution that was the embodiment of reciprocity in IHL. Based on this, some have asserted the demise of reciprocity in the laws of war.[25]

The International Criminal Tribunal for the former Yugoslavia (ICTY) weighed in on the reciprocity debate in its *Kupreskic* judgment. In that case, the defence had raised the fact that the opposing side had carried out atrocities of its own, thereby suggesting that the responsibility of the accused ought to be diminished to some extent. There were two possible legal strands to this suggestion. The first was a doctrine termed *tu quoque*, according to which an individual may not be found guilty of a war crime if the enemy has behaved in a similar manner. Although there are some limited elements supportive of such a doctrine, including part of the judgment of the Nuremberg International Military Tribunal, the ICTY denied that such a principle could shield the accused from criminal liability.[26] The second legal strand related to belligerent reprisals. Again the ICTY denied any applicability of such rules in the *Kupreskic* context because several conditions of reprisals were not met, including, most fundamentally, the rule that civilians may never be the target of such retaliatory measures. The tribunal not only rejected the argument but also took the opportunity to underline, in very general terms, the fact that "the bulk of [IHL] lays down absolute obligations, namely obligations that are unconditional or in other words not based on reciprocity."[27] The ICTY Appeals Chamber endorsed this approach in its 2008 judgment in the *Martic* case, writing that "arguments based on reciprocity, including the *tu quoque* argument are no defence to serious violations of international humanitarian law."[28]

The dismissal of the *tu quoque* doctrine appears entirely sound, but the overly general rejection of the relevance of reciprocity for obligations under IHL is arguably both unwarranted and unwise. I have previously challenged the soundness of such a general rejection, chiefly on the basis of a distinction between immediate and systemic reciprocity and the bilateralizable nature of many obligations under IHL. Briefly stated, international norms are said to be bilateralizable if the web of relations created by a treaty or pursuant to customary law can be broken down into a series of parallel bilateral relations. International trade treaties such as the General Agreement on Tariffs and Trade (GATT) offer a good example of bilateralizable obligations, in that they allow for the regulation of bilateral trade relations between states or blocs of states. On the other hand, the *Convention on the Prevention and Punishment of the Crime of Genocide* does not stand for an aggregate of synallagmatic relations but rather for a collective undertaking to abstain from engaging in acts of genocide, and to try to stop them if they occur. In such a treaty, obligations are non-bilateralizable in that the parallel relations created between each and all state parties is clearly peripheral to the object and purpose of the treaty. Non-bilateralizable obligations overlap to a significant extent with the concept of obligations *erga omnes,* although the latter concept gives greater emphasis to the interests of third states in universal compliance with a given norm. Bilateralizable obligations tend to correspond to a model of immediate reciprocity, in which the obligations of a given party are connected to those of another to varying degrees. In circumstances in which the equality of all parties is not assured, there tends to be greater reliance on immediate reciprocity to ensure the viability of the regime. Non-bilateralizable obligations are more common in situations in which the regime is centralized to a greater extent, reflecting a systemic reciprocity. In such models, the equality of participants is presumed, and each undertakes obligations under the assumption that a central force will ensure that all are treated in roughly the same manner. Non-bilateralizable obligations based on systemic rather than immediate reciprocity tend to foster a greater degree of institutionalization of the regime, so that a central body can track compliance and act on behalf of all parties to sanction any cases of non-compliance.

Analyzing in detail the norms surrounding the creation, application, and sanction of IHL, I concluded in an earlier study that there was no basis on which to make a general claim that reciprocity played no role in the architecture of the laws of war.[29] States have indeed insisted on a direct *quid pro quo* in agreeing to be bound by humanitarian law, and reciprocity creeps up in numerous places to ensure the stability of a regime intended to regulate what is surely one of the legal relationships least amenable to stability. Reciprocity's role is complex, and a conclusion that it remains a significant force does not lead to the conclusion that IHL is entirely grounded in immediate reciprocity. There is thus no inconsistency between this conclusion

and the ICTY's narrower finding that violations of the laws of war committed by an opposing party should in no way diminish the criminal responsibility of a person accused of war crimes. Indeed, the criminal lens through
which the ICTY is compelled to consider IHL may well explain its desire to
exorcise reciprocity as completely as possible.[30] There is, however, a danger
in reducing IHL to the prosecution of war crimes. Individual criminal responsibility, as important as it might be, plays a rather marginal role in the
life of the laws of war. In fact, few have ever claimed that the mere threat of
criminal liability may be sufficient on its own to bring about full compliance
with IHL. Given the reality that only an extraordinarily small number of all
war crimes are ever criminally sanctioned, it is crucial to consider other factors that may induce greater compliance with humanitarian law. Although
reciprocity is not necessarily systematically central to a belligerent's decision to comply with the laws of war, it is nevertheless an important factor
in inducing compliance. For instance, the Canadian Armed Forces in Afghanistan apply IHL as a matter of policy, regardless of what the Taliban
does.[31] What this tells us is that reciprocity is not the only force motivating
compliance with the laws of war. That said, the policy reasons that push for
Canadian compliance with humanitarian law in Afghanistan do not seem to
produce the same effect for the Taliban in that country or for Russian troops
in Chechnya. If increased compliance with the laws of war by every party to
any armed conflict remains our target, as it should, then we must broaden
our horizon to tap other forces that can be harnessed to induce compliance.
Reciprocity, it is argued, should be high on our list.

The sovereign equality of states is a legal fiction forming one of the bed-
rocks of the international legal system. The fact that states are often unequal
in non-legal ways explains why reciprocity cannot be shed altogether from
IHL, in which it still plays an important role. If we turn from interstate
armed conflicts to consider either non-international armed conflicts or conflicts in which other non-state actors, such as private military contractors,
play a role, the standard then becomes one of legal inequality. Given my
earlier remarks on the link between immediate reciprocity and the uncertain equality of participants in any given regime, one would expect that the
laws of war would make an even more significant space for reciprocity in
internal wars than in international armed conflicts. Interestingly, the accused in the *Hadzihasanovic* case presented an argument to the ICTY
Appeals Chamber alleging that the doctrine of command responsibility reflected the normative reciprocity of humanitarian law applicable in international armed conflict, but that no such reciprocity existed in internal

wars. As a result, the accused argued, the doctrine of command responsibility had no place in internal armed conflicts.[32] Judge Theodor Meron, writing for the Appeals Chamber, agreed with the proposition that "internal armed conflict is now the concern of international law without any question of reciprocity," but concluded that command responsibility did not depend on notions of reciprocity.[33]

The terms of Common Article 3 of the *Geneva Conventions* do not frame the duties of belligerents in an internal armed conflict as being conditioned on reciprocity. Rather, Article 3 states in absolute terms the prohibitions binding on combatants ("each Party to the conflict shall be bound to apply, as a minimum, the following provisions"). What is specified in the provision relates to equality instead of reciprocity: it is stated that the application of IHL to belligerents during a non-international armed conflict "shall not affect the legal status of the Parties to the conflict." In a recent article, David Kretzmer takes this to means that there is symmetry between the state and rebels in that the provision makes no apparent distinction between them in defining applicable standards.[34] This is true only insofar as each belligerent is similarly required not to inhumanely treat non-combatants and to refrain from torture, hostage taking, and other similar abuses. Even within the scope of the provision, however, it is not at all clear that the execution of an individual by a rebel group could ever be validly grounded in the pronouncement of a "regularly constituted court."[35] The very complexity of the argument needed to advance such a claim belies any notion of symmetry between state and rebels. More generally, Common Article 3 must be taken within the context of the *Geneva Conventions* and the international legal regime as a whole, rooted in the principle of state sovereignty. Although formulated in neutral terms, the reference to the "legal status of the Parties" was clearly not directed at a state party to a conflict but rather at non-state groups. In its barest forms, the asymmetry between the parties to the armed conflict is maintained and, further, that reciprocity is denied any significant role. The solution is unchanged in the context of an armed conflict in which the presumably failed state plays no part, involving only various non-state groups fighting one another. Somalia provides perhaps the best example of such a situation, regulated only by Common Article 3 and, to an extent that is not entirely clear, by customary international law. In such circumstances, again with no incorporation of reciprocity in the framework of the laws of war, practice appears to indicate nearly a return to ground zero, with very little compliance with even minimal humanitarian standards.[36] Protocol II, Additional to the *Geneva Conventions* of 1949 (Protocol II), applying only to non-international armed conflicts, does not depart significantly from the model of asymmetrical non-reciprocity, adding only the condition that the insurgent be sufficiently organized and in control of a territory so as to be able to implement the protocol. This corresponds to a capacity requirement on the part of the insurgent rather than the application of immediate reciprocity in non-international armed conflicts. There is nothing to suggest that customary humanitarian law as applicable to civil wars functions according to different principles in this respect.

The model quite clearly seems based on asymmetrical non-reciprocity. The question is whether it stands a reasonable chance of being actually applied by belligerents during an armed conflict. In a non-international armed conflict, hostilities will be governed by both the domestic legal system and IHL. Under the domestic laws of nearly any state, the act of taking up arms against the government will be a crime calling for the most severe punishment available, including the death penalty if it has not been abolished in the country in question. As a result, whether insurgents fight in accordance with or in violation of IHL does not seem to matter radically from a legal standpoint. One difference is that serious violations of IHL can amount to war crimes, which can be punished by any state acting on the basis of universal jurisdiction or, in some circumstances, by an international criminal tribunal without possibility of amnesty or prescription. Given the limited appetite of states for universal jurisdiction and the limitations on the competence and capacities of international tribunals, the likelihood of either type of prosecution appears too remote to suggest a significant compliance pull attached to the international criminality of an act. Indeed, at a more general level, the significance of individual criminal responsibility as an enforcement tool for IHL may well be overstated.[37] For the state party to a non-international armed conflict, the situation is somewhat different but not necessarily more conducive to better compliance with IHL. Government troops fighting an insurgent force will benefit from domestic legitimacy, the parameters of which can be defined with some degree of elasticity by the state. The application of IHL to the conflict will regulate the state's lawful repression of an insurgency, subject members of the armed forces to the theoretical possibility of international prosecution, and possibly provide a measure of political legitimacy to the insurgency. Not surprisingly perhaps, states have proven extremely reluctant to characterize situations on their territory as non-international armed conflicts and thus acknowledge the application of Common Article 3, Protocol II, or customary humanitarian norms. More often than not, governments will label an insurgency as banditry, terrorism, internal disturbances, or tensions not calling for the application of IHL – often despite large-scale military operations and loss of control over part of the national territory.[38] While there is no basis to suggest that a state has a legal right to block the *de jure* applicability of IHL to an internal armed conflict on its territory, there is no denying that state refusal to characterize the situation as such can have a significant *de facto* impact on compliance and on the fundamental objective of protecting the victims of war.[39]

Given the serious shortcomings of a model based on asymmetrical non-reciprocity, is there another model to be found in IHL for regulating asymmetrical wars such as non-international armed conflicts? One response has been to attempt to correct the asymmetry by way of a legal fiction whereby belligerents are deemed equal, paving the way for adopting a framework in which reciprocity can play its role. This is the model embodied in Article 1(4) of Protocol I, Additional to the *Geneva Conventions* of 1949 (Protocol I), which characterizes as international armed conflicts those situations in which peoples are fighting colonial domination, alien occupation, or a racist regime in furtherance of their right to self-determination. Analogous to the act of ratification by a state, the condition for applicability of this article is one of reciprocity, in that, according to Article 96(3), the national liberation movement must make a declaration that it will comply with the *Geneva Conventions* and with Protocol I. Beyond this formal distinction, both parties to an armed conflict of national liberation are basically subject to the same rules, as if the conflict involved two states. The very notions of "state" and "peoples" are, of course, themselves legal fictions. Thus, equality from a strictly legal standpoint does not raise particular problems beyond those of possible incoherence between this particular norm and the state-centred international legal regime. More troubling when considering compliance with IHL is the chasm between the legal equality thus created among belligerents and the radical asymmetry that usually obtains in military and political terms.[40] The failure of IHL to reflect this asymmetry is part of the reason that Article 1(4) of Protocol I has generated so much opposition and has failed to be applied in any armed conflict in the more than three decades since the adoption of the protocol.

I will argue that what is needed is not to attempt to create, with the force of law, an equality that does not correspond to facts on the ground, but rather that forms of reciprocity that acknowledge existing asymmetries should be built into the architecture of IHL.

Asymmetrical Reciprocity in IHL

Civil wars, the archetype of asymmetrical conflict, stand as perhaps the greatest compliance challenge in the field of IHL today. While there are other asymmetries in armed conflicts, the much-discussed difficulty in regulating the behaviour of both powerful states, such as Russia in Chechnya, and weaker insurgents, such as the Taliban in Afghanistan, can provide a useful laboratory in which to study the possible positive impact of reciprocity. The manner in which parties to a civil war need to be engaged may yield lessons that can bring other peripheral players, such as private military companies, more fully into the fold of IHL.

At the outset, it is useful to recall that the International Committee of the Red Cross (ICRC) had proposed in the negotiations leading to the adoption of the 1949 *Geneva Conventions* that these be simply applicable to internal as well as international armed conflict. This was a model based purely on the equality of belligerents, opening avenues for compliance fuelled to some extent by mutual expectations of reciprocity.[41] This approach proved politically unacceptable to states present at the Geneva conference, for reasons that would surface again three decades later in discussions around Article 1(4) of Protocol I, as discussed earlier. The minimalist provision eventually adopted, Common Article 3, denied any notion of legal equality and formally rejected a role for reciprocity. The negotiation of Protocol II in 1977 tells a similar story, with the ICRC putting forward a quite ambitious proposal to more fully regulate internal armed conflict only to see it rejected by states, which agreed only to a bare-bones protocol. Given the sustained opposition of states to the adoption of a treaty regime containing the notion of equality, it seems unrealistic to suggest broadly revamping IHL for non-international armed conflicts to make it more evenly balanced. This is unfortunate, as a more balanced regime would naturally allow for a greater role for reciprocity as a force for compliance, as it does for international armed conflicts. For instance, the adoption of prisoner-of-war status for rebel combatants could prove more effective in promoting respect for the laws of war than the threat of eventual criminal prosecution, especially as the rarity of such prosecution is often compounded by domestic amnesties granted as part of peace negotiations to end the conflict. As it is, state reluctance to seriously consider such changes in humanitarian law applicable to civil wars leads to a situation where there is neither a reciprocal pull to compliance nor a credible threat of enforcement, leaving victims of war gravely underprotected.

Short of such a sweeping revision of the laws of war applicable to non-international armed conflicts, is it possible to better exploit the particular asymmetrical dynamics of civil wars to emphasize belligerents' reciprocal interest in improved compliance with IHL norms? The manner in which reciprocity operates within IHL will reflect the normative framework of that legal regime. IHL is structured around the existence of a hostile relationship among belligerents, seeking to reconcile the interest of belligerents in effectively pursuing the conflict with the entitlement of victims of war to be protected from unnecessary suffering. At the level of norms, humanitarian law operates primarily by way of the imposition of obligations on every category of agent involved in an armed conflict, from the state to the individual combatant, rather than by recognizing individual rights to protection for victims, as in human rights law.[42] Relationships governed by humanitarian law are those related to the conflict, and as such marked by hostilities, a requirement that ensures that humanitarian law does not entirely displace other legal regimes, including human rights law and domestic law. Thus a bar brawl in a conflict zone may well have no link to the war and, as such, should not attract the application of the laws of war but rather domestic criminal law, military codes of conduct, or human rights law. With a trend towards the "humanization" of IHL and its resulting focus on the individual interest of victims, the fundamental features of IHL are at risk of being lost. When turning to reciprocity as a force that may influence compliance with humanitarian law, the relationship to which it can attach will likewise be one marked by enmity and, as such, necessarily have a collective dimension. Beyond that, however, the specific relationship touched by reciprocity may be more individualized or more purely collective.

It is an observable fact that soldiers on the battlefield confronted with a violation that affects them or their comrades will be tempted to, and in some circumstances will, react in kind. This version of immediate reciprocity will exist in a range of ways, depending on the types of norms at play. For instance, certain norms may have a more localized nature, leaving more possibilities for individual reactions (such as using bullets doctored to explode on impact), whereas others may play out on a wider field, leaving fewer opportunities for individual acts of retaliation (such as using banned chemical weapons).[43] Within localized norms, James Morrow's statistical analysis suggests that norms that do not attract reciprocity have a weaker compliance pull than norms that do. For example, rules protecting civilians, the violation of which is unlikely to trigger a counter-violation by civilian victims, have less influence on compliance than rules surrounding the prohibition of killing an enemy *hors de combat,* which risks being answered in kind.[44] Although relevant to actual compliance with IHL, this type of immediate reciprocity is not reflected in the laws of war. On the contrary, legal norms regulating retaliation at that level seek to limit individual agency and assign the power to authorize reciprocal actions – that is, belligerent reprisals – to superior officers.[45] The framework written into IHL tends to elevate reciprocity to a more collective level, even in the case of reactions to more localized or individualized violations. It is worth noting, however, that the source of the initial violation (collective or individual) appears to have a less clear bearing than might have been anticipated. Given the collectivizing tendency within the framework of humanitarian law, one might expect that retaliation would occur more readily in response to initial violations reflecting an enemy policy rather than the uncontrolled actions of individuals. Again, Morrow's study suggests that battlefield "noise" often makes it unclear to a belligerent whether an initial violation reflects a deliberate enemy policy or a lack of discipline among enemy troops.[46] More broadly, a belligerent may be equally tempted to alter an established enemy policy or to put an end to indiscipline among enemy troops that leads to violations of the laws of war of which it is the target. This focus on reciprocity can play a positive role by providing a belligerent with a means to pressure the enemy to stop violations and resume compliance with humanitarian law. At the same time, it risks simply echoing one violation with another, starting a spiral of non-compliance that may threaten to unravel the whole fabric of IHL.

The modelling of the role of reciprocity described above is predicated on a starting situation of compliance with IHL, with an analysis of the potential impact of reciprocity on the resumption of full compliance or the acceleration of the trend towards greater disrespect for the laws of war. The initiation of any kind of compliance remains a critical challenge in asymmetrical wars such as the vast majority of non-international armed conflicts. The fact that insurgents such as the Taliban in Afghanistan are by and large excluded from the benefits of working within the parameters of humanitarian law means that they have, from the outset, very little incentive to do so. To stress an earlier point, given that taking up arms against the government constitutes treason and is normally punished with the utmost severity, why would insurgents bother to comply with IHL? The fact that states have elected to call these norms "law" does not in itself exert a very strong moral or ethical claim upon rebels fighting to topple a particular government. Indeed, explaining the process whereby IHL can impose obligations on rebel groups and individual insurgents has remained a challenge to that regime. The best explanation available is that under public international law, states may elect to directly create rights and obligations for other actors under their jurisdiction. Although I myself have advanced such an argument in the past, I now view it as persuasive only within a strictly positivist reading of law. The broad failure of insurgents in non-international armed conflicts to comply with the laws of war stands as the strongest indictment of such a view. Instead, it can be argued that international law imposes real constraints on states' liberty to do as they please because it emerges from a process in which they are centrally implicated. In other words, international law is a collective project in the construction of which states are continuously involved. As constructivists in international relations have put it, the reality of international law corresponds to the solidity of a community of practice.[47] Between states, deemed sovereign equals by the most fundamental principle of international law, there is at least a formal symmetry that facilitates interactions and suggests that law is more than a conduit for the exercise of raw power. How does this reading of international law inspired by legal pluralism transpose to IHL in the context of non-international armed conflicts, marked by radical asymmetry between belligerents? The question is fascinating because law in this context is nearly entirely stripped of all institutions that normally come to cloud the visibility of the impact of legal norms alone, and because it applies to a setting in which resort to raw power is already occurring but is unable to bring a resolution to the issues at hand (there is no way to "force" rebels to comply with the laws of war).

The starting point, then, is the existence of a community of practice. Such a community is both grounded in and a breeding ground for shared understandings as to the proper ordering of society. Can it be said that the Taliban and NATO forces in Afghanistan, Russian troops and rebels in Chechnya, and Blackwater operatives and insurgents in Iraq all belong to either one global community or several regional communities of practice? The mere suggestion may seem provocative, if not ludicrous, but the insight of legal pluralism suggests that an affirmative answer is an absolute precondition to a meaningful legal order encompassing these various actors. In other words, the imposition of legal norms from above, whether by a state or by a more amorphous international community, is unlikely to ground the existence of a regime that will successfully alter behaviour. Law is not handed down but rather continuously constructed by all who are involved in its creation and application. Whereas positivism may countenance a responsibility to the law, commanding obedience under certain conditions, legal pluralism speaks to a responsibility for the law, demanding engagement with legal norms over and above compliance. Within that scheme, formal norms can play a role if they are not rejected outright. Formal law can provide the architecture, underpinning the elaboration of norms by a plurality of actors.[48] How that elaboration takes place has been described by Lon Fuller as intersecting expectancies, whereby practices gradually come to be considered by all parties as something that can be relied upon.[49] Importantly, Fuller took pains to show that no type of law could escape this process of normative accretion, whether it be contracts or criminal law, custom or administrative law. There is no required symmetry among the various actors thus linked by way of this process of norm creation. Indeed, Fuller specifically refers to the intersecting expectancies between the state and its citizens.[50] Thus, there can be reciprocity between widely divergent actors, each with interconnected albeit asymmetrical expectations.[51] Zones of convergence map communities of practice supporting legal norms that can have an impact on an actor's behaviour. To the thinness of the community will correspond the thinness of effective legal normativity. If there is no community of practice at all, then there is likely to be no meaningful law either. As noted by Jutta Brunnée and Stephen Toope, "if there is no agreement on even the parameters of coordinated social action, legal normativity cannot emerge."[52] A complete absence of shared understanding among belligerents would amount to a situation of absolute "unrelatedness," something difficult to imagine occurring in today's society. Several centuries ago, it could perhaps have been argued that Islam and Christianity operated under such unrelatedness, meaning that there was not only no overarching international legal system but, more broadly, no shared understanding of any kind bridging the divide between the two polities. Islam, for instance, is said to have been grounded in a fundamental opposition between Dar al-Harb and Dar al-Islam so that, in its formative period, Islamic law regulated the relationship between Muslims and others purely on the basis of a unilateral normative projection rather than by any shared regime.[53] Whether or not this construction of the historical relationship between Christianity and Islam could withstand close scrutiny, it is difficult to imagine that any such situation of absolute unrelatedness can be said to exist today. The question is, rather, whether the understandings we share extend with sufficient specificity to limits on the conduct of war.

In order for legal norms to blossom, there must be wide-ranging participation by all actors whose behaviour we seek to regulate, as well as communication among these actors to allow for expectancies to intersect. How does this play out on a battlefield marked by radical asymmetry, far removed from the model of international armed conflicts in which two or more states are involved, ineluctably linked by a web of institutions and practices brought about by globalization? In non-international armed conflicts, asymmetrical in political as well as legal and strategic terms, insurgents are typically shut out from the web of institutions and practices. If we hope to bring them into the fold of IHL, a space must be created for them so that their voices are taken into consideration when assembling shared understandings about the limits of warfare.[54]

At the global level, the invitation of a small number of national liberation movements to the diplomatic conference negotiating the Additional Protocols in Geneva in 1977 represents an interesting model. The choice of liberation movements invited to the conference undeniably betrayed a very specific political agenda, which can be readily deciphered in the careful wording of Article 1(4) of Protocol I. Beyond that, however, the comparatively more sophisticated provisions on participation in hostilities owes something to the contribution of these liberation movements, resulting in a more complex but surely more balanced regime setting out the parameters of legitimate participation in hostilities for guerrilla forces.[55] More recently, private military companies (PMCs) and civil society organizations were included in the negotiations that resulted in the adoption of the *Montreux Document*.[56] Such participation arguably broadened the scope of perspectives granted consideration, resulting in a soft-law instrument that may turn out to be more relevant to the practice of PMCs and NGOs than a more formal agreement arrived at solely by states.[57]

Although broadening participation complicates negotiations, the added hurdle may nevertheless bring an important normative dividend in the greater compliance pull of any norms so agreed upon. This may be so even in the absence of formal equality among participants in the negotiations leading up to the adoption of a document. The *Montreux Document* once again provides an interesting illustration: the instrument is the outcome of a Swiss-ICRC initiative that brought together representatives from states, the security industry, and civil society. At one point, however, all non-state participants save the ICRC were excluded from further negotiations, and ultimately only states were invited to sign the document.[58] The shared nature of the understanding thus embodies a form of reciprocity, however asymmetrical, that will strengthen each party's commitment to the norm and make such a document more effective than one that originates in a single category of participants, even if that category comprises the agents whose behaviour is thought central to compliance. It is too early to assess the influence of the *Montreux Document,* but we can anticipate that it will have a more wide-ranging effect than industry codes of conduct prepared by the private security firms themselves.[59] That being said, in the field of IHL there are few opportunities for multilateral negotiations that would broadly revisit the status of insurgents and applicable rules in a non-international armed conflict. In any case, states are likely to remain as resistant as ever to politically "elevating" rebel groups by way of an invitation to Geneva to participate in a diplomatic conference. One alternative would be to encourage the ICRC or another humanitarian organization, such as Geneva Call, to convene a global conference on IHL to which only insurgent groups and possibly civil society organizations would be invited. While this could result in significant normative benefits in identifying practices and areas of consensus, legitimate concerns over the wisdom of creating a networking opportunity for organizations devoted to destabilizing governments around the world would likely prevent it from happening.

Beyond the inclusion of non-state actors in the shaping of global shared understandings relating to the humanitarian law regime, it is possible to prop up more confined communities of practices that relate to smaller regions or particular conflicts. At the outset, it is worth recalling that Common Article 3 provides that the parties to an armed conflict "should further endeavour to bring into force, by means of special agreements, all or part of the other provisions" of the *Geneva Conventions.* What is envisaged is the creation of an ad hoc legal regime among the parties to a non-international armed conflict, where belligerents jointly select, *à la carte,* as it were, which humanitarian norms ought to be applicable in the given conflict. This is to be contrasted with the approach embodied in the substantive paragraphs of Common Article 3 and in the whole of Protocol II, meant to become automatically applicable to a non-international armed conflict involving a state that has ratified these instruments. Opposed to the model of asymmetrical non-reciprocity in the body of Common Article 3 and Protocol II is a model of symmetrical reciprocity for special agreements under Common Article 3. What this stands for is an invitation to create by legal agreement an equality between belligerents that does not correspond to the asymmetrical disparity in the field. This disconnect, which we also observed earlier in the structure of Article 1(4) of Protocol I, surely helps to explain why there have been very few recorded instances of the adoption of special agreements under Common Article 3 relative to the prevalence of internal conflicts.[60] The formality of such bilateral special agreements is taken by states as ineluctably endowing the signatory insurgents with a significant dose of the political legitimacy that states are keen to deny them. In conclusion, therefore, it appears that greater humanitarian protection for victims of war will come neither from a regime rejecting reciprocity altogether nor from one seeking to artificially create among belligerents a symmetry not corresponding to reality on the ground.

Leaving aside a model that embraces formalism and the resulting legal equality among signatories to a contractual agreement, are there other processes to identify and nurture shared understandings about norms applicable in non-international armed conflicts? It is possible that state and non-state parties to a civil war may each unilaterally undertake to apply the same humanitarian norms. In the protracted internal conflict in El Salvador, both the government and the rebel FMLN[61] pledged to respect Common Article 3 and Protocol II.[62] They did so not in a joint fashion but rather independently, although it is clear that the undertakings are connected and, as such, represent a form of reciprocity. The most interesting treasure trove of practice in this respect may be the campaign mounted by Geneva Call, an NGO seeking to engage with insurgent groups to convince them to abandon the use of anti-personnel landmines.[63] Since 2000, Geneva Call has managed to induce more than three dozen non-state groups engaged in armed conflicts in Asia and Africa to sign a "deed of commitment" whereby they renounce the use of landmines. Although the work of the organization finds inspiration in the 1997 *Ottawa Convention* banning anti-personnel landmines,[64] its activities are not part of the regime directed at states, and indeed most insurgent groups who have signed the deed of commitment operate in the territory of a state that has not ratified the *Ottawa Convention.* Interestingly, however, Geneva Call reports that Sudan and Iraq decided to ratify the *Ottawa Convention* in light of rebel undertaking to abandon the use of landmines in accordance with their commitment to Geneva Call.[65] Sri Lanka, for its part, was reported as being at one point open to ratification of the *Ottawa Convention* if the LTTE[66] rebels were to sign the Geneva Call deed of commitment. This is a model in which there is clear asymmetry, as state and rebels are subject to norms that are different in both form and substance, yet reciprocity can be seen to operate in a positive way to attract compliance in certain situations. Geneva Call reported in 2008 that it was expanding its mandate to initiate discussions with non-state actors regarding the recruitment of child soldiers and the protection of women during armed conflict.[67] There is no reason to believe that any part of IHL is unsuitable for this type of undertaking by rebel groups. As was the case with the use of anti-personnel landmines in Sudan and Iraq, belligerents of all sides in an armed conflict may well realize that however differently situated they may be, some zones of normative convergence can be identified.

What is striking about this approach is not the engagement with rebel groups *per se,* which is something that the ICRC has been doing for many years as part of its dissemination campaign. The novelty lies in the normative dimension of the endeavour, in seeking to trigger the type of normative commitment that Robert Cover identified as essential to give meaning to any legal standard.[68] It is not altogether clear whether Geneva Call considers its deed of commitment to be legally binding on the rebels, although the very label and formal signing ceremony unambiguously signal a ritualistic invocation of the force and majesty of the law. I would suggest that in agreeing to live by certain humanitarian norms, whether such agreement is expressed in the formal signing of a deed of commitment or simply in the oral undertaking of a rebel leader, non-state actors are creating IHL in a fashion that is as real and possibly as effective as states ratifying an international treaty on the same matter. All contribute in an asymmetrical but interrelated way to the creation of a community of practice that can attest to shared understandings of the acceptable limits of war.

Conclusion

The asymmetrical nature of contemporary armed conflicts is a reality that cannot be overlooked. At the same time, the reciprocal nature of IHL is a feature that remains a central force of that regime, and there is significant peril in models that seek to jettison it altogether in the interests of a greater humanization of that body of law. The result of such action may well be a humanitarian regime even more inefficient than the one we have now, resulting in weaker rather than stronger protection of the victims of war. As I have argued here, reciprocity and asymmetry are not mutually inconsistent concepts; indeed, they are not analogs: symmetry is a description of relative positions, whereas reciprocity is a type of interaction.[69] If we hope to construct a normative regime that will effectively influence the behaviour of belligerents during an asymmetrical armed conflict, then that asymmetry must be woven into the reciprocity that will ineluctably be found to operate in humanitarian norms. Public international law, structured around states deemed sovereign equals, may not appear especially amenable to such an arrangement. The idea of common but differentiated responsibilities and obligations, however, is one that has made progress in recent years, especially in the field of international environmental law. Asymmetry, accepted only to a limited extent, remains a phenomenon countenanced only between states, and only in some sectors of activity. In the regulation of war, the dissociation of *jus ad bellum* and *jus in bello* and the attendant equality of belligerents under the latter remains a basic principle. Within that context, it may be wondered whether IHL as it stands now is really structured in a fashion that allows for the effective regulation of internal armed conflict. When the shortcomings of IHL are seen through the lens of legal pluralism, the emptiness of a purely positivistic grounding of these norms is revealed. Ordering rebels and other non-state actors to behave in compliance with the laws of war is not likely to change their behaviour, regardless of the number of international tribunals we create. The solution is to expose the hollowness of a state monopoly on the power to create rules in relation to the law of armed conflict. This then paves the way for a pluralization of the norm creation process to attract, from all classes of agents, normative commitments on the basis of understandings shared in a community of practice.

NOTES

1 Fuerzas Armadas Revolucionarios de Colombia (Revolutionary Armed Forces of Colombia).
2 See Eyal Benvenisti, "Rethinking the Divide Between Jus ad Bellum and Jus in Bello in Warfare against Nonstate Actors" (2009) 34 Yale J. Int'l L. 541 at 545: "warfare between a regular army and nonstate actors is not subject to the dyadic reciprocity rationale. The asymmetric relationship in fact incentivizes *both* sides to eschew reciprocal considerations" [emphasis in original]; Toni Pfanner, "Asymmetrical Warfare from the Perspective of Humanitarian Law and Humanitarian Action" (2005) 857 Int'l Rev. Red Cross 149 at 158: "it is debatable whether the challenges of asymmetrical war can be met with the current law of war"; Marco Sassoli, "The Implementation of International Humanitarian Law: Current and Inherent Challenges" (2007) 10 Y.B. Int'l Human. L. 45 at 49: "reciprocity ... does not work in asymmetrical conflicts."
3 In an attempt to abstain from positioning myself in that particular debate, I will use all these terms interchangeably throughout this chapter.
4 Theodor Meron, "The Humanization of Humanitarian Law" (2000) 94 A.J.I.L. 239.
5 On the relationship, see generally: René Provost, *International Human Rights and Humanitarian Law* (Cambridge: Cambridge University Press, 2002). On the *lex specialis/lex generalis* question, see William Schabas, "Lex Specialis? Belt and Suspenders? The Parallel Operation of Human Rights Law and the Law of Armed Conflict, and the Conundrum of Jus ad Bellum" (2007) 40 Isr. L.R. 592.
6 Emanuele Calò, *Il principio di reciprocità* (Milan: Giuffrè, 1993); Emmanuel Decaux, *La réciprocité en droit international* (Paris: LGDJ, 1980); Bruno Simma, *Das*

Reziprozitätselement im Zustandekommen völkerrechtlicher Verträge (Berlin: Duncker & Humblot, 1972); Alvin Gouldner, "The Norm of Reciprocity: A Preliminary Statement" (1960) 25 American Sociological Review 161; Robert Keohane, "Reciprocity in International Relations" (1986) 40 International Organization 1.

7 Herfried Münkler, *Der Wandel des Krieges. Von der Symmetrie zur Asymmetrie* (Weilerswist: Velbrück Wissenschaft, 2006); Herfried Münkler, *The New Wars* (Cambridge: Polity Press, 2004) at 66-70; Herfried Münkler, "The Wars of the 21st Century" (2003) 849 Int'l Rev. Red Cross 7 at 20; David Kretzmer, "Rethinking Application of IHL in Non-International Armed Conflicts" (2009) 42 Isr. L.R. 1 at 5; Rod Thornton, *Asymmetric Warfare* (Cambridge: Polity Press, 2007).

8 Münkler, "The Wars of the 21st Century," *ibid.* at 19; Andreas Paulus and Mindia Vashakmadze, "Asymmetrical War and the Notion of Armed Conflict – a Tentative Conceptualization" (2009) 91 Int'l Rev. Red Cross 95.

9 See René Provost, "The International Committee of the Red Widget? The Diversity Debate and International Humanitarian Law" (2007) 40 Isr. L.R. 614.

10 Frédéric Mégret, "From 'Savages' to 'Unlawful Combatants': A Postcolonial Look at International Law's 'Other'" in Anne Orford, ed., *International Law and Its Others* (Cambridge: Cambridge University Press, 2006) 265-317.

11 It was recognized that a state could grant rebels recognition of belligerency or insurgency, to thus trigger the application of rules regulating international armed conflicts, but such acts of recognition were entirely at the discretion of the concerned state and, as a result, rare in practice. See Hersh Lauterpacht, *Recognition in International Law* (Cambridge: Ams Press, 1948) at 175-76 and 240-46; Victor Duculesco, "Effet de la reconnaissance de l'état de belligérance par les tiers, y compris les organisations internationales, sur le statut juridique des conflits armés à caractère non-international" (1975) 79 Revue générale de droit international public 125.

12 See Benjamin Perrin, "Promoting Compliance of Private Security and Military Companies with International Humanitarian Law" (2007) 88 Int'l Rev. Red Cross 613; Peter Singer, "Outsourcing War" (2005) 84 Foreign Affairs 119.

13 There are reportedly more than 30,000 military contractors out of a total of 120,000 contractors in Iraq.

14 Terrorists are deliberately not included in this list. There may be acts of terrorism in war, carried out by either combatants or non-combatants belonging to one of the categories mentioned already. Much has been written about the fact that organizations like al-Qaeda do not feel bound by any rules in the "war" on terror, and that reliance on any form of reciprocity would undermine compliance with international law by states in their efforts to thwart terrorist attacks. Terrorism detached from armed conflicts does not call for the application of international humanitarian law, and developing an analysis on the place of reciprocity in the laws of war around issues connected to anti-terrorism is unwarranted: see, *e.g.*, Mark Osiel, *The End of Reciprocity: Torture, Terror and the Law of War* (Cambridge: Cambridge University Press, 2009); Anthony Dworkin, "The Laws of War in the Age of Asymmetric Conflict" in George Kasimmeris, ed., *The Barbarisation of Warfare* (New York: NYU Press, 2006) 220-37. International humanitarian law is a regime aiming to regulate armed hostilities that reach a certain level of intensity and aim towards a military

victory. An internal armed conflict may already challenge these assumptions to some extent, but a terrorist campaign reflects a wholly different paradigm both with regard to intensity and the possibility of a military victory: Mary Ellen O'Connell, "Defining Armed Conflict" (2008) 13 J. Confl. & Sec. L. 393.

15 Pfanner, *supra* note 2 at 158. See also Knut Ipsen, "Humanitäres Völkerrecht und asymmetrische Konfliktparteien – ein Ausschlussbefund?" in Andrea Fischer-Lescano *et al.*, eds., *Freiden in Freiheit* (Baden-Baden: Nomos, 2008) 445-63; Herfried Münkler, "Asymmetrie und Kriegsvölkerrecht: Die Lehren des Sommer-krieges 2006" (2006) 81 Friendens-Warte 62.

16 See Pfanner, *ibid.* at 169 ("reciprocity can scarcely be expected in asymmetrical wars, as the weaker party is usually neither able nor willing to take prisoners").

17 I explored this question at significant length in Provost, *supra* note 5 at 119-238. See also Sean Watts, "Reciprocity and the Law of War" (2009) 50 Harvard Int'l L.J. 365.

18 See Lon Fuller, *The Morality of Law* (New Haven, CT: Yale University Press, 1969) at 20-22.

19 P. Bogaïewsky, "Les secours aux militaires malades et blessés avant le XIX siècle" (1903) 10 Revue générale de droit international public 202; Henri Coursier, "L'évolution du droit international humanitaire" (1960) 99 Recueil des cours 371.

20 Jean Pictet, ed., *Geneva Convention Relative to the Protection of Civilian Persons in Time of War* (Geneva: ICRC, 1958) at 15.

21 Laurence Boisson de Chazournes and Luigi Condorelli, "Common Article 1 of the Geneva Conventions Revisited: Protecting Collective Interests" (2000) 82 Int'l Rev. Red Cross 67-88; Hans-Peter Gasser, "Ensuring Respect for the Geneva Conventions and Protocols: The Role of Third States and the United Nations" in Hazel Fox and Michael Meyer, eds., *Armed Conflict and the New Law – Effecting Compliance* (London: British Institute of International and Comparative Law, 1993) at 28-30; Nicholas Levrat, "Les conséquences de l'engagement pris par les hautes parties con-tractantes de 'faire respecter' les conventions humanitaires" in Fritz Klashoven et al., eds., *Implementation of International Humanitarian Law* (Dordrecht, Netherlands: Martinus Nijhoff, 1989) at 263; René Provost, "Starvation as a Weapon: Legal Implications of the United Nations Food Blockade against Iraq and Kuwait" (1992) 30 Colum. J. Transnat'l L. 577 at 600-1.

22 Provost, *supra* note 5 at 138.

23 See generally Fritz Kalshoven, "Belligerent Reprisals Revisited" (1990) 21 Netherlands Yearbook of International Law 43.

24 See Françoise Hampson, "Belligerent Reprisals and the 1977 Protocols to the Geneva Conventions of 1949" (2008) 37 I.C.L.Q. 818.

25 See Jean de Preux, "The Geneva Conventions and Reciprocity" (1985) 244 Int'l Rev. Red Cross 25.

26 On *tu quoque*, see Provost, *supra* note 5 at 227-35.

27 International Criminal Tribunal for the former Yugoslavia (ICTY), *Prosecutor v. Kupreskic et al.*, Trial Judgment, IT-95-16-T (14 January 2000) at para. 517, online: UNHCR <http://www.unhcr.org/refworld/>.

28 ICTY, *Prosecutor v. Milan Martic*, Appeal Judgment, IT-95-11-A (8 October 2008) at para. 111, online: UNHCR <http://www.unhcr.org/refworld/>.

29 See Provost, *supra* note 5 at 236-40.

30 The ICTY's eagerness to pronounce on reciprocity is highlighted by the fact that the accused in *Kupreskic* never actually did plead a defence of *tu quoque*. On appeal, the accused sought to challenge as an error of law the Trial Chamber's initiative in rejecting a defence never advanced by him. The Appeals Chamber concluded, in a guarded fashion, that if such an initiative had been taken, it was inconsequential for the defence. ICTY, *Prosecutor v. Kupreskic et al.*, Appeal Judgment, IT-95-16-A (23 October 2001) at para. 25, online: UNHCR <http://www.unhcr.org/refworld/>.

31 See Michael Schmitt, "Asymmetrical Warfare and International Humanitarian Law" (2008) 62 A.F.L. Rev. 1 at 37.

32 ICTY, *Prosecutor v. Hadzihasanovic*, Interlocutory Appeal on Decision on Joint Challenge to Jurisdiction, IT-01-47-PT (27 November 2002) at paras. 39-50.

33 ICTY, *Prosecutor v. Hadzihasanovic*, Interlocutory Appeal on Decision Challenging Jurisdiction in Relation to Command Responsibility, IT-01-47-AR72 (16 July 2003) at paras. 19-20.

34 Kretzmer, *supra* note 7 at 25-26.

35 See the very detailed analysis offered by Jonathan Somer, "Jungle Justice: Passing Sentence on the Equality of Belligerents in Non-International Armed Conflict" (2007) 867 Int'l Rev. Red Cross 655; Sandesh Sivakumaran, "Courts of Armed Opposition Groups: Fair Trials or Summary Justice?" (2009) 7 Journal of International Criminal Justice 489.

36 See Louis Lafrance, *Droit humanitaire et guerres déstructurées – l'exemple africain* (Montréal: Éditions Liber, 2006) at 90-100; Pfanner, *supra* note 2 at 154.

37 Daniel Muñoz-Rojas and Jean-Jacques Frésard, *The Roots of Behaviour in War: Understanding and Preventing IHL Violations* (Geneva: ICRC, 2004).

38 See, *e.g.*, France in Algeria and Russia in Chechnya: Provost, *supra* note 5 at 268.

39 A government characterizes factual situations at its own risk, and the state and individuals may be found internationally responsible if their judgment does not stand scrutiny at a later point: Provost, *ibid.* at 279-84. We are once again sent to a liability model in which there is little solace to be found.

40 On this generally, see Schmitt, *supra* note 31.

41 See Jean Pictet, *Geneva Convention for the Amelioration of the Condition of the Wounded and Sick in Armed Forces in the Field: Commentary* (Geneva: ICRC, 1952), commentary to Common Article 3; David Elder, "The Historical Background of Common Article 3 of the Geneva Conventions of 1949" (1979) 11 Case W. Res. J. Int'l L. 37.

42 For a full argument on this point, see Provost, *supra* note 5.

43 James Morrow, "When Do States Follow the Laws of War?" (2007) 101 American Political Science Review 559 at 561.

44 *Ibid.* at 569.

45 See, *e.g.*, Judge Advocate General, *The Law of Armed Conflict at the Operational and Tactical Level*, B-GG-005-027/AF020 (Ottawa: Department of National Defence, 1999) at ss. 15-13.

46 *Supra* note 43 at 570.

47 See Emanuel Adler, *Communitarian International Relations* (London: Routledge, 2005) at 11. This is brought to bear on international law in a fascinating way by Jutta

Brunnée and Stephen Toope, *Legitimacy and Legality in International Law* (Cambridge: Cambridge University Press, 2010) at c. 1.

48 Gerald Postema, "Implicit Law" (1994) 13 Law & Phil. 361 at 368.

49 Lon Fuller, "Human Interaction and the Law" (1969) 14 Am. J. Juris. 1.

50 *Ibid.* at 19.

51 See Adler, *supra* note 47 at 15; Brunnée & Toope, *supra* note 47 at 7.

52 Brunnée & Toope, *ibid.* at 27.

53 See Hans Kruse, "The Islamic Doctrine of International Treaties" (1954) 1 Islamic Quarterly 152 at 155; Edmond Rabbath, "Pour une théorie du droit international musulman" (1950) 6 Revue égyptienne du droit international 1 at 14.

54 See Marco Sassoli, "Possible Legal Mechanism to Improve Compliance by Armed Groups with International Humanitarian law and International Human Rights Law" (2003), online: Geneva Call <http://www.genevacall.org/resources/other-documents-studies/>.

55 Yves Sandoz, Christophe Swinarski, and Bruno Zimmermann, eds., *Commentary on the Additional Protocols of 8 June 1977 to the Geneva Conventions of 12 August 1949* (Geneva: Martinus Nijhoff, 1987) at 520.

56 *The Montreux Document on Pertinent International Legal Obligations and Good Practices for States Related to Operations of Private Military and Security Companies during Armed Conflict* (Montreux: Government of Switzerland, 2008), online: ICRC <http://www.icrc.org/web/>.

57 See James Cockayne, "Regulating Private Military and Security Companies: The Content, Negotiation, Weaknesses and Promise of the Montreux Document" (2008) 13 J. Confl. & Sec. L. 401.

58 See *ibid.* for a description of these negotiations.

59 See Perrin, *supra* note 12.

60 Examples of internal armed conflicts in the context of which an agreement was arrived at would include Yemen (1962), Nigeria (1967), El Salvador (1990), Bosnia-Herzegovina (1992), Guatemala (1994), and the Philippines (1998): Adama Dieng, "La mise en oeuvre du droit international humanitaire: les infractions et les sanctions, ou quand la pratique désavoue les textes" in *Law in Humanitarian Crises – How Can International Humanitarian Law Be Made Effective in Armed Conflicts?* vol. 1 (Luxembourg: EC, 1995) at 339-40; ICRC, *Increasing Respect for International Humanitarian Law in Non-International Armed Conflicts* (Geneva: ICRC, 2008) at 16-18. In other conflicts, insurgent proposals for such an agreement were rebuffed by the state. Thus, the FLN (Front de Libération Nationale, or National Liberation Front) in Algeria floated the idea of a special agreement under Common Article 3, but this was not endorsed by the French government: Lindsay Moir, *The Law of Internal Armed Conflict* (Cambridge: Cambridge University Press, 2002) at 71.

61 Frente Farabundo Martí para la Liberación Nacional (Farabundo Martí National Liberation Front).

62 FMLN, *Le legitimidad de nuestros métodos de lucha* (El Salvador: Secretaria de promoción y protección de los derechos humanos del FMLN, 1989) at 89; El Salvador, *Informe de la Fuerza Armada de El Salvador sobre el respecto y la vigencia de las normas del derecho humanitario durante el periodo de septiembre de 1986 a agosto de 1987* (1987).

63 See <http://www.genevacall.org/>.

64 *Convention on the Prohibition of the Use, Stockpiling, Production and Transfer of Anti-Personnel Mines and on Their Destruction,* 1997, 36 I.L.M. 1507 (entered into force 1 March 1999) [*Ottawa Convention*].

65 See Pascal Bongard, "Engaging Armed Non-State Actors in Landmine Ban: A Review of Geneva Call's Action, 2000-2007" (2008) 12 Journal of Mine Action.

66 Liberation Tigers of Tamil Eelam.

67 See *Annual Report 2008* (2008), online: Geneva Call <http://www.genevacall.org/resources/> at 6-9.

68 Robert Cover, "Nomos and narrative" (1983) 97 Harv. L. Rev. 4.

69 See Chae-Han Kim, "Reciprocity in Asymmetry: When Does It Work?" (2005) 31 International Interactions 1.

The Pragmatic Value of Reciprocity
Promoting Respect for International Humanitarian Law among Non-State Armed Groups

SOPHIE RONDEAU

[A] man be willing, when others are too, as far forth for peace and defense of himself, ... be contented with so much liberty against other men as he would allow other men against himself.

– The second law of nature, according to Thomas Hobbes

The Twenty-First Century International Legal Order

The international legal order set forth in the Peace of Westphalia in the seventeenth century rests on three main pillars: the state as the subject of law, state sovereignty,[1] and reciprocity. Alongside this more traditional conception, over the last centuries a new model of the international community has emerged. Antonio Cassese refers to this as "the Kantian Model":

> A ... feature of [this] model is the belief in a core of universal values (peace, respect for human rights, and self-determination of peoples) that all members of the international community must respect. In other words, alongside national interests and reciprocal relations among States, there also exist common interests and concerns that transcend each single State and unite the whole of mankind.[2]

The Westphalian/Anzillotian model[3] and the Kantian model offer two very different outlooks on international relations, making their coexistence somewhat uneasy. These tensions are further amplified when armed conflicts arise. If war is considered "the ontological underpinning of the State,"[4] then the Westphalian model may seem better suited to address it, the very nature of war putting the state at the centre of it all. But even with the existence of the UN Security Council and the cross-fertilization provided by regional human rights institutions, a central mechanism for lawmaking or law enforcement is still lacking in international humanitarian law (IHL). Although the International Criminal Court shows tremendous potential on that front, it still needs to deliver. Furthermore, state sovereignty is challenged when peoples – members of the international community that compose the "invisible layer" of public international law[5] – assert their right to self-determination, or even when, in the name of the common interest of mankind, heads of states are held personally accountable for violations of law and customs of war.

So where does the international legal order stand today? How does it adapt to the ever-growing presence and participation of the invisible layer in contemporary warfare? Are we at a crossroads where tradition and modernism meet to propose a combination of the Westphalian and Kantian models?

Furthermore, in the context of IHL, the definition of the elements that compose this invisible layer is fundamental. Even though all parties to non-international armed conflicts, whether state actors or armed groups, are bound by the relevant rules of IHL, the term "non-state armed groups" itself is not defined in treaty law. "Parties" to an armed conflict indeed vary widely in character. Organized armed groups, in particular, are extremely diverse, as explained by the International Committee of the Red Cross (ICRC):

> They range from those that are highly centralized (with a strong hierarchy, effective chain of command, communication capabilities, etc.) to those that are decentralized (with semi-autonomous or splinter factions operating under an ill-defined leadership structure). Groups may also differ in the extent of their territorial control, their capacity to train members, and the disciplinary or punitive measures that are taken against members who violate humanitarian law.[6]

For the purpose of this chapter, we will be aligning ourselves with the broad description of "organized armed groups" provided by the ICRC above. More specifically, the term "non-state armed groups" (NSAGs) should be understood as it is defined by the United Nations Office for the Coordination of Humanitarian Affairs (OCHA) in its *Manual on Humanitarian Negotiations with Armed Groups.*[7]

The fact that NSAGs do not participate in drafting treaties *per se* could be perceived as a disincentive to enforcement of IHL, potentially leading them towards feeling unconstrained by their "international" obligations. In order to minimize the state-centric nature of public international law, many innovative strategies to directly engage NSAGs have arisen in the last decades. One very successful example is Geneva Call (set out in Chapter 3). Also, there are mechanisms that can be found right within the corpus of IHL that deal directly with those groups. For example, when national liberation movements are parties to a conflict, they can draft unilateral declarations to apply the *Geneva Conventions* in accordance with Article 96(3) of Protocol I, Additional to the *Geneva Conventions* of 1949 (Protocol I). Since 1963, more than half a dozen NSAGs have used this mechanism.[8] Additional ways to get NSAGs to participate in the formation of IHL rules will be discussed in greater detail in Chapters 3 to 5, notably surrounding concepts such as the practice of engagement and the ownership of IHL. These are all relevant examples of tools created to make up for the absence of NSAGs from the table when the obligations binding all parties during an armed conflict were defined. The impact of those initiatives is not to be underestimated.

Furthermore, even if we set aside the question of participation of NSAGs – under varied forms – in the formation of IHL rules, it cannot be denied that, throughout history, the rules of war have become increasingly grounded in core universal values, somewhat to the detriment of state interests. Even before the Peace of Westphalia, there existed the Babylonian cardinal rule of "preventing the strong from oppressing the weak," as followed in numerous treaties signed at St. Petersburg,[9] Brussels,[10] Geneva,[11] Nuremberg,[12] and, more recently, Rome,[13] where universal humanitarian values were referred to as a crucial element to take into account in the waging of war. Of course, some might say that strategic, and not humanitarian, interests were at stake when heads of states negotiated humanitarian treaties. For example, by fixing the technical limits for the use of certain projectiles in the *St. Petersburg Declaration* of 1868, Czar Alexander II may not really have wanted to "alleviat[e] as much as possible the calamities of war"; more likely, he knew he did not have sufficient funds to purchase the explosive projectiles that the declaration banished. Although it is necessary to acknowledge this perspective, too much importance should not be given to such analysis.

Deconstructing the negotiation of international instruments through the study of egocentric and tactical considerations is not necessarily relevant, when the end result is positive in terms of commitment to the spirit of IHL.

A cross-fertilization of human rights law and IHL has also been gradually occurring, mutually influencing both systems. This has given rise to a movement offering a rereading of IHL that "humanizes" that regime.[14] One aspect of the humanization of IHL has been an attempt to minimize the role of reciprocity and to cast the obligations created by that regime as absolute and unilateral. Such an approach raises important questions: Is this a misguided effort? Is IHL now beyond reciprocity? Does it now solely rest on the requirements of humanity and the objective application of the law?

A Definition of Reciprocity in the Context of IHL

A related question worthy of exploring is the definition of reciprocity in the context of IHL. A general definition proposed by Cassese is "the idea that all interstate relations are based on self-interest, and that States engage in international legal dealings primarily to promote their own interests by reconciling them with those of any other State they wish to engage with."[15] This definition coincides with the seventeenth-century Westphalian/Anzillotian model of the international legal order, as described above: a legal order that encompasses only state actors and, to a certain extent, addresses almost only treaty law. With a narrow, interstate definition such as this one, reciprocity can be considered, to a certain extent, as a "toxic factor ... importing conditionality and offering excuses to match any violation committed by the other side," as René Provost puts it in Chapter 1. The next section will offer an analysis of two of what could be considered toxic factors, namely, the concepts of reservations and participation clauses. It will be argued that they have only very limited impact nowadays, as the "classic" notion of reciprocity linked to treaty law excludes all entities that are not states, hardly reflecting the reality of today's armed conflicts.

In addition, in trying to define reciprocity in the context of IHL, a distinction between two types can be made: reciprocity that is immediate and reciprocity that is systemic.[16] This distinction, which better mirrors the realities of a contemporary legal order that goes beyond interstate relations, opens the door to the inclusion of NSAGs.

Immediate reciprocity is tied to the interests of the state and is grounded in the bilateral nature of the obligations. This type of reciprocity is, for instance, at the centre of a *quid pro quo* agreement, where an exchange of one thing is required in return for another. It is argued that this type of reciprocity constitutes a transitional stage towards systemic reciprocity that allows for "the attainment of full equality."[17] Indeed, systemic reciprocity is linked to obligations that are tied to the continued existence of the system, not only to the states.[18] This type of reciprocity can be found in centralized systems, such as national criminal law, where there are legitimate expectations that all members of the system will bear similar obligations. As René Provost explains:

> In centralized systems, there is a much smaller need to rely on reciprocity, given the presence of a central authority which can act to both impose norms and enforce them. Equality among participants is usually a requirement for this type of system, and immediate reciprocity between participants becomes less essential. Relationships stemming from multilateral agreements which cannot be construed as creating a multiplicity of parallel bilateral relationships tend to lead to the establishment of institutionalized systems. Such non-bilateralisable relationships are not grounded in immediate reciprocity, but in the fashioning of a normative public order, a bundle of shared commitments and values which underlie systemic reciprocity.[19]

The emergence of the Kantian conception of the international legal order and the fact that IHL is a decentralized system suggest that, even though immediate reciprocity may no longer play a major role in this system, it may still be relevant. On the other hand, the lack of a central authority to enforce IHL is a barrier to the full attainment of systemic reciprocity. This provides the basis of our analysis: the extent to which these perceptions are well founded is investigated in this chapter, as an attempt will be made to situate the corpus of IHL within these two types of reciprocity. The potential of systemic reciprocity as a reinforcement mechanism of IHL for NSAGs will also be explored, even if, as Provost concluded, "it is clear that ... humanitarian law is [not] a perfect regime in which systemic reciprocity can effectively protect all fundamental interests of participants."[20]

In this chapter, I will look at the *Geneva Conventions* of 1949[21] and their Additional Protocols of 1977 (Protocol I, Protocol II)[22] to determine whether reciprocity – understood in its broader meaning, including both immediate and systemic reciprocity – is still an efficient way of generating compliance with IHL. This will be followed by a reflection on the validity and legality of an argument that could be invoked by parties to an international or non-international armed conflict: that non-reciprocity in the application of IHL rules (in the conduct of hostilities, for instance) gives rise to the right of reprisal. I will then conclude with a reflection on the links between humanitarian treaty law, reciprocity, and NSAGs.

Reciprocity and Humanitarian Treaty Law: The Imperative Call of Civilizations, beyond Reservations and *Clausa si Omnes*

In the general corpus of public international law, certain authors[23] assert that reciprocity is a "principle of international law," as understood under the United Nations *Statute of the International Court of Justice.*[24] It could indeed be argued that reciprocity is one of the basic concepts of this system, or at least treaty law, through the notion of reservations.

As stated in the *Vienna Convention on the Law of Treaties,*[25] when a state ratifies (or signs, accepts, approves, or accedes to) an international instrument, it can formulate a reservation to some of the treaty's provisions in order to protect its sovereign will. Such reservations modify the provisions in question to the same extent for other parties in relation to the reserving state. Hence, reservations are part of a fundamentally reciprocal mechanism and allow parties to clearly state their intention to apply and respect – or not – the provisions of a treaty. This is a form of immediate reciprocity, focused on the bilateral effects of the enforcement of the mechanism. Indeed, a reservation does not directly impact the treaty as an "institution"; rather, it provides boundaries for the relationships that the parties build together *around* the treaty.[26]

Under conventional IHL, reservations that are compatible with the object and purpose of the instruments are not prohibited *per se* by the *Geneva Conventions* and the Additional Protocols. In fact, twenty-two state parties to the *Geneva Conventions*[27] and thirty-six state parties to the Additional Protocols[28] made reservations upon signature or ratification of those instruments. With that many reservations, immediate reciprocity is reinforced; as Provost proposed, "particular relationships are created between State parties, the content of which varies according to reservations made by each State."[29] Here, however, the pragmatic weight of reciprocity is of little significance with respect to the promotion of respect for IHL among NSAGs, since reservations are mechanisms accessible only to states. By not having the possibility of entering reservations, NSAGs miss out on the possibility of influencing the application of the rules they are otherwise requested to observe and respect. In this context, the less inclusive the process is, the less motivation there is to respect the emerging norms. Of course, legally speaking, lack of motivation will never justify violations of IHL rules by NSAGs, since the rules bind all parties to the conflict, whether they agree or not. Nevertheless, moral and psychological incentives might be lacking.

It is worth recalling, however, that *erga omnes* obligations are non-bilateralizable norms. This considerably limits the impact of the reservation mechanism in IHL treaty law. Examples of such norms are those contained in Common Article 3; Part II of the *Fourth Geneva Convention*, which provides for the general protection of populations against certain consequences of war; sections of Protocol I regarding the treatment of refugees and stateless persons in the power of a party to the conflict (Article 73) and the fundamental guarantees of all persons in the power of a party to the conflict (Article 75); and Protocol II as a whole.[30] These obligations formulate basic norms that are owed to all other states and to the international community as a whole. Even if a state party were to submit reservations to those key humanitarian obligations, it would have no significant impact. This levels the field between state and non-state armed groups, as both of them cannot substantially modify the content of these humanitarian obligations. With *erga omnes* obligations, we are getting closer to the notion of systemic reciprocity where Provost's "bundle of shared commitments and values" are interacting.

On a related note, it should be added that the *clausa si omnes* (the participation clause) originally found in the 1899 *Convention with Respect to the Laws and Customs of War on Land*,[31] which allowed state parties to ignore the conventions if one or more parties to the conflict did not ratify them, can no longer be found in IHL treaty law.[32] Indeed, the content of Article 2 of the 1907 *Hague Convention IV*[33] and Article 24 of the 1906 *Convention for the Amelioration of the Condition of the Wounded and Sick in Armies in the Field*[34] was not repeated in subsequent treaties. Furthermore, it was reversed in the 1929 *Geneva Convention* on prisoners of war,[35] and then in Common Article 2(3) of the 1949 *Geneva Conventions*,[36] which provides for the application of the conventions between powers who are parties and are involved in a conflict, even if one of the belligerents is not a party to the convention. The article goes even further by stating that a power that is not party to the treaty but is involved in the conflict can recognize the convention for a specific conflict only. It is of interest that at the Diplomatic Conference of Geneva of 1949, it was suggested – but not accepted – that the following sentence be added to Common Article 2:

In the event of an international conflict between one of the High Contracting
Parties and a Power which is not bound by the present Convention, the
Contracting Party shall apply the provisions thereof. This obligation shall
stand unless, after a reasonable lapse of time, the Power not bound by the
present Convention states its refusal to apply it, or in fact fails to apply it.[37]

This proposition did not survive the process of the Diplomatic Conference.
This could be interpreted as signifying that, regarding the non-application
of the convention by a party that was officially bound to it, there was no
desire to allow for "*de facto* reciprocity" (meaning, lawfully disregarding
the law if the other party is, in fact, not respecting it itself) or *de jure* reciprocity (meaning, lawfully disregarding the law if the other party clearly and
officially stated its intention not to respect it). The most recent version of
Common Article 2 of the *Geneva Conventions* states that parties to the
conventions need to respect the rules they chose to abide by, notwithstanding the position of a party to the armed conflict that is not party to the
conventions.

Still, it cannot yet be said that Common Article 2 is a robust foundation
for the establishment of systemic reciprocity. Indeed, just like the mechanism of reservation discussed above, Common Article 2 is, in the end, a
manifestation of immediate reciprocity, applicable *only to state parties towards one another.* The fact that "under the Conventions High Contracting
Parties have no obligations toward non-party States" may lead to the conclusion that "particular bilateral relationships are created between State
parties," each relationship varying according to the reservations made at
ratification, hence reinforcing IHL as a "contractual-like" system.[38] Even if
this observation contains many striking and relevant points, in the context
of the present analysis it is not a major impediment to enforcement of IHL
by all parties to an armed conflict; indeed, it should be noted that IHL could
still be implemented outside systemic reciprocity.

Additionally, the issue of relations between contracting and non-
contracting state parties in armed conflicts is now moot, the *Geneva
Conventions* having been universally ratified by all member states of the
United Nations: no state can invoke the *clausa si omnes*, even if it could still
be found under treaty law. Even beyond treaty law, Dieter Fleck argues that
"the general participation clause has become obsolete insofar as the underlying treaty provisions have subsequently developed into customary law, as
was the case for the Hague Regulation of Land Warfare."[39] Fleck used the
1991 Gulf War as an example: the White House stated at that time that the

main provisions of the Protocol I were applied by the United States as if they constituted customary law, even if the US was not party to the instrument. This caused Fleck to conclude that "humanitarian protection standards were applied for policy reasons even in a situation in which treaty obligations did not exist."[40] This is at the core of the reflection on reciprocity and the engagement of all actors in an armed conflict, be they state or non-state: reciprocity, or lack thereof, touches upon fundamental principles of humanity that are beyond the realm of the legal norm. Can these principles be enforced? Is conscience the only judge of infringement of such principles?

Over the years, IHL has evolved away from the model of "if someone does not agree with the rules, then they are no longer rules" and closer to the notion of unilateral application, according to which, under all circumstances, even war has limits. Even if the participation clause no longer bears any relevance to contemporary IHL, the evolution that led to its extinction speaks volumes about the will of the international community to unconditionally undertake engagements that speak directly to the heart of humanity.

The *Commentaries to the Geneva Conventions* spell out the unilateral application of the 1949 *Geneva Conventions* (for ratifying states) through their interpretation of Common Article 1:

> By undertaking at the very outset to respect the clauses of the Convention, the Contracting Parties draw attention to the special character of that instrument. It is not an engagement concluded on a basis of reciprocity, binding each party to the contract only in so far as the other party observes its obligations. It is rather a series of unilateral engagements solemnly contracted before the world as represented by the other Contracting Parties. Each State contracts obligations "vis-à-vis" itself and at the same time "vis-à-vis" the others. The motive of the Convention is such a lofty one, so universally recognized as an imperative call of civilization, that one feels the need for its assertion, as much because of the respect one has for it oneself as because of the respect for it which one expects from one's opponent, and perhaps even more for the former reason than for the latter.[41]
>
> ...
>
> It has already been said that the Conventions are coming to be regarded ... more and more as solemn affirmations of principles respected for their own sake, and as a series of unconditional engagements on the part of each of the Contracting Parties "vis-à-vis" the others. A State does not proclaim the

principle of the protection due to wounded and sick combatants in the
hope of saving a certain number of its own nationals. It does so out of respect for the human person as such.[42]

The "epitomizing of the rejection of [immediate] reciprocity"[43] found in
Common Article 1 was reinforced by the International Court of Justice
when it stated that the undertaking of the High Contracting Parties to respect and ensure respect for the 1949 *Geneva Conventions* in all circumstances was not just an obligation under treaty law but also declaratory of
general principles of humanitarian law.[44] The International Criminal Tribunal for the former Yugoslavia (ICTY) followed the same path when it
stated in 2000 that the bulk of IHL lays down absolute obligations that are
unconditional and not based on reciprocity.[45] More specifically, the ICTY
judges examined in the *Kupreskic* case the *tu quoque* ("you too" in Latin)
defence, which rests not on the proof that the accused did not commit the
offence he is charged with but on the fact that the adversary has also committed similar crimes.

The ICTY made a very strong statement against the *tu quoque* defence
and, more generally speaking, in favour of the absolute and unconditional
nature of humanitarian obligations, going as far as evoking the Kantian conception of international relations (discussed above), as shown by the following excerpt from the judgment:

Individual criminal responsibility for serious violations of international
humanitarian law may not be thwarted by recourse to arguments such as
reciprocity. The absolute nature of most obligations imposed by rules of
international humanitarian law reflects the progressive trend towards the
so-called "humanisation" of international legal obligations, which refers to
the general erosion of the role of reciprocity in the application of humanitarian law over the last century. After the First World War, the application
of the laws of war moved away from a reliance on reciprocity between belligerents, with the consequence that, in general, rules came to be increasingly applied by each belligerent despite their possible disregard by the
enemy. The underpinning of this shift was that it became clear to States that
norms of international humanitarian law were not intended to protect State
interests; they were primarily designed to benefit individuals *qua* human
beings. Unlike other international norms, such as those of commercial
treaties which can legitimately be based on the protection of reciprocal interests of States, compliance with humanitarian rules could not be made

dependent on a reciprocal or corresponding performance of these obligations by other States. This trend marks the translation into legal norms of
the "categorical imperative" formulated by Kant in the field of morals: one
ought to fulfill an obligation regardless of whether others comply with it or
disregard it.[46]

Even if the ICTY makes the *tu quoque* argument completely irrelevant
from the basis of IHL,[47] it is still interesting, in the context of this chapter, to
assess further the implications of doctrines that rely similarly on reciprocity,
such as the reprisal doctrine. This will be one of the main topics of the following section.

Inadimplenti non est adimplendum? (Non-)Reciprocity, Extinction or Suspension of Obligations, and Reprisals

Is the condition of reciprocity found in the *Vienna Convention on the Law of
Treaties* an obstacle to the promotion of respect for IHL by all of its actors,
both states and NSAGs?[48] Since traditionally treaty law is fundamentally an
interstate institution steering away from NSAGs and reflecting the content
of the Westphalian/Anzillotian model, referred to above, too much focus
should not be placed on this issue. Nevertheless, it remains important to
look at the specifics of IHL under this perspective, as it risks reinforcing the
position that the concept of reciprocity – as a pragmatic argument, beyond
its actual legal value in the traditional international legal order – does entail
a practical strategy for enticing NSAGs to follow the rules.

The *Vienna Convention* states that a "material breach"[49] of a treaty by one
of its parties entitles the others to invoke the breach as a ground for termin-
ating the treaty or suspending its operations.[50] Here, "non-reciprocity in the
application of a treaty" is a valid legal argument that could be invoked by a
party if its counterpart, who solemnly engaged itself not to breach it, commits a violation or unauthorized rejection of the treaty. Generally speaking,
this mechanism could strongly reinforce an immediate bilateral and reciprocal response under international public law. Under the specific corpus
of IHL, however, this provision has very limited application, hence little impact on NSAGs, who would otherwise be marginalized. Indeed, the condition of reciprocity as defined under the *Vienna Convention* finds very few
uses in IHL.

First, it is important to note that, under Article 60(1) of the *Vienna Convention,* the condition of reciprocity can apply to situations of international
armed conflict only. Indeed, even if NSAGs can be considered parties to the

conflict subject to IHL norms, they cannot be considered "a party who *solemnly* engages itself not to breach" [emphasis added] the said norms. Second, and more important, the *Vienna Convention* expressly provides that the valid motives for suspension or extinction of an international treaty do "not apply to provisions relating to the protection of the human person contained *in treaties of a humanitarian character*, in particular to provisions prohibiting any form of reprisals against persons protected by such treaties"[51] [emphasis added]. Thus, this article dictates that obligations pertaining to the protection of the human person must be respected regardless of whether the counter-party respects said obligations.

An interesting element of Article 60 concerns the prohibition of reprisals. Paragraph 5 brings to light the fact that, in some cases, the beneficiaries of IHL still deserve some level of protection, even if they themselves violate those norms. Although it is not the purpose of this chapter to differentiate between the condition of reciprocity and reprisals, it is useful to take this opportunity to discuss the latter in the context of IHL and NSAGs. The issue of reprisals must be addressed as it risks constituting one of the "dark sides" of pushing for reciprocity – even pragmatically – to ensure respect for IHL. Simply put, if all parties to a conflict are expected to respect humanitarian imperatives in a reciprocal fashion (without the humanitarian obligations necessarily being subject to reciprocity *per se*[52]), it should also be taken into consideration that, in the conduct of hostilities, an "in-kind" response to the breach of reciprocity in the form of an attack on the civilian population would be to retaliate by attacking civilian targets. IHL strictly prohibits such actions, but education and reinforcement of the values underpinning IHL are essential to prevent breaches.

Reprisals[53] are against the law in principle, but are considered lawful by those who carry them out when used as a response and a sanction to a breach committed by the adversary.[54] There are notable exceptions, however:

- Reprisals against protected people, prisoners of war, civilians, and wounded, sick, and shipwrecked combatants are explicitly prohibited by the *First Geneva Convention* (Article 46), *Second Geneva Convention* (Article 47), *Third Geneva Convention* (Article 13), *Fourth Geneva Convention* (Article 33), and Protocol I (Articles 20 and 51[6]).
- In the *Convention for the Protection of Cultural Property in the Event of Armed Conflict*,[55] reprisals against cultural property are expressly prohibited in Articles 4(4) and 4(5), although it is possible to attack such property, but only if the enemy is "exposing it to destruction or damage"

and if the case presents itself where military necessity imperatively requires such an attack (Articles 4[1] and [2]).

- Finally, customary IHL, as stated in an ICRC study,[56] prohibits belligerent reprisals in international armed conflicts, but not entirely; it affirms that reprisals that are allowed are subject to stringent conditions (Rule 145), and confirms that belligerent reprisals against persons and objects protected by the *Geneva Conventions* are prohibited (Rules 146 and 147). In cases of non-international armed conflicts, even if Protocol II is silent on the matter of reprisals, customary law states that parties to the conflict do not have the right to resort to belligerent reprisals (Rule 148).

As part of the *Martic* decision, the ICTY Trial Chamber looked into customary international humanitarian law and concluded that any reprisals conducted in the context of a non-international armed conflict against civilians (whether individuals or populations) "are prohibited in all circumstances, even when confronted with wrongful behavior of the other party."[57]

These rules imply that, for example, the fact that a wounded soldier from Army A uses the emblem of the International Red Cross and Red Crescent Movement with perfidy to lure soldiers from Army B into a trap does not allow Army B to attack the hospital where the enemy combatants are being treated. Since not all reprisals are prohibited, however, those carried out during combat against combatants who otherwise violate IHL might be allowed in this context. Since there are no explicit rules on the matter in IHL treaty law, the principles of proportionality and humanity should always guide the parties to an armed conflict when conducting hostilities between combatants and considering reprisals, to make sure they are compatible with IHL requirements.[58]

The rationale for the prohibition of reprisals is easy to understand and shows the influence of human rights law on IHL: reprisals are often aimed at persons who are innocent of the crime that the perpetrators of the said reprisals intended to prevent or punish, and are therefore contrary to the modern idea of justice.[59] As Frits Kalshoven notes:

While there is ... a theoretical basis for the justification of belligerent reprisals, there are also grave objections, particularly from the point of view of human rights. It is of course easy to refer to reprisals as acts of one belligerent party against the other, but in reality the acts will affect the interests, or even the life or health, of human beings.

Belligerent reprisals, in other words, rest on the idea of solidarity, of holding the members of a community jointly and severally liable for the deeds of some of them. It hardly needs emphasizing that this goes to the roots of the concept of human rights, as fundamental rights of the human being as an individual, as distinct from his position as a member of the collectivity.[60]

Humanitarian Treaty Law, Reciprocity, and NSAGs: In Favour of a Culture of Compliance

The key issue to address while discussing the respect for IHL by NSAGs is whether the above reflection regarding treaty law is transposable to non-international armed conflicts where NSAGs are parties to the conflict and hence bound by the rules of IHL, but have not expressed their will to be bound by ratifying the applicable treaties.

It is reported in the ICRC *Commentaries* that at the Preliminary Conference of National Red Cross Societies in 1946, the International Committee proposed that, in the event of civil war, the parties should be invited to state that they were prepared to apply the principles of the convention on the basis of reciprocity.[61] This "second-best to ratification" solution was based on the assumption that an explicit declaration would "encourage ... the parties to line up with the advocates of humanitarian ideas, and that the sufferings arising out of civil wars thereby be appreciably reduced."[62] The national societies did not approve the suggestion, however. Instead, they recommended inclusion of an article normalizing the idea that silence meant consent: unless a party to a non-international conflict expressly announced its intention not to follow them, the conventions would apply to all parties.[63] The Conference of Government Experts were not willing to go as far as the national societies wanted. As a result, an article under which the principles of the conventions were to be applied in civil wars by the contracting party, provided that the adverse party did the same, was drafted, leading us back onto the reciprocity wagon.

A few years later, the pendulum swung back towards unilateralism. The Stockholm Conference, which comprised a mixed group of government and national society representatives, proposed the following text to the Diplomatic Conference of 1949 regarding non-international armed conflicts:

In all cases of armed conflict which are not of an international character, which may occur in the territory of one or more of the High Contracting

Parties, the implementing of the principles of the present Convention shall be obligatory on each of the adversaries. The application of the Convention in these circumstances shall in no way depend on the legal status of the Parties to the conflict and shall have no effect on that status.[64]

Common Article 3, as we know it today,[65] is in line with what was proposed by the "Stockholm contingent": the text is automatically applicable without any condition of reciprocity. The mere fact that non-signatory parties – parties that were not yet in existence in 1949 – are bound by this norm is innovative, to say the least, in public international law. The ICRC *Commentaries* state:

> If an insurgent party applies Article 3, so much the better for the Victims of the conflict. No one will complain. If it does not apply it, it will prove that those who regard its actions as mere acts of anarchy or brigandage are right.[66]

This affirmation echoes the words of Claude Bruderlein when speaking of the treatment to be afforded to those not committed to the basic principles of IHL: "We should not engage with them. They should be marginalized, seen as other 'génocidaires,' further isolated, ostracized and to a large extent, neutralized as being a main obstacle to the protection of the victims of war."[67]

While one might consider the use of the isolation strategy by states and non-state actors such as humanitarian groups and members of the international civil society as an effective way to show commitment towards the basic principles of IHL, it should remain a last resort. If the "insurgent" wants to be looked at as a brigand and anarchist, because it keeps the international community away or because it makes it "easier" for him to violate basic principles of humanity, marginalization may not be the strategy to adopt. Additionally, before ostracizing a party, it is important to ensure that all other parties to the armed conflict are waging war in a way that does not create expectations of non-reciprocity. If NSAGs are treated as criminals rather than lawful combatants and are denied the favourable treatment that they might be entitled to from the very beginning under IHL, any motivation they might have had to observe the law is likely to be drastically diminished. Simply put, "the culture of compliance with the law"[68] needs to be enforced before marginalizing a party to the conflict. Perhaps this is what

US President Barack Obama had in mind during his inaugural address on 20 January 2009 when, addressing the Muslim world, he stated: "We seek a new way forward, based on mutual interest and mutual respect."[69]

Fleck, who developed the idea of a "culture of compliance," has an interesting comment on the connection between the practical aspect of reciprocity and the conduct of military operations:

> Air campaigns are fought to concentrate forces and scrupulously avoid own casualties. Respect for public opinion in the sending state makes such consideration mandatory. But this practice may lead to an acceptance of greater risks for civilians in the battlefield ... Decision-makers must not only act in the interest of their own state, but they should also consider themselves as guardians of the people in the area of conflict. In choosing the means and methods of their operations, they must consider public opinion in all countries affected.[70]

It has already been argued that although reciprocity traditionally formed a fundamental basis of the law of armed conflicts, the harsh realities of the impact of war on people not directly taking part in hostilities, along with the influence of human rights law, has shifted it towards a more unilateral model of application. One major problem is that, as Michael F. Noone stated, human rights law is designed to treat "rational" criminals, whereas in many non-international armed conflicts the opponents are "irrational" (for instance, deterrence will have little effect on a suicide bomber).[71] Even if this rings true, it is of utmost importance to look at the big picture if one wishes to evaluate the relevance of current IHL. Suicide bombers are but one of the new contemporary challenges and, as Fleck stated, allowing individual actors to dictate a change of a valid rule shows weakness rather than strength.[72] It is by establishing and coherently reinforcing the "culture of compliance with the law" referred to earlier that parties to armed conflicts will truly embody humanitarian principles. Only after such a framework is established will it be feasible to use the pragmatic weight of reciprocity that encourages state and non-state parties to an armed conflict to auto-regulate the way they wage war in a fashion compatible with humanitarian considerations.

Reciprocity can be leveraged in non-international armed conflicts to encourage compliance, but not without some important caveats. In some specific contexts, reciprocity can constitute a constructive force and generate greater compliance with IHL, resulting in greater protection for the most vulnerable – the victims of war. Again, however, extreme caution is warranted. Reciprocity can be extremely difficult to use in practice, even more so in non-international armed conflicts where asymmetrical warfare is being waged. In some extreme cases, reciprocity is rejected and even, one could say, betrayed. For example, Osama bin Laden's "Letter to America," published in 2002, declares:

> The American army is part of the American people ... the American people are the ones who employ both their men and their women in the American forces which attack us. That is why the American people cannot be innocent of all the crimes committed by the Americans and the Jews against us. Allah, the Almighty, legislated the permission and the option to take revenge ... And whoever has killed our civilians, then we have the right to kill theirs.[73]

Toni Pfanner pondered this statement and wrote, in a 2005 contribution to the *International Review of the Red Cross:* "Not only is the fundamental distinction not made between combatants and civilians, but it is systematically used for the very purpose of placing the adversary at a disadvantage. In such cases, the other side begins to feel that it might be more in its interest not to consider itself bound by the law of war ... To level the battlefield, the military-wise stronger party is tempted to resort as well to unconventional warfare and covert operations."[74] From there, reciprocity in the asymmetrical conduct of hostilities leads us onto a very slippery slope, where "in-kind" reprisals to an attack on civilian populations take the form of blunt violations of the laws of armed conflicts, such as retaliation attacks on civilian targets.

Understanding reciprocity in IHL contexts requires looking beyond the legal sphere and into the practical, tactical, and political issues it entails. From that perspective, the theory of law and economics, which considers that reciprocity remains important, brings back to the table fundamental considerations, such as the lack of an overarching legal authority to enforce rules and the important weight of national self-interest in the behaviour of states. For instance, when Parisi sets up a taxonomy of social interactions in a game-theoretic framework to examine the role of reciprocity in the functioning of international law,[75] he makes a strong case that reciprocity is a meta-rule for the system of international law. Likewise, the words of Franck about the "age of pragmatic power politics" still confront some contemporary humanitarian assertions, even though those words were written forty years ago.[76] Thus, although the state of IHL is, strictly speaking in the legal sense, adequate with regard to reciprocity, we should not turn a blind eye to the reality of political contexts and decisions.

Moreover, granting of combatant immunity for mere participation in internal armed conflicts or mitigation of sentences by national courts are examples of mechanisms relying on some sort of reciprocity. Article 6(5) of Protocol II provides this option by "encourag[ing] gestures of reconciliation which can contribute to re-establishing normal relations in the life of a nation which has been divided."[77] Even though I do not necessarily endorse the amnesty solution beyond what Protocol II proposes, I recognize that many non-international armed conflicts end in combatant, even war criminal, amnesties. In the latter situation, immunity is granted after the violations have been committed, which shows the failure of the system of victim protection. Nevertheless, if this measure could influence the motivation of insurgents to observe the law today, it should be considered.

Along the same lines, the recognition of belligerency for NSAGs should not be rejected at the first occasion by a state on whose territory a non-international armed conflict is being waged. One key reason is that it prevents "any subordination of jus in bello to jus ad bellum," and triggers the application of virtually the whole range of the laws and customs of war.[78] This type of recognition can be qualified as a kind of "positive reciprocity," where the same rights are granted for all parties involved in the armed conflict (combatants from both sides will be equally treated as prisoners of war, for instance, even if the conventional threshold of what qualifies as an international armed conflict is not necessarily met).

Of course, this is a difficult and intricate decision for the state, and humanitarian reasons may not be sufficient in themselves to justify such a choice: recognition of belligerency may indeed weaken the sovereign authority of the government, as it could be perceived as having failed at securing the integrity of its territory. This might explain, at least partially, why this mechanism has not been used for the past thirty years (the last documented use being during the declaration of independence by the "Republic of Biafra").[79] Also, since implementation of fundamental humanitarian guarantees such as those found in Protocol II and Common Article 3 "does not constitute recognition of belligerency even implicitly nor does it change the legal nature of the relations between the parties engaged in the conflict,"[80] there are not that many incentives for a state to opt for the recognition of belligerency. Such recognition, however, does nothing to jeopardize the state's ability to fully enforce the rule of law and prosecute breaches of

IHL committed by the belligerent. Furthermore, on the military strategic front, this decision may be just what the Psychological Operations branch of the military needs: the state acting as "a reasonably diligent man" and winning the hearts and minds of its population by providing a safe and secure environment for them.

Even though the recognition-of-belligerency mechanism seems currently out-of-touch and is somewhat controversial, it still offers a "positive" form of reciprocity that is to be encouraged: it promotes higher humanitarian values and not bilateral relations, and brings about greater buy-in to a culture of compliance from all parties to a conflict.

Conclusion

> Even if obligations under international humanitarian law today are not subject to reciprocity, the expectation of reciprocal adherence by the adversary can be a driving force to motivate compliance. It is common sense that only those who themselves comply with the rules of international humanitarian law can expect the adversary to observe the dictates of humanity in an armed conflict. The expectation of mutual advantages is one of the guarantees for the implementation of international humanitarian law as much as it supports the implementation of international law in general.[81]

When deterrence and the threat of criminal liability or "chivalry and principles of humanity" do not create a full counterbalance to military necessity,[82] increased reliance on reciprocity – beyond treaty law – should be considered as a possible means of generating greater compliance with IHL, especially in a non-international armed conflict. In order for NSAGs to be truly engaged in this process, reciprocity needs to be understood in a broad, contemporary sense and closely linked to the concepts of culture of compliance and ownership of the rules, which means a gradual distancing from a bilateral model where adherence can be achieved only through direct participation in the initial drafting of the rules.

Contemporary non-international armed conflicts are more often than not waged asymmetrically by two groups with significantly different capabilities. The asymmetries, whether in the form of military power or general resources, are almost always in favour of the state. Terrorist attacks – acts used to frighten the population and influence the behaviour of a government or organization – provide an example of how NSAGs attempt to overcome this imbalance by using unconventional methods for maximum impact when faced with a significantly greater state arsenal. In this situation (which should not be perceived only as a new phenomenon of the twenty-first century[83]), there are examples where state military forces are reacting by stepping further away from the practices enforced in symmetrical warfare.[84] As Fleck notes, "given such trends, it is difficult to see how relevant the core principles of humanitarian protection are in practice for fighters in today's war."[85]

It has been proposed that terrorist acts and counterterrorist operations conducted outside of an armed conflict should be treated as law enforcement issues following a criminal justice model. Indeed, IHL is applicable to some terrorist acts and counterterrorist operations, but not all of them and certainly not those acts clearly committed outside of an armed conflict:

> [T]he ICRC believes that international humanitarian law is applicable when the "fight against terrorism" amounts to, or involves, armed conflict ... It is submitted that, absent more factual evidence that would enable further legal analysis, acts of transnational terrorism and the responses thereto must be qualified on a case-by-case basis. In some instances the violence involved will amount to a situation covered by IHL (armed conflict in the legal sense), while in others, it will not. Just as importantly, whether armed conflict in the legal sense is involved or not, IHL does not constitute the only applicable legal framework. IHL does not – and should not be used – to exclude the operation of other relevant bodies of law, such as international human rights law, international criminal law and domestic law.[86]

That being said, finding out what motivates NSAGs to observe IHL and its basic humanitarian principles is a complex question that we can scarcely tackle in this chapter. Earlier, we commented on a few incentives of "positive reciprocity," such as granting of amnesties and recognition of belligerency. At the core of it all, what is needed in order for reciprocity to be a strong enforcement tool is for a minimum but universally valid level of humanity to be enforced by all parties to a conflict. Still, it is very difficult to define to what extent parties are willing to abide by it. For instance, we do not possess sufficient reliable data to fully understand whether it is humanitarian duties or respect that is expected from their opponents that motivates certain states[87] and NSAGs[88] to refer to the policy of "calibrated reciprocity," which justifies, in the eyes of the perpetrator, systematic retaliation for the belligerents' actions, as defensive measures.

All parties to an armed conflict need to "walk the talk" of humanitarian norms. This is an important element in order for NSAGs to line up with the advocates of humanitarian ideas beyond the realm of conventional legal norms and treaty law. In order to build a culture of compliance towards IHL norms, all parties to a conflict need to hear the "imperative call of civilization" and act upon it. State actors must also actively contribute to this culture, given their privileged position in the international legal order.

Furthermore, the participation of NSAGs in the formation and enforcement of the rules is an appropriate area for investment of efforts in order to better address the intrastate nature of armed conflicts and better tackle the question of asymmetrical warfare. A broader, more contemporary and adapted definition of reciprocity based on the concept of ownership of the rules by NSAGs, through their participation in the formation and enforcement of those rules, could indeed further the cause of the imperative call of civilization. Of course, for the future, NSAGs should be involved – in one way or another – in the initial drafting of new treaties.

As Marco Sassòli stated, "[i]f ... rules are to apply to non-international armed conflicts, preliminary research should be done on what is realistic for non-State actors, because if the rules are designed exclusively for the needs of States, these non-State actors will simply ignore them."[89] To build on ownership of already existing rules, one needs to rely on mechanisms that formalize the commitments of NSAGs (action plans, agreements, deeds of commitment, codes of conduct, etc.): this is one key element that will be thoroughly addressed in Chapters 3 to 5. Other possibilities, as brought up by Sassòli,[90] are to look for inspiration from analogous branches of international law between non-state actors, such as cyberlaw, international sports law, or *lex mercatoria,* to develop, in consultation with non-state actors, applicable soft law; to negotiate specific codes of conduct with given non-state actors that would apply only to the specific conflict in which the actor is engaged; and to allow or encourage armed groups to publicly commit themselves to respecting IHL or show formal acceptance. All these possibilities provide for a stronger ownership of the rules by NSAGs.

One of the key ideas behind the reinforcement of ownership is that it is feeding into something positive and building on a culture of compliance. Looking at achievements such as those of Geneva Call, I believe optimistically that ownership of the rules of IHL by non-state armed groups is attainable through mechanisms outside the traditional state-centric model of the international legal order. If NSAGs are permitted to use their judgment and their reasoning to decide whether and how they will be bound by rules, a context is created where reciprocal adherence is seen as a positive tool and not a toxic justification to legally validate violations. In this sense, reciprocity will generate greater compliance with IHL by all parties to the conflict.

NOTES

1 *Contra:* the Peace of Westphalia did not put an end to multilayered authority in Europe, but simply constituted a case of redistribution of authority within the Holy Roman Empire: Stéphane Beaulac, "The Westphalian Model in Defining International Law: Challenging the Myth" (2004) 7 Australian Journal of Legal History 181.

2 Antonio Cassese, "A Big Step Forward for International Justice" (December 2003), online: Crimes of War Project <http://www.crimesofwar.org/>.

3 *Ibid.* It should be noted that, although Cassese refers to the "Grotian model" (which embodies the modern natural law theory), the term "Westphalian/Anzillotian model" and its dualist/voluntarist positivism doctrine is preferred here.

4 See Philip S. Golub, "Cinq années de 'guerre au terrorisme' – état d'urgence permanent" *Le monde diplomatique* (September 2006) at 18 and 19, online: Le monde diplomatique <http://www.monde-diplomatique.fr/>. Golub states that "l'état d'urgence permet à l'État de transcender la société et d'établir son autonomie dictatoriale. Ayant ainsi acquis le monopole de l'action et de la décision politiques, l'Etat, incarné par le dictateur qui décide de l'exception et qui, de ce fait, devient véritablement souverain, jouit de pouvoirs illimités. Étant donné que la guerre représente la forme la plus pure de l'état d'urgence, elle devient le fondement ontologique de l'Etat."

5 This conception of public international law is composed of two layers: "a traditional layer consisting of the law regulating the co-ordination and the co-operation between the members of the international society [... states ...] and a new layer consisting of the constitutional and administrative law of the international community of 6.5 billion human beings," as explained in Marco Sassòli and Antoine Bouvier, *How Does Law Protect in War?* 2d ed. (Geneva: ICRC, 2006) at 89 and 90.

6 Michelle Mack, "Increasing Respect for International Humanitarian Law in Non-International Armed Conflicts" (Geneva: ICRC, February 2008) at 11, online: ICRC <http://www.icrc.org/>.

7 Gerard McHugh and Manuel Bessler, "Humanitarian Negotiations with Armed Groups – a Manual for Practitioners" (UN, January 2006) at 6; see also s. 2.3, p. 14, online: OCHA <http://ochaonline.un.org/>. Non-state armed groups are defined as groups that have the potential to employ arms in the use of force to achieve political, ideological, or economic objectives; are not within the formal military structures of states, state-alliances, or intergovernmental organizations; and are not under the control of the state(s) in which they operate.

8 Declaration of 23 May 1968 in Kampala by the rebel Biafran authorities; Declaration of 16 June 1977 by Joshua Nkomo of the African National Congress and the Zimbabwean African People's Union (ANC-ZAPU); Declaration of 8 September 1977 by Ndabaningi Sithole of the African National Congress (ANC, Zimbabwe); Declaration of 23 September 1977 by Bishop Muzorewa of the United African National Council (UANC); Declaration of 25 July 1980 by the União Nacional para a

Independencia Total de Angola (UNITA); Declaration of 28 November 1980 by the African National Congress (ANC, South Africa); Declaration of the South West Africa People's Organization (SWAPO); Declaration of 5 April 1988 by the UNITA; Declaration in June 1988 by John Garang (Sudan); Declaration of 6 October 1988 in Geneva by the SWAPO; Declaration of 22 October 1992 by the Rwandese Patriotic Front: Churchill Ewumbue-Monono, "Respect for International Humanitarian Law by Armed Non-State Actors in Africa" (2006) 88 Int'l Rev. Red Cross 907.

9 *Declaration Renouncing the Use, in Time of War, of Explosive Projectiles under 400 Grammes Weight,* Saint Petersburg, 29 November/11 December 1868, Preamble, original text in French: "an International Military Commission ... having by common agreement fixed the technical limits at which *the necessities of war ought to yield to the requirements of humanity*" [emphasis added], reprinted from Dietrich Schindler and Jiri Toman, *The Laws of Armed Conflicts,* 4th ed. (Leiden and Boston: Martinus Nijhoff, 2004) at 91, online: ICRC <www.icrc.org/ihl> [*St. Petersburg Declaration*].

10 *Project of an International Declaration Concerning the Laws and Customs of War,* Brussels, 27 August 1874, original in French; *e.g.,* art. 12: "The laws of war do not recognize in belligerents an unlimited power in the adoption of means of injuring the enemy," reprinted from Schindler and Toman, *ibid.* at 22, online: ICRC <www. icrc.org/ihl> [*Brussels Declaration*].

11 *Convention for the Amelioration of the Condition of the Wounded and Sick in Armed Forces in the Field,* Geneva, 12 August 1949, 75 R.T.N.U. 31 [GCI]; *Convention for the Amelioration of the Condition of Wounded, Sick and Shipwrecked Members of Armed Forces at Sea,* Geneva, 12 August 1949, 75 R.T.N.U. 85 [GCII]; *Convention Relative to the Treatment of Prisoners of War,* Geneva, 12 August 1949, 75 R.T.N.U. 135 [GCIII]; and *Convention Relative to the Protection of Civilian Persons in Time of War,* 12 August 1949, 75 R.T.N.U. 287 [GCIV], online: ICRC <http://www.icrc.org/ihl.nsf/>.

12 *Principles of International Law Recognized in the Charter of the Nüremberg Tribunal and in the Judgment of the Tribunal,* 1950, Report of the International Law Commission Covering Its Second Session, 5 June – 29 July 1950, Document A/1316, online: ICRC <http://www.icrc.org/ihl.nsf/>.

13 *Rome Statute of the International Criminal Court,* 17 July 1998, 2d para. of the Preamble: "Mindful that during this century millions of children, women and men have been victims of unimaginable atrocities that deeply shock the conscience of humanity," in A/CONF.183/9 as corrected by the procès-verbaux of 10 November 1998 and 12 July 1999 in PCNICC/1999/INF/3, online: ICRC <http://www.icrc. org/ihl.nsf/>.

14 Theodore Meron, "The Humanization of Humanitarian Law" (2000) 94 A.J.I.L. 239.

15 Cassese, *supra* note 2.

16 This distinction has been proposed and thoroughly researched by René Provost, *International Human Rights and Humanitarian Law* (Cambridge: Cambridge University Press, 2002) at 122. See also Robert Keohane, "Reciprocity in International Relations" (1986) 40 International Organization 1 at 4 (distinction between specific and diffuse reciprocity), as quoted in Provost, *ibid.;* also see Peter M. Blau, *Exchange and Power in Social Life,* 3d ed. (Edison, NJ: Transaction Publishers, 1992) (theory of social exchange).

17 Provost, *ibid.* "Immediate reciprocity" might be what Mark Osiel describes as "real reciprocity [that] entails contributing to an emergent global contract that encompasses the law of war and from which all peoples may mutually benefit" in *The End of Reciprocity: Terror, Torture, and the Law of War* (Cambridge: Cambridge University Press, 2009).

18 Robert Keohane applies Blau's concepts to international politics and distinguishes two types of reciprocity: specific reciprocity ("situations in which specified partners exchange items of equivalent value in a strictly delimited sequence") and diffuse reciprocity ("a definition ... less precise [where] one's partner may be viewed as a group rather than as particular actors, and the sequence of events is less narrowly bounded"), as quoted in Yongnian Zheng, "China's De Facto Federalism" in Baogang He, Brian Galligan, and Takashi Inoguchi, eds., *Federalism in Asia* (Northampton, MA: Edward Elgar, 2007) at 234.

19 Provost, *supra* note 16 at 123 [footnotes omitted].

20 *Ibid.* at 237.

21 GCI, GCII, GCIII, and GCIV, *supra* note 11.

22 *Protocol Additional to the Geneva Conventions of 12 August 1949, and Relating to the Protection of Victims of International Armed Conflicts (Protocol I)*, 8 June 1977, 1125 U.N.T.S. 3 (entered into force 7 December 1978) [API]; *Protocol Additional to the Geneva Conventions of 12 August 1949, and Relating to the Protection of Victims of Non-International Armed Conflicts (Protocol II)*, 8 June 1977, 1125 U.N.T.S. 609 (entered into force 7 December 1978) [APII].

23 See, *e.g.*, Michael Byers, *Custom, Power and the Power of Rules* (Cambridge: Cambridge University Press, 1999) at 90; Jianming Shen, "The Basis of International Law: Why Nations Observe" (1999) 17 Dick. J. Intl. L. 287; Francesco Parisi and Nita Ghei, "The Role of Reciprocity in International Law" (2003) 36 Cornell Int'l L.J. 93, online: Social Science Research Network (SSRN) <http://papers.ssrn.com/sol3/>.

24 26 June 1945, 59 Stat. 1055 at art. 38(1)(c).

25 *Vienna Convention on the Law of Treaties*, 23 May 1969, 1155 U.N.T.S. 331 (entered into force 27 January 1980) at art. 21(b) [*Vienna Convention*].

26 *Ibid.* at art. 21(2).

27 Albania, Angola, Australia, Bangladesh, Barbados, China, Czech Republic, Guinea-Bissau, Islamic Republic of Iran, Israel, Democratic Republic of Korea, Republic of Korea, Kuwait, New Zealand, Pakistan, Portugal, Russian Federation, Suriname, United Kingdom, United States of America, Vietnam, and Yemen all made reservations upon signature or ratification of the 1949 *Geneva Conventions*. See Final Record of the Diplomatic Conference of Geneva of 1949, vol. 1, Federal Political Department, Berne, at 342-57, online: ICRC <http://www.icrc.org/ihl.nsf/>.

28 Out of the 167 states that ratified Protocol I, Albania, Angola, Argentina, Australia, Austria, Belgium, Canada, China, Denmark, Egypt, Finland, Former Yugoslav Republic of Macedonia, France, Germany, Greece, Holy See, Iceland, Ireland, Italy, Japan, Republic of Korea, Kuwait, Liechtenstein, Malta, Mauritius, Mongolia, Netherlands, Oman, Portugal, Qatar, Saudi Arabia, Spain, Sweden, Syrian Arab Republic, United Arab Emirates, and United Kingdom all made reservations upon signature or ratification: see list of State parties under the Introduction to "Protocol

Additional to the Geneva Conventions of 12 August 1949, and relating to the Protection of Victims of International Armed Conflicts (Protocol I), 8 June 1977," online: ICRC <http://www.icrc.org/ihl.nsf/>. Out of the 163 states that ratified Protocol II, Argentina, Austria, Canada, China, Egypt, France, Germany, Holy See, Ireland, Liechtenstein, Malta, Mauritius, Oman, Portugal, Russian Federation, and United Arab Emirates all made reservations upon signature or ratification: see list of State parties under the Introduction to "Protocol Additional to the Geneva Conventions of 12 August 1949, and relating to the Protection of Victims of Non-International Armed Conflicts (Protocol II), 8 June 1977," online: ICRC <http://www.icrc.org/ihl.nsf/>.

29 Provost, *supra* note 16 at 147.

30 *Ibid.* at 150.

31 The Hague, 29 July 1899, reprinted from Schindler and Toman, *supra* note 9 at 69, online: ICRC <www.icrc.org/ihl>.

32 As Theodore Meron explains, this clause threatens the integrity of the Nuremberg prosecutions, but the tribunal countered that argument by stating that the rules laid out in the 1907 *Hague Convention IV* were, by 1939, considered customary, making the general-participation clause fall into desuetude: Meron, *supra* note 14 at 247 *in fine* and 248.

33 18 October 1907, 36 R.T.S.N. 539: "The provisions contained in the Regulations referred to in Article 1, as well as in the present Convention, do not apply except between Contracting Powers, and then only if all the belligerents are parties to the Convention."

34 6 July 1906, 35 Stat. 1885: "The provisions of the present Convention are obligatory only on the Contracting Powers, in case of war between two or more of them. The said provisions shall cease to be obligatory if one of the belligerent Powers should not be signatory to the Convention."

35 118 L.N.T.S. 303 (entered into force 19 June 1931), art. 82: "In time of war if one of the belligerents is not a party to the Convention, its provisions shall, nevertheless, remain binding as between the belligerents who are parties thereto."

36 "Although one of the Powers in conflict may not be a party to the present Convention, the Powers who are parties thereto shall remain bound by it in their mutual relations. They shall furthermore be bound by the Convention in relation to the said Power, if the latter accepts and applies the provisions thereof."

37 *Remarks and Proposals Submitted by the International Committee of the Red Cross,* Geneva, February 1949, at 9, as reported in Jean Pictet, ed., *The Geneva Conventions of August 12 1949: Commentaries,* Geneva, ICRC, 1958 at 31, online: ICRC <http://www.icrc.org/ihl.nsf/> [ICRC's *Commentaries GC*]. It should also be noted that, after this proposal did not go through, the Canadian delegation suggested that the convention should be applicable to a power not party to the convention so long as that power complied with its provisions. Under this proposal, the signatory powers were automatically bound, and continued to be bound, so long as the non-signatory power complied with the convention. Since no agreement was possible, the proposal was discarded in favour of the compromise wording of the present text.

38 Provost, *supra* note 16 at 147.

39 Dieter Fleck, "International Humanitarian Law after September 11: Challenges and the Need to Respond" (2003) 5 Y.B. Int'l Human. L. 41 at 60.
40 *Ibid.* at 61.
41 ICRC's *Commentaries GC, supra* note 37 at 25.
42 *Ibid.* at 28.
43 Meron, *supra* note 14 at 248.
44 *Military and Paramilitary Activities in and against Nicaragua (Nicaragua v. United States)*, Merits, [1986] I.C.J. Rep. 14 at 114.
45 International Criminal Tribunal for the former Yugoslavia (ICTY), *Prosecutor v. Kupreskic et al.*, Trial Judgment, IT-95-16-T (14 January 2000) at paras. 515-20, online: UNHCR <http://www.unhcr.org/refworld/>.
46 *Ibid.* at paras. 517-18. It should also be noted that the *tu quoque* defence, although invoked indirectly, was dismissed once again in ICTY, *Prosecutor v. Kunarac*, Judgment, IT-96-23-T & IT-96-23/1-T (22 February 2001) at para. 580 : "As the Defence was reminded many times during the trial, the fact that the Muslim side may have committed similar atrocities against Serb civilians, an argument brought up mutatis mutandis by almost every Serb accused and Defence counsel before the Tribunal, is irrelevant in the context of this case." See also ICTY, *Prosecutor v. Kunarac*, Judgment (appeal), IT-96-23 & IT-96-23/1-A (12 June 2002) at para. 87 and ICTY, *Prosecutor v. Limaj*, Judgment, IT-03-66-T (30 November 2005) at para. 193.
47 *Contra:* There were a few occasions at the Nuremberg and Dachau Trials where the *tu quoque* defence was accepted. For more information on this element and on the *tu quoque* defence, see Sienho Yee, "The *Tu Quoque* Argument as a Defence to International Crimes, Prosecution, or Punishment" (2004) 3 Chinese Journal of International Law 87.
48 The Latin in this section's title is translated as "Has one no need to respect his obligation if the counter-party has not respected his own?"
49 Being a "repudiation of the treaty or a violation of a provision essential to the accomplishment of the object or the purpose of the treaty": see *Vienna Convention, supra* note 25 at art. 60(3).
50 *Ibid.* at art. 60(1).
51 *Ibid.* at art. 60(5). See also Christopher Greenwood, "Historical Development and Legal Basis" in Dieter Fleck, ed., *The Handbook of Humanitarian Law in Armed Conflicts* (Oxford: Oxford University Press, 1995) 1 at para. 102(2) (the non-reciprocity of humanitarian undertakings is reflected in the *Vienna Convention*, art. 60[5]).
52 Fleck, *supra* note 39 at 61: "Reciprocity in compliance by warring parties is not a condition for humanitarian protection today. It may even be questioned whether and to what extent such reciprocity was important in earlier stages of history. There might be no conclusive evidence that 'civilized' societies, as they saw themselves strictly required reciprocity for every action vis-à-vis each other" [footnotes omitted].
53 See Steven R. Ratner, "Rethinking the Geneva Conventions" (30 January 2003), online: Crimes of War Project <http://www.crimesofwar.org/>. It should be noted that the complete prohibition of reprisals under Protocol I does present difficulties.

Indeed, states such as Italy and the United Kingdom issued reservations to this protocol, allowing for the possibility of measured reprisals against civilians if the opposing party itself engaged in serious, deliberate attacks on civilians: Frits Kalshoven, "Human Rights, the Law of Armed Conflicts, and Reprisals" (1971) 121 Int'l Rev. Red Cross 183 at 186.

54 Yves Sandoz, Christophe Swinarski, and Bruno Zimmermann, eds., *Commentary on the Additional Protocols of 8 June 1977 to the Geneva Conventions of 1949*, Genève, ICRC (1987) at 982, online: ICRC <www.icrc.org/ihl/> [ICRC's *Commentary AP*].

55 The Hague, 14 May 1954, reprinted from Schindler and Toman, *supra* note 9 at 747, online: ICRC <www.icrc.org/ihl/>.

56 Jean-Marie Henckaerts, "Study on Customary International Humanitarian Law: A Contribution to the Understanding and Respect for the Rule of Law in Armed Conflict" (March 2005), online: ICRC <http://www.icrc.org/>.

57 ICTY, *Prosecutor v. Martic*, Decision (Review of the Indictment under Rule 61), IT-95-11, (8 March 1996) at paras. 17 and 18.

58 See ICRC's *Commentary AP, supra* note 54 at 985, para. 3457, for more information on guiding principles on reprisals: "1) subsidiarity: reprisals may only be taken in the case of imperative necessity when all other means have proved ineffective and after a specific, formal and prior warning has been given that such measures would be taken if the breach did not cease or if it recommenced, and the warning remained ineffective; such a decision can only be taken by the highest authorities of the Party to the conflict; the reprisals will end as soon as they have achieved their purpose, *i.e.*, the cessation of the breach which provoked them; 2) proportionality: in deciding upon the way in which reprisals will be applied and upon their extent the utmost restraint must be exercised consistent with the purpose they are to serve, namely, to lead the adversary to respect the law; the degree of severity of the reprisals shall in no case exceed that of the breach committed by the enemy; 3) humanity: in all cases Parties to the conflict must respect the laws of humanity and the dictates of the public conscience." See also Crimes of War Project, the Book, Definition of Reprisal by Frits Kalshoven, online: Crimes of War Project <http://www.crimesofwar.org/a-z -guide/reprisal/>: "if a commander wishes to exercise a 'right to retaliate' against his enemies in conformity with IHL – under the condition that it is not otherwise prohibited – he must apply the principle of subsidiarity, emit a valid notice, exercise his actions in accordance with the principle of proportionality and enforce the temporary character of the retaliatory action."

59 *Contra:* Michael A. Newton "Reconsidering Reprisals" (2010) 20 Duke J. Comp. & Int'l L. 361 (abstract): "Thoughtful and multilateral reassessment of the lawful scope and rationale for reasonable reprisals is overdue."

60 Kalshoven, "Human Rights," *supra* note 53 at 183.

61 ICRC's *Commentaries GC, supra* note 37 at 41.

62 *Ibid.*

63 *Ibid.:* "In the case of armed conflict within the borders of a State, the Convention shall also be applied by each of the adverse Parties, unless one of them announces expressly its intention to the contrary."

64 ICRC's *Commentaries GC, supra* note 37 at 42 and 43.

65 GCI, GCII, GCIII, and GCIV, *supra* note 11: "In the case of armed conflict not of an international character occurring in the territory of one of the High Contracting Parties, each Party to the conflict shall be bound to apply, as a minimum, the following provisions:

    (1) Persons taking no active part in the hostilities, including members of armed forces who have laid down their arms and those placed 'hors de combat' by sickness, wounds, detention, or any other cause, shall in all circumstances be treated humanely, without any adverse distinction founded on race, colour, religion or faith, sex, birth or wealth, or any other similar criteria.

    To this end, the following acts are and shall remain prohibited at any time and in any place whatsoever with respect to the above-mentioned persons:

    (a) violence to life and person, in particular murder of all kinds, mutilation, cruel treatment and torture;

    (b) taking of hostages;

    (c) outrages upon personal dignity, in particular humiliating and degrading treatment;

    (d) the passing of sentences and the carrying out of executions without previous judgment pronounced by a regularly constituted court, affording all the judicial guarantees which are recognized as indispensable by civilized peoples.

    (2) The wounded and sick shall be collected and cared for.

    An impartial humanitarian body, such as the International Committee of the Red Cross, may offer its services to the Parties to the conflict.

    The Parties to the conflict should further endeavour to bring into force, by means of special agreements, all or part of the other provisions of the present Convention.

    The application of the preceding provisions shall not affect the legal status of the Parties to the conflict."

66 ICRC's *Commentaries GC, supra* note 37 at 52.

67 Transcript from Claude Bruderlein's presentation in *International Panel on the Future of International Humanitarian Law, Humanitarian Policy and Conflict Research* (18 July 2008), online: Humanitarian Law and Policy Forum <http://ihlforum.ning.com>.

68 Fleck, *supra* note 39 at 64.

69 President Barack Obama's speech in full is available online: White House <http://www.whitehouse.gov/>.

70 Fleck, *supra* note 39 at 64.

71 The notion of lack of effect of deterrence in asymmetrical warfare has been discussed by Prof. Michael F. Noone, at the 7th International Security Forum (ISF) in April 2007. To consult the paper capturing the panel discussions, see: Vivian Fritschi, *The Law of Armed Conflict and the Principle of Sovereign Equality of States* (Zurich: Center for Security Studies [CSS] and ETH Zurich, 2007), at 106, online: International Relations and Security Network, Swiss Federal Institute of Technology: <http://www.isn.ethz.ch/isn/Digital-Library/Publications/>.

72 Fleck, *supra* note 39 at 62.

73 "A letter from Osama bin Laden to the American people": the letter appeared first on the Internet in Arabic on 17 November 2002 and was subsequently translated into English. "Full text: bin Laden's 'letter to America,'" online: Guardian <http://www.guardian.co.uk/>, as quoted in: Toni Pfanner, "Asymmetrical Warfare from the Perspective of Humanitarian Law and Humanitarian Action" (2005) 87 Int'l Rev. Red Cross 149 at 162.

74 *Ibid.*

75 Parisi and Ghei, *supra* note 23.

76 Thomas Franck, "Who Killed Article 2(4)?" (1970) 64 A.J.I.L. 809 at 836: "National self-interest, particularly the national self-interest of the super-Powers, has usually won out over treaty obligations. This is particularly characteristic of this age of pragmatic power politics. It is as if international law, always something of a cultural myth, has been demythologized. It seems this is not an age when men act by principles simply because that is what gentlemen ought to do." See also Thomas Franck, "What Happens Now? The United Nations after Iraq" (2003) 97 A.J.I.L. 607.

77 ICRC's *Commentary AP, supra* note 54 at 1400, para. 4618.

78 Francois Bugnion, "*Jus ad Bellum, Jus in Bello* and Non-International Armed Conflicts" (2003) 4 Y.B. Int'l Human. L. 167 at 181.

79 *Ibid.*

80 ICRC's *Commentary AP, supra* note 54 at 1344, para. 4440 [footnotes omitted].

81 Fleck, *supra* note 39 at 61 [footnote omitted].

82 Meron, *supra* note 14 at 243.

83 Pfanner, *supra* note 73 at 150 and 151.

84 *Ibid.* at note 37, where the existence of a new American organization, called the Strategic Support Branch, is mentioned. This organization is designed to operate without detection and under the direct control of the Secretary of Defense, deploys small teams of case officers, linguists, interrogators, and technical specialists alongside newly empowered Special Operations Forces: "The Secret Unit Expands Rumsfeld's Domain" *Washington Post* (23 January 2005); and US Department of Defense release no. 062-0523, "Statement from Pentagon Spokesman Lawrence DiRita on Intelligence Activities of the Defense Department" (23 January 2005), online: US Department of Defense <http://www.defense.gov/>.

85 Fleck, *supra* note 39 at 61.

86 *International Humanitarian Law and the Challenges of Contemporary Armed Conflicts,* report prepared by the ICRC for the 28th International Conference of the Red Cross and Red Crescent, Geneva, 2-6 December 2003, at 18 and 19, online: ICRC <http://www.icrc.org/>.

87 For instance, the Philippine government is enforcing the policy in its conflict with the Moro Islamic Liberation Front (MILF). See "PGMA's speech during the Mindanao Island Conference" (18 July 2003), online: Office of the President, Republic of the Philippines <http://www.beatingtheodds.ph/op/>.

88 For instance, Hezbollah is enforcing this policy. Online: Transnational and Non-State Armed Groups Project (TAGS Project) <http://www.tagsproject.org/>.

89 Marco Sassòli, "Legal Mechanisms to Improve Compliance with International Humanitarian Law by Armed Groups" in Marc Vuijlsteke, Anja Fiedler, and Jan Rovny, eds., *Proceedings of the Bruges Colloquium – Improving Compliance with International Humanitarian Law – 11th-12th September 2003*, Special Edition of *Collegium* (Winter 2004) 97 at 98, online: College of Europe <http://www.coleurop.be/>.
90 *Ibid.*

Armed Non-State Actors and Humanitarian Norms
Lessons from the Geneva Call Experience

ELISABETH DECREY WARNER, JONATHAN SOMER, AND PASCAL BONGARD

This chapter is presented partly as an introduction to the methodology employed by the international non-governmental organization (NGO) Geneva Call in trying to get "armed non-state actors" (ANSAs)[1] to respect humanitarian norms, and partly as a reaction to the other chapters in Part 1 of this book. It begins by providing the context for the process of engagement with ANSAs, describing the Geneva Call approach, and discussing some of its achievements and challenges. It then analyzes the influence of reciprocity on ANSA behaviour according to Geneva Call's experience, and compares its impact with that of a formal mechanism under which ANSAs can commit to international humanitarian law (IHL) and international human rights law (IHRL) norms.[2] As its scope is limited to the Geneva Call experience, this chapter does not attempt to draw global conclusions about the role of reciprocity. Instead, it should be considered as sharing practice-based observations on some aspects of a complex issue.

Engaging with ANSAs on Humanitarian Issues

The Practice of Engagement
Most armed conflicts today are non-international and involve one or more ANSAs fighting government forces or other ANSAs or both. The Stockholm International Peace Research Institute (SIPRI) records that in 2009 all major armed conflicts waged worldwide were intrastate.[3] Yet, while ANSAs

play an increased role in contemporary warfare and are responsible for many abuses of humanitarian norms, the state-centric nature of international law poses challenges for addressing their behaviour. First, existing treaties and their enforcement mechanisms remain primarily focused on states. Second, even though they are bound by IHL, ANSAs cannot negotiate or become parties to relevant international treaties, and there is no agreement on whether they contribute to the formation of customary IHL.[4] There is therefore little opportunity for ANSAs to express their adherence to humanitarian norms, which may indeed limit the incentive to respect them. ANSAs may not feel bound by rules that they have not been involved in making and are not allowed to sign on to.

Despite these challenges, humanitarian organizations such as the International Committee of the Red Cross (ICRC) have long had to deal with ANSAs in order to fulfill their missions.[5] Over the last decade, however, the practice of humanitarian engagement with ANSAs – which can be defined as a non-coercive process of interaction for the purposes of ensuring the provision of humanitarian assistance to populations affected by armed conflicts, the safety of humanitarian workers, and better respect for IHL and IHRL – has developed significantly.[6] International human rights NGOs, which traditionally focused their attention on governments, have since the 1990s increasingly reported on abuses committed by ANSAs and advocated their compliance with international standards.[7] United Nations agencies have negotiated a growing number of humanitarian agreements with ANSAs, such as the "Ground Rules Agreement" signed in 1995 with the Sudan People's Liberation Movement/Army (SPLM/A);[8] at about the same time, a Special Representative of the Secretary-General for Children and Armed Conflict was mandated by the UN General Assembly to promote the rights of the child with respect to parties to armed conflicts, including ANSAs.[9] In 2000, members of the International Campaign to Ban Landmines (ICBL) created a specialized NGO, Geneva Call, exclusively dedicated to getting ANSAs to adhere to the ban on anti-personnel (AP) mines and to other humanitarian norms.

Geneva Call's Approach

Geneva Call was launched in response to the realization that the AP mine problem would not be effectively addressed if only states were engaged. In recent years, this weapon has been used by ANSAs in more countries than by government forces, and some ANSAs have been manufacturing their own mines or mine-like explosive devices. Research conducted by Geneva Call identified at least forty ANSAs that reportedly employed these weapons between 2003 and 2005.[10] Moreover, many of them control mine-affected territories. Local communities living in such areas suffer from the presence of mines and often receive little or no assistance. It is therefore important that ANSAs undertake, support, or at least permit mine action. Finally, the 1997 *Convention on the Prohibition of the Use, Stockpiling, Production and Transfer of Anti-Personnel Mines and on Their Destruction* (also known as the *Ottawa Convention*) does not apply directly to ANSAs, unlike Common Article 3 of the *Geneva Conventions,* and the mechanism provided to prevent and suppress prohibited activities – adoption of domestic legal and administrative measures, including the imposition of penal sanctions – has not proven to be effective against ANSAs. The latter may not be aware of the law or willing to abide by the obligations taken by the very state they are fighting against, especially since the act of rebellion itself will invariably be criminalized domestically.

As ANSAs cannot become parties to the *Ottawa Convention,* Geneva Call developed an innovative mechanism, the "Deed of Commitment for Adherence to a Total Ban on Anti-Personnel Mines and for Cooperation in Mine Action" (hereafter *Deed of Commitment*), which allows ANSAs to adhere to its provisions.[11] This universal and standard unilateral declaration by and large mirrors state obligations under the convention. Signatory ANSAs formally pledge to prohibit the use, production, and transfer of AP mines, to destroy stocks they may have, to cooperate in humanitarian mine action, and to take measures to enforce compliance.[12] The *Deed of Commitment* also contains a monitoring provision, which includes a self-reporting requirement and, more radically, an agreement on the part of the signatory ANSA to allow for external monitoring of compliance, including field verification missions by Geneva Call.[13] In addition to these clauses, which form the core obligations of the *Deed of Commitment,* signatory ANSAs agree to consider their pledge to the AP mine ban as one step or part of a broader commitment to humanitarian norms.[14] They also acknowledge that adhering to the *Deed of Commitment* will not affect their legal status, pursuant to Common Article 3 of the 1949 *Geneva Conventions.*[15] Finally, they agree that, in cases of confirmed violations, Geneva Call may publicize such violations as a means of sanctioning their non-compliance.[16]

The *Deed of Commitment* is signed by the ANSA leadership and countersigned by Geneva Call and the Government of the Republic and Canton of

Geneva, usually at a ceremony in the Alabama Room in Geneva's City Hall, the locale where the first *Geneva Convention* was adopted in 1864. The Canton of Geneva acts as the custodian for the signed documents.

Geneva Call's engagement effort continues after signature through its support of implementation of the *Deed of Commitment* and monitoring of its compliance. Recently, the organization has begun to engage ANSAs in two other areas of humanitarian concern: the protection of children and women in armed conflict.[17]

Achievements and Challenges

Since its inception, Geneva Call, in partnership with national campaigns of the ICBL and other local NGOs, has been in dialogue with about seventy ANSAs worldwide. As of today, forty-one ANSAs from ten countries and territories (Burma/Myanmar, Burundi, India, Iraq, Iran, the Philippines, Somalia, Sudan, Turkey, and Western Sahara) have signed the *Deed of Commitment* banning AP mines.[18] Overall, signatories have complied with their obligations. Except in one case, no conclusive evidence of violation of the prohibition on the use, production, and transfer of AP mines has been found by Geneva Call. Most of them have also carried out or facilitated mine action activities, such as de-mining, victim assistance, and mine risk education. Altogether, signatories have destroyed nearly twenty thousand stockpiled AP mines to date, along with thousands of unexploded ordnances (UXO). In addition, several other ANSAs that have not signed the *Deed of Commitment* have nevertheless pledged to prohibit or limit the use of such mines, either unilaterally or within a ceasefire agreement with the concerned government. Furthermore, in some countries, ANSA commitments have precipitated the launch of much-needed mine action programs by specialized agencies.

Although much progress has been made, engaging ANSAs in a mine ban has not been without its challenges. Analogous to certain states, some ANSAs have resisted renouncing this weapon. Among them are major AP mine users, notably in Colombia and Burma/Myanmar. In several cases, Geneva Call has experienced difficulties in engaging ANSAs due to their internal divisions or for security reasons. Another issue has been to secure the support of concerned states. Although most states have cooperated with Geneva Call, in some cases it has been challenging to gain access to the ANSA on the territory where it operates. Moreover, ANSAs that have signed the *Deed of Commitment* have often lacked technical support from the international community to carry out mine action activities, such as stockpile destruction or de-mining, in areas under their control.[19] Similar challenges, in particular ensuring resources to support victims, can be foreseen as Geneva Call expands its operations towards the protection of children and women in armed conflict.

Some Observations on the Pragmatic Effect of Reciprocity

In Chapter 2, Sophie Rondeau refers to the notion of systemic reciprocity as a network of shared commitments rather than parallel bilateral relationships. She cites René Provost as stating: "Equality among participants is usually a requirement for this type of system, and immediate reciprocity between participants becomes less essential."[20] Thus, Provost breaks down reciprocity into two notions: systemic and immediate. Immediate reciprocity refers to the common understanding of the term, where obligations are based on a *quid pro quo*. Systemic reciprocity, on the other hand, is based on the idea that the system generally imposes similar or corresponding obligations on all its members, where obligations are no longer contingent upon the commitment of other parties. The Provost model envisions immediate reciprocity as a transitional stage towards the attainment of full equality, and ultimately systemic reciprocity.[21]

Using Geneva Call's experience, this chapter now turns to ANSA and state practice to expand upon both parts of this proposition: the relationship between equality and systemic reciprocity, and the impact of systemic reciprocity on immediate reciprocity. It will then consider the relative importance of the availability of a mechanism for ANSAs to express their commitment to humanitarian norms. As a caveat, the analysis of ANSA practice and opinion will be more anecdotal than scientific, as little data are available. A more comprehensive mapping of ANSA policies (such as codes of conduct, unilateral declarations, bilateral agreements, and so on) will provide greater insight not only into the weight of reciprocity but also into the motivation of ANSAs to respect humanitarian norms in general. Together with other partners, Geneva Call is in the process of collecting such policies.

Systemic and Immediate Reciprocity

Insight into the relationship between systemic and immediate reciprocity can be gained through an example that does not involve bilateral and reciprocal relationships between states and ANSAs but does allow both types of actors to express their willingness to be bound by shared commitments. This is the combined effect of the AP mine ban, as represented for states by the *Ottawa Convention* and for ANSAs by the Geneva Call *Deed of Commitment*. Note that one important aspect of systemic reciprocity, the presence of a central authority (at the international as opposed to the domestic level), is absent; such is the reality of the international legal order. The example may, however, be the closest there is to one of systemic reciprocity between states and ANSAs, as the universal and standard commitments are not based on a *quid pro quo*. In terms of the Provost model, it could represent the process of sliding from immediate towards systemic reciprocity.

As is typical of international treaties, the *Ottawa Convention* is open to states only. Unlike certain IHL treaties, however, it does not directly incorporate ANSAs through the term "each Party to the conflict." Each *state* party undertakes to "never under any circumstances" use, develop, produce, otherwise acquire, stockpile, retain, or transfer anti-personnel mines.[22] No reservations are allowed,[23] and an instrument of withdrawal from a state party involved in an armed conflict will not have effect until its end.[24] In relation to opposing ANSAs, therefore, state parties commit to be bound without resort to reciprocity.

As described in Part I, the Geneva Call *Deed of Commitment* is a standard and universal instrument under which ANSAs are provided the opportunity to make commitments similar to state obligations under the *Ottawa Convention*. There are no provisions for either reservations or withdrawal. Due to these standard and universal qualities,[25] as well as the custodial role of the Republic and Canton of Geneva, the *Deed of Commitment* may be considered a special type of non-state unilateral declaration. It is also non-reciprocal in nature.

The combined force of the *Ottawa Convention* and the *Deed of Commitment* may be revealing in the discussion on the pragmatic weight of reciprocity. As is the case under IHL treaties, the obligations extend to both the state and ANSA in a non-bilateral manner. Unlike IHL treaties, the ANSA is able to express its willingness to be bound. In fact, it is arguable that the practical effect begins to approach that of systemic reciprocity, in that equal and parallel, rather than bilateral, obligations are created.[26] A series of questions on the notion of reciprocity in its broad sense thereby come to mind: (1) Are there examples of either states or ANSAs that have refused to sign their respective appropriate instrument until or unless the opposing party has signed its appropriate instrument? (2) Are there examples of states and ANSAs that did in fact become signatories in spite of the opposing party's refusal to do so? If so, did this have any impact on the subsequent decision of the opposing party? (3) Are there examples of states or ANSAs that applied reciprocity (in the form of a breach of their commitment) following the breach of the commitment of the other?

With respect to the first question, a case in point was Sri Lanka, where the government declared in past years that it would join the *Ottawa Convention* when the Liberation Tigers of Tamil Eelam (LTTE) agreed to make a similar commitment.[27] In Sudan, according to senior officials, the government would not have felt able to ratify the convention if the SPLM/A had not made a prior commitment to observe its provisions in the territory under its control by signing the Geneva Call *Deed of Commitment*.[28] Rather than reciprocity, however, the rationale of the Sudanese government may have been the inability to implement its obligations in areas under its jurisdiction but not control.[29] Other states not party to the convention have explicitly pointed to such lack of control as a justification for remaining outside of it.[30]

For their part, ANSAs have cited a variety of reasons to justify their refusal to sign the *Deed of Commitment*. There are no clear examples, however, of an ANSA that has based its justification exclusively on the refusal of the opposing state to become party to the *Ottawa Convention*. Many have pointed to such a refusal, but it has generally been combined with other reasons, such as the contention that the means (*e.g.*, cluster bombs) or methods (*e.g.*, indiscriminate bombings) of warfare employed by the opposing state have similar or worse effects compared with AP mines,[31] the lack of alternative weapons available to resist the overwhelming firepower of the state,[32] and/or the anticipated refusal of the state to allow for monitoring of the commitment.[33] Some ANSAs have said that they would renounce AP mines only when the conflict had been resolved.[34]

On the second question, there are many examples of both states and ANSAs that have signed the appropriate instrument even though the opposing party has not done so. In fact, at the time of their signature, thirty-six out of forty-one signatories to the *Deed of Commitment* were operating in states not party to the *Ottawa Convention*, and many state parties to the convention have non-signatory ANSAs operating on their territory. Signatory ANSAs routinely express their dissatisfaction when the opposing state has not assumed a similar obligation, however. Although some of these ANSAs were hesitant to take on such commitments unilaterally, once they had done so, none failed to meet its obligations as a result of such dissatisfaction. Among other reasons, some ANSAs have signed the *Deed of*

Commitment to seize a higher moral ground than the governments they are fighting, and indirectly put pressure on the enemy to reciprocate. The SPLM/A, for example, called upon the international community to "bring pressure to bear on the government of the Sudan to ratify the Ottawa Convention on the ban on the use of landmines and to allow free access for co-ordinated cross-conflict mine action operations."[35] Similarly, the Polisario Front and the Chin National Front (CNF)/Chin National Army (CNA), both signatories to the *Deed of Commitment*, have consistently urged Morocco and Burma/Myanmar, respectively, to accede to the *Ottawa Convention.*

The third question addresses something akin to "reprisals."[36] There is no evidence that any state or ANSA has carried out "reprisals" as a result of a breach of the appropriate instrument by the opposing side. In one example from Turkey, both the government and the ANSA – the Kurdistan People's Congress (Kongra Gel)/People's Defence Force (HPG), also known as the Kurdistan Workers' Party (PKK) – made allegations against each other, although each party purports to have maintained its own commitment, and neither has made reference to a right of "reprisals." The PKK has explicitly restated its adherence to the *Deed of Commitment* and called for an international fact-finding mission to investigate its compliance.[37] Another ANSA, however, has expressed its concern that the *Deed of Commitment*'s provision requiring ANSAs to allow for and cooperate in monitoring and verification by Geneva Call goes beyond that which is required of states in terms of alleged IHL violations in general. It argues that if it is to be scrutinized regarding its use of AP mines, then the opposing state should be scrutinized for alleged IHL violations such as indiscriminate bombing. So far, though, this ANSA has given no indication that it would use such an argument as a justification for refusing to cooperate in a verification process.[38]

While it would be presumptuous to draw conclusions on the basis of such limited practice, the lessons related to reciprocity learned from the AP mine ban are instructive:

- Commitments by ANSAs can have a positive influence on state policy.
- Both states and ANSAs have made humanitarian commitments even though the opposing party has not.
- As a matter of principle, neither states nor ANSAs have resorted to "reprisals" with respect to commitments they have made.
- ANSAs have referred to state practices that have effects similar to the use of AP mines (such as cluster bombs or indiscriminate bombing) to justify their refusal to commit to the AP mine ban.

Equality and Systemic Reciprocity

The equality of belligerents is a fundamental underpinning of traditional IHL between states, but its transition to the law of non-international armed conflict has not necessarily been smooth. This is because under international law, as noted above, ANSAs do not have the same legal status or capacities as states, even though they are deemed to be bound by IHL. Here we will look at one example, namely the recruitment and use of children in hostilities, where international law regulating armed conflict, despite the equality-of-belligerents principle, treats ANSAs differently from states either with respect to substantive obligations or with respect to participation in norm formation. Such an analysis will help test the proposition that equality is a requirement for systemic reciprocity. In other words, how likely is systemic reciprocity when the state and non-state parties are expected to follow different norms?

The recruitment and use of children in hostilities is regulated by both IHL and IHRL. The most protective standards are found in the *Optional Protocol to the Convention on the Rights of the Child on the Involvement of Children in Armed Conflict* (OPAC), which is generally considered to be a human rights rather than humanitarian treaty. While the OPAC does not purport to bind ANSAs directly, it creates prejudicial standards with which ANSAs "should" comply. First, states are allowed to recruit children between sixteen and eighteen years of age who volunteer for non-combat roles, whereas ANSAs may not. Second, the standard applicable to ANSAs on the prohibition of child participation is the broader "use in hostilities," compared with "direct participation in hostilities" for states.[39]

Many commentators on the OPAC have warned that ANSAs will object to the prejudicial treatment.[40] In one of the few documented expressions of ANSA opinion, the National Democratic Front of the Philippines (NDFP) accuses the UN Secretary-General of applying against NDFP armed forces use and recruitment standards "that are not even made absolutely applicable to States."[41] Geneva Call's experience in dialogue with ANSAs on child use and recruitment indicates that these concerns over inequality are warranted. For example, one ANSA questioned why the opposing government was permitted to recruit children under eighteen years into its military academies. It is not known to what extent inequality in itself will be used by ANSAs to justify non-application of these standards, however. Geneva Call is in the process of gathering the perspectives of ANSAs on the issue of child use and recruitment, which will lead to a better understanding of their policies and motivations,[42] and will work towards inclusive solutions wherein

ANSAs can express their commitments towards the respect and protection of children in armed conflict.[43]

In Chapter 2, Sophie Rondeau suggests that the lack of legal capacity for ANSAs to participate in treaty making is the main obstacle to the pragmatic effect of reciprocity. The same could be said for customary international law, where the capacity for ANSAs to participate in its formation is an unsettled issue.[44] Other than situations of inequality as discussed above, Geneva Call's experience to date does not necessarily support these propositions. In its operations, the organization has not confronted a situation where an ANSA cited its exclusion from norm formation as a reason for not agreeing to comply with humanitarian standards, although there are other examples of ANSAs that have done so.[45] In addition to the *Deed of Commitment* on AP mines, many ANSAs have made statements or declarations adhering to IHL as a body of law, without objecting to their lack of participation. Moreover, the non-recognized Republic of Somaliland has recently passed "legislation" conforming to the norms of the *Ottawa Convention,* even though it was not involved in drafting the convention and cannot become party to it.

The sparse evidence available indicates that equality with respect to substantive provisions and enforcement mechanisms may well play a role in an ANSA's willingness to commit to a regime of systemic reciprocity. It appears from Geneva Call's experience that ANSA participation in international norm formation is less important than ensuring that (1) there is a mechanism for ANSAs to express their adherence to, and ownership of, such norms; and (2) international law applicable to ANSAs is responsive to the realities of ANSAs.[46] If so, substantive equality would be more important to systemic reciprocity than equality in norm formation. This is another question that could benefit from a greater understanding of ANSA perspectives.

Conclusion

So far, there have been few systematic efforts to understand the motivations of ANSAs to comply with humanitarian norms. Based on sparse information about ANSA practices, this analysis suggests that although reciprocity can play a role in inducing formal commitments from both states and ANSAs, it has not been seen to play a significant role in ensuring compliance once formal commitments have been made. This tendency points to the importance of formal commitments themselves, whether reciprocal or not, in efforts to improve compliance.

It is therefore critical to grant ANSAs the opportunity to declare their adherence to humanitarian norms so that they take ownership of the rules they are expected to respect. Once ANSAs agree to be bound by international standards and pledge to observe them, it becomes possible to measure their ensuing behaviour against their declaration of intent. Their commitment provides a benchmark that can be used to hold them accountable and ensure that they keep their promises. Such an inclusive approach is believed to be instrumental in securing compliance. For example, many ANSAs would not have committed to the ban on AP mines or destroyed their stockpiles without the *Deed of Commitment* mechanism. Moreover, as mentioned above, ANSA commitments can encourage states to reciprocate. Nevertheless, it would be imprudent to conclude that commitments in themselves will generally ensure compliance in the absence of reciprocity.[47]

To strive towards what Fleck calls a "culture of compliance with the law,"[48] one needs to consider a wide range of approaches vis-à-vis ANSAs. There is reason to be optimistic that the international climate is becoming more open towards innovative efforts.[49] This is a crucial development, because a culture of compliance requires that international law applicable to ANSAs, despite (or in fact because of) its state-centric nature, be responsive to the particular realities and status of ANSAs. It should not be prejudicial towards them, but rather should encourage ownership of norms. Although such a proposition may seem counterintuitive to some, improved protection of civilians from the effects of armed conflict may depend on it.

NOTES

1 For its operational purposes, Geneva Call uses the term "armed non-state actors" to refer to organized armed entities that are primarily motivated by political goals, operate outside effective state control, and lack legal capacity to become party to relevant international treaties. This includes armed groups, *de facto* governing authorities, national liberation movements, and non- or partially internationally recognized states.

2 IHL and IHRL are the main bodies of international law providing for the protection of civilians in situations of armed conflict. IHL equally binds both state and non-state parties to a conflict, which is considered a significant development of international law in that it addresses ANSAs directly. Traditionally, IHRL has placed obligations on states only, but there is currently a movement towards making IHRL standards applicable to ANSAs. In this chapter, unless a distinction is made, the term "humanitarian norms" will be used to cover both IHL and those IHRL standards relevant to ANSAs.

3 SIPRI, *SIPRI Yearbook 2010: Armaments, Disarmament and International Security* (Oxford: Oxford University Press, 2010).

4 For further discussion, see Jonathan Somer, "Jungle Justice: Passing Sentence on the Equality of Belligerents in Non-International Armed Conflict" (2007) 89 Int'l Rev. Red Cross 661 at 662.

5 The ICRC has recently published accounts of its experience and lessons learned in engaging ANSAs in situations of armed conflicts. See *Improving Respect for International Humanitarian Law in Non-International Armed Conflicts* (Geneva: ICRC, 2007), and Olivier Bangerter, "The ICRC and Non-State Armed Groups" in Geneva Call, Program for the Study of International Organizations (PSIO), and United Nations Institute for Disarmament Research (UNIDIR), *Exploring Criteria and Conditions for Engaging Armed Non-State Actors to Respect Humanitarian Law and Human Rights Law* (Geneva: Geneva Call, 2007).

6 The issue of ANSA compliance with humanitarian norms has also attracted growing academic attention in recent years. See, *inter alia,* the studies of Claude Bruderlein, *The Role of Non-State Actors in Building Human Security: The Case of Armed Groups in Intra-State Wars* (Geneva: Centre for Humanitarian Dialogue, 2000); David Petrasek, ed., *Ends and Means: Human Rights Approaches to Armed Groups* (Geneva: International Council on Human Rights Policy, 2000); Liesbeth Zegveld, *Accountability of Armed Opposition Groups in International Law* (Cambridge: Cambridge University Press, 2002); Andrew Clapham, *Human Rights Obligations of Non-State Actors* (Oxford: Oxford University Press, 2006); Marco Sassòli, *Transnational Armed Groups and International Humanitarian Law. Occasional Paper Series No. 6* (Cambridge, MA: Program on Humanitarian Policy and Conflict Research, Harvard University, 2006).

7 Pablo Policzer, *Neither Terrorists nor Freedom Fighters.* Working Paper 5 (Calgary: Armed Groups Project, 2005) at 2.

8 Gerard McHugh and Manuel Bessler, *Humanitarian Negotiations with Armed Groups: A Manual for Practitioners* (New York: United Nations, 2006). The increased need for humanitarian agencies to negotiate with ANSAs has been reflected since 1999 in successive reports of the UN Secretary-General on the protection of civilians in armed conflict.

9 *Children and Armed Conflict: Report of the Secretary-General,* UN Doc. A/60/335 (7 September 2005) at paras. 18-20. See also Coalition to Stop the Use of Child Soldiers, *International Forum on Armed Groups and the Involvement of Children in Armed Conflict* (London: Coalition to Stop the Use of Child Soldiers, 2007).

10 Anki Sjöberg, *Armed Non-State Actors and Landmines. Volume I: A Global Report Profiling ANSAs and their Use, Acquisition, Production, Transfer and Stockpiling of Landmines* (Geneva: Geneva Call, 2005). See also International Campaign to Ban Landmines (ICBL), *Landmine Monitor Report 2009: Toward a Mine-Free World* (Ottawa: Mine Action Canada, 2009) at 10.

11 The full text of the *Deed of Commitment for Adherence to a Total Ban on Anti-Personnel Mines and for Cooperation in Mine Action* is available online: Geneva Call <http://www.genevacall.org/> [*Deed of Commitment*].

12 *Deed of Commitment* at arts. 1, 2, and 4.

13 *Ibid.* at art. 3.
14 *Ibid.* at art. 5.
15 *Ibid.* at art. 6.
16 *Ibid.* at art. 7.
17 In 2010, Geneva Call developed a new deed of commitment on the protection of children from the effects of armed conflict.
18 The list of signatories is available online: Geneva Call <http://www.genevacall.org/>.
19 For details on both achievements and challenges, see Geneva Call, *Engaging Armed Non-State Actors in a Landmine Ban: The Geneva Call Progress Report (2000-2007)* (Geneva: Geneva Call, 2007), and Pascal Bongard, "Engaging Armed Non-State Actors on Humanitarian Norms: The Experience of Geneva Call and the Landmine Ban" in Geneva Call, PSIO, and UNIDIR, *Exploring Criteria and Conditions for Engaging Armed Non-State Actors to Respect Humanitarian Law and Human Rights Law* (Geneva: Geneva Call, 2008).
20 René Provost, *International Human Rights and Humanitarian Law* (Cambridge: Cambridge University Press, 2002) at 123, quoted in Chapter 2 of this book (see p. 47).
21 *Ibid.* at 122-23.
22 *Convention on the Prohibition of the Use, Stockpiling, Production and Transfer of Anti-Personnel Mines and on Their Destruction,* 1997, 2056 U.N.T.S. 211, 36 I.L.M. 1507 (entered into force 1 March 1999) [*Ottawa Convention*].
23 *Ibid.* at art. 19.
24 *Ibid.* at art. 20(3).
25 It is described as "standard" as it is a single, non-adaptable text, and "universal" as it is open to all ANSAs throughout the world who meet Geneva Call's engagement criteria. Cf. supra note 1.
26 The obligations contained in the *Deed of Commitment* differ in some aspects from *Ottawa Convention,* but these differences have so far not had substantial practical effect.
27 ICBL, *Landmine Monitor Report, Report 2006: Toward a Mine-Free World* (Ottawa: Mine Action Canada, 2008) at 1076.
28 See the preface of Martin Barber, Director of United Nations Mine Action Service, 2000-5, to Sjöberg, *supra* note 10 at 1.
29 *Ottawa Convention* at art. 4.
30 See, *e.g.,* the following statement of a Georgian Ministry of Defence official: "Over the years one of the principal reasons for not [acceding] to the convention has been the existence of the territories uncontrolled by central authorities of the state," quoted in ICBL, *Landmine Monitor Report 2006: Toward a Mine-Free World* (New York: Human Rights Watch, 2006) at 889.
31 Letter to Geneva Call from the National Democratic Front of the Philippines (NDFP), 27 October 2005, on file with Geneva Call.
32 For example, on the Ejército de Liberación Nacional (ELN), see Philippe Gazagne, "Engaging Armed Non-State Actors on the Issue of Child Recruitment and Use" in David Nosworthy, ed., *Seen but Not Heard* (Zurich: Lit Verlag, 2009) at 240.

33 For example, the Aceh Sumatra National Liberation Front (ASNLF)/Free Aceh Movement (GAM) in Indonesia; see Geneva Call *Annual Report 2003* and *2004*.

34 For example, the Abkhazian authorities; see *Landmine Monitor Report 2004: Toward a Mine-Free World* (New York: Human Rights Watch, 2004) at 1179.

35 Statement of the SPLM/A on the occasion of the signing of the *Deed of Commitment*, delivered by Commander Nhial Deng Nhial, Chairman of the SPLM/A Commission for External Relations, Information and Humanitarian Affairs, Geneva, 4 October 2001.

36 The term appears in quotation marks to signify *de facto* rather than *de jure* reprisals.

37 General Command of HPG, letter to Geneva Call, 29 October 2008, on file with Geneva Call.

38 Confidential Geneva Call mission report.

39 See *Optional Protocol to the Convention on the Rights of the Child on the Involvement of Children in Armed Conflicts*, New York, 25 May 2000, 2173 U.N.T.S. 222, 39 I.L.M. 1285 (entered into force 12 February 2002) at arts. 1, 3, and 4.

40 See, *e.g.*, Gazagne, *supra* note 32, and Daniel Helle, "Optional Protocol on the Involvement of Children in Armed Conflict to the Convention on the Rights of the Child" (2000) 82 Int'l Rev. Red Cross 797.

41 Letter of Luis G. Jalandoni, Chairperson of NDFP Negotiating Panel, addressed to Secretary-General Ban Ki-moon, 24 November 2008, on file with Geneva Call.

42 The study was published under the title *In Their Words : Perspectives of Armed Non-State Actors on the Protection of Children from the Effects of Armed Conflict* (Geneva: Geneva Call, 2010).

43 There are other areas of international law applicable to armed conflict where the equality principle comes into question. Examples are the passing of sentences and exemption of armed forces from certain terrorist offences.

44 Somer, *supra* note 4.

45 For examples from the Frente Farabundo Martí para la Liberación Nacional (FMLN) and Colombian ANSAs, see Sandesh Sivakumaran, "Binding Armed Opposition Groups" (2006) 55 I.C.L.Q. 55 at 393.

46 See Marco Sassòli, "Engaging Non-State Actors: The New Frontier for International Humanitarian Law" in Geneva Call, PSIO, and UNIDIR, *Exploring Criteria and Conditions for Engaging Non-State Armed Actors to Respect Humanitarian Law and Human Rights Law* (Geneva: Geneva Call, 2008).

47 For example, Hezbollah Secretary General Hasan Nasrallah has stated: "As long as the enemy undertakes its aggression without limits or red lines, we will also respond without limits or red lines": Amnesty International, "Israel/Lebanon: Hezbollah's Attacks on Northern Israel" (2006) at 6, online: Amnesty International <http://www.amnesty.org/en/>.

48 See Chapter 2, p. 58.

49 For example, see *Report of the Secretary-General on the Protection of Civilians in Armed Conflict*, UN Doc. S/2009/277 (29 May 2009) at paras. 38-47.

The Ownership of International Humanitarian Law
Non-State Armed Groups and the Formation and Enforcement of IHL Rules

SANDESH SIVAKUMARAN

In Chapter 2, Sophie Rondeau notes that often non-state armed groups (NSAGs) do not feel bound by their international obligations. She notes that despite all the innovative strategies for engaging with armed groups formulated in recent years, NSAGs still do not participate in drafting treaties. In her view, the less inclusive the process, the less motivation there is to respect the norms emerging from that process.

In purely legal terms, NSAGs remain bound by international humanitarian law (IHL) regardless of the degree of their participation in its formation.[1] As far as compliance with the law is concerned, the issue is very different, with the actual degree of participation likely proving influential. Indeed, it has been said that "it is psychologically easier to have [rules] accepted and respected by persons who were involved – or represented – in their development."[2] That participation in the formation of rules is linked to compliance is evidenced by the practice of some non-state armed groups. For example, in El Salvador the Frente Farabundo Martí para la Liberación Nacional (FMLN) took the view, at one point in time, that it was not bound by certain rules contained in Protocol II, Additional to the *Geneva Conventions* of 1949 (Protocol II), as it had not concluded an agreement to that effect.[3] Similarly, some NSAGs operating in Colombia have expressed the view that they do not accept Protocol II "since it was not negotiated directly with them."[4]

Assuming, then, that there is a link between participation in a process
and respect for the results of that process, it is crucial that all relevant actors
participate in the formation of IHL. This is not to say that they necessarily
have to play an equal role in the process or a role at the time of the inception
of the rule, but some form of participation must occur in order to give them
a sense of ownership of the rules.[5] Accordingly, we will begin by ascertaining
the degree of involvement of NSAGs in the formation of IHL.[6] As respect
for IHL is also linked to its enforcement, we will then consider the role
played by NSAGs in the enforcement of IHL, focusing on courts established
by such groups to prosecute, among other things, violations of IHL.

Ownership of the Rules through Participation in Their Formation

The sources of IHL, like those of public international law more broadly, are
treaties, customary international law, and general principles of law.[7] Judicial
decisions and the writings of publicists are not sources of international law
in and of themselves, but are of considerable assistance in determining the
law on point.[8] Of all the sources, treaties and customary international law
remain by far the most important.

Treaties and Custom

In the last decade, IHL with respect to non-international armed conflicts has
changed almost beyond recognition. Non-international armed conflicts are
no longer governed by the very minimum of humanitarian law treaty provisions, namely, Common Article 3 of the 1949 *Geneva Conventions,* the 1977
Protocol II additional to the same, and Article 19 of the *Hague Convention* of
1954 on the protection of cultural property.[9] Recently concluded treaties –
the *Ottawa Convention* banning anti-personnel landmines, the *Protocol on
Explosive Remnants of War,* and the *Convention on Cluster Munitions,* for
example – have been designed so as to include non-international armed
conflicts within their ambit.[10] Others, notably the *Convention on Certain
Conventional Weapons,* have been revised and expanded so as to regulate
non-international conflicts.[11] Generally there has been little dissent on the
part of states regarding these extensions.

There has been a similar growth in the rules of customary international
humanitarian law applicable to non-international armed conflicts. The *Tadić*
interlocutory appeal on jurisdiction was unquestionably the turning point
in this regard, with its recognition that "[w]hat is inhumane, and consequently proscribed, in international wars, cannot but be inhumane and

inadmissible in civil strife."[12] The *Tadić* approach was then essentially put before states at the diplomatic conference on the establishment of the International Criminal Court and accepted and endorsed by them.[13] The unprecedented growth of customary international humanitarian law rules applicable to non-international armed conflicts has been confirmed by the study on customary international humanitarian law conducted under the auspices of the International Committee of the Red Cross (ICRC). In that important work, all but a handful of the rules identified were considered applicable to international and non-international armed conflicts alike.[14]

If we are to take the idea of ownership seriously – the view that being included in a process leads to greater compliance with the outcome of that process – then it would be expected that NSAGs should be able to participate fully in the negotiation of IHL treaties as well as in the formation of customary international humanitarian law. Yet NSAGs do not participate in the conclusion of multilateral treaties, and their practice is rarely considered for the formation of customary rules. The methodology adopted by the customary international humanitarian law study in drawing up its list of customary rules is a case in point. The study consigned the practice of NSAGs to a category of "other practice," giving it an intermediate status by which it should count for something but could not be weighed equally with the practice of states. There was no place for it in the orthodox explanation of the formation of customary international law; at the same time, there was recognition that it could not simply be ignored. Thus, there is recognition that the practice should fit somewhere, although that somewhere is yet to be identified. Some two decades ago, the legal adviser of the ICRC asked "whether the practice and the *opinio juris* of insurgent groups in a civil war carry any significance in the creation and ascertainment of customary law."[15] It seems that we are still awaiting an answer.

The growth in IHL rules applicable in non-international armed conflicts has not been accompanied, then, by a corresponding change in the methodology for determining those rules. For the purposes of this chapter, a focus on conventional and customary international law, at least insofar as they are traditionally formulated, is problematic given the lack of involvement on the part of NSAGs in their formation. Although this traditional methodology may be appropriate for the determination of the rules of international armed conflicts, which are traditionally fought between states,[16] it does little to foster a sense of ownership of the rules on the part of the armed group in a non-international armed conflict, fought between a state and a NSAG, or between two or more armed groups. To utilize the practice of states alone is to miss out on at least one half of what is going on in each and every non-international armed conflict, and to limit the possibility of truly engaging with armed groups.

There are of course difficulties in giving NSAGs a more formal role in the norm creation process.[17] Allowing such groups to conclude treaties with states may grant them a certain status over and above that which states are willing to offer. Sitting around a table with NSAGs may confer on them a degree of legitimacy, thus presenting difficulties for the states with which they are in conflict. Although precedent-setting initiatives exist, such as the invitation of certain national liberation movements to the diplomatic conference on the reaffirmation and development of IHL that gave rise to the two Additional Protocols of 1977, they are difficult to apply given that the movements invited were those with observer status to regional organizations. States that jealously guard their sovereignty may also consider there to be something untoward about signing the same sheet of paper as that signed by an armed group. Furthermore, the purported signature and ratification of treaties by NSAGs presents difficult questions for the depositary of the treaty.[18]

There are equal if not greater difficulties involved in the participation of NSAGs in the formation of customary international humanitarian law. Issues that would have to be considered include:

- Which armed groups' practices would be deemed relevant for the formation of customary law?
- How much weight should be attributed to their practices?
- How should this weight compare with the weight afforded to the practices of states?
- What about other interested actors?
- What if states acted in one way and non-state armed groups in another?

Besides being fundamental, the above questions are somewhat complex. Nevertheless, this should not stop us from seeking creative solutions.

These difficulties, and the approach of the customary international humanitarian law study, suggest that international law may not be ready for a significant restructuring of its foundations. If that turns out to be the case, attention would need to shift to other means by which NSAGs could possibly be involved in the formation of the rules.

Alongside the growth of treaty and customary rules applicable to non-international armed conflicts, a good number of bilateral agreements are concluded between states and armed groups, and an assortment of unilateral declarations and codes of conduct are issued by armed groups on an ad hoc basis. A recent article lists a significant collection of agreements concluded with, and declarations made by, armed groups in Africa in the last few decades alone.[19] These instruments can potentially offer a useful means through which NSAGs can participate in the formation of the rules and thus feel a sense of ownership over them.

Bilateral Agreements, Unilateral Declarations, and Codes of Conduct

During armed conflicts, agreements relating to IHL may be concluded between the warring parties. Among the most high-profile of these is the 22 May 1992 agreement concluded between representatives of the presidents of the Republic of Bosnia-Herzegovina, the Serbian Democratic Party, the Party of Democratic Action, and the Croatian Democratic Community.[20] Much of the time, however, ad hoc bilateral agreements may be difficult to conclude, with the warring factions refusing to sit around a table with the opposing side. The issuance of unilateral declarations committing the respective parties to the rules of IHL goes some way towards addressing this problem. There are many examples of unilateral declarations made by NSAGs during non-international conflicts, such as the commitment of the Liberation Tigers of Tamil Eelam (LTTE) in Sri Lanka to abide by the *Geneva Conventions* and the Additional Protocols.[21] NSAGs also issue instructions or codes of conduct, such as the Three Main Rules of Discipline and the Eight Points for Attention promulgated by the Chinese People's Liberation Army (CPLA).[22] More recently, the Revolutionary United Front (RUF) in Sierra Leone issued, among others, its Eight Codes of Conduct.[23] A study of armed groups has demonstrated the value of these codes of conduct, concluding that armed groups that have committed themselves to such codes are more likely to comply with the law.[24] Codes of conduct are also important, as they may later be adopted by armed groups fighting in altogether different conflicts, as was in fact the case with the RUF Eight Codes of Conduct and the CPLA Eight Points for Attention.

Despite their existence, these instruments – the bilateral agreements, the unilateral declarations, and the codes of conduct – have an uncertain legal status. There is some debate as to whether bilateral agreements between a state and a non-state armed group constitute treaties for the purposes of international law.[25] Unilateral declarations, for their part, are more firmly accepted as part of the fabric of public international law, with certain declarations having been held by international courts to bind the state that made them.[26] These concern declarations on the part of states, however, and even then there remains much mystery surrounding when such declarations would likely be considered binding on their author and when they risk being considered mere puffery.[27] The legal status of codes of conduct, outside of being evidence of *opinio juris*, is less well understood, with some querying even the status of states' military manuals.[28]

In light of the foregoing, the international system would seem to be operating at two different levels. At one level, treaties are increasingly regulating non-international armed conflicts, and the scope of customary rules of international armed conflict are being broadened to cover non-international armed conflicts. Yet neither treaties nor custom, as traditionally formulated, envisage the participation of non-state armed groups in their formation. At another level, bilateral agreements, unilateral declarations, and codes of conduct continue to be concluded, but in many cases without any formal international legal status attaching to them. At some point, the two levels will need to converge if NSAGs are going to be drawn into the norm-creation process. Two recent initiatives have, to some extent, sought to develop linkages across these two levels.

Deeds of Commitment and Plans of Action

Given that armed groups are currently unable to sign and ratify multilateral humanitarian treaties, the organization Geneva Call[29] enables them to express their adherence to the norms laid down in the *Ottawa Convention* through signature of a deed. This deed commits the signatory to adhere to the "complete prohibition on all use, development, production, acquisition, stockpiling, retention and transfer of [anti-personnel] mines" and to cooperation in mine action.[30] At the time of writing, some forty-one armed groups from Burundi, India, Iran, Iraq, Myanmar, the Philippines, Somalia, Sudan, Turkey, and Western Sahara have signed the Geneva Call deed of commitment.[31]

The status of the deed should not be minimized. Signature takes place with all the pomp and circumstance of a treaty signing,[32] and the Government of the Republic and Canton of Geneva acts as the custodian of the deed.[33] As far as enforcement is concerned, the deed provides for the monitoring and verification of the commitment by Geneva Call or other bodies associated with the organization.[34] Occasionally, monitoring is to be conducted through on-site verification missions.[35] The deed also provides that Geneva Call may publicize an armed group's non-compliance with its commitment.[36] It further provides that the signatory will treat "this commitment as one step or part of a broader commitment in principle to the ideal of humanitarian norms, particularly of IHL and human rights, and to contribute to their respect in field practice as well as to the further development of humanitarian norms for armed conflicts."[37]

A second initiative that has started to bridge the gap consists of United Nations Security Council–mandated plans of action. The Security Council has required certain entities party to a conflict to draw up "concrete time-bound action plans to halt recruitment and use of children in violation of the international obligations applicable to them."[38] A working group of the Security Council has been established, among other things, to monitor the development and implementation of these action plans.[39] This has proven effective in part with action plans being drawn up by armed forces and groups in the Central African Republic (Forces démocratiques pour la rassemblement); Ivory Coast (Forces de défense et de sécurité des Forces nouvelles, Front pour la libération du Grand Ouest, Mouvement ivoirien de libération de L'Ouest de la Côte d'Ivoire, Alliance patriotique de l'ethnie Wé, Union patriotique de résistance du Grand Ouest); Myanmar; Sri Lanka (Liberation Tigers of Tamil Eelam); Sudan (Sudan Liberation Army/Minni Minawi); and Uganda.[40]

Should the relevant parties fail to prepare an action plan, or if they do not live up to the commitments expressed therein, the Security Council has warned that it intends "to consider imposing targeted and graduated measures ... such as, *inter alia,* a ban on the export or supply of small arms and light weapons and of other military equipment and on military assistance, against these parties."[41] This has proven not to be an empty gesture. The working group recommended to the Security Council that it consider imposing targeted sanctions on the leaders of the Mouvement Révolutionnaire Congolais "for repeated violations of Security Council resolutions on children and armed conflict."[42] The working group also referred Laurent Nkunda, a rebel leader fighting in the Democratic Republic of the Congo notorious for the use of child soldiers, to the Security Council sanctions committee concerning that country, which placed him on the list of individuals and entities subject to a travel ban and asset freeze.[43] The Security Council has also expressed its expectation that there will be compliance with any commitments made to the Special Representative of the Secretary-General for Children and Armed Conflict, UNICEF, or other UN agencies.[44]

Ownership of the Rules through Their Enforcement

Non-state armed groups are frequently called upon by the international community to respect IHL.[45] In response to reports of atrocities, the Security Council often demands that all parties cease their violations and stresses "the need to bring to justice those responsible."[46]

There are various options for the NSAG in considering how best to bring those responsible to justice. The accused, whether a member of the state's armed forces or a "fighter" of the NSAG, could be tried by the armed group, handed over to the state for trial by its judicial system, or transferred to another state for trial. Trial by the authorities of the state is often the preferred approach,[47] but it is singularly unrealistic. It would be remarkable were a non-state armed group to hand over one of its own "fighters," or indeed a captive of the opposing side, to its enemy for prosecution when the distrust between the two sides runs deep. The matter may be referred to the International Criminal Court, but there is no guarantee of jurisdiction and admissibility. The focus of the Court to date on members of NSAGs rather than on state officials does not help. Thus, encouraging NSAGs to prosecute violations of IHL may be the only means by which to avoid a climate of impunity.

Encouraging prosecution by the non-state armed group also takes us back to the idea of ownership. Ownership of the rules suggests not only participation in their creation but also the ability to enforce them. In order to foster a sense of ownership of IHL, NSAGs must be able to enforce the rules themselves. If enforcement always comes from the outside – for example, from the state or the international community – there will be a danger that the law becomes viewed as serving primarily those entities. IHL becomes something extrinsic to the armed group, an alien system being foisted upon it, a creation of the other. Any sense of ownership of the rules is significantly reduced, if not lost altogether. Accordingly, calls such as those of the former Special Rapporteur on the situation of human rights in Sudan directly to the leadership of NSAGs to enforce IHL may be more likely to result in positive outcomes.[48]

Capacity to Enforce IHL

All this presupposes that NSAGs have the capacity to enforce IHL. Given that the material resources of these groups are sometimes limited, it is necessary to consider whether such an assumption is valid. This can be answered by analyzing the definition of a non-international armed conflict. A non-international armed conflict has been defined as "protracted armed violence between governmental authorities and organized armed groups or between such groups within a State."[49] Accordingly, a non-international armed conflict presupposes a certain intensity in the level of violence exhibited and a certain measure of organization on the part of the armed group.[50]

One of the indicia of organization is "the existence of a command structure and disciplinary rules and mechanisms within the group."[51] Although the disciplinary procedures need not be elaborate – indeed, a Trial Chamber of the International Criminal Tribunal for the former Yugoslavia has held that the mere existence of such procedures may allow us to overlook their limited use[52] – mechanisms for enforcing IHL are an indication that the armed group is organized. Because an organized armed group is one of the two requirements of an armed conflict, the capacity of an armed group to enforce IHL is bound up in the very idea of an armed conflict.

This becomes even more apparent in relation to conflicts governed by Protocol II additional to the 1949 *Geneva Conventions,* on the protection of victims of non-international armed conflicts. In order for Protocol II to apply, the organized armed group must be under responsible command, exercise such territorial control "as to enable them to carry out sustained and concerted military operations and" – importantly for our purposes – "to implement [the] Protocol."[53] The ability to implement the protocol is therefore crucial. It is for this reason that the ICRC has opined that "anarchic" conflicts – those in which the structure of the state is disintegrating – may not fall within the ambit of the protocol because factions acting therein may not "have a strong enough chain of command to enable them to implement Protocol II."[54] The capacity of the armed group to implement Protocol II is thus a prerequisite for its application.

Courts of Non-State Armed Groups[55]

If ownership of the rules arises in part from their enforcement, and if prosecution is the high-water mark of enforcement, then it follows that with prosecution comes a heightened sense of ownership. This suggests that close attention needs to be paid to trials conducted by NSAGs.

NSAGs have, not infrequently, established their own courts to try, among other things, violations of IHL. In the last decade alone, courts of one form or another have been convened by the Fuerzas Armadas Revolucionarias de Colombia (FARC) and the National Liberation Army (ELN) in Colombia, the Liberation Tigers of Tamil Eelam (LTTE) in Sri Lanka, Maoist rebels (CPN-M) in Nepal, and the Revolutionary United Front (RUF) in Sierra Leone. The courts of the Frente Farabundo Martí para la Liberación Nacional

(FMLN) in El Salvador and the National Liberation Front (FLN) in Algeria are earlier examples.

That NSAGs convene courts is unsurprising given that provision is explicitly made for them in the principal IHL instruments. Common Article 3 of the *Geneva Conventions* prohibits "the passing of sentences and the carrying out of executions without previous judgment pronounced by a regularly constituted court, affording all the judicial guarantees which are recognized as indispensable by civilized peoples."[56] Protocol II contains a similar provision, reading in part: "No sentence shall be passed and no penalty shall be executed on a person found guilty of an offence except pursuant to a conviction pronounced by a court offering the essential guarantees of independence and impartiality."[57]

What is more surprising is that when NSAGs do seek to enforce IHL through prosecution before their own courts, they face a barrage of criticism. The UN Office of the High Commissioner for Human Rights in Nepal has been critical of Maoist courts for failing to provide "minimum guarantees of due process and fair trial."[58] The United Nations Observer Mission in El Salvador (ONUSAL) has criticized FMLN courts for failing to provide various due process guarantees.[59] The same is true of Human Rights Watch with regard to FARC and ELN courts,[60] and the United States Department of State with regard to LTTE courts.[61] The problem is not so much the content of the criticism – which is often fair – but the fact that the criticism is not constructive. If NSAGs are expected to enforce IHL, it is rather more helpful to provide constructive ways by which they can improve their systems so as to meet international standards of due process than it is simply to point out flaws in their systems.

Providing assistance to NSAGs does pose its own set of problems. Material assistance may be seen as providing support to a terrorist group. Training on due process standards may be viewed as unwarranted interference in the domestic affairs of the state. Establishing that the courts of NSAGs meet international human rights standards will not be in the interests of the state, as it may offer some degree of legitimacy to the armed group. For this reason, active engagement with the courts of NSAGs has encountered resistance. A proposed judicial monitoring system of LTTE courts in the north and east of Sri Lanka, originally envisaged to be based on the Judicial System Monitoring Programme in East Timor, was scrapped for fear of legitimizing the courts. Fear of legitimization may also explain why ONUSAL did not offer any constructive suggestions to the FMLN on improving its courts.[62] There is, then, a tension between engaging with these courts and legitimizing them. This is a tension that must be acknowledged, but its existence should not mean the immediate dismissal of these courts.

Courts of NSAGs offer some very real advantages. They constitute a forum in which to prosecute alleged violators of IHL, going some way towards reducing the climate of impunity that often develops during a non-international armed conflict. They provide an opportunity to engage with armed groups on issues relating to IHL and the rule of law more generally. Above all, as far as this chapter is concerned, they provide armed groups with a sense of ownership of the rules, which may in turn lead to increased compliance.

Conclusion

The involvement of NSAGs in the creation and enforcement of IHL brings with it a host of problems. States may view it as encroaching into their space and infringing on their sovereignty. Public international law may not be ready for such changes, viewing the participation of NSAGs as the start of a slippery slope towards the inclusion of any number of non-state actors. Yet, if ownership of the rules does lead to increased compliance, then despite these concerns the involvement of NSAGs in the norm-creating process needs to be taken very seriously indeed. After all, as Marco Sassòli puts it, how can non-state armed groups be expected "to abide by a special set of laws designed to cover conflicts if they are not ... involved in the law-making process?"[63]

NOTES

1 See Sandesh Sivakumaran, "Binding Armed Opposition Groups" (2006) 55 I.C.L.Q. 369.
2 Marco Sassòli, "Possible Legal Mechanisms to Improve Compliance by Armed Groups with International Humanitarian Law and International Human Rights Law" (Paper presented at the Armed Groups Conference, Vancouver, November 2003) at 6.
3 Liesbeth Zegveld, *Accountability of Armed Opposition Groups in International Law* (Cambridge: Cambridge University Press, 2002) at 17, fn. 27.
4 Human Rights Watch, *War without Quarter: Colombia and International Humanitarian Law* (New York: Human Rights Watch, 1998) at 25.
5 See Sassòli, *supra* note 2 at 6-13. For a different idea of ownership of IHL, see Kenneth Anderson, "Who Owns the Rules of War?" *New York Times Magazine* (13 April 2003), online: New York Times <http://www.nytimes.com/>.
6 This part draws on Anthea Roberts and Sandesh Sivakumaran, "Law-Making by Non-State Actors: Engaging Armed Groups in the Creation of International Humanitarian Law" (2011) 37 Yale J. Int'l L. (forthcoming).

7 *Statute of the International Court of Justice*, 1945, 3 Bevans 1179; 59 Stat. 1031; T.S.
   993; 39 AJIL Supp. 215 (1945) (entered into force 24 October 1945) at art. 38.
8 On the doctrine of sources in the context of IHL, see Robert Cryer, "Of Custom,
   Treaties, Scholars and the Gavel: The Influence of the International Criminal
   Tribunals on the ICRC Customary Law Study" (2006) 11 Journal of Conflict and
   Security Law 239.
9 *Convention for the Amelioration of the Condition of the Wounded and Sick in Armed
   Forces in the Field*, Geneva, 12 August 1949, 75 R.T.N.U. 31 [GCI]; *Convention for the
   Amelioration of the Condition of Wounded, Sick and Shipwrecked Members of Armed
   Forces at Sea*, Geneva, 12 August 1949, 75 R.T.N.U. 85 [GCII]; *Convention Relative
   to the Treatment of Prisoners of War*, Geneva, 12 August 1949, 75 R.T.N.U. 135
   [GCIII]; and *Convention Relative to the Protection of Civilian Persons in Time of War*,
   12 August 1949, 75 R.T.N.U. 287 [GCIV], online: ICRC <http://www.icrc.org/>;
   *Protocol Additional to the Geneva Conventions of 12 August 1949, and Relating to
   the Protection of Victims of Non-International Armed Conflicts (Protocol II)*, 8 June
   1977, 1125 U.N.T.S. 3 (entered into force 7 December 1978) [APII]; *Convention for
   the Protection of Cultural Property in the Event of Armed Conflict*, 14 May 1954, 249
   U.N.T.S. 240 (entered into force 7 August 1956) at art. 19 [*Hague Convention*].
10 *Convention on the Prohibition of the Use, Stockpiling, Production and Transfer of
   Anti-Personnel Mines and on Their Destruction*, 1997, 36 I.L.M. 1507 (entered into
   force 1 March 1999) [*Ottawa Convention*]; *Protocol on Explosive Remnants of War to
   the Convention on Prohibitions or Restrictions on the Use of Certain Conventional
   Weapons Which May Be Deemed to Be Excessively Injurious or to Have Indiscriminate
   Effects (Protocol V)*, 2003, 2399 U.N.T.S. 100 (entered into force 12 November 2006);
   Convention on Cluster Munitions, 2008, C.N.776.2008.TREATIES-2 (entered into
   force 1 August 2010).
11 *Convention on Prohibitions or Restrictions on the Use of Certain Conventional
   Weapons Which May Be Deemed to Be Excessively Injurious or to Have Indiscriminate Effects (with Protocols I, II and III)*, 1980, 1342 U.N.T.S. 137 (entered into force
   2 December 1983) [*Convention on Certain Conventional Weapons*]. Art. 1 originally
   provided that the "Convention and its annexed Protocols shall apply in the situations
   referred to in Article 2 common to the Geneva Conventions ... including any situation described in paragraph 4 of Article 1 of Additional Protocol I to these Conventions." This was amended during the second review conference to "also apply to
   situations referred to in Article 3 common to the 1949 Geneva Conventions."
12 International Criminal Tribunal for the former Yugoslavia (ICTY), *Prosecutor v.
   Tadić*, Decision on Interlocutory Appeal on Jurisdiction, IT-94-1-AR72 (2 October
   1995) at para. 119 [*Tadić*].
13 Claus Kress, "War Crimes Committed in Non-International Armed Conflict and the
   Emerging System of International Criminal Justice" (2001) 30 Israel Yearbook on
   Human Rights 103.
14 Jean-Marie Henckaerts and Louise Doswald-Beck, *Customary International Humanitarian Law. Volume I: Rules* (Cambridge: Cambridge University Press, 2005).
15 "Determining Customary International Law Relative to the Conduct of Hostilities in
   Non-International Armed Conflicts: Remarks of HP Gasser" (1987) 2 Am. U. J. Int'l
   L. & Pol'y 471 at 477.

16 Though the potential for participation of national liberation movements suggests that it may not be appropriate.

17 See Sassòli, *supra* note 2 at 6-7.

18 François Bugnion, "*Jus ad Bellum, Jus in Bello* and Non-International Armed Conflicts" (2003) 6 Y.B. Int'l Human. L. 167.

19 Churchill Ewumbe-Monono, "Respect for International Humanitarian Law by Armed Non-State Actors in Africa" (2006) 88 Int'l Rev. Red Cross 905.

20 Reproduced in Marco Sassòli and Antoine Bouvier, *How Does Law Protect in War? Volume II* (Geneva: ICRC, 2006) at 1765.

21 Letter from Vellupillai Prabhakaran, Leader, Liberation Tigers of Tamil Eelam, to Members and Observers, United Nations Commission on Human Rights, Forty-fourth session, 24 February 1988.

22 Three Main Rules of Discipline and Eight Points for Attention, cited in He Xiaodong, "The Chinese Humanitarian Heritage and the Dissemination of and Education in International Humanitarian Law in the Chinese People's Liberation Army" (2001) 841 Int'l Rev. Red Cross 141 at 153.

23 Special Court for Sierra Leone, *Prosecutor v. Sesay, Kallon and Gbao,* Judgment, SCSL-04-15-T (2 March 2009) at para. 705.

24 International Council on Human Rights Policy, *Ends and Means: Human Rights Approaches to Armed Groups* (Geneva: International Council on Human Rights Policy, 2000) at 52.

25 See Sivakumaran, *supra* note 1 at 389-91.

26 *Nuclear Tests (Australia v. France),* [1974] I.C.J. Rep. 253 at para. 43; *Nuclear Tests (New Zealand v. France),* [1974] I.C.J. Rep. 457 at para. 44.

27 See, *e.g.,* the position taken by the International Court of Justice in *Military and Paramilitary Activities in and against Nicaragua (Nicaragua v. United States of America)* [1986] I.C.J. Rep. 14 at para. 261; *Case Concerning the Frontier Dispute (Burkina Faso/Republic of Mali),* [1986] I.C.J. Rep. 554 at paras. 39-40; *Application of the Convention on the Prevention and Punishment of the Crime of Genocide (Bosnia and Herzegovina v. Serbia and Montenegro),* [2007] I.C.J. Rep. 43 at paras. 377-78.

28 See the comments of William J. Fenrick, "Determining Customary International Law Relative to the Conduct of Hostilities in Non-International Armed Conflicts" (1987) 2 Am. U. J. Int'l L. & Pol'y 471 at 493.

29 For more on Geneva Call, see Chapter 3.

30 *Deed of Commitment for Adherence to a Total Ban on Anti-Personnel Mines and for Cooperation in Mine Action* at art. 1, online: Geneva Call <http://www.genevacall.org/> [*Deed of Commitment*].

31 See "Signatories to the *Deed of Commitment* banning anti-personnel mines (at 20 September 2011)," online: Geneva Call <http://www.genevacall.org/>.

32 Andrew Clapham, *Human Rights Obligation of Non-State Actors* (Oxford: Oxford University Press, 2006) at 296-97, notes that "[i]n some cases the signing has been in the presence, not only of a representative of the Republic and Canton of Geneva, but also of an Ambassador from the state against which the rebels are fighting," and that "[a]t least one negotiation and signing took place in the Alabama Room in Geneva – the room where the first Geneva Convention was signed in 1864."

33 *Deed of Commitment* at art. 10.
34 *Ibid.* at art. 3.
35 See *Report of the Geneva Call Mission to the Moro Islamic Liberation Front (MILF) in Central Mindanao, Philippines* (Geneva and Mindanao: Geneva Call, 2002).
36 *Deed of Commitment* at art. 7.
37 *Ibid.* at art. 5.
38 SC Res. 1539, UN SCOR, UN Doc. S/RES/1539 (2004) at para. 5(a).
39 SC Res. 1612, UN SCOR, UN Doc. S/RES/1612 (2005) at para. 8.
40 See *Children and Armed Conflict: Report of the Secretary-General,* UN Doc. A/61/529-S/2006/826; *Children and Armed Conflict: Report of the Secretary-General,* UN Doc. A/62/609-S/2007/757.
41 SC Res. 1539, *supra* note 38 at para. 5(c). This was reiterated in SC Res. 1612, *supra* note 39 at para. 9.
42 *Children and Armed Conflict, supra* note 40. See also Security Council Working Group on Children and Armed Conflict, *Conclusions on Parties in the Armed Conflict of the Democratic Republic of the Congo,* UN SCOR, UN Doc. S2006/724, Annex.
43 *Children and Armed Conflict, ibid.* at para. 124.
44 SC Res. 1539, *supra* note 38 at para. 4.
45 See, *e.g.,* SC Res. 814, UN SCOR, UN Doc. S/RES/814 (1993) at para. 13.
46 See, *e.g.,* SC Res. 1509, UN SCOR, UN Doc. S/RES/1509 (2003) at para. 10.
47 This was the view of the United Nations Observer Mission in El Salvador. See Tathiana Flores Acuña, *The United Nations Mission in El Salvador: A Humanitarian Law Perspective* (The Hague: Kluwer, 1995) at 61, fn. 247.
48 *Report of the Special Rapporteur on the Situation of Human Rights in Sudan,* UN Human Rights Council, UN Doc. E/CN.4/1996/62 (1996) at para. 87.
49 *Tadić, supra* note 12 at para. 70.
50 On these elements, see Sandesh Sivakumaran, "Identifying an Armed Conflict Not of an International Character" in Carsten Stahn and Göran Sluiter, eds., *The Emerging Practice of the International Criminal Court* (Leiden: Brill Academic Publishers, 2008) at 363.
51 ICTY, *Prosecutor v. Haradinaj, Balaj and Brahimaj,* Judgment, IT-04-84-T (3 April 2008) at para. 60; ICTY, *Prosecutor v. Limaj, Bala and Musliu,* Judgment, IT-03-66-T (30 November 2005) at para. 171.
52 This is the reading of the *Limaj* trial judgment by the *Haradinaj* Trial Chamber, at para. 56.
53 APII, *supra* note 9 at art. 1(1).
54 ICRC, "Armed Conflicts Linked to the Disintegration of State Structures" (Preparatory document drafted by the ICRC for the first periodical meeting on international humanitarian law, Geneva, 19-23 January 1998).
55 For more on the courts of non-state armed groups, see Sandesh Sivakumaran, "Courts of Armed Opposition Groups: Fair Trials or Summary Justice?" (2009) 7 Journal of International Criminal Justice 489; Jonathan Somer, "Jungle Justice: Passing Sentence on the Equality of Belligerents in Non-International Armed Conflict" (2007) 89 Int'l Rev. Red Cross 655.

56 GCIII, *supra* note 9 at art. 3, para. 1(d).

57 APII, *supra* note 9 at art. 6(2).

58 UN Office of the High Commissioner for Human Rights in Nepal, *Human Rights Abuses by the CPN-M: Summary of Concerns* (September 2006) at 4.

59 *Third Report of the United Nations Observer Mission in El Salvador (ONUSAL)*, UN Doc. A/46/876-S/23580 (19 February 1992) at paras. 112-14.

60 Human Rights Watch, *supra* note 4, c. 5.

61 United States Department of State, *Country Reports on Human Rights Practices: 2006* (Washington, DC: Department of State, 2007), chapter on Sri Lanka.

62 On the omission, see Acuña, *supra* note 47 at 60; Zegveld, *supra* note 3 at 74.

63 Marco Sassòli, "Transnational Armed Groups and International Humanitarian Law," Program on Humanitarian Policy and Conflict Research, Harvard University, Occasional Paper Series (Winter 2006) at 40.

Armed Groups and the Arms Trade Treaty
Challenges and Opportunities

PABLO POLICZER AND VALERIE YANKEY-WAYNE

Regulating the purchase, transfer, and use of small arms and light weapons (SALW) is a critical but difficult humanitarian challenge. On the one hand, states require SALW to uphold the rule of law and their status as states, with a monopoly over coercive force. On the other hand, states are not the only actors with access to SALW, whose low cost and ease of use make them accessible to a wide range of non-state groups. Moreover, unlike landmines, it is difficult to conceive of an outright ban on SALW: the goal instead must be their appropriate regulation. Nevertheless, because of the wide range of state and non-state groups with access to SALW, such regulation is especially challenging. For example, an outright prohibition of the transfer of conventional arms[1] to non-state armed groups (NSAGs) has been a controversial issue in the disarmament debate, and raised a number of political and analytical challenges. With some exceptions (for example, Man Portable Air Defence Systems, or MANPADS), prohibition of transfers to armed groups has proven either unacceptable (for some) or undesirable (for others). Given the controversies surrounding the subject and given that states are likely to avoid a subject that risks stalemating negotiations, the probability that a discussion of this issue will be ignored during the deliberations of arms transfer control regimes (for example, the Arms Trade Treaty [ATT] deliberations[2]) is high.

This impasse does not mean that the problem of arms transfers to, and use by, armed groups need be ignored. For any international transfer regime to be effective, it has to consider the full range of end users, and this must include not just states but also non-state armed groups. With this in mind, we argue that it is possible to address the issue of arms transfers to armed groups as well as the regulation of their end use by improved end-user controls, particularly among states (the primary producers, suppliers, and holders). Ensuring that states meet their commitments with regard to arms transfers and end use remains the most promising avenue for improving the overall arms control regime. This chapter offers a framework for thinking about how to do this by better understanding the types of armed groups whose end use must be regulated, as well as some of the options available for doing so.

We make two central claims. The first is that the best available research shows that most non-state armed groups get their weapons from poorly controlled state stockpiles and through sophisticated criminal networks. This means that monitoring end-user controls, particularly among states, promises to address a significant part of the problem of weapons acquisition and use by armed groups. Second, acknowledging that at least some NSAGs may continue to acquire weapons through either legal or illegal means, it is also essential to improve existing regulatory methods and explore ways to address the end use of difficult cases through traditional and non-traditional regulatory mechanisms.

We start by offering a typology of armed actors in the disarmament debate – including both states and NSAGs – followed by a discussion of what the available research indicates about the dynamics of weapons transfers to armed groups. Based on this, we then propose ways to regulate states' end use through different command-and-control mechanisms, and conclude by exploring emerging ways of engaging NSAGs in regulating their own weapons end use that are compatible with improved state regulations.

Distinguishing among Different Types of Armed Groups

From a legal perspective, the distinction between states and non-state groups can be understood as a dichotomy: states are (mostly) recognized as such by other states, and there is little ambiguity as to which entities count as states and which do not. Notwithstanding this, a wide range of different actors beyond states buy, sell, and use weapons. In contrast to the legal perspective, these actors can be better understood as a spectrum rather than in dichotomous terms. They include states, state agents, and different types of non-state armed groups. Building on Muggah and Jütersonke, we suggest in this section a way of conceptualizing armed groups in the disarmament debate.[3]

A group's ability to access weapons and the nature of their end use can be understood according to two key dimensions. The first is a group's degree of organization. Some groups are highly organized, operating sophisticated bureaucracies with significant executive capacity. Many states obviously fall into this category, but so do many non-state groups. For example, some private security groups, including mercenaries and security companies, are highly organized. This is also true of some rebel groups. By contrast, some groups have very little organizational capacity and operate as largely informal organizations. Certainly many non-state groups fall into this category, such as groups that form spontaneously as protests or movements in response to particular events or crises. In certain instances, groups may be more long-standing but still lack a clear or formal organization. This includes not only non-state actors: some states also have very little organizational capacity. In other words, degree of organization is independent of whether or not a group is affiliated with a state.

The second dimension of a group's ability to access weapons and the nature of the weapons' end use is whether an actor operates primarily in the public or private sphere (or for public or private ends). Generally, states are the primary actors operating in the public sphere – and indeed in defining its boundaries. But many non-state groups may also operate in this sphere. For example, a rebel group that seeks to overthrow a particular government technically operates outside the public sphere, but because it aims to take over the public sphere, it is useful to include them in this space as well. The private sphere, by contrast, is occupied by actors that operate strictly private enterprises, for private ends. These again include a range of legal and illegal actors, from businesses to criminal enterprises.

Neither of these dimensions is dichotomous, since both states and non-state groups can fall on any point of the organizational matrix shown in Figure 5.1.[4] It bears restating that neither the degree of organization nor the particular sphere in which different actors operate map directly to the legal distinctions between states and non-state groups. We contend that we can build on this insight both to understand some of the dynamics of weapons flows between states and non-state groups and to build a more effective regulatory mechanism for these dynamics.

The Dynamics of Weapons Transfers to Non-State Armed Groups

There are two main methods of weapons diversion to non-state armed groups: unintentional diversion from government stockpiles, and state-sanctioned transfers ("intentional" stockpile diversion).[5] As we outline below,

FIGURE 5.1

Types of armed actors

	Private sphere	Public sphere
High organization	Private security companies Criminal and vigilante groups Armed groups	State armed forces Police forces Paramilitaries/militias Private security companies Armed groups
Low organization	Paramilitaries/militias Armed groups Criminal groups	Paramilitaries/militias Armed groups

a growing body of evidence suggests that weapons reaching the wrong hands come mostly from state stockpiles. It would therefore be inappropriate for any international efforts aimed at curbing proliferation to ignore this method of diversion while focusing solely on the manufacture and international transfers of new weapons from state-to-state entities. Although a large part of the arms trade does consist of transfers between state actors, groups operating in the public sphere with access to state stockpiles can easily transfer arms to the wrong hands. Thus, in terms of Figure 5.1, diversion from state stockpiles allows arms to flow from the public to the private sphere.

In many cases, armed groups acquire their weapons either through corruption or through stockpiles that are poorly controlled. Some groups in the private sphere occasionally associate with elites in the public sphere to facilitate diversion. Often weapons are easily available as a result of a political-criminal nexus, which consists of varying degrees of cooperation among military, national law enforcement, and criminal participants. These may involve elements of the state armed forces, police, special forces, or political elites. In the context of domestic diversion from government stockpiles, research by Small Arms Survey and other organizations illustrates how ammunition originally intended exclusively for state forces is diverted to armed groups.[6] In Colombia, such diversion and distribution networks are associated with government-licensed or authorized groups such as private security companies,[7] where arms and ammunition are also stolen from military and police units.[8]

Unintentional Diversion from Government Stockpiles
In the case of international diversion from government stockpiles, seizures of weapons held by illegal groups in Colombia, for example, indicate that armaments intended for exclusive use by the armed forces of countries like Venezuela, Ecuador, and Peru ended up in the hands of local or international arms dealers.[9] It is alleged that corruption in the Peruvian armed forces provided a steady stream of arms and munitions to Colombian rebels.[10] According to *Jane's Terrorism and Security Monitor,* there have been several incidents where corrupt members of the Peruvian security forces were implicated in smuggling military equipment to the FARC (Fuerzas Armadas Revolucionarias de Colombia, or Revolutionary Armed Forces of Colombia).[11] A network involving police officers was unravelled in September 2006, when 31,300 Kalashnikov rounds were seized. Naval personnel were implicated in another network uncovered in December 2006. During internal audits on a marine battalion stationed at Ancon, 34,700 rounds were found to be missing, with the ammunition boxes filled with stones and sand to make them appear full. Seven members of the battalion, including a captain and a lieutenant, were tried by the military justice system in connection with the theft. In September 2007, the Peruvian anti-terrorist agency, Dirección Contra el Terrorismo, broke up another alleged arms-smuggling network, arresting eight people, among them two serving and two retired members of the army.[12]

A United Nations panel of experts report regarding the Democratic Republic of the Congo (DRC) suggest that weapons used in the remaining conflict zones in the northeast of the country were diverted from military stockpiles as a result of poor command and control exercised over the Congolese national army.[13] Yet another example of international diversion from government stockpiles is the proliferation of MANPADs from the poorly secured Warsaw Pact arms depots to armed groups following the collapse of the former Soviet bloc. Since 2002, armed groups "have acquired hundreds, possibly thousands, of missiles from a variety of sources, including ... poorly secured government depots, and government patrons."[14]

To better understand how arms flow across these spheres, it is useful to consider the second dimension of the typology, namely, a group's degree of organization. As mentioned earlier, an actor's degree of organization is not related to whether it is a state or a non-state group. Highly organized groups might be intensely entrepreneurial, with business portfolios spanning the illegal to legal spheres, enabling them to cover up arms transfers. In other cases, groups may lack a clear or formal organization and may range from a long-standing group to loosely organized individuals. These networks do not generally have leaders in the accepted sense, but are made up of individuals or small groups that operate largely autonomously. They are elusive and fluid, and can often function across national boundaries with great ease.

State-Sanctioned Transfers to Armed Groups

Some non-state armed groups, particularly in the Horn of Africa and parts of the Middle East and Asia, still benefit from covert arms supplies through varying degrees of cooperation among political actors and transnational intermediaries. A number of states or state officials continue to exploit the rationale that they have the right to interfere in the internal affairs of other unstable or weak states to safeguard their own national security interests. Certain governments transfer weapons directly to armed groups; in other cases, key political or military stakeholders divert weapons from their national stockpile to armed groups through criminal networks at the local, national, and transnational levels.

For instance, in the past, both Rwanda and Uganda maintained security arrangements with leaders of armed groups in the embargoed regions of the DRC under the excuse that the DRC had failed to disarm rebel forces. The UN group of experts on the DRC (2005) concluded that arms continued to be supplied to Ituri from Uganda in violation of Security Council Resolution 1552 (2004). For example, the group of experts received information from eyewitnesses that a Uganda-based aircraft operating from Entebbe delivered cases of arms and ammunition to Union des Patriotes Congolais (UPC) positions on 3 October and 14 November 2004.[15]

Evidence also suggests that Ethiopia, Djibouti, Eritrea, and Yemen supported different factions in Somalia. For example, the Eritrean government has been accused of providing support to armed groups led by the Islamic Courts Union (ICU) in opposition to Ethiopian military support to the Somali Transitional Government.[16] The UN Monitoring Group on Somalia (2007) has provided evidence relating to the purchase of cargo aircraft by Eriko Enterprises in Asmara, which is believed to be a front company of the Eritrean government used to make regular weapons deliveries to Somalia.[17] The report states that the Eritrean government delivered a consignment of six SA-18 surface-to-air missiles to the ICU.[18] In another case, a US Senate Foreign Relations Committee report dated 15 December 2006 explicitly stated that the government of Eritrea reportedly provided direct assistance to the Liberation Tigers of Tamil Eelam (LTTE) in Sri Lanka.[19]

Other Potential Sources

In addition to transfers or smuggling from government stockpiles (whether state-sanctioned or otherwise), some arms are smuggled by local or international arms dealers often associated with "ant trails" involving small quantities of weapons in trunks of cars, on backs of trucks, on backs of animals, and so on, passing across land borders; or multiple shipments of small quantities of arms entering a country numerous times over the year. Most "ant trails" between the United States and Mexico are allegedly linked to Mexican drug cartels.[20] The weapons are often bought at gun shows in Arizona and other border states, where criminals take advantage of legal loopholes.[21] It is alleged that corrupt customs officials also help smuggle weapons into Mexico.[22] According to intelligence reports on Colombia, one of the main characteristics of the country's traffic in arms is that it takes place in the form of multiple shipments of small quantities of arms – an average of fifteen to twenty weapons per shipment.[23]

It is generally economically unprofitable and risky for armed groups to manufacture their own weapons, and only a few likely engage in this practice. Nevertheless, a number of armed groups have the capability to manufacture improvised explosive devices (IEDs) and to repair weapons. It is alleged that the LTTE had advanced weapons-manufacturing capacity and had succeeded in making sophisticated IEDs.[24] Colombian authorities have allegedly found that the FARC has developed a semi-industrial capacity to produce light artillery materials, especially mortars and grenades. The FARC also has a series of workshops and repair centres where they manufacture parts for various rifles and provide maintenance for arms.[25] Some blacksmiths and locksmiths in Africa have the capability to repair and manufacture pistols, shotguns, and single-barrel guns with relative sophistication. Such weapons appear to be increasingly used for criminal activities within the region.[26]

In addition, there are a number of arms markets where recycled and locally produced weapons are sold. The Bakaaraha arms markets in Somalia, particularly Mogadishu, continue to play a central role as one of the primary sources of arms to various armed factions in the country.[27] The village of Durra in northwestern Pakistan is known for its weapons-making skills and is the world's largest market for craft-produced weapons. It is alleged that it is possible to find everything from a handgun to a rocket launcher at the gun market. Gunsmiths in the village manufacture replicas of ammunition and different types of handguns and rifles with scrap metals using primitive tools.[28]

For reasons of economy of scale, only rich armed groups or groups with active state sponsorship or strong links to criminal networks can afford to acquire heavy and expensive weapons systems. Smaller groups and common criminal groups acquire their weapons through domestic and regional arms trafficking. Most armed groups often resort to small arms and light weapons because they lack the resources to buy heavy and sophisticated weaponry, or lack the skills and training to operate advanced weapons systems.[29]

There appears to be no limit to the type of weapons that armed groups can have access to (surface-to-air missiles, fighter jets, anti-aircraft weaponry, armoured personnel carriers, and so on). The LTTE, for example, proved to be the first rebel group in the world with an offensive air capability.[30] In 2007, Sri Lankan intelligence sources alleged that three light aircraft were purchased from Jakarta through intermediaries; two of them were disassembled and packed into shipping containers that were then smuggled to northern Sri Lanka by LTTE vessels. One of the aircraft was identified as a Czech-built Zlin Z-143.[31] In another case, military police in the Brazilian city of Rio de Janeiro seized a 0.50-calibre "anti-aircraft" weapon from a drug gang in April 2008. This seizure appears to confirm that criminal gangs have access to military-grade weaponry and will continue to present a challenge to police attempts to reduce armed violence.[32] The potential for non-state armed groups to acquire sophisticated weaponry indicates that the scope of a comprehensive arms transfer regime – such as the proposed ATT – should consider or reflect the conventional arms used by armed groups. These may include a diverse range of land, air, and sea-based weapons, including heavy weapons, light weapons, ammunition, explosives, battle tanks, and dual-use items and technology.

To summarize the main points concerning the dynamics of the arms trade to armed groups, we argue that the degree of organization presents both a challenge and an opportunity. On the one hand, highly organized groups are able to mount increasingly sophisticated operations, to acquire more and better weapons, and to better hide their tracks. On the other hand, these same groups are increasingly able to control the behaviour of their agents, meaning that policies set at the top of their hierarchy are more likely to be followed at the bottom by all members. We highlight the fact that most undesirable NSAGs obtain their weapons from states, often through illegal diversion from state stockpiles. Thus, if we can improve states' own internal controls, we will have taken steps towards addressing an important part of the problem.

Command, Control, and Monitoring

The previous section identified a number of cases where diversion from state stockpiles could have been either state-sanctioned or unintentional. With the legality of state-sanctioned transfers to armed groups still being debated at both the national and international levels, this section focuses on how states can best meet their commitments in preventing unintentional diversion of weapons to armed groups. Our argument is that the states best able to meet their commitments to combat illegal arms transfers are those with strong command-and-control structures, namely, those that are highly organized and best able to ensure that their agents follow the directives set out at the top by their leaders.

The problem of ensuring that agents follow orders and directives is generally known as the "principal-agent problem." This refers to how principals (or leaders) ensure that their policies are carried out by hiring suitable agents, by paying them fittingly, and especially by appropriately monitoring their activities. Indeed, there is increasing consensus that of all the things that principals need to do to ensure that agents implement their policies, monitoring is the most important. Here we offer a way to apply some of the insights from the principal-agent literature to the problems faced by the arms transfer regime.

Since it is not possible for the principal to be aware of all of its agents' activities all the time, the principal relies on a number of methods to monitor them. In arms control, transparency and oversight are essential to monitoring arms transfers and its misuse in any organization. This can be done through two main methods: internal monitoring (IM), where transparency and oversight are ensured from within the principal's own organization, and external monitoring (EM), where the same are ensured by participants outside the direct control of the principal, such as regional organizations, the UN, or civil society. Internal and external monitoring are not mutually exclusive strategies, and it is possible to have different combinations of the two. Indeed, many organizations rely on such combinations. The implication here is that in order to limit the diversion of weapons in the international arms trade, it is likely necessary to allow both internal mechanisms and some form of external monitoring mechanism. Such an approach limits internal monopolization of information and guards against corruption. External monitoring also provides a wealth of independent information, enabling the principal to analyze information from various sources.[33]

We suggest the following five aspects are central to effective monitoring of the international arms trade.

Coordination and Oversight

Coordination on arms procurement by relevant government agencies reduces duplication and improves transparency and oversight not only with respect to arms procurement but also with respect to the activities of government and the private agents involved. In most countries, several agencies are involved in arms procurement. This has long been recognized as a source of potential unintentional diversion, simply because of the significant difficulties in coordinating government agencies or departments, particularly coordination between defence departments, the executive branch, and law enforcement agencies.

Reporting

Periodic and reliable reporting procedures on arms transfers are also essential for improved monitoring of activities and agents. For example, under the *ECOWAS Convention on Small Arms and Light Weapons, Their Ammunition and Other Related Materials*,[34] member states are to provide annual reports to the regional body detailing their orders or purchases of small arms and light weapons. For the European Union countries, reporting on arms exports is strongly influenced by the European Union Code of Conduct on Arms Exports. In this sense, most European countries have dramatically changed their reporting procedures and policies, including industry reporting to government and publication of annual arms export reports by governments. The United Nations Register of Conventional Arms established in January 1992 calls on all member states to provide annual data on imports and exports of conventional arms, such as battle tanks, armoured combat vehicles, large-calibre artillery systems, combat aircraft, attack helicopters, warships, and missiles and missile launchers. Since 2006, the register has included, albeit with limited results, an optional reporting on transfers of small arms and light weapons.[35]

A number of non-governmental agencies play a critical role in external public monitoring of states. For example, Small Arms Survey has developed the Small Arms Trade Transparency Barometer to assess and compare countries' export reports data that have been made public. Although varying forms of reporting makes it difficult to get a complete picture of a country's arms exports, the barometer nevertheless provides a useful assessment of small arms and light weapons export data.

End-Use and Arms Transfer Certification

International arms export control regimes implicitly monitor the command-and-control procedures within states. For example, most arms export control measures are designed to limit the proliferation of weapons and sensitive technologies that could threaten the security of states.[36] States have a shared interest in greater responsibility between the principal and the agent to prevent arms diversion that undermines peace and stability.

Similarly, post-transfer certification is sometimes integrated into the end-use certification process for arms exports to ensure that arms authorized for export are delivered to the stated end user and not diverted to areas under embargo or groups likely to commit human rights violations. This places an indirect responsibility on state agents to ensure responsible command-and-control measures. Post-delivery verification includes reviewing proposed transfers to foreign recipients (through pre-delivery checks) and verifying that recipients of arms exports receive and/or use these weapons as intended (through post-delivery checks). Many major exporters require a guarantee by the importing agency that it will not re-export the arms without the prior written consent of the exporting country. The guarantee also states that the recipient will not use the arms for proscribed purposes, including abuses of human rights or violations of international humanitarian law.

Sweden, for example, has a good practice of end-use monitoring. The Swedish Inspektionen för Strategiska Produkter (ISP),[37] which is responsible for administering export controls in Sweden, requires a "Declaration by End-User," printed on special banknote-quality paper bearing a unique number, for exports of military equipment for combat purposes to the armed forces in the recipient country. This type of certificate is sent by the exporter to the end user, who upon completion delivers it to the Swedish embassy in the country of end use. The embassy must verify that the request and the signature are legitimate before the export is authorized. Included in the certification process is a commitment by end users not to re-export without permission. Requests to re-export are routed through the ISP, which applies similar criteria to such requests as it does to direct exports. In cases where it is known that end-use undertakings have been broken, Sweden reserves the right to halt further contracted supplies.

While post-delivery checks may be difficult for some states, civil society groups can serve a critical role in external monitoring of post-delivery goods. Groups such as International Crisis Group, Amnesty International, and Human Rights Watch also provide independent reports, which complement states' efforts at transparency, particularly on end use.

Monitoring State Agents

The issue of end use suggests that monitoring state agents is a critical problem. A growing body of evidence suggests that illegal diversion occurs less during international transfers between states and more through leaks from government stockpiles. To prevent weapons diversion, governments must take an interest in adequately securing the stockpile of all imports and exports. This should be complemented by good command and control over their agents. Principals ensure that their policies are carried out by hiring appropriate agents, by paying them appropriately, and especially by appropriately monitoring their activities. This means that states should consider introducing security sector governance into the broader framework of arms control.

Monitoring Stockpiles

Effective recordkeeping systems and monitoring and verification of stockpiles indicate whether the principal has oversight over:

- any leakage/diversion of arms and ammunition from the stockpile(s) and/or breach of security measures
- any surplus, damaged, or obsolete arms and ammunition likely to be diverted to undesirable groups
- unauthorized individuals with access to government stockpile(s)
- recordkeeping systems, processes, and standards that allow for surveillance, inspections, and audits of the inventories on a regular basis.

In conclusion, monitoring and adequate control over government stockpiles are essential to prevent diversion. Monitoring of state agents and weapons stockpiles must be an important component of any security sector governance program, including the proposed ATT. External monitoring also provides the international community with a mechanism for preventing intentional and unintentional transfers to groups likely to commit human rights violations.

Emerging Ways to Engage Non-State Armed Groups

Very few conflicts around the world today are between states, and most currently involve at least one non-state actor.[38] Although improving states' monitoring and end use will contribute significantly to reducing the proliferation of weapons, it will not address the entire problem. Many groups, whether in the private or public spheres, will continue to obtain weapons either legally or illegally. Even though a major arms control initiative such as the ATT is primarily directed at states, the standards developed under international law may also apply to armed groups. Furthermore, it is worth noting that there are also emerging codes of conduct particularly for armed groups sanctioned by, or associated with, the state, such as state armed forces, police and special forces, paramilitary/militia, and private security companies or mercenaries. In addition, many international humanitarian organizations have long recognized the benefits of engaging armed groups in a dialogue on the principles of international humanitarian law (IHL). The humanitarian community is increasingly urging non-state armed groups to respect international norms. The question, however, is how, given the asymmetries of the state-centric system, to hold armed groups responsible or accountable for violations of human rights and humanitarian norms when they are not in a position to sign regional or international agreements.[39]

Arguably, armed groups are unlikely to abide by any international arms transfer regime that seeks to limit transfers of weapons to them. Access to weapons is fundamental to the sustainability and survival of these groups, so it may seem absurd to require them to prohibit the use, production, acquisition, transfer, and stockpiling of such weapons, or to compel the destruction of the stockpiles. Moreover, such groups may lack capacity or be simply unwilling to respect standards of IHL and international human rights law (IHRL) in their operations. Strategically targeting, terrorizing, and displacing innocent civilians are their way of exerting pressure on the opposing party.[40] Efforts to engage these groups to get them to respect national or international standards, particularly on limiting their supply of weapons, may appear fruitless. Nevertheless, there is room to engage them in humanitarian end-user activities that are compatible with the broad aims of an international arms control regime.

The long-standing experience of major humanitarian organizations has demonstrated the potential benefits of such an engagement. Examples can be found in various agreements and memorandums of understanding on humanitarian standards. Despite political obstacles, humanitarian organizations such as the United Nations Development Programme (UNDP), the United Nations Children's Fund (UNICEF), the Office of the UN High Commissioner for Refugees (UNHCR), the United Nations Office for the Coordination of Humanitarian Affairs (UNOCHA), the International Committee of the Red Cross (ICRC), and Médecins Sans Frontières (MSF) engage armed groups on a daily basis in their humanitarian work. Such organizations negotiate access agreements and arrange ceasefires or safe passages to conduct humanitarian work. In doing so, they are *de facto* experimenting with various policy tools to pressure armed groups to limit human rights abuses.[41]

Engaging armed groups in the landmine debate offers some potentially useful lessons. The Swiss NGO Geneva Call[42] has conceived an innovative mechanism for armed groups who were excluded from the drafting of the 1997 anti-personnel *Mine Ban Treaty* (also known as the *Ottawa Convention*)[43] and thus may not feel bound by the convention. The organization provides non-state actors with the possibility of subscribing to the same obligations through a "Deed of Commitment for Adherence to a Total Ban on Anti-Personnel Mines and for Cooperation in Mine Action." Although politically contentious for some states, Geneva Call has helped groups set what is essentially a clear external monitoring benchmark that can be used to ensure that armed groups meet their commitments. Thus, another way to regulate weapons proliferation and misuse by armed groups is to increase external monitoring of their activities. Groups such as the International Crisis Group, Amnesty International, and Human Rights Watch, among others, regularly publish reports on different armed groups' actions and responsibilities under international law, in many cases shaming those that violate international standards. The UN Security Council has also taken a similar stance, naming and shaming groups that violate internationally accepted standards, such as those pertaining to the use of child soldiers.

Conclusions and Recommendations

In order to ensure a comprehensive solution to the problem of transfers to undesirable end users, arms transfer regimes must consider all types of armed actors, from states to non-state groups. The evidence gathered by those who monitor weapons acquisitions and transfers indicates that improving states' own internal controls – especially through better internal monitoring – is a critical component of a better regulatory regime. Research indicates that the majority of weapons reaching the wrong hands that undermine peace and security come from poorly controlled state stockpiles. Weapons are easily available as a result of the political-criminal nexus, characterized by varying degrees of cooperation among military, national law enforcement, and different criminal participants. In order to counteract the political-criminal nexus, it is essential to have an organization with both stringent internal and external monitoring mechanisms that adequately cover information gathering, reporting, coordination, and post-delivery verification. In end-use monitoring, it should not be left to the discretion of states to decide when a certificate is required. Documentary proof of end use must be compulsory for all transfers, and restrictions on end use and re-export must be clearly set out. States should consider sharing resources for pre-licensing evaluations and post-export delivery verification and monitoring – such cooperation will prevent future misuse or diversion. In addition, better and timely reporting will ensure increased transparency and accountability.

States also have to improve their monitoring of the activities of agents responsible for both arms transfers and stockpiles. The broader framework of the arms control debate and implementation should include security sector governance and codes of conduct for armed groups: state armed forces, police and special forces, paramilitary/militia, and private security companies or mercenaries.

Non-state groups will continue to acquire weapons through legal or illegal means. It is therefore possible, and indeed useful, to consider non-traditional ways to regulate end use by armed groups – such as setting clear monitoring benchmarks for armed groups who are not signatories to arms transfer regimes – to ensure that they respect IHL and IHRL. States should recognize the complementary role of research and humanitarian non-governmental agencies in monitoring the activities of non-state armed groups. Strategies for engaging such groups will remain largely experimental, as situations and tactics of armed groups evolve constantly. Engaging these groups on humanitarian issues should not be considered of limited value, however, considering the progress that has been made on mine action by organizations such as Geneva Call.

We end by restating that for an arms transfer regime to be effective, it needs to consider the full range of armed actors: not just states but also non-state groups. We have argued that even though the issue of armed groups is politically contentious, it makes sense from a regulatory perspective to think of a world that is not strictly divided between states and non-state groups, but rather one that is closer to a continuum. The continuum of regulatory possibilities offered by different degrees of internal and external monitoring by both state and non-state actors is a promising way to help the international community limit the illegal proliferation, diversion, and misuse of weapons.

NOTES

1 The term "conventional arms" generally includes small arms and light weapons, non-nuclear bombs, shells, rockets, missiles, and cluster munitions, as well as sea and land mines. Certain types of conventional weapons are prohibited under the *Convention on Cluster Munitions*, 2008, C.N.776.2008.TREATIES-2 (entered into force 1 August 2010), and the *Convention on the Prohibition of the Use, Stockpiling, Production and Transfer of Anti-Personnel Mines and on Their Destruction*, 1997, 36 I.L.M. 1507 (entered into force 1 March 1999) [*Ottawa Convention*]. The United Nations *Convention on Prohibitions or Restrictions on the Use of Certain Conventional Weapons Which May Be Deemed to Be Excessively Injurious or to Have Indiscriminate Effects (with Protocols I, II and III)*, 1980, 1342 U.N.T.S. 137 (entered into force 2 December 1983) [*Convention on Certain Conventional Weapons*] prohibits the use of certain conventional weapons that are considered excessively injurious or whose effects are indiscriminate.

2 In December 2006, United Nations member states began a drive to develop an international legally binding Arms Trade Treaty (ATT) to regulate international state-to-state transfers of conventional arms: *Towards an Arms Trade Treaty: Establishing Common International Standards for the Import, Export and Transfer of Conventional Arms*, GA Res. 89, UN GAOR, 61st Sess., UN Doc. A/61/89 (2006). Two one-week meetings per year were scheduled from 2009 to 2011 to start discussions focused on a possible arms trade treaty. The first two Arms Trade Treaty Preparatory Committee meetings were held 12-23 July 2010. They established the outline of a draft treaty, a draft preamble, draft goals and objectives, and three substantial papers on the treaty's scope, parameters, and implementation. The third Preparatory Committee meeting took place 28 February-3 March 2011.

3 Robert Muggah and Oliver Jütersonke, "Considering the Contribution of Public and Private Security Providers to Endemic Urban Violence" (Paper presented at the Human Security and Cities Conference, Canadian Consortium of Human Security and Department of Foreign Affairs and International Trade Canada, Liu Institute for Global Issues, University of British Columbia, Vancouver, BC, 3-4 March 2008).

4 Source: Adapted from *ibid.*

5 Throughout this section, we avoid using the terms "legal" or "illegal" arms transfers. We simply discuss the ways in which armed groups obtain weapons. We restrict ourselves in this sense because the term "legal" can mean either according to national law or according to international law. The manner in which international law applies to arms transferred and used by non-state armed groups is discussed in the section "Emerging Ways to Engage Non-State Armed Groups" below. Although there is a substantial body of international law that can be applied to the international

arms trade, there is little agreement on the manner in which this might be done. One of the challenges for an arms transfer regime is how to supplement and strengthen existing international law as it applies to the arms trade. Instead of "legal" and "illegal" transfers and use of arms, we use pejorative terms such as "the wrong hands," "diversion," or "misuse," which will need to be properly defined in any future treaty.

6 See James Bevan and Pablo Dreyfus, "Enemy Within: Ammunition Diversion in Uganda and Brazil" in Eric G. Berman, Keith Krause, Emile LeBrun, and Glenn McDonald, eds., *Small Arms Survey 2007: Guns and the City* (Cambridge: Cambridge University Press, 2007) at 288-315.

7 See United Nations Office on Drugs and Crime, *Violence, Crime, and Illegal Arms Trafficking in Colombia* (Bogota: United Nations Office on Drugs and Crime, 2006), online: UNODC <http://www.unodc.org/>.

8 *Ibid.* at 32.

9 *Ibid.* at 34.

10 In the largest recorded arms shipment to the FARC, 10,000 Kalashnikov rifles from Peru were parachuted into the jungles of eastern Colombia in 1999. Estimated to be worth US$8 million, the deal was brokered by Vladimiro Montesinos, Peru's intelligence chief at the time. Montesinos was also at the centre of a conspiracy to buy rifles from Jordan and transfer them to the Colombian rebels. In September 2006, he was sentenced to twenty years in prison for the deal. See "FARC Rearms from Peru, Eyes Venezuela" *Jane's Terrorism & Security Monitor* (28 September 2007).

11 *Ibid.*

12 *Ibid.* The soldiers are being held on suspicion of stealing rifles, pistols, bullets, binoculars, and telescopic sights from armouries in Lima.

13 *Final Report of the Group of Experts on the Democratic Republic of Congo Submitted in Accordance with Paragraph 18(d) of Security Council Resolution 1807 (2008)*, UN SCOR, UN Doc. S/2008/773 (2008) at 6-7.

14 Matt Schroeder, "Manpad Proliferation in Latin America: An Analysis of the Threat and Regional Response" *En la mira – the Latin American Small Arms Watch* (4 January 2008), online: Comunidade Segura <http://www.comunidadesegura.org/>. Taken from "Rogue Missiles: Tracking Manpads Proliferation Trends" *Jane's Intelligence Review* (November 2007).

15 See *Report of the Group of Experts Submitted Pursuant to Resolution 1552 (2004)*, UN SCOR, UN Doc. S/2005/30 (2005) at 34.

16 See *Report of the Monitoring Group on Somalia Pursuant to Security Council Resolution 1676 (2006)*, UN SCOR, UN Doc. S/2006/913 (2006) at 15 [*Report of the Monitoring Group on Somalia 2006*]. Also see United Nations Office of the Special Adviser on Africa, "Overview of DDR Process in Africa" (Paper presented at the Second International Conference on DDR and Stability in Africa, Kinshasa, Democratic Republic of Congo, 12-14 June 2007) at 13, online: United Nations <http://www.un.org/africa/osaa/>.

17 See *Report of the Monitoring Group on Somalia Pursuant to Security Council Resolution 1724 (2006)*, UN SCOR, UN Doc. S/2007/ (2007) 436 at 9.

18 *Ibid.* at 15. Also see Jon Swain and Brian Johnson-Thomas, "Exposed: The Somalia Arms Boycott Breaker" *Sunday Times* (18 February 2007), online: Timesonline <http://www.timesonline.co.uk/>.

19 *Senate Foreign Relations Committee Staff Report* (15 December 2006), online: Federation of American Scientists <http://www.fas.org/>.
20 See Manuel Roig-Franzia, "U.S. Guns Behind Cartel Killings in Mexico" *Washington Post Foreign Service* (29 October 2007) A01, online: Washington Post <http://www.washingtonpost.com/>.
21 In Arizona and Texas, some unlicensed vendors can sell personal collections at weekend gun shows without background checks. See Paul Helmke, "U.S. Guns Behind Cartel Killings in Mexico" *Huffington Post* (6 November 2007), online: Huffington Post <http://www.huffingtonpost.com/paul-helmke/>; also see James McKinley Jr., "U.S. Is Arms Bazaar for Mexican Cartels?" *New York Times* (25 February 2009), online: New York Times <http://www.nytimes.com/2009/02/26/us/26borders.html>.
22 Franzia, *supra* note 20.
23 *Violence, Crime, and Illegal Arms Trafficking, supra* note 7 at 28.
24 Mines Action Canada, "Non-State Armed Groups and the Mine Ban," *Landmine Monitor Fact Sheet* (June 2005), online: Landmine Monitor <http://lm.icbl.org/>.
25 *Supra* note 7 at 33.
26 Christiane Agboton-Johnson, Adedeji Ebo, and Laura Mazal, "Small Arms Control in Ghana, Nigeria and Senegal, West Africa Series No. 2," International Alert (London: Security and Peacebuilding Programme: Monitoring the Implementation of Small Arms Control [MISAC], 2004) at 12.
27 *Report of the Monitoring Group on Somalia 2006, supra* note 16.
28 It needs to be noted that Durra's weapons industry has existed for over a century, and it is a tradition in Durra to carry a small weapon for self-defence. See also "Durra – the World's Largest Illegal Firearms Market" *France 24* (25 April 2008), online: France 24 <http://observers.france24.com/en/>.
29 The AK-47 is the assault rifle of choice for armed groups because it is cheap, easily available, easy to carry, durable, and easy to use with its discharge of six hundred rounds per minute.
30 This was confirmed when the main base of the Sri Lankan Air Force was bombed on 25 March 2007.
31 "Flying Tigers Strike at Night" *Jane's Terrorism and Security Monitor* (11 April 2007), online: Jane's <http://www.janes.com/>.
32 "'Anti-aircraft' weapon seized from Brazilian drugs gang" *Jane's Security News* (14 April 2008), online: Jane's <http://www.janes.com/>.
33 For a fuller discussion of the tensions and complementarities of internal and external monitoring, see Pablo Policzer, *The Rise and Fall of Repression in Chile* (South Bend, IN: University of Notre Dame Press, 2009), chap. 2.
34 *ECOWAS (Economic Community of West African States) Convention on Small Arms and Light Weapons, Their Ammunition and Other Related Materials* (Abuja, Nigeria: ECOWAS Executive Secretariat, 2006), online: ECOWAS Small Arms Control Programme <http://www.ecosap.ecowas.int/>.
35 Paul Holtom, "Reporting Transfers of Small Arms and Light Weapons to the United Nations Register of Conventional Arms, 2007" (February 2009), online: SIPRI <http://books.sipri.org/>; see also "UN Register of Conventional Arms," online: United Nations Office for Disarmament Affairs <http://www.un.org/disarmament/>.

36 For example, the European Code of Conduct (1998), Wassenaar Arrangement (1996), EU Dual Use Regulation (1995), and the Missile Technology Control Regime (1987).

37 For more information on arms exports, see Inspektionen för Strategiska Produkter <http://www.isp.se/sa/node.asp?node=410>.

38 The 2008 *SIPRI Yearbook* reports fourteen major conflicts in thirteen countries in 2007, all of which were intrastate. Among the more than thirty major conflicts between 1998 and 2007, only three were interstate.

39 Pablo Policzer, "Human Rights and Humanitarian Norms beyond the State: The Problem of Non State Armed Groups" (Memo prepared for the seminar Human Rights at War: A Comparative Study of the Effectiveness of the Geneva Conventions, Cornell University, Ithaca, NY, 9-19 November 2007); see also "Ends and Means: Human Rights Approaches to Armed Groups" (Versoix, Switzerland: International Council on Human Rights Policy, 2001).

40 See *Report of the Secretary-General to the Security Council on the Protection of Civilians in Armed Conflict*, UN SCOR, UN Doc. S/1999/957 (1999) at 2. Armed groups are certainly not accountable for all violence perpetrated against civilians, but their presence among civilians plays a definite role in blurring the dividing line between combatants and non-combatants.

41 David Capie and Pablo Policzer, *Keeping the Promise of Protection: Holding Armed Groups to the Same Standard as States*. Working Paper 3 (Calgary: Armed Groups Project, 2004), online: Armed Groups Project <http://www.armedgroups.org/>.

42 Geneva Call is an international humanitarian organization dedicated to persuading armed non-state actors to respect and adhere to humanitarian norms, starting with the ban on anti-personnel mines.

43 *Convention on the Prohibition of the Use, Stockpiling, Production and Transfer of Anti-Personnel Mines and on Their Destruction*, 1997, 36 I.L.M. 1507 (entered into force 1 March 1999).

PART 2

PRIVATE MILITARY AND SECURITY COMPANIES AND HUMANITARIAN ORGANIZATIONS

Private Security Companies and Humanitarian Organizations
Implications for International Humanitarian Law

BENJAMIN PERRIN

*Without security, there can be no humanitarian aid or
assistance, no reconstruction, no democratic development.
To suggest, as some have, that we can do one without the other
is nothing short of pure folly and, in fact, it's dangerous.*

– *The Honourable Peter MacKay, Minister of National Defence,
Government of Canada*

Although it has long been recognized that "[t]he safety and security of humanitarian relief personnel is an indispensable condition for the delivery of humanitarian relief to civilian populations,"[1] there is a quiet but intense debate in the humanitarian community about when, if ever, humanitarian organizations should resort to private security providers for the defensive armed protection of humanitarian personnel, property, and materiel.

Unfortunately, the literature on private military and security companies has overwhelmingly focused on states as clients. Comparatively little attention has been paid to other customers, such as humanitarian organizations.[2] Those studies that have been undertaken on the prevalence of private security usage by humanitarian actors have not engaged in any sustained analysis of the international humanitarian law (IHL) implications of this practice. A 2008 study found that there was a "critical absence of policy and guidance" and that "field staff are making decisions in a policy vacuum."[3] This chapter aims to contribute towards addressing this gap, while highlighting the tension between classical humanitarian principles of independence, impartiality, and neutrality and the imperatives of delivering humanitarian aid in the complex security environments of today.

This chapter first examines the historical approach to the protection of humanitarian actors during armed conflict and occupation. It also explores how contemporary manifestations of armed conflict, such as those arising from non-international ethnically-based violence, failed and failing states, and insurgency-based warfare, have increased the security risks to humanitarian actors since the end of the Cold War.

Following this, alternative approaches taken in the last two decades with respect to the delivery of humanitarian assistance and ensuring the security of those delivering such aid are identified in order to situate the use of private security by humanitarian organizations within the menu of available options. The main strengths and weaknesses of alternatives are described, as well as the rationales cited by leading humanitarian organizations for choosing among these approaches.

Next, the potential consequences under IHL of humanitarian actors relying on private security providers for defensive armed protection are analyzed. The focus of this analysis is on issues of protected status and humanitarian access. Finally, the chapter concludes with preliminary recommendations for managing some of the risks involved in the hiring of private security companies by humanitarian organizations.

Historical Context and Modern Challenges to Humanitarian Aid Delivery

Humanitarian organizations exist to alleviate suffering during, and in the aftermath of, armed conflict. As a result, they inevitably operate in dangerous situations where their personnel are at risk of being harmed. In order for these organizations to do their job, humanitarian personnel, premises, and materiel must be protected. The historical consent-based approach to delivering humanitarian aid is described in this section, followed by an exploration of the implications of the changing nature of armed conflict for security in humanitarian aid delivery.

Historical Approach to Protection of Humanitarian Actors

The world has changed dramatically since the birth of the modern humanitarian movement in 1859.[4] During the international armed conflicts of the Westphalian state-centric world order, humanitarian organizations relied on the consent, goodwill, and assurances of national militaries to protect relief workers. Safe passage agreements, together with clear identification, generally helped to ensure the safety of humanitarian actors in the field.

One hundred fifty years after the Battle of Solferino, Henry Dunant's International Committee of the Red Cross (ICRC) remains committed to a classical approach towards protecting its humanitarian personnel, based on the negotiated consent of parties to the armed conflict. Consent of the parties is viewed by the ICRC as a basis for ensuring both security of its personnel and respect for its neutral and impartial mandate: "It is very dangerous if not impossible to organize a large-scale relief effort in secret or against the wishes of a fighting party. The ICRC operates on the principle of neutrality, which means that in theory, and in fact *99 percent of the time,* it does not allow any weapons in the vicinity of its operations" [emphasis added].[5] The remaining 1 percent of the time where the ICRC has departed from its general policy against armed protection will be explored below.

Other humanitarian actors that emerged after the Second World War, particularly after the end of the Cold War, have not been as stringent in requiring state consent before initiating humanitarian relief efforts. This was most pronounced with Dr. Bernard Kouchner's *sans frontierism* movement in the late 1960s and early 1970s, where "Kouchner and others asserted the right to intervene for humanitarian purposes whether or not governmental permissions were granted."[6] The emergence of a willingness to intervene without the consent of the state or parties to the conflict gives primacy to the humanitarian needs of the civilian populace over state sovereignty, and perhaps over the principles of neutrality and impartiality. Where humanitarian action is pursued in this manner, the security of humanitarian personnel can no longer depend on the assurances and goodwill of the state or parties to the conflict. The unwillingness or inability of the parties to guarantee the safety of humanitarian personnel and materiel created the impetus for alternative approaches for enhancing the security of humanitarian actors, but the call for humanitarian action regardless of state consent is only one of many factors that have driven the need for alternative security arrangements for humanitarians.

Changing Nature of Armed Conflict and Humanitarian Assistance
Non-international armed conflicts, including ethnically motivated attacks, and the growth of insurgency warfare has tragically cost many humanitarians their lives. These contemporary forms of armed conflict have taken

place alongside a significant expansion in the number and scope of humanitarian organizations. Estimates put the number of people assisted by nongovernmental organizations (NGOs) at 250 million,[7] and the "total value of assistance delivered by NGOs now outweighs that disbursed by the UN system."[8] Humanitarian actors "regularly enter high-threat locations, arriving on scene before the military and remaining after the military departs."[9]

The assumptions underlying the consent-based approach to security for humanitarian actors eroded substantially after the end of the Cold War. Consent of the parties to a conflict typically involved the ICRC negotiating with representatives of two or more states, both of which had ratified basic IHL instruments. In the five years following the collapse of the Berlin Wall, however, at least seventy-nine out of eighty-two armed conflicts were non-international in nature, involving state militaries and a litany of non-state armed groups (NSAGs).[10] During this period, NGOs disbursed approximately US$8-10 billion in aid, half of it earmarked for emergency relief. This represented a sixfold increase in humanitarian activity over the prior decade.[11]

These conflicts posed a serious challenge to humanitarian actors, since it became difficult to identify representatives of NSAGs with whom to negotiate humanitarian access (as many of these groups did not have recognizable command structures). The parties engaged in many conflicts also lacked the knowledge or respect for the protected status of humanitarian personnel under IHL. Mary Ellen O'Connell observes that, compounding these difficulties, "[r]ebel groups have been known to dishonor agreements intentionally to create new occasions to negotiate. These groups believe that negotiating with international aid organizations enhances their status."[12]

In addition to these challenges, many non-international armed conflicts involved ethnically motivated attacks on civilians, to the point that the delivery of relief assistance was viewed as an opposing factor to be confronted.[13] Indeed, "where the objective [of a party to the conflict] is to obliterate a particular group (ethnic or otherwise), impartial humanitarian intervention is difficult to achieve."[14]

An even more fundamental challenge to the consent-based approach to humanitarian security arose with the problem of failed and failing states. Somalia was a watershed, both because of the number of humanitarian actors involved and because of the complex security situation that this failed state presented. Between 1991 and 1993, over fifty NGOs participated in humanitarian relief in Somalia.[15] Without a Somali central authority with which to negotiate humanitarian access and protection, the ICRC was forced to decide between refusing to provide humanitarian assistance or obtaining alternative security for its personnel in order to stave off a catastrophe. The ICRC chose the latter. In a recent account of this departure from the organization's general policy against armed protection, David Forsythe and Barbara Rieffler-Flanagan write:

> For the first time in its history, the ICRC took the decision to operate as part of a military mission, because that was the only way, in [the] view of the top decision-makers of the organization, that widespread starvation could be checked in Somalia. Previously the ICRC had required even military transports carrying its relief goods to be weapons-free, even as the organization then turned and hired local security forces to guard its facilities and resources on the ground.[16]

The ICRC was not alone in securing alternative security arrangements in Somalia. Even more controversially, other humanitarian organizations associated themselves with different tribal factions in order to bring relief aid to civilians, an indication that the principle of impartiality may have been compromised by reliance on security personnel holding vested interests in the conflict. Those organizations that did not hire local armed guards reportedly lost up to 50 percent of aid supplies to theft. Other Western aid representatives that had hired local guards were threatened when they attempted to terminate the arrangement, suggesting that a "protection racket" had been established as part of the war economy.[17]

More recently, insurgency warfare in Afghanistan and Iraq has presented new challenges for humanitarians. While counterinsurgency warfare is not "new,"[18] the presence of a large number of humanitarian actors in the midst of this type of conflict is a relatively recent phenomenon. For example, as Andrew Bearpark explains, in Iraq during 2003-4 there occurred the "tragic bombing of the UN, and a few weeks later ... the attack on the ICRC office and the kidnappings and murders of individual aid workers, with the tragic death of Margaret Hassan from CARE as one example. There was a total change in atmosphere – from being neutral do-gooders, the aid workers had suddenly become perceived as part of the war environment, and that's where the need for security arose."[19]

Understanding the Increased Risk to Humanitarian Personnel
The combined effect of these complex modern security environments and the increasing number and scope of humanitarian actors has, in some cases,

been deadly. Sean Greenaway and Andrew Harris observe that "[i]n virtually every part of the world, those providing aid to distressed populations have been robbed, beaten, raped, abducted and murdered ... Only 6% of those interviewed – which included development workers – recorded no security problems at their work location."[20] The study identified four types of security risks facing humanitarian personnel: accident, criminality, banditry, and targeting. Banditry "refers to armed factions seeking to plunder aid agency assets with an economic value in order to feed their war machine or for personal gain ... [as well as][h]ostage-taking for ransom," while targeting "refers to deliberate attacks or threats aimed at an agency in order to disrupt its activities or to influence the behavior of third party, mainly international, actors."[21] Based on the state of affairs prevailing in 1998, Greenaway and Harris considered "that, apart from accident, the criminality and banditry categories predominate" but that targeting "probably constitutes the greatest threat to humanitarian action in the instances where it occurs."[22]

The number of attacks against humanitarian aid workers worldwide shows an upward trend. Between 1997 and 2007, the incidence of major violence against humanitarian personnel more than doubled.[23] Although the number of humanitarian personnel operating worldwide has also increased during this period, the growth in major incidents has outpaced the growth in number of aid workers overall.[24] Between 2005 and 2007, there were 253 incidents of violence against humanitarian aid workers worldwide, compared with 94 incidents from 1997 to 1999.[25]

Additionally, statistics maintained by the United Nations of attacks on its personnel offer insight into the types of security incidents that humanitarian personnel are affected by in the field:

> Over the past decade, threats against the safety and security of UN personnel have escalated at an unprecedented pace. Forced to operate in increasingly dangerous environments and in complex emergencies, the mortality and distress rates of field staff have increased dramatically. From January 1992 to April 2003, 220 civilian UN staff members lost their lives through the deliberate machinations of perpetrators ... Between January 1994 and October 2002, 74 incidents involving hostage-taking or kidnapping involving 262 staff occurred – eight in 2002 in separate incidents in Somalia, the Sudan and Guyana ... This list does not include the growing number of incidents of rape, sexual assault, armed robbery, car-jacking, attacks on humanitarian convoys and operations and harassment perpetrated upon UN staff.[26]

The reasons behind these statistics are far more complex than the numbers suggest. In addition to the contribution of modern forms of armed conflict, discussed above, the following factors are believed to have increased the security risks facing humanitarian actors in recent years:

- lack of situational awareness and local knowledge among humanitarian personnel in their initial period of deployment[27]
- competition between humanitarian organizations, resulting in the placing of inexperienced staff in the field and increased risk taking[28]
- targeting of civilians by combatants, with aid workers viewed as a threat to achievement of this objective[29]
- targeting of humanitarian workers directly because they are not perceived as neutral, due to their foreign nationality, perceived cooperation/ relationship with opposing military forces, or their human rights advocacy[30]
- targeting of humanitarian workers to discredit the ability of the occupying authority to protect civilians,[31] "a desire to influence a third party, force withdrawal of the agency, or invite greater force in the conflict"[32]
- lack of respect for the protected status of humanitarian workers under IHL
- economic motivations of belligerents or "criminal profiteering"[33] to obtain materiel and supplies directly, or because the aid, if delivered, would negatively affect their economic power in the conflict.[34]

Humanitarian Assistance and the Private Security Debate

Responding to the complexity and instability of modern armed conflict, two trends with respect to humanitarian assistance and security may be observed. First, humanitarian organizations no longer have a monopoly on the delivery of humanitarian assistance in difficult security environments. Other actors, including state armed forces and, more rarely, private military and security companies now deliver humanitarian aid directly. Second, many humanitarian organizations have managed their security risks by adopting an array of new, sometimes controversial approaches to protection. As a result of these twin phenomena, there has been an expansion of both the actors delivering humanitarian assistance and those providing security for such assistance. The direct delivery of humanitarian assistance by state armed forces and private security companies as independent actors is explored in this section, followed by a consideration of the security alternatives facing humanitarian organizations themselves.

Other Actors Delivering Humanitarian Assistance

State and non-state actors that specialize in providing security have assumed a greater role in directly delivering humanitarian assistance themselves, without necessarily involving humanitarian organizations at all. The
counterinsurgency doctrines pursued by state armed forces in countries
such as Iraq and Afghanistan consider humanitarian relief aid and longer-
term development assistance as part of a military strategy, recognizing that
soldiers "are expected to be nation builders as well as warriors."[35]

Less frequent but also notable is the contracting out of humanitarian aid
to private military and security companies themselves. With relatively little
publicity to date, such companies have received contracts to directly deliver
humanitarian assistance, based on their capability to rapidly deploy and
provide their own security. These firms see business opportunities in a vast
array of operations, including "state-building, supporting and even providing humanitarian and disaster relief, which includes logistics, communications and energy services."[36] The companies have also reportedly advised
and provided protection for displaced populations.[37] Although state armed
forces and private military and security companies bring a particular expertise in security, humanitarian activists argue that "as a matter of principle
and practice, humanitarian action is – and should remain – first and foremost civilian in character."[38]

Ensuring the Safety of Humanitarian Personnel

As discussed above, humanitarian organizations have proliferated since the
end of the Cold War. To enter or remain in the business of delivering humanitarian aid during modern armed conflicts, these organizations have
been compelled to consider an array of alternative approaches to protecting
their personnel, property, and materiel. This problem is further complicated
by the addition of new actors to the humanitarian arena. Thus, many humanitarian organizations are no longer content to simply rely on their protected status under IHL or the traditional consent-based approach to
protection.

In confronting today's complex security climate, humanitarian organizations have a diverse menu of alternatives to consider:

• withdraw, or never enter, due to unacceptable risk
• utilize "soft security": training, policies, procedures, security information
  management, infrastructure, collaboration with other organizations
• engage state armed forces to mitigate security risks

- engage non-state armed groups to mitigate security risks
- engage the populace or community to mitigate security risks ("acceptance" strategy)
- integrate in-house security officers
- hire local guards to provide armed or unarmed protection
- hire a private security company to provide armed or unarmed protection
- align with a state to obtain armed security from state armed forces.

Most humanitarian organizations share the common goal of providing "safe, effective delivery of relief and provision of temporary protection to those in need,"[39] but many disagree on which of the above security alternatives actually satisfy this objective, in both the short and long term.

The threshold security question that all humanitarian organizations face is whether to enter a conflict or post-conflict area at all. Although they have a responsibility to deliver relief, they also have obligations to protect their staff and conduct due diligence on the security risks involved. A potential consequence of refusing to enter a theatre of operations to deliver humanitarian assistance is the damning observation that "[t]he resulting loss of life in the affected population is significant – both from lack of access to relief programs and from the protection international agencies offer as 'witnesses' to deter atrocities."[40] Typically, the option of withdrawal, suspension of operations, or refusal to enter the area where humanitarian relief is required will be based on the failure of parties to the conflict to provide a secure environment, and an organization's unwillingness or inability to pursue alternatives to mitigate the security risks. In the case of long-standing humanitarian organizations, fundamental philosophies about the use of defensive armed security loom larger than the immediate conflict, but, as witnessed in Somalia, there are exceptions to every such policy.

Between refusing to enter an area of operations and resorting to external security options, humanitarian organizations have adopted a range of "soft" approaches to security. Security training, procedures, and awareness education each play a role in mitigating risks. Many larger organizations have become increasingly adept at developing internal capacity in this area, besides bringing in outside security consultants. Some organizations, however, lack the expertise and information to adequately provide such training. Coordination between humanitarian organizations, including with respect to evacuation planning, is one way to overcome these shortcomings.[41]

"Engagement" is a broad category of proactive approaches to mitigate security risks, with humanitarian organizations directly consulting and negotiating with state armed forces, non-state armed groups, and the local populace.[42] For some organizations, engagement or "acceptance" as a security strategy is intended to overcome the need for physical "hard" security alternatives.

Pragmatic considerations related to obtaining access to contested areas of operations have long led the UN and ICRC to negotiate access agreements with various non-state armed groups. As Nuchhi Currier has noted, for these agreements to succeed, they must be "transparent, neutral and a humanitarian necessity."[43] The challenges of obtaining such agreements in contemporary armed conflicts as part of the consent-based strategy have been discussed earlier.

Although engaging the populace[44] as a security strategy is considered by some to be the alternative "closest to humanitarian principles," its effectiveness may be quite limited in practice. To succeed in providing timely information to humanitarian actors and to foster community protection, this approach requires early and sustained effort by experienced humanitarian personnel.[45]

Beyond these "soft" security alternatives, humanitarian organizations have at least three external "hard" security options: (1) local "guards," (2) state armed forces, and (3) foreign private security contractors. The decision of a humanitarian organization to rely on any of these alternatives is inextricably linked to the broader debate about the use of armed protection by humanitarians.

The Armed Protection Debate

The use of armed protection has sharply divided the humanitarian community. On one side of the debate, organizations such as the ICRC and Médecins Sans Frontières (MSF) have resisted the use of armed protection. The ICRC's general view is that security is best achieved through adherence to its core principles of neutrality, impartiality, and independence. Its *Report on the Use of Armed Protection for Humanitarian Assistance* states: "[T]he ability to deliver humanitarian assistance and to carry out humanitarian activities in violent situations is a product first and foremost of our ethical and professional standards and the way we conduct ourselves. It is not a function of armed escorts and flak-jackets."[46] As a result of this approach, the ICRC has had to temporarily suspend operations (as in Bosnia and the Democratic Republic of the Congo) due to security risks that it was unable to manage within the confines of its general policy against armed protection.[47]

MSF has also resisted armed protection by "robustly defending the right of intervention on the principle[s] of impartiality and neutrality."[48] These principles were painfully tested in June 2004 when five MSF staff were killed in northwestern Afghanistan, and other members received threats of further violence from the Taliban. The organization chose to withdraw from the country shortly thereafter.[49]

Conversely, organizations like CARE and the World Food Programme (WFP) have used armed escorts extensively in transporting aid to populations in need. An International Alert study found that these armed escorts are usually provided by the host government, but in some cases where the state authorities lack effective control, the organizations have hired private security companies to provide armed protection to aid convoys.[50]

Security by State Armed Forces

Humanitarian organizations have resisted reliance on state armed forces for close protection on the basis that it undermines impartiality, neutrality, and independence.[51] For example, with respect to the ICRC, the *Commentaries on Protocol I, Additional to the Geneva Conventions* of 1949 (Protocol I), take the view that "the neutrality of the emblem should preclude them from being escorted by members of the armed forces."[52]

Fred Schreier and Marina Caparini argue that the "use of military protection in support of humanitarian operations should only occur when there is no comparable civilian alternative."[53] There is also the concern that being in such close proximity to military personnel will undermine the effectiveness of the protected status of humanitarian actors as civilians under IHL.[54]

From the perspective of state armed forces, Major Lisa Turner and Major Lynn Norton highlight two competing views on providing protection to humanitarian organizations. On the one hand, while noting the independence of humanitarian organizations, military commanders may see a strategic advantage in being able to influence humanitarian action – doing so through logistical support, security, and communications. On the other hand, requests for security by humanitarian organizations may be viewed as "unreasonable, unnecessary, and untenable in their effects upon the military mission."[55]

Local Guards as Private Security

In an attempt to balance security concerns with the principles of neutrality and impartiality, some humanitarian organizations have hired local "guards"

– armed and unarmed – to escort personnel and supply convoys, or to provide security at fixed locations.

An International Alert study found that American NGOs typically hire local guards to deter banditry by providing (usually) unarmed protection at fixed sites, such as warehouses.[56] There are instances, however, where these "flashlight and radio" guards are able to call in armed response teams on short notice. In such cases, humanitarian workers may be surprised to find that these guards play a role in rapidly escalating an incident.[57] Many of the NGOs in the International Alert study also expressed a greater willingness to use armed guards to "ride shotgun" for convoys in unstable areas.[58] Even the ICRC (in Somalia and the Northern Caucasus) and MSF (in Somalia and Pakistan) have reportedly hired local guards to escort aid convoys.[59]

The use of locally hired guards has been a preferred option among certain humanitarian organizations for several reasons. For one thing, they are presumed to be knowledgeable about the players, politics, and language of the area of operations. It is assumed that they promote the neutrality and independence of humanitarian organizations because they are presumed not to be affiliated with state armed forces or non-state armed groups, who may otherwise have to be relied upon to provide protection.

There are several serious concerns, however, with hiring local individuals to provide armed or unarmed protection to humanitarian organizations. First, local personnel may have ethnic or tribal affiliations with parties to the conflict.[60] James Cockayne has characterized the ICRC's approach in Somalia as building "a small army out of a patchwork of different clansmen, in an effort to ensure humanitarian access for aid convoys."[61] At the time that a Western humanitarian organization is attempting to initially establish its operations, local affiliations will be very difficult to fully appreciate. As a result, the image of the humanitarian organization may be tarnished if it hires unsavoury local characters as "guards"; even worse, the organization may unwittingly associate itself with a party to the conflict and thus become the target of attacks.

Second, a 2008 Humanitarian Policy Group study found widespread concern among humanitarian actors about the calibre of local private security providers. Specifically, most aid workers interviewed expressed serious reservations about the "overall poor quality of skills and training, low payment, high turnover, weak incentive structures and patchy oversight of these security actors."[62]

A third set of concerns has to do with the broader impact of this practice. There is the risk that hiring local guards will result in a localized "arms race" because in order to provide credible deterrence, the guards must be equipped to ward off local security threats.[63] Further, hiring local guards may fuel the local war economy and encourage a protection racket. The lack of thought given to what these guards will do to make a living after their contract has ended is problematic – there is a risk that they will turn to criminality or join one of the parties to the armed conflict.

Hiring a Private Security Company

The extent to which humanitarian organizations hire private security companies is only beginning to be discerned. Neither the literature on private military and security companies[64] nor industry surveys, which suffer from poor response rates and which are too general,[65] provide detailed information on the prevalence of private security company usage by humanitarian organizations. Tim Cross has gone so far as to say that the hiring of private security firms by humanitarian organizations has "taken place under a veil of silence, in an *ad hoc* way."[66]

Typically, statements about the use of private security firms by humanitarian organizations are very general in nature, withholding the identity of the organization and the firm, and the scope of the contract.[67] For example, Larry Minear states that "humanitarian organizations have contracted with international security firms to provide protection for operations and personnel in places such as Sierra Leone, Angola and the Congo."[68] It has been apparent for several years that private security companies are engaged in a wide range of activities for humanitarian organizations, of which armed protection is likely to be only a very small aspect.[69]

Armour Group International, a British private security company, has been a notable exception to this "veil of silence" and has been quite open about working for humanitarian organizations. The company has a client list that reads like a who's who of the humanitarian and development community, including UN agencies, the European Community Humanitarian Office (ECHO), US Agency for International Development (USAID), UK Department for International Development (DFID), ICRC, International Rescue Committee, CARE, and Caritas.[70] Armour Group has been quite vocal about the need for accountability for private security contractors and claims that it does not seek immunity for its personnel.[71]

The demand for private security services by reputable "blue chip" clients such as humanitarian organizations may provide incentive for such firms to ensure that they maintain an excellent record of compliance with human rights and international humanitarian law. The strength of such an incentive is limited, however, due to the relatively small portion of the market that such clients comprise.[72]

It is plausible, at least in theory, that foreign private security contractors are more neutral and impartial players than either locally hired guards or members of state armed forces,[73] but this argument is becoming less persuasive as such firms hire an increasing percentage of local staff. For example, at the height of the intervention in Iraq, the ratio of expatriate to local staff employed by private military and security companies was 1:10.[74] Furthermore, "very few PSPs [private security providers] appear to have developed an understanding of the unique operating principles that guide humanitarians in their operations in conflict contexts."[75]

Similar to the concerns surrounding the practice of hiring local guards, there are also worries about the impact in a given theatre of operations of hiring private security companies. Some argue that it can have the unintended consequence of increasing the security threat to humanitarian organizations, since "the introduction of another armed faction inside an already unstable region would only increase the probability of the use of armed force,"[76] and because the presence of armed personnel makes the protected personnel or assets more visible to belligerents or criminal elements.

In September 2008, a much-needed study released by the Humanitarian Policy Group (HPG) provided greater insight into the prevalence of humanitarian organizations' practice of hiring armed private security contractors. Based on interviews with leading international humanitarian organizations,[77] the study found that although the use of private security contractors by humanitarian actors has been growing, armed protection remained the exception rather than the rule. Withdrawal or suspension of operations was the preferred option for many organizations when faced with the most insecure of environments. Despite this trend, the HPG study found:

> No major humanitarian provider – UN, NGO or Red Cross – can claim that it has never paid for armed security. According to consolidated organisational responses, over the past year at least 41% of the major humanitarian organisations contracted some form of armed protective services (guards, escorts or bodyguards) for one or more of their operations. Exceptional or not, armed security has been and stands to remain an incontestable reality for the international humanitarian community.[78]

The reality of this practice warrants much greater attention, particularly because of its implications for IHL.

Implications for International Humanitarian Law

The changing nature of armed conflict, the complex security risks facing humanitarian organizations, and the shortcomings of relying on local guards or state armed forces for protection have combined to make the use of private security companies the least-worst alternative for some humanitarian organizations. While the extent of the practice is difficult to assess, it is clear that private security companies have been hired for a range of activities, including armed defensive protection. The consequences of this trend in terms of the rights and obligations of humanitarian actors under IHL have received little attention to date.

Intentionally directing attacks against personnel, installations, materiel, units, or vehicles involved in a humanitarian assistance mission constitutes a war crime in both international and non-international armed conflicts. For an attack against a humanitarian mission to be considered a war crime, two requirements must be met: (1) the humanitarian mission must be conducted in accordance with the UN Charter, and (2) the humanitarian personnel and objects must be "entitled to the protection given to civilians or civilian objects under the international law of armed conflict."[79] In other words, if the protected status of humanitarian personnel or objects as civilians is suspended or lost, then any intentional attack will not constitute a war crime. Thus, protected status is a pivotal concept in this aspect of the legal protection regime for humanitarian personnel.

When the Additional Protocols to the 1949 *Geneva Conventions* were adopted in 1977, the use of private security firms as an alternative means of ensuring security for humanitarian action was not envisaged. As a result, there is no explicit directive in either the *Geneva Conventions* or the Additional Protocols as to whether humanitarian organizations retain their protected status when they hire armed private security companies to provide protection for humanitarian personnel, property, or materiel.

In order to assess the legal consequences for a humanitarian organization's protected status when employing private military companies, it is necessary to go back to first principles. Two threshold issues must be addressed:

- Is the protected status of humanitarian personnel under IHL suspended or lost if they use armed private security contractors?

- Is humanitarian access to provide relief affected by the decision to hire a private security company for armed protection of relief consignments?

Protected Status

Obligations to Protect Humanitarian Personnel

Parties to an international armed conflict have a legal obligation under IHL to protect humanitarian relief consignments and personnel. This has been recognized as a rule of customary international law.[80] With respect to international armed conflicts, Article 70(4) of Protocol I provides that "[t]he Parties to the conflict shall protect relief consignments and facilitate their rapid distribution," while Article 71(2) states that personnel participating in relief actions "shall be respected and protected."[81] The *Commentaries* on Article 70(4) follow the traditional consent-based approach to humanitarian security:

> If the authorities do not have the means to ensure such protection, particularly if they cannot prevent looting and diversion of relief consignments, the whole question whether the relief action can continue is obviously put in jeopardy, first from the point of view of the donors, then the Parties allowing the passage over their territory, and finally, and most of all, the adverse Parties of the receiving Party.[82]

Likewise, Article 71(2) of Protocol I confers only modest protection for humanitarian personnel, such that the parties to the conflict must "inform and instruct their armed forces not to attack such personnel."[83] Banditry and riots by a starving population are risks recognized in the *Commentaries*, and may be dealt with by reliance on the local police force, if it is necessary and requested.[84]

The relevant party to an international armed conflict is also required to provide security and access to civilian medical personnel where medical services are needed.[85] Additionally, "[i]f needed, all available help shall be afforded to civilian medical personnel in an area where civilian medical services are disrupted by reason of combat activity."[86]

During a non-international armed conflict, the obligation to respect and protect humanitarian relief personnel and consignments has been recognized under customary international law, despite the general lack of treaty-based provisions analogous to those applicable to international armed conflicts.[87] Article 9(1) of Protocol II, Additional to the *Geneva Conventions* of 1949 (Protocol II) explicitly states, however, that medical personnel "shall be respected and protected."[88] Article 11(2) states that "[t]he protection to which medical units and transports are entitled shall not cease unless they are used to commit hostile acts, outside their humanitarian function."[89]

Since the end of the Cold War, the increase in the number of attacks on UN humanitarian aid workers has also prompted the international community to take additional action to protect those engaged in UN operations. The *Convention on the Safety of United Nations and Associated Personnel*[90] was adopted in 1994 and requires state parties to criminalize attacks on humanitarians and assist in prosecuting offenders.[91] Notably, the convention specifies: "Nothing in this Convention shall be construed so as to derogate from the right to act in self-defence."[92] At the same time, however, the convention also requires that United Nations and associated personnel[93] "[r]efrain from any action or activity incompatible with the impartial and international nature of their duties."[94]

Protected Status as Civilians

Humanitarian personnel are civilians under IHL and thus have protected status, which grants them immunity from attack during international and non-international armed conflicts.[95] Persons denied civilian status under IHL are identified in Articles 4A(1), (2), (3), and (6) of the *Third Geneva Convention* and Article 43 of Protocol I; in those cases where an individual's status is in doubt, "that person shall be considered a civilian."[96] Humanitarian personnel are thus clearly civilians. On the basis of Article 50(1) of Protocol I, security personnel accompanying them should similarly be considered as having civilian status unless and until such time as they directly participate in hostilities.

Protected status as a civilian subsists "unless and for such time as they take a direct part in hostilities."[97] A significant consequence of the suspension or loss of protected status is that the individual may legally be subject to attack.[98] Consistent with this principle, as noted above, the ICRC study on customary international humanitarian law has recognized that military personnel delivering humanitarian aid are not afforded protected status as humanitarian personnel.[99] While the meaning of "direct participation in hostilities" remains complex in IHL, recent attempts have helped to provide a clearer interpretation of this pivotal concept.[100]

Starting from first principles, the ICRC *Commentaries* to Protocol I state that direct participation "means acts of war which by their nature or purpose are likely to cause actual harm to the personnel and equipment of the enemy armed forces,"[101] and that "[h]ostile acts should be understood to be acts which by their nature and purpose are intended to cause actual harm to the personnel and equipment of the armed forces."[102] The *Commentaries* express the view that on a temporal basis, "the word 'hostilities' covers not only the time that the civilian actually makes use of a weapon, but also, for example, the time that he is carrying it, as well as situations in which he undertakes hostile acts without using a weapon."[103]

Essentially, the same approach applies to civilians in non-international armed conflicts. The *Commentaries* on Protocol II "impl[y] that there is a sufficient causal relationship between the act of participation and its immediate consequences"[104] for a civilian to be found to have taken a direct part in hostilities.

Armed Private Security and Direct Participation in Hostilities

The private military and security company literature does not include an in-depth analysis of whether the use of armed private security by humanitarian actors for defensive purposes constitutes "direct participation in hostilities."[105] There are, however, two positions that have been staked out on the matter. Schreier and Caparini state that armed escorts by a private security company "would in practice constitute a military operation," according to the ICRC's view.[106] Conversely, Emanuela-Chiara Gillard, a legal advisor to the ICRC itself, has written that "all employees of PMCs/PSCs [private military and security companies] present in situations of armed conflict and hired by entities *other* than states" [emphasis added] will be entitled to civilian status, unless and for such time as they take a direct part in hostilities.[107]

The validity of physical armed protection for various humanitarian activities has received some recognition in treaty law. For example, civilian medical units retain their protected status as civilians under Article 13(2) of Protocol I when they "are equipped with light individual weapons for their own defence or for that of the wounded and sick in their charge" and are "guarded by a picket or by sentries or by an escort."[108] Medical aircraft personnel are permitted under Article 28(3) of Protocol I to carry "light individual weapons as may be necessary to enable the medical personnel on board to defend themselves and the wounded, sick and shipwrecked in their charge."[109] Additionally, civil defence forces, which may be responsible for a wide range of humanitarian tasks during occupation, are *not* considered to have undertaken an act harmful to the enemy when their personnel "bear light individual weapons for the purpose of maintaining order or for self-defence."[110] However, the occupying forces "may disarm civil defence personnel for reasons of security."[111] Likewise, the more recent *UN Safety Convention* recognizes "the right to act in self-defence"[112] of UN and associated personnel, which may include humanitarian personnel. These international treaty provisions suggest that a civilian does *not* take a direct part in hostilities simply on account of carrying light weapons for individual self-defence against, at least, banditry and criminality.

Blanket assertions that humanitarian personnel *automatically* lose their protected status as civilians by using armed private security contractors are therefore not consistent with international humanitarian law. The contextual nature of the inquiry into the suspension or loss of civilian status through "direct participation in hostilities" and recognition in treaty law of certain rights of armed individual self-defence by civilians, discussed above, require a case-by-case assessment into whether the use of private security contractors in a given situation entails the loss or suspension of protected status for humanitarian personnel and premises that are the subject of defensive armed protection.

As a result of this conclusion, the key to whether humanitarian personnel or objects lose their protected status, or their safety is put at risk because their private security contractors are in close proximity and have lost their protected status, is the nature of the *conduct* of the armed private security contractor.

A civilian who uses armed force in self-defence that is a necessary and proportionate response to a threat by an individual or group not party to the armed conflict would not lose protected status because such use is not directed at the personnel and equipment of the enemy armed forces. Therefore, if armed private security contractors hired by a humanitarian organization fire their weapons in legitimate self-defence to protect their client against banditry and criminality by individuals or groups that are not parties to the armed conflict, there will be no loss of protected status. Taking this further, Michael Schmitt argues that a situation where a private security company defends civilians or civilian objects against an attack by unlawful combatants engaged in criminal activities or war crimes would similarly not constitute direct participation in hostilities.[113]

If a civilian fires a weapon at a combatant without provocation, certainly they would be taking a direct part in hostilities, and their protected status is lost for the duration of the participation. The more controversial issue is whether civilians lose their protected status if they fire a weapon at a combatant in order to defend themselves against the unlawful acts of the combatant. In other words, does the retention of protected status as a civilian preclude the use of armed force in self-defence against a combatant who is illegally targeting the civilian?

On the one hand, Lindsey Cameron argues that if a private security guard returns fire to defend against a party to the conflict, the guard will be directly participating in hostilities and lose protected status.[114] Cameron relies on Article 49(1) of Protocol I, which states that "'[a]ttacks' means acts of violence against the adversary, whether in offence or in defence." With respect, this analysis is misplaced. The definition of attacks in Article 49(1) does not relate to the concept of what types of acts will constitute "direct participation in hostilities" by a civilian. Rather, the definition of "attacks" is related to the *prohibition* against an attack on civilians, as in Article 51(2) and (4). In other words, Article 49(1) ensures that civilians are protected from acts of violence perpetrated by the adversary, in either defence or offence, and therefore does not offer any assistance for the present analysis.

On the other hand, Michael Schmitt argues that civilians have a right to self-defence against unlawful actions by combatants, and retain their protected status:

> Civilians may also always defend themselves (because they are not legitimate targets under humanitarian law). In such cases, the civilian is acting either to enforce the law or in accordance with their right to defend persons and property in domestic and international criminal law. It would be absurd to hold that the law disallows defense against illegal actions by the victims thereof or by those who might come to their aid ... Of course, any lawful use of force must be necessary and proportionate.[115]

Schmitt's position has gained international support and is the better view. The *Interpretive Guidance on the Notion of Direct Participation in Hostilities under International Humanitarian Law* adopted by the Assembly of the International Committee of the Red Cross on 26 February 2009 states that civilians acting in defence of themselves (or others) in response to an unlawful violent attack lacks the "belligerent nexus" required to constitute direct participation in hostilities. This belligerent nexus requires that "an act must be specifically designed to directly cause the required threshold of harm in support of a party to the conflict and to the detriment of another."[116]

Under international criminal law, "an imminent and unlawful use of force" – such as the intentional targeting of humanitarian personnel – may be repelled with force that is reasonable and proportionate to protect oneself or another, or property essential for the survival of that person or another.[117] As with the "direct participation in hostilities" test, however, any argument related to self-defence under international criminal law "must be assessed on its own facts and in the specific circumstances."[118] A private security contractor using armed force against a combatant to defend humanitarian personnel against an unlawful attack would not be criminally responsible under international law.

It would be incongruous for international criminal law to authorize a civilian to respond with reasonable, necessary, and proportionate force to an imminent unlawful attack by a combatant, only to have IHL deem that that very act of self-defence authorizes the illegal attacker to then legitimately attack the civilian, on the grounds that the civilian is directly participating in hostilities at that time. If the initial attack on the civilian was illegal under IHL, it would be inconsistent with general principles of law for attackers to rely on their own breach of law to justify their continued attack. Consequently, neither the private security contractor nor the humanitarian personnel they are protecting would be taking a direct part in hostilities, which would entail a loss of protected status, if they use reasonable, necessary, and proportionate force to defend themselves against illegal intentional targeting by any individual or group, including parties to the conflict.

Regardless of whether humanitarian personnel retain their protected status as civilians *de jure* under IHL, it has been argued that such status will be of little effect as a matter of practice. For example, "[b]oth ICRC and MSF refuse to use security contractors in Afghanistan and Iraq, on the basis that to do so would in fact decrease staff security by risking associating them with Parties to an armed conflict."[119]

Likewise, although the US military "asserts that it does not violate international law for a civilian employee or a contractor with an armed force to carry a weapon for personal defense ... Joint Publication 4-0 acknowledges that the wearing of arms by contractors in an 'uncertain or hostile environment can cloud their status, leaving them open to being targeted as a combatant.'"[120] An even more serious problem is where private security firms are retained to provide services to both civilian and military clients in the same area of operations. In such circumstances, problems with the principle of distinction between combatants and civilians are likely to arise.[121]

Humanitarian Access

A second issue related to the rights and obligations of humanitarian organizations that hire private security contractors is whether access to provide relief is affected by the decision to employ such a company for armed protection.

Under IHL, the delivery of humanitarian assistance must be neutral and impartial in both international and non-international armed conflicts.[122] In *Nicaragua v. United States of America,* the International Court of Justice emphasized that humanitarian aid is not unlawful intervention, so long as it is neutral and non-discriminatory:

> There can be no doubt that the provision of strictly humanitarian aid to persons or forces in another country, whatever their political affiliations or objectives, cannot be regarded as unlawful intervention, or as in any other way contrary to international law. The characteristics of such aid were indicated in the first and second of the fundamental principles declared by the Twentieth International Conference of the Red Cross, that "The Red Cross, born of a desire to bring assistance without discrimination to the wounded on the battlefield, endeavours – in its international and national capacity – to prevent and alleviate human suffering wherever it may be found. Its purpose is to protect life and health and to ensure respect for the human being."[123]

As discussed under "The Armed Protection Debate" above, resort to local armed guards or state armed forces to protect humanitarian personnel, property, or materiel is arguably more likely to offend the principle of neutrality than hiring a foreign private security company for such services.

There are, however, countervailing concerns related to state sovereignty in Protocol I that would require a humanitarian organization that has hired a private security company for defensive armed protection to obtain the approval of the state of operation. Article 71(4) of Protocol I states: "Under no circumstances may relief personnel exceed the terms of their mission under this Protocol. In particular they shall take account of the security requirements of the party in whose territory they are carrying out their duties. The mission of any of the personnel who do not respect these conditions may be terminated."[124] The *Commentaries* to Article 71 of Protocol I state that personnel participating in relief actions "do not have a 'right' to carry out a particular task, and the reason for granting them a status in international humanitarian law is to allow them to 'act' effectively for the benefit of a civilian population lacking essential supplies."[125]

Contemporary international opinion continues to reflect the stance taken in the *Commentaries*. In response to the 19 August 2003 bombing of the UN headquarters in Baghdad, the Security Council passed Resolution 1502, which reaffirms the protected status and right of humanitarian access of humanitarian personnel, as well as the need for neutrality and impartiality in situations of armed conflict.[126] It also explicitly mentions, however, an additional constraint on these organizations, namely, "the obligation of all humanitarian personnel and United Nations and its associated personnel to observe and respect the laws of the country in which they are operating, in accordance with international law and the Charter of the United Nations."[127] This language reflects the limits set out under Article 71 of Protocol I, and reveals a compromise between humanitarian protection and the sovereignty of the territorial state. Under this UN resolution, humanitarian access is tied to (1) respect for local law – at least to the extent that it is not inconsistent with the UN Charter and international law, and (2) the principles of neutrality and impartiality.[128]

Conclusion

Non-international armed conflict, ethnically motivated violence, failed and failing states, and insurgency-based violence have come to dominate modern armed conflict. The traditional humanitarian security paradigm, premised on a state-centric world order with a limited number of players, has been stretched to the breaking point in many instances. Lack of respect for IHL by certain non-state armed groups, intentional targeting of humanitarian personnel, and the numerous other factors explored in this chapter have rendered the consent-based approach to ensuring protection of humanitarian personnel, property, and materiel obsolete in many cases.

The inadequacy of the consent-based model of humanitarian protection, coupled with the increased risk to humanitarian personnel in the field, has resulted in a proliferation of both the actors involved in delivering humanitarian aid and the security options humanitarian organizations have resorted to. The armed protection debate in the humanitarian community is only likely to grow more intense given these realities.

Before a humanitarian organization hires a private security company to protect its personnel, property, or materiel, a number of factors should be considered to ensure that its rights and obligations under IHL are respected. This chapter has focused on two threshold issues: the impact on the protected status of humanitarians, and their ability to access populations in need. Debate on these issues and further research to identify other potential IHL implications would be welcome in order to bring some clarity to this murky and complex area of law.

As a result of the findings regarding protected status, a case-by-case assessment of the nature of the conduct of private security contractors hired by a humanitarian organization will determine whether protected status is maintained as a matter of law. Given this realization, we are concerned with how private security contractors *actually* behave in practice, as opposed to what the terms of their contract and rules of engagement specify. In other words, if the agreed terms between a private security company and humanitarian organization specify rules of engagement that would, on paper, prevent contractors from engaging in conduct that could be interpreted as direct participation in hostilities, humanitarian personnel or premises could nevertheless be harmed in a legal attack if their contractors exceeded their rules of engagement and directly participated in hostilities. In the pitch of such a firefight, it would be of no avail for a humanitarian organization to simply rely on the language of the contract in an attempt to distance its humanitarian personnel from the private security contractors it hired.

Consequently, ensuring proper conduct by private security contractors requires a range of preventative and reactive measures before a humanitarian organization can reasonably manage the risk of retaining such a firm.[129] A preliminary list of such measures, similar to those that would be required for other clients, could include the following:

1 Preventative approaches

- obtaining information on the human rights record and past performance of the company
- well-defined scope of activities covered under the contract
- clear and appropriate rules of engagement, including rules on carrying and use of firearms, as well as disclosure of whether armed force will be on hand, or on call
- requirements for contractors to be subject to, and compliant with, local laws

- clauses to remove contractors from duty and terminate contract (with penalties to the contractor) for improper conduct
- vetting of individual contractors
- training requirements for contractors in IHL and human rights
- monitoring and reporting of activities to determine whether the contractual terms and rules of engagement are followed in practice.

2   Reactive approaches

- investigation of alleged misconduct
- suspension or removal from duty of contractors for misconduct
- contract termination for misconduct
- reporting misconduct to the state of operation, state of incorporation of company, state of nationality of perpetrator
- ensuring full cooperation with relevant investigations.

A challenge facing many humanitarian organizations is a lack of capacity to conduct these due diligence steps, which is a cause for concern. Although enhanced collaboration and information sharing between humanitarian organizations about the private security companies they hire is a positive step, there are mixed reviews on the extent to which this is happening in practice.[130] A concrete proposal by Cross is the creation of an "updated register/database of financially transparent firms with a good track record."[131]

On an individual organization basis, Cockayne's study found that most non-governmental organizations do not take sufficient measures within their power to enhance accountability of the private security contractors they hire and, as a result, there is a "significant lack of control, increasing risk for users."[132] For example, his study found only one general reference in contracts between humanitarian organizations and private security companies to the international standards on use of force and firearms.[133]

Currently, there are several guidelines that could be adapted by humanitarian organizations, either individually as an internal policy document or jointly as a statement of best practices, to ensure accountability from private security companies. These documents generally suffer from a lack of specificity,[134] however, or a lack of understanding of the current state of IHL as it applies to humanitarian organizations, especially in relation to their use of private security companies.[135]

The role of donors in enhancing the policies and procedures of humanitarian organizations hiring private security companies is likely to focus attention on ensuring that due diligence is observed.[136] At the same time, it must be noted that humanitarian organizations have limited bargaining power to secure contractual concessions from private security companies due to the relatively small segment of the market that they represent.

Finally, to ensure humanitarian access, humanitarian organizations should obtain authorization from the state in which relief is to be delivered before using private security companies for defensive armed protection. It also bears mentioning that without recognized status under a status of forces agreement, a separate agreement with the host government, or an explicit exemption, humanitarian personnel and private security contractors will be fully subject to local laws, which may affect the legality of the organizations' use of private security contractors.[137]

Delivering humanitarian assistance in the midst of the diverse and complex forms of modern armed conflict is a significant challenge that strikes at the core assumptions of the early humanitarian movement. Understanding how the changing nature of armed conflict has affected the risks of humanitarian action and expanded alternative approaches to security is an important starting point. Factors affecting the decision to hire private security contractors are likely to vary between organizations, based largely on their philosophical underpinnings.

The use of private security contractors by humanitarian organizations is a topic that deserves greater attention because of its impact on the broader humanitarian community and the potential impact that this practice has on the decision of state armed forces to directly deliver humanitarian assistance. Humanitarian organizations that choose to hire private security contractors would benefit from an exchange of information and sharing of best practices with one another. Bringing together representatives of humanitarian organizations, state armed forces, private security companies, policy makers, and academics with diverse viewpoints on these matters could also assist in confronting these issues.

At the end of the day, as Greenaway and Harris have emphasized, what must be forefront in our minds throughout this debate is the common goal of effective and safe delivery of humanitarian assistance to those in need.[138]

ACKNOWLEDGMENTS

The author is pleased to acknowledge the support of the Canadian Red Cross, the Liu Institute for Global Issues at the University of British Columbia, and the Department of Foreign Affairs and International Trade

(Canada), as well as research assistance from Jacky Sin, Tyson Stiege, Bethany Hastie, and Brendan Naef. The views expressed in this chapter represent only those of the author.

NOTES

1 Jean-Marie Henckaerts and Louise Doswald-Beck, *Customary International Humanitarian Law*, vol. 1 (Cambridge: Cambridge University Press, 2005) at 105.

2 Three main studies undertaken on this topic will be referred to throughout this chapter: Abby Stoddard, Adele Harmer, and Victoria DiDomenico, "The Use of Private Security Providers and Services in Humanitarian Operations," HPG (Humanitarian Policy Group) Report 27 (2008) at 2, online: ReliefWeb <http://www.reliefweb.int/>; James Cockayne, *Commercial Security in Humanitarian and Post-Conflict Settings: An Exploratory Study* (New York: International Peace Academy, 2006); and Tony Vaux, Chris Seiple, Greg Nakano, and Koenraad Van Brabant, *Humanitarian Action and Private Security Companies: Opening the Debate* (2002), online: International Alert <http://www.globalpolicy.org/>. A conference on this topic in 2001 found "no consensus amongst participants at the workshop on the way forward, and how aid agencies could best address the use of private security companies": Feinstein International Famine Center and International Alert, "The Politicisation of Humanitarian Action and Staff Security: The Use of Private Security Companies by Humanitarian Agencies" (International Workshop Summary Report, Tufts University, Boston, MA, 23-24 April 2001) at 5, online: <http://www.sces.msh-paris.fr/>.

3 Stoddard *et al.*, *supra* note 2 at 2: "Protocols or guidance on whether, when and how to contract and manage private security companies, as a special category of vendor requiring special criteria and oversight, are almost completely absent among humanitarian organizations."

4 See Hans Haug *et al.*, *Humanity for All: The International Red Cross and Red Crescent Movement* (Berne: Paul Haupt Bern Publishers, 1993) at 27.

5 David P. Forsythe and Barbara Ann J. Rieffler-Flanagan, *The International Committee of the Red Cross: A Neutral Humanitarian Actor* (London: Routledge, 2007) at 57.

6 Sheri Fink, "Protection of Civilians in Armed Conflict: A Decade of Promises" in Kevin M. Cahill, ed., *The Pulse of Humanitarian Assistance* (New York: Fordham University Press, 2007) 22 at 34.

7 Major Lisa L. Turner and Major Lynn G. Norton, "Civilians at the Tip of the Spear" (2001) 51 A.F.L. Rev. 1 at 14.

8 Thomas G. Weiss, "The UN's Prevention Pipe-Dream" (1996) 14 Berkeley J. Int'l L. 423 at 431.

9 Turner and Norton, *supra* note 7 at 14.

10 United Nations Development Programme, *Human Development Report 1994* (New York: Oxford University Press, 1994), cited in Weiss, *supra* note 8 at 427.

11 Weiss, *ibid.* at 431.

12 Mary Ellen O'Connell, "Enhancing the Status of Non-State Actors through a Global War on Terror?" (2005) 43 Colum. J. Transnat'l L. 435 at 442.

13 More recently, civilians and humanitarian personnel alike have been attacked and killed in Darfur, Sudan: see Fink, *supra* note 6 at 33.

14 Lindsay Jill Suttenberg, "Recent Developments: Curing the Humanitarian Crisis: Resolution 1502" (2005) 4 Washington University Global Studies Law Review 187 at 194.

15 As an indicator of the growth of humanitarian organizations, "during the 1999 Kosovo crisis, already more than 400 NGOs participated in the humanitarian relief effort. Currently [2005], UNHCR efforts are implemented by more than 600 NGOs, receiving almost $270 million, more than one fifth of UNHCR's annual budget." Liesbet Heyse, *Choosing the Lesser Evil: Understanding Decision Making in Humanitarian Aid NGOs* (Aldershot, UK: Ashgate, 2006) at 3 [citations omitted].

16 Forsythe and Rieffler-Flanagan, *supra* note 5 at 70-71.

17 Vaux *et al., supra* note 2 at 23.

18 "Rebels in the American Revolution took thirteen years to defeat the British armed forces and adopt the Constitution. American armed forces took seventeen years to pacify the Philippines. British armed forces took twelve years to subdue Malaysian communist guerrillas." See Commander Albert S. Janin, "Engaging Civilian-Belligerents Leads to Self-Defense/Protocol I Marriage" *Army Lawyer* (July 2007) 82, online: <http://www.loc.gov/rr/frd/Military_Law/>.

19 "Interview with Andrew Bearpark" (2006) 863 Int'l Rev. Red Cross 449 at 450.

20 Sean Greenaway and Andrew J. Harris, "Humanitarian Security: Challenges and Responses" (Paper presented to the Forging Peace Conference, Harvard University, Cambridge, MA, 13-15 March 1998), online: ReliefWeb <http://www.reliefweb.int/library/>.

21 *Ibid.*

22 *Ibid.*

23 This information is drawn from studies made by the Humanitarian Policy Group. See Stoddard *et al., supra* note 2 at 7. Additional data and the methodology used in compiling this information can be found in Abby Stoddard, Adele Harmer, and Katherine Haver, "Providing Aid in Insecure Environments: Trends in Policy and Operations," HPG (Humanitarian Policy Group) Report 23 (2006) at 5, online: Overseas Development Institute <http://www.odi.org.uk/resources/>.

24 *Ibid.*

25 *Ibid.*

26 Nuchhi Currier, "Protecting the Protectors – Strengthening Staff Security: Priorities and Challenges" (2003) 2 UN Chronicle 5, online: United Nations <http://www.un.org/Pubs/>.

27 "A study of deaths among aid workers showed that most occur within the first three months of arrival in a country, rather than after they have spent time and made enough mistakes to make some enemies on one side of a conflict or another or have angered some black marketers or local authorities." See Barbara Smith, "The Dangers of Aid Work" in Yael Danieli, ed., *Sharing the Front Line and the Back Hills – International Protectors and Providers: Peacekeepers, Humanitarian Aid Workers and the Media in the Midst of Crisis* (Amityville, NY: Baywood Publishing, 2002) 171 at 175.

28 Greenaway and Harris, *supra* note 20.

29 Suttenberg, *supra* note 14 at 194.

30 Bearpark, *supra* note 19 at 450; Vaux *et al.*, *supra* note 2 at 12; Suttenberg, *ibid.* at 193.

31 Suttenberg, *ibid.* at 193-94.

32 Currier, *supra* note 26.

33 *Ibid.*

34 Suttenberg, *supra* note 14 at 194.

35 United States Department of the Army and Marine Corps, *The U.S. Army / Marine Corps Counterinsurgency Field Manual* (Chicago: University of Chicago Press, 2007) at ix. Along the same line, humanitarian assistance is perceived as a "force multiplier" when combined with military action; see Turner and Norton, *supra* note 7 at 14.

36 Bearpark, *supra* note 19 at 451.

37 Vaux *et al.*, *supra* note 2 at 8.

38 Larry Minear, *The Humanitarian Enterprise: Dilemmas and Discoveries* (Bloomfield, CT: Kumarian Press, 2002) at 105.

39 Greenaway and Harris, *supra* note 20.

40 *Ibid.*

41 *Ibid.*

42 For example, the US military has worked with humanitarian organizations through the Combined Military Operations Center (CMOC) in Somalia, Haiti, and northern Iraq. Daily meetings between commanders and representatives from relevant humanitarian organizations and NGOs take place with the CMOC. See Turner and Norton, *supra* note 7 at 46.

43 Currier, *supra* note 26.

44 Also referred to as the "acceptance" strategy or "anthropological" approach.

45 Feinstein International Famine Center, *supra* note 2 at 3.

46 International Committee of the Red Cross, *Report on the Use of Armed Protection for Humanitarian Assistance*, Extract from Working Paper 95/CD/12/1, ICRC and International Federation, Council of Delegates (Geneva, 1-2 December 1995), online: ICRC <http://www.icrc.org/Web/eng/siteeng0.nsf/html/57JNEG> [*Report on the Use of Armed Protection for Humanitarian Assistance*].

47 Forsythe and Rieffler-Flanagan, *supra* note 5 at 57.

48 Vaux *et al.*, *supra* note 2 at 14.

49 Médecins Sans Frontières, "MSF Leaves Country Following Staff Killings and Threats" in *MSF Activity Report 2003/04* (16 December 2004) at 49, online: Médecins Sans Frontières <http://www.msf.org/msfinternational/>.

50 Vaux *et al.*, *supra* note 2 at 15.

51 Greenaway and Harris, *supra* note 20.

52 International Committee of the Red Cross, *Commentaries: Protocol Additional to the Geneva Conventions of 12 August 1949, and Relating to the Protection of Victims of International Armed Conflicts (Protocol I)* (8 June 1977) at 827, paras. 2858 to 829, para. 2864 [API *Commentaries*].

53 Fred Schreier and Marina Caparini, *Privatising Security: Law, Practice and Governance of Private Military and Security Companies,* Geneva Centre for the Democratic Control of Armed Forces, Occasional Paper No. 6 (Geneva: DCAF, 2005) at 93.
54 Turner and Norton, *supra* note 7 at 26.
55 *Ibid.* at 64-65.
56 Vaux *et al., supra* note 2 at 24.
57 *Ibid.* at 17, 24-25.
58 *Ibid.* at 26.
59 Cockayne, *supra* note 2 at 6.
60 Minear, *supra* note 38 at 110.
61 Cockayne, *supra* note 2 at 6.
62 Stoddard *et al., supra* note 2 at 12.
63 Cockayne, *supra* note 2 at 11.
64 Vaux *et al., supra* note 2 at 9.
65 See, *e.g.,* Peace Operations Institute, *State of the Peace and Stability Operations Industry: Second Annual Survey 2007* (Washington, DC: Peace Operations Institute, 2007) at 11 (6.10 percent response rate, with 23 of 334 companies responding; "contracting entities" are not described in a manner to identify humanitarian organizations directly).
66 Major General Tim Cross, "The Humanitarian Community and the Private Sector" in Kevin M. Cahill, ed., *The Pulse of Humanitarian Assistance* (New York: Fordham University Press, 2007) 79 at 100.
67 "Some humanitarian organizations regularly hire them [private security companies] to provide security for their operations, in addition to the many reconstruction firms that hire them in Iraq and elsewhere": Lindsey Cameron, "Private Military Companies: Their Status under International Humanitarian Law and Its Impact on Their Regulation" (2006) 863 Int'l Rev. Red Cross 573 at 576.
68 Minear, *supra* note 38 at 110.
69 Feinstein International Famine Center, *supra* note 2 at 4; Stoddard *et al., supra* note 2 at 1.
70 Vaux *et al., supra* note 2 at 16.
71 Paul Keilthy, "Private Security Firms in War Zones Worry NGOs" *AlertNet* (11 August 2004), online: AlertNet <http://www.alertnet.org/>.
72 Benjamin Perrin, "Promoting Compliance of Private Security and Military Companies with International Humanitarian Law" (2006) 863 Int'l Rev. Red Cross 613 at 624.
73 Schreier and Caparini, *supra* note 53 at 93.
74 Perrin, *supra* note 72 at 618.
75 Stoddard *et al., supra* note 2 at 2.
76 Vaux *et al., supra* note 2 at 25.
77 These findings were based on a series of surveys answered by 13 UN agencies and 47 NGOs, as well as 241 interviews conducted with staff from UN agencies, NGOs, private security companies and academics working on the subject. See Stoddard *et al., supra* note 2 at 5.
78 *Ibid.* at 12.

79 United Nations Diplomatic Conference of Plenipotentiaries on the Establishment of an International Criminal Court, *Rome Statute of the International Criminal Court*, UN Doc. A/CONF.183/9 (17 July 1998) at arts. 8(2)(b)(iii) (international armed conflict), 8(2)(e)(iii) (non-international armed conflict) [*Rome Statute*]; "Statute of the Special Court for Sierra Leone" in *Report of the Secretary-General on the Establishment of a Special Court for Sierra Leone*, UN SCOR, 55th Sess., UN Doc. S/2000/915 (2000), art. 4(b). See also International Criminal Court, *Elements of Crimes*, ICC-ASP/1/3 at 131, 149.

80 Henckaerts and Doswald-Beck, *supra* note 1 at 105-11 (Rules 31 and 32).

81 *Protocol Additional to the Geneva Conventions of 12 August 1949, and Relating to the Protection of Victims of International Armed Conflicts (Protocol I)*, 8 June 1977, 1125 U.N.T.S. 3 (entered into force 7 December 1978) at arts. 70(4), 71(2) [API].

82 API *Commentaries, supra* note 52 at 827, paras. 2858 to 829, para. 2864.

83 *Ibid.* at 834, para. 2885.

84 *Ibid.* at 829, para. 2864.

85 API, *supra* note 81 at art. 15(4).

86 *Ibid.* at art. 15(2).

87 Henckaerts and Doswald-Beck, *supra* note 1 at 105-11 (Rules 31 and 32).

88 *Protocol Additional to the Geneva Conventions of 12 August 1949, and Relating to the Protection of Victims of Non-International Armed Conflicts (Protocol II)*, 8 June 1977, 1125 U.N.T.S. 609 (entered into force 7 December 1978) at art. 9(1) [APII].

89 *Ibid.* art. 11(2).

90 This convention was adopted in response to the "growing number of deaths and injuries resulting from deliberate attacks against United Nations and associated personnel." See *Convention on the Safety of United Nations and Associated Personnel*, 1994, 2051 U.N.T.S. 363 (entered into force 15 January 1999), Preamble, online: United Nations <http://www.un.org/law/> [*UN Safety Convention*].

91 *Ibid.* at arts. 7, 9.

92 *Ibid.* at art. 21.

93 "Associated personnel" includes only persons deployed by humanitarian NGOs that are specifically engaged to support UN operations. While this definition is narrowly focused, it nevertheless may cover a large number of organizations. For example, the UNHCR alone implements its programs through the work of over six hundred NGOs. See *UN Safety Convention, supra* note 90 at art. 1(b)(iii); see also Heyse, *supra* note 15 at 3.

94 *UN Safety Convention, ibid.* at art. 6(1)(b).

95 Henckaerts and Doswald-Beck, *supra* note 1 at 17-19 (Rule 5).

96 See API, *supra* note 81 at arts. 43, 50(1).

97 *Ibid.* at art. 51(3).

98 There are other consequences (such as capture, detention, prisoner-of-war status, and prosecution under domestic criminal law for acts that do not violate international humanitarian law) that may flow from suspension or loss of protected status, depending on whether the conflict is international or non-international in character.

99 Henckaerts and Doswald-Beck, *supra* note 1 at 105.

100 A series of expert consultations co-organized by the ICRC and the TMC Asser
     Institute have culminated in: International Committee of the Red Cross, "Interpretive
     Guidance on the Notion of Direct Participation in Hostilities under International
     Humanitarian Law" (2008) 90 Int'l Rev. Red Cross 991 [*Interpretive Guidance*]
     (adopted by the Assembly of the International Committee of the Red Cross on 26
     February 2009).
101 API *Commentaries, supra* note 52 at 619, para. 1944. See also API *Commentaries* at
     516, para. 1679: attacks are defined as "acts of war which are intended by their nature
     or their purpose to hit specifically the personnel and the 'matériel' of the armed
     forces of the adverse Party ... Direct participation in hostilities implies a direct causal
     relationship between the activity engaged in and the harm done to the enemy at the
     time and the place where the activity takes place."
102 *Ibid.* at 618, para. 1942.
103 *Ibid.* at 618-19, para. 1943.
104 International Committee of the Red Cross, *Commentaries: Protocol Additional to
     the Geneva Conventions of 12 August 1949, and Relating to the Protection of Victims
     of Non-International Armed Conflicts (Protocol II)* (8 June 1977) at 1453, para. 4788
     [APII *Commentaries*].
105 Recent articles on "direct participation in hostilities" by private military/security
     companies focus on state armed forces as clients: see, *e.g.,* Michael N. Schmitt,
     "Humanitarian Law and Direct Participation in Hostilities by Private Contractors or
     Civilian Employees" (2004) 5 Chicago J. Int'l L. 511; Cameron, *supra* note 67;
     Shannon Bosch, "Private Security Contractors and International Humanitarian Law
     – a Skirmish for Recognition in International Armed Conflicts" (2007) 16 African
     Security Review 34.
106 Schreier and Caparini, *supra* note 53 at 94.
107 Emanuela-Chiara Gillard, "Business Goes to War: Private Military/Security
     Companies and International Humanitarian Law" (2006) 863 Int'l Rev. Red Cross
     525 at 539.
108 API, *supra* note 81 at art. 13(2)(a)-(b).
109 *Ibid.* at art. 28(3).
110 *Ibid.* at arts. 65(3), 67(1)(d).
111 *Ibid.* at art. 63(3).
112 *UN Safety Convention, supra* note 90 at art. 21.
113 Schmitt, *supra* note 105 at 538.
114 Cameron, *supra* note 67 at 589-90.
115 Schmitt, *supra* note 105 at 539.
116 *Interpretive Guidance, supra* note 100 at 1025, 1028. One of the experts in the ICRC
     consultative meetings on direct participation in hostilities stated that "if a private
     security contractor's role is defensive and involves defending persons who are not
     legitimate targets themselves, then they should not be regarded as engaged in DPH
     [direct participation in hostilities] even if they have to use considerable force to do
     so": *Second Expert Meeting: Direct Participation in Hostilities under International
     Humanitarian Law* (Co-organized by the ICRC and the TMC Asser Institute, The
     Hague, 25-26 October 2004) at 14, online: ICRC <http://www.icrc.org/>.

117 *Rome Statute, supra* note 79, art. 31(1)(c).
118 International Criminal Tribunal for the former Yugoslavia (ICTY), *Prosecutor v. Kordić and Čerkez,* Trial Judgment, IT-95-14/2 (26 February 2001) at para. 452.
119 Cockayne, *supra* note 2 at 14.
120 Turner and Norton, *supra* note 7 at 56, 58.
121 Cockayne, *supra* note 2 at 13.
122 See O'Connell, *supra* note 12 at 440; see also APII, *supra* note 88 at art. 18(2).
123 *Case Concerning Military and Paramilitary Activities in and against Nicaragua (Nicaragua v. United States of America),* [1986] I.C.J. Rep. 14 at para. 242.
124 API, *supra* note 81 at art. 71(4).
125 API *Commentaries, supra* note 52 at 832, para. 2871.
126 Protection of United Nations personnel, associated personnel, and humanitarian personnel in conflict zones, SC Res. 1502, UN SCOR, UN Doc. S/RES/1502 (2003) Preamble at paras. 3-4.
127 *Ibid.,* Preamble.
128 It is, of course, routine for insurgents who have kidnapped and/or murdered humanitarian aid workers to claim, without any evidence, that those workers were spies for a foreign government that they have committed themselves to destroying by any means necessary.
129 See discussion in Cockayne, *supra* note 2 at 10-12; see also *Report on the Use of Armed Protection for Humanitarian Assistance, supra* note 46; K. Van Brabant, *Operational Security Management in Violent Environments: A Field Manual for Aid Agencies* (London: Overseas Development Institute, 2000); see generally Michael Cottier, "Elements for Contracting and Regulating Private Security and Military Companies" (2006) 863 Int'l Rev. Red Cross 637.
130 Vaux *et al., supra* note 2 at 23 (discussing collaborating through the InterAction Security Working Group); see, *contra,* Cockayne, *supra* note 2 at 10.
131 Cross, *supra* note 66 at 101.
132 Cockayne, *supra* note 2 at ii.
133 *Ibid.* at 11.
134 The guidelines published by the European Community Humanitarian Aid and Civil Protection provides some guidance on selecting, preparing, and managing the use of armed guards by a humanitarian organization. However, this guideline fails to consider the IHL implications for hiring such guards, and it does not provide any suggestions for developing best practices and ensuring accountability. See European Community Humanitarian Aid and Civil Protection (ECHO), *Generic Security Guide for Humanitarian Organizations* (European Community, 2004), online: <http://ec.europa.eu>.
135 *The Montreux Document on Pertinent International Legal Obligations and Good Practices for States Related to Operations of Private Military and Security Companies during Armed Conflict* (Montreux: Government of Switzerland, 2008), online: ICRC <http://www.icrc.org/web/>, is one of the most comprehensive assessments on IHL and its application to private military and security companies to date. However, this document was not designed for humanitarian organizations, and several enforcement guidelines may not be relevant for humanitarian actors. Nevertheless, it

presents a reasonable starting point for developing a set of guidelines for humanitarian organizations wishing to employ private military companies.

136 Greenaway and Harris, *supra* note 20.

137 Turner and Norton, *supra* note 7 at 93; see also SC Res. 1502, *supra* note 126, Preamble.

138 Greenaway and Harris, *supra* note 20.

The Case for Humanitarian Organizations to Use Private Security Contractors

ANDREW BEARPARK

Since the end of the Cold War, there has been a shift in the security landscape. Two characteristics of this are an increase in private actors working in conflict and disaster zones[1] and the shrinking of "humanitarian space."[2] This shrinkage is putting aid workers and humanitarian efforts at increased risk. Although the private security industry has had a difficult relationship with humanitarians in the past, the simultaneous occurrence of increased activity of private actors and the shrinking of humanitarian space has created a convergence of interests. In this chapter, I make the case for humanitarian organizations to use the services of private security companies (PSCs) for functions beyond simple asset protection. By hiring companies for risk consultancy, pre-deployment training, and other functions aside from straightforward close and static protection, humanitarians can mitigate risks for their staff without compromising their image and objectives. I also illustrate additional ways in which PSCs may contribute to humanitarian goals, by carrying out, for example, security sector reform (SSR) and service delivery. I do not contend, however, that PSCs should, as some claim, be hired to run humanitarian operations *per se*, nor do I advocate the hiring of PSCs to stabilize regions such as Darfur, for example.

Why Humanitarian Workers Face Increased Risk

The concept of humanitarian space is based on the principle that neutral humanitarians occupy a unique place in crisis and conflict and are, in theory, afforded the space to address humanitarian needs without being considered a party to the conflict or a legitimate target.[3] Traditionally, humanitarian space was the remit of civilians, and by operating within it one was automatically considered to be a civilian. As new trends are identified in contemporary armed conflicts, however, there is evidence that humanitarian workers are less safe than they previously were and that they are often deliberately targeted.[4] Thus, as conflicts change, so do the perceptions of the roles of humanitarian workers.

While there are many strands in the debate as to how wars have changed in the post–Cold War globalized climate, understandings of "new" or "postmodern" warfare provide particularly pertinent insight into the reasons behind the shrinking humanitarian space. This is because such understandings address the nature of non-state warfare. In its statistical overview of war, the *Final Report of the Commission on Human Security*[5] illustrates that although conflicts are declining globally, interstate war has declined more sharply than intrastate war. Intrastate wars are typically of low intensity and, unlike their militaristic interstate counterparts, are often engaged in by (and inflicted upon) civilians and non-state actors. This is key to the "new wars" definition advanced by Mary Kaldor, based upon the three primary facets of funding (global political economies), cause (identity politics), and method (increasing targeting of civilians).[6]

Developing this further, theories of postmodern war[7] highlight the importance of the proliferation of non-state actors as an inextricable part of the global "parcelling out" of power. This parcelling out is not only due to the thickening of global networks and economic globalization but also a consequence of failing states, where non-state actors – be they warlords, corporations, non-governmental organizations (NGOs), and humanitarians or otherwise – move in to fill the power vacuum left by failed government systems. Crucially, in these types of conflicts the distinctions between peace, war, crime, and human rights violations are difficult to discern, leading to some confusion over the status of civilians working in conflict theatres. It is particularly unclear who is taking part, and who *should* be taking part, either in forging the conflict or in attempting to mitigate it. As Jan Angstrom summarizes of the non-state warfare debate, "wars conducted by irregular militias will be fought differently and therefore have a different nature than wars conducted by States and their armies."[8]

This results in the traditional place of humanitarians becoming one of risk, leading some to turn to PSCs to ensure the safety of their staff, infrastructure, and projects.[9] Humanitarian space is thus shrinking, which is prompting reflection into the manner in which humanitarian organizations operate in conflicts and disasters. In addition, as non-state actors have moved further into the conflict and security landscape, the blurring between military and civilian and between security and development has meant that traditional notions of who should perform which roles in conflict mitigation and disaster relief are being challenged. With their array of expertise, and given their military and civilian capabilities, there are questions about whether PSCs can assume a role in humanitarian work.

Private Security Companies and Their Services

The private security industry is being scrutinized as PSCs become recognized as important actors in conflicts and high-risk environments. Despite the increased attention, however, a high proportion of the studies focus on the impact of the private security industry on the state's monopoly on violence, with research and analysis tending to assume that states are the sole clients. Similarly, there is little acknowledgment of the differential effect of PSC hiring by a developed or a weak state.[10] In fact many PSCs, particularly British ones, work almost exclusively for the private sector and provide a range of services beyond close protection and static armed guarding.

Although the main preoccupation in the past concerned whether or not PSCs were distinguishable from mercenaries,[11] the discussion has moved on. Mercenaries conduct offensive operational activities, are illegal under international law, and are not legally or morally comparable to PSCs. Moreover, while there is some question about whether or not humanitarians hiring PSCs compromise their status (see Chapter 6), there is no doubt that hiring mercenaries would. This chapter has therefore been written with the understanding that the mercenary question is now moot.

There remains, however, some difficulty in categorizing an industry that provides such a diverse range of services. Various labels for sectors within the industry reflect this: private military companies, private intelligence companies, private security companies, risk consultancies, and so on. To understand the industry as we see it today, a brief history is necessary. Contemporary PSCs have their roots in the post–Cold War period, where there was a general move towards military downsizing.[12] This created a surplus of both weapons and military trained personnel while low-intensity and complex intrastate conflicts were on the rise. Insecurity became increasingly multifaceted without the glue of the superpowers; many low-intensity, protracted conflicts characterized by non-state militia and insurgency involvement broke out in volatile and at-risk regions, including conflicts in the Balkans, Chechnya, and Sudan.

This led to a somewhat "experimental" phase for privatized security. At first there were attempts by several companies to move into counterinsurgency operations in the wake of stalled state interventions, as seen in early forays in Angola, Sierra Leone, and Papua New Guinea.[13] This was not generally considered to be successful, however, and the industry as we see it today developed along a different model. Control Risks Group is the most obvious early example of the post–Cold War PSC. Set up as a kidnap and ransom consultancy for private sector workers in high-risk areas, it eventually expanded to provide a comprehensive range of services across the security spectrum, including armed guarding, intelligence provision, risk analysis, and so on. Other companies developed in a similar fashion, starting off with one core service in response to post–Cold War security risks and eventually expanding into related services. Most of the industry has adopted this broad-services approach, particularly in response to the Iraq War, when the industry boomed. The logic is simple. Entry barriers to becoming a major international PSC (as opposed to a single-function niche operator) are high due to the costs of equipment, skilled personnel, international locations, and the size of operation needed to make some services viable. Thus, it is sensible for a comprehensive range of services to be provided to the client by a single company – a security and risk "powerhouse" that can look after the client at all stages.

Services provided by the industry may now include static protection, mobile armed protection, mobile unarmed protection, risk analysis, kidnap and ransom consultancy, military infrastructure provision, catering and laundry services for the military, high-tech engineering services, due diligence, specialist insurance, infrastructure protection, emergency communications provision, mine clearance, hostile environment training, intelligence gathering, business intelligence strategy, crisis management and response, pre-deployment training, Disarmament, Demobilization, and Reintegration (DDR), security sector reform (SSR), forensic services, and more.

There have been several attempts to categorize the industry according to the types of services a company provides. Notable examples include those by Christopher Kinsey[14] and Peter Singer,[15] who attempt to classify the industry by service provision and through a "tip of the spear" categorization, respectively. Categorization efforts are complicated, however, by the fact that companies often provide services across the spectrum. Indeed, industry officials have identified ambiguities in deciding what constitutes the private security industry, so diverse are its undertakings. This should not, however, prevent constructive analysis of the activities of PSCs and their interaction with humanitarian agencies.

In this chapter, the term "private security company" is used as it best reflects the character of the British industry. The British Ministry of Defence does not outsource in the way that its US counterpart does, and this has influenced the nature of British PSCs. Many of them apparently work largely for private sector civilian clients, and the British industry does not feature the large military logistics firms providing, for example, military catering and housing in the manner of KBR, Inc. and other military provider firms in the US market. The emphasis among British companies is mostly on security services and risk analysis; however, as the industry is diversifying in response to market pressures (since the collapse of the "Iraq bubble"[16]), PSCs are increasingly seeking opportunities in SSR and DDR work. Although traditional critiques of the industry centre on the acceptability of breaking the state's monopoly on the use of force,[17] the overview of industry services provided above illustrates that their range of both tasks and clients often renders this argument unhelpful. Rather, PSCs are part of a more general trend towards non-state activity in the humanitarian, development, and security spheres.

How PSCs and Humanitarian Organizations Can Work Together

There have been several high-profile incidents in recent years where humanitarians have been targeted by insurgents and spoilers in-theatre.[18] We are witnessing a trend towards PSCs being hired by and providing consulting to humanitarian organizations in order to address this growing vulnerability.[19] There are concerns in some quarters that by turning to PSCs for protection, humanitarians will exacerbate the conditions making them unsafe in the first place, and consequently *contribute* to the shrinking of humanitarian space.[20] Although formal data on the incidence of humanitarian agencies hiring PSCs are not available, many of the major PSCs have admitted to having humanitarian organizations as clients, and a few humanitarian organizations acknowledge having used the services of PSCs.[21] Much of the current debate focuses on the merits and drawbacks of the use of PSCs by humanitarian organizations to provide armed guards in-theatre. As the previous section illustrates, however, the industry provides a more diverse range of services, a fact that must be considered when addressing the questions surrounding the relationship between humanitarian organizations and PSCs.

Physical Protection

As mentioned, it is the hiring of static and mobile guards, both armed and unarmed, that has caused the most discussion in the humanitarian community, as it fits more generally into debates about the blurring of the distinction between humanitarians, civilians, and parties to the conflict. As Benjamin Perrin illustrates in Chapter 6, humanitarians do not lose their status as civilians simply by employing PSCs; the threat is reputational rather than legal. Humanitarian entities fear they may be increasingly targeted if they are seen to be too closely allied with PSCs, which themselves inhabit an ambiguous position in the perceptions of the public in terms of whether or not they are combatants or civilians. Legally, PSC personnel are civilians, but this does not prevent there being some negative perception about their use. Although there is no statistical evidence that using PSCs will damage the reputation of humanitarian organizations and therefore increase their risk, there are concerns about overall future trends. There are also concerns over humanitarian agencies tying their reputation to companies whose other contracts they have no control over.[22] On the other hand, extreme insecurity, such as in Somalia, has left some humanitarian organizations little choice but to hire armed or unarmed guards for their buildings and staff.

Consultancy, Training, and Behind-the-Scenes Services

Besides providing highly visible armed guards, there are many ways in which PSCs can support the work of humanitarians. Anecdotally, we know that there is a general perception in the humanitarian community that PSCs operate in a culturally blind way, and that they have a poor understanding of local customs. Local milieu partly determines security needs, however, and because of this, many of the large PSCs have armies of analysts and intelligence collectors, both in their headquarters and on location, which can make them ideal sources of expertise and advice on local conditions. This is essential for providing a holistic security service to the client; PSCs are now becoming powerhouses of expertise on the conflicts in which they work. Thus, contrary to the caricature of PSC personnel as sunglass-wearing, gun-toting thugs (likely the result of the presence of less than scrupulous operators during the market bubble of Iraq), today's PSCs exude a high degree of professionalism and now have access to sophisticated and comprehensive pictures of high-risk theatres.

As demonstrated in the cases of Afghanistan and the Democratic Republic of the Congo (DRC), PSCs can provide invaluable pre-deployment training to humanitarian workers. Knowledge of how to avoid risks while in the field as well as how to respond to a crisis is essential.[23] Such training reduces the need for visible guards and therefore entails little risk to the reputations of humanitarian organizations. Similarly, PSCs can make organizational contingency plans in case of emergency.

Emergency communications are another key area. Several companies provide advice on emergency communications devices to keep staff reachable and therefore extractable in the field. PSCs can also recruit local intelligence providers. This sort of consultancy service should be considered by organizations that have to be reactive in terms of where they locate their efforts – that is, they cannot strategically plan far in advance where they will be needed next. PSCs have the size and reach to store expertise regarding any region experiencing insecurity, whether or not it has developed into a full-fledged humanitarian disaster.

PSCs and the Humanitarian "Service"

A third option for humanitarian organizations is to use PSCs for the actual "end service" – that is, instead of hiring a PSC to guard headquarters, protect staff, or even facilitate their work, there is discussion about hiring PSCs to carry out the actual main humanitarian work, such as food drops or peacekeeping.[24] This is already occurring to some extent. Clearance of unexploded ordnance has been carried out by PSCs such as ArmorGroup International, which has brought PSCs together with UXO-related charities and, to some extent, the UN. This has been less controversial than other PSC forays into humanitarian work, largely because de-mining is still seen as a military activity even if responsibility for it has been taken on by humanitarian agencies. The guarding of refugees is another case of PSCs working towards humanitarian goals. For example, in Albania during the Kosovo crisis, PSCs were hired to work with humanitarian organizations to protect refugee camps and to prevent them from becoming a training ground for militias.

PSCs are increasingly trying to break in to the SSR and DDR markets.[25] This is being done largely through their training capabilities, and thanks in part to the fact that many PSC staff are ex-British military. Moreover, with

the establishment of the United States African Command (AFRICOM), it
has been speculated that PSCs will play an increased role away from Iraq
and Afghanistan, as has been made clear from discussions with the US
Department of Defense (DOD), in which the Pentagon has expressed its
desire for an increased role for PSCs and, perhaps most important, African
PSCs.[26] The debate is therefore shifting to how small, indigenous PSCs can
be brought into the Montreux Process. Perhaps the most prominent example of PSCs' potential contribution to humanitarian aims is found in
the ongoing debate concerning the hiring of a PSC to be deployed in
Darfur.[27] In the absence of humanitarian intervention in Sudan, there are
calls from some quarters for a PSC to be hired to protect tribes at risk of
ethnic cleansing. This is not the first time such an issue has arisen; former
UN Secretary-General Kofi Annan allegedly considered contracting out
Rwandan peacekeeping during the 1994 Rwandan genocide when the UN
machinery operated too slowly to prevent the atrocities. The controversy
that would accompany the hiring of a private company to effectively run
such an operation has made it unviable, however.

Policy Recommendations
Humanitarian organizations are still understandably reluctant to discuss
their use of PSCs and show little willingness to formalize the process of
commissioning them. There remains little awareness among NGOs and
other humanitarian entities of how to properly procure risk management
and security services. This is due to a lack of dialogue between PSCs and
humanitarian organizations, lack of research and openness about contracts
between them, and lack of formal structures within which humanitarians
can learn and gather information about PSC services. It is also due to great
uncertainty within the humanitarian community regarding their position
on the progress of a relationship with the private security industry. As
Cockayne states:

> Users of commercial security in the humanitarian space have no formal
> arrangements for sharing information about the performance history or
> socio-economic profile of [PSCs] they work with. Even global NGO fam-
> ilies (such as Save the Children) seem to rely heavily on informal infor-
> mation sharing between different family members. Respondents cited a
> number of reasons for this: a still nascent NGO security community; the
> habitual protection of operational independence; an unwillingness to dis-
> close involvement with sub-standard providers; concern over defamation

liability; and competition between actors in the humanitarian space for the best security services.[28]

Several steps can be taken to remedy this situation. The first is the creation of a working group or a series of roundtables to provide a forum for PSCs and humanitarian entities. This would need to be held under Chatham House rules to mitigate fears of reputational risk on the part of humanitarian organizations taking part in the discussions. Such a series would enable the humanitarian community to explore its relationship with PSCs in a structured setting and possibly foster a consensus. There are now several organizations that are well placed to manage the PSC side of this. The British Association of Private Security Companies (BAPSC)[29] is a self-regulatory trade association for British PSCs, and the so-called Swiss Initiative[30] is currently providing an international forum for discussion of standards and regulation of PSCs. It is essential that humanitarian groups have increased dialogue with these initiatives to discuss their own needs.

The findings of any forum should be used to provide a guide for humanitarians in procuring an array of PSC services. Data and information are crucially lacking at the moment, and the working group should aim to redress this and provide some definitive guidelines. A second outcome of a forum's ongoing work should be guidance to the PSC industry itself. Humanitarian clients have specific needs, and PSCs will need some education on the particular requirements of this somewhat new group of clients. This will protect humanitarians as clients, ensuring quality and appropriateness of service.

Conclusions

This chapter has presented the case for humanitarian organizations to use private security contractors. The current debate about shrinking humanitarian space and the blurring of civilian and non-civilian roles is symptomatic of wider trends in protracted intrastate conflict, but it would be advantageous for the humanitarian community to develop a consensus on the hiring of PSCs. Lack of consensus is causing fragmented, ad hoc procurement policies that do nothing to encourage consistency or an improvement in standards among PSCs, leaving humanitarians vulnerable to poor or, worse, damaging services. There is also speculation that the hiring of PSCs by some organizations endangers others that eschew such a practice. The ultimate recommendations of this chapter are twofold: (1) that humanitarian organizations utilize the broad expertise of PSCs, rather than hiring them only for static and close protection; and (2) that a dialogue between humanitarians and PSCs be encouraged, extended, and formalized.

NOTES

1 Mary Kaldor, *New and Old Wars: Organized Violence in a Global Era*, 2d ed. (Cambridge: Polity Press, 2006).
2 Ulrike von Pilar, "Humanitarian Space under Siege" (Background paper for the symposium "Europe and Humanitarian Aid – What Future? Learning from Crisis," 22-23 April 1999, Bad Neuenahr).
3 Michael Pugh "Military Intervention and Humanitarian Action: Trends and Issues" (1998) 22 Disasters 339-51.
4 Abby Stoddard, Adele Harmer, and Victoria DiDomenico, "Private Security Contracting in Humanitarian Operations," HPG (Humanitarian Policy Group) Policy Brief 33 (2009), online: Overseas Development Institute <http://www.odi.org.uk/resources/>.
5 *Final Report of the Commission on Human Security* (2003), online: Commission on Human Security <http://www.humansecurity-chs.org/>.
6 Kaldor, *supra* note 1.
7 Mark Duffield, *Global Governance and the New Wars*, 4th ed. (London: Zed Books, 2006).
8 Isabelle Duyvesteyn and Jan Angstrom, eds., *Rethinking the Nature of War* (Oxford: Frank Cass, 2005) at 7.
9 Stoddard *et al.*, *supra* note 4.
10 Elke Krahmann, "Security Governance and the Private Military Industry in Europe and North America" (2005) 5 Conflict, Security and Development 247.
11 See, *e.g.*, Gerry Cleaver, "Subcontracting Military Power: The Privatisation of Security in Contemporary Sub-Saharan Africa" (2000) 33 Crime, Law and Social Change 131.
12 Caroline Holmqvist, "Private Security Companies: The Case for Regulation," Policy Paper 9 (2005), online: SIPRI <http://books.sipri.org/>.
13 Christopher Kinsey, *Corporate Soldiers and International Security* (London: Routledge, 2006).
14 *Ibid.*
15 Peter Warren Singer, *Corporate Warriors: The Rise of the Privatized Military Industry* (Ithaca, NY: Cornell University Press, 2003).
16 As predicted in Dominick Donald, "After the Bubble: British Private Security Companies after Iraq," Whitehall Paper, Royal United Services Institute (25 July 2006).
17 Simon Chesterman and Chia Lehnardt, eds., *From Mercenaries to Market: The Rise and Regulation of Private Military Companies* (New York: Oxford University Press, 2007).
18 Xan Rice, "Médecins Sans Frontières Workers Kidnapped in Darfur" *Guardian* (12 March 2009), online: Guardian <http://www.guardian.co.uk/>; IRIN (Integrated

Regional Information Networks "Philippines: Fresh Appeals to Release ICRC Hostages" *AlertNet* (17 March 2009), online: AlertNet <http://www.alertnet.org/>.

19 Stoddard *et al., supra* note 4.

20 James Cockayne, "Commercial Security in the Humanitarian Space" (New York: International Peace Academy, 2006), online: Ralph Bunche Institute for International Studies <http://web.gc.cuny.edu/ralphbuncheinstitute/>.

21 *Ibid.*

22 Tony Vaux, Chris Seiple, Greg Nakano, and Koenraad Van Brabant, "Humanitarian Action and Private Security Companies: Opening the Debate," International Alert (2002), online: Alexander Hamilton Institute for International Trade <http://www.alexanderhamiltoninstitute.org/>.

23 European Community Humanitarian Aid and Civil Protection (ECHO), *Generic Security Guide for Humanitarian Organizations* (European Community, 2004), online: <http://ec.europa.eu>.

24 Jakkie Cilliers, "A Role for Private Military Companies in Peacekeeping?" (2002) 2 Conflict, Security and Development 145.

25 Sabrina Schulz and Christina Yeung, *Private Military and Security Companies and Gender (Tool 10)* (Geneva: DCAF, OSCE/ODIHR, UN-INSTRAW, 2008), online: DCAF <http://www.dcaf.ch/publications/>.

26 Bruce Falconer and Daniel Schulman, "Blackwater's New Frontier: Their Own Private Africa" *Mother Jones* (12 March 2009), online: Mother Jones <http://www.motherjones.com/>.

27 Harvey Morris, "Activists Turn to Blackwater for Darfur Help" *Financial Times* (19 June 2008), online: Financial Times <http://us.ft.com/ftgateway/>.

28 Cockayne, *supra* note 20 at 24.

29 British Association of Private Security Companies <http://www.bapsc.org.uk/>.

30 *The Montreux Document on Pertinent International Legal Obligations and Good Practices for States Related to Operations of Private Military and Security Companies during Armed Conflict* (Montreux: Government of Switzerland, 2008), online: ICRC <http://www.icrc.org/web/>.

The Use of Armed Security Escorts
A Challenge to Independent and Neutral Humanitarian Action

JAMIE WILLIAMSON

During times of armed conflict, whether characterized as international or non-international, international humanitarian law (IHL), also known as the law of armed conflict, is applicable.[1] As a body of law, IHL does not question the lawfulness of a conflict (*jus ad bellum*) but seeks to apply humanitarian principles in warfare (*jus in bello*). IHL recognizes that even war has its limits, regardless of its cause, and strives to establish humanitarian parameters for the means and methods of warfare and to alleviate the suffering that conflict so often causes to persons taking no part in the hostilities.

The core IHL instruments are the four *Geneva Conventions* of 1949, their two Additional Protocols of 1977, and the 2005 Additional Protocol III.[2] The specific mandate of the International Committee of the Red Cross (ICRC) has been entrusted to it by states party to the four *Geneva Conventions* and their Additional Protocols,[3] as well as in the Statutes of the International Red Cross and Red Crescent Movement.[4]

The ICRC's mission is to protect and assist the civilian and military victims of armed conflicts and internal disturbances on a strictly neutral and impartial basis and to promote compliance with IHL. The ICRC's global presence is adjusted to respond to armed conflicts and other situations of violence. It currently has offices in eighty countries, with over twelve thousand staff worldwide.

The ICRC's most important operational challenge is to ensure access to victims of armed conflict and other situations of violence. Direct access to these people is essential if the ICRC is to understand their situation and address their needs. In a changing conflict environment, however, this access is becoming more difficult because of security constraints.

With the characteristics of modern-day conflicts changing, it was reported in the early 1990s that humanitarian workers were increasingly targeted by the warring factions and by bandits profiting from the chaos prevailing in conflict regions. As a result, a number of humanitarian organizations sought recourse to private security firms for protection. Although at first glance this may appear logical in the increasingly dangerous operational environments, from a humanitarian perspective the long-term disadvantages may actually outweigh the advantages of using private security.

Modern-Day Conflicts

Contemporary armed conflicts are vastly different creatures from those prevailing in the early part of the twentieth century, when states negotiated the texts of the *Geneva Conventions.* Gone are the days when, as during the World Wars, the belligerents were easily recognizable and were mostly members of the regular armed forces of the states confronting one another. Those actively engaged in the fighting were usually soldiers who were easily distinguishable from civilians and others not in combat. They wore military uniforms and bore their arms openly. By contrast, most contemporary armed conflicts are not fought between states. Interstate wars are being replaced by a wide range of highly complex and drawn-out internal conflicts of low intensity. Most conflicts usually involve at least one organized non-state armed group, and often several, which may split or shift alliances in the course of the conflict. Moreover, there is neither a clear start nor end to the hostilities, and the question of transnational terrorism adds fuel to the fire of violence.

The metamorphosis of conflicts and the way they are fought has given rise to new challenges. It has become increasingly difficult to identify the various actors, their allegiances, and motivations, and often the warring factions are not easily distinguishable from the civilian population. More worrisome, though, and as a consequence of the myriad actors in the theatre of hostilities, is the increased number of civilian casualties as well as the targeting of humanitarian actors.

To be sure, working in a war zone is inherently dangerous, and humanitarian organizations should be fully aware of the risks that they run when operating in these areas. For its part, the ICRC makes essential risk assessments before deploying. Security presupposes acceptance of the ICRC's presence and activities by all belligerents, as well as recognition and respect of the emblem. Without this acceptance, the ICRC's humanitarian operations would be put at risk. Thus, to remain close to the victims and to communicate with all existing or potential parties to a conflict, the ICRC has developed a network of more than 230 delegations, subdelegations, and offices throughout the world. The ICRC strives to continuously expand its network of contacts with all weapons bearers, and with those who can influence them. In order to assist people affected by armed conflict, the ICRC speaks with all parties with a view to disseminating IHL so that arms carriers understand and better respect IHL, other fundamental rules protecting persons in situations of violence, and the role of the ICRC as a neutral and independent humanitarian organization.

Notwithstanding these efforts, contemporary armed conflicts are plagued with new risks and realities. They are more complex, and often ethnic and religious differences are the driving forces in the seemingly endless cycles of violence. New actors, greater availability of unregulated weapons, the instrumentalization of humanitarian activities for military or political purposes, and asymmetrical warfare are just some of the factors that have led to increased risks for civilians, medical personnel, and humanitarian workers in combat zones.

Some organizations have therefore considered seeking the services of private industry for the provision of armed security for their humanitarian activities. The use of armed escort services entails many risks, however, and could be prejudicial to the humanitarian organization's activities in the long term. Perception as a hostile entity associated with arms carriers rather than as an independent and neutral humanitarian organization is but one of these risks. As some researchers have concluded, using private security companies (PSCs) "creates particular vulnerabilities for humanitarian organisations, and requires special consideration in regard to contracting, management and oversight."[5]

The Use of Private Armed Security Escorts

The functions of PSCs vary and have included the provision of logistical, communication, and security services, the protection of convoys and personnel for multinational companies, the staffing of checkpoints, and in some situations even the interrogation of prisoners, collection of intelligence, and direct participation in combat operations. One recurring view is that these individuals are merely glorified mercenaries whose activities are contrary to a number of international and regional instruments. Another point of view is that these private security firms are legitimate corporate entities providing essential security services in conflict and post-conflict zones. Although many in the industry argue that the companies operate within and in full respect of applicable law, even in conflict zones such as Iraq, over the past few years many accusations have been levied against some companies for using excessive force in carrying out their activities. At times, the alleged overzealous protection by the personnel of certain security contractors of their VIP or convoy has put civilians in harm's way, endangering their lives. These situations have given rise to numerous issues – legal, ethical, and practical. Passions aside, with an increase in the number of humanitarians being targeted by parties to a conflict and by banditry, the issue is whether humanitarian organizations operating in armed conflict zones should contract the services of such private entities, whose image and reputation have been somewhat tarnished recently.

In providing a viewpoint on this issue, for the purposes of this chapter a distinction is made between, on the one hand, the provision of security services such as armed security escorts to enable humanitarian organizations to gain access to various localities, and, on the other, security services such as guards and alarm systems to safeguard facilities and households of humanitarian organizations. The use of the former will be addressed here.

A general argument is that the use of armed escort services will in many contexts affect the perception that victims and parties to armed conflict have of a humanitarian organization using such security, calling into question the organization's neutrality and impartiality. With this in mind, it could be said that, as a rule, humanitarian organizations such as the ICRC should not be using private security firms in times of armed conflict.

Although the role and imprint of PSCs have gained prominence only recently in such contexts as Iraq and Afghanistan, the International Red Cross and Red Crescent Movement studied the issue of armed protection for humanitarian assistance back in the 1990s. As early as 1993, the Council of Delegates called upon the ICRC and the International Federation of Red Cross and Red Crescent Societies (IFRC) to form a joint working group to look into this issue.[6]

In its report, the working group recognized that with the end of the Cold War, the world had undergone many major changes. The subsequent collapse of social structures, the fragmentation of power, the weakening of states, the development of ethnic intolerance and tensions, the widespread availability of and trade in weapons, the continuing rural exodus, increasing economic turmoil, and the rise in illegal trading – such as raw materials or drugs – were cited by the working group as examples of the pressures being exerted upon people and society in the 1990s. As a result, war, social unrest, and indeed all forms of violence were on the increase. At the time of writing of the report, there were more than thirty-one armed conflicts, in places such as Afghanistan, Liberia, Somalia, Rwanda, Angola, and Sudan in the South to the former Yugoslavia and parts of the former Soviet Union in the North. With these new conflicts came new tactics and means, namely, the deliberate and intentional destruction of the very fabric of human dignity, the family and other social structures. With greater chaos and anarchy, conflicts became more complex, the suffering of civilians increased, and humanitarian workers and the international community became generally ever more helpless.[7]

For the components of the Red Cross/Red Crescent Movement and other humanitarian organizations, this new tapestry made operations more difficult and dangerous. The multitude of actors, including "groups, clans, bandits, militias and weekend fighters," created new challenges in negotiating access to victims and ensuring security for humanitarian workers.[8] Independent research found that humanitarian workers were increasingly victims of attacks and that the emblem of the Red Cross and Red Crescent no longer provided the necessary protection. Certain studies showed that 382 humanitarian workers were killed between 1985 and 1998; approximately 68 percent of these deaths were due to intentional violence (from guns or other weapons) and many were associated with banditry.[9] As the working group concluded:

> [In] carrying out their duty to provide assistance and protection to those most vulnerable, whether it be in times of conflict, natural disaster or chronic need, Red Cross and Red Crescent Societies acting within the framework of their domestic programmes or through the International Federation, or the ICRC (working with national societies or by itself in times of armed conflict or internal violence) have increasingly become targets of violence and face growing difficulties in commanding respect for the emblem.[10]

Clearly, the increased risk to humanitarian workers hampers their organizations' capability and capacity to deliver humanitarian assistance to victims and other persons in need. The concerned organizations had to make a difficult choice: on the one hand, the safety of their staff and volunteers and the overall security of their operations were vital; on the other hand, the provision of humanitarian assistance to those in need was equally necessary. One obvious solution that was raised was the use of armed escorts to deter and to protect against hostile acts, and to enable organizations to safely access their intended beneficiaries.

As the working group noted, however, the use of armed protection by any component of the Red Cross/Red Crescent Movement may endanger the neutrality and ultimate safety of other components, as well as place at risk the lives of the persons receiving the aid.

In its conclusions, therefore, the working group stated that any armed protection for any component of the movement was in conflict with its fundamental principles of humanity, independence, impartiality, and neutrality, and stipulated as a general rule that the different components of the movement should not use armed protection, particularly armed escorts, or deterrent force against those tempted to use violence. The working group noted that the use of private escorts might in some exceptional circumstances be justified, for instance, situations where "human lives may be saved only by accepting an armed escort because the refusal of such an escort would lead to the paralysis of humanitarian activities, and consequently the possibility that the victims would die."[11] In such cases, argued the working group, "the principle of humanity requires that the components of the Movement thoroughly assess the situation, attempt to find the best solution and, in certain circumstances, accept changes to their normal operating procedures."[12] The working group was careful to point out, however, that use of an armed escort "may help get one aid convoy through but eventually jeopardise the operation as a whole," given that such use can affect the image of all the components of the movement, now and in the future, and jeopardize acceptance of the emblem as well as future access and action.[13]

The working group proposed certain criteria, called "minimal conditions," to be met in cases where a component of the Red Cross/Red Crescent Movement is considering the use of an armed escort:

- Are the needs so pressing (*e.g.*, saving lives on a large scale) as to justify an exceptional way of operating, and can they be met only with the use of an armed escort?
- Is the Red Cross/Red Crescent Movement's component sure that the use of an armed escort will not have a detrimental effect upon the security of the intended beneficiaries?

- Is the component the most capable of covering the identified needs? Is there no other agency or body external to the movement that is in a position to carry out the same activities or to cover the same needs?
- Is armed protection being considered primarily for its deterrent value and not for its firepower, recognizing the extreme reluctance with which the movement would condone the use of violence and the threat of violence to deter attack?
- Has the party or authority controlling the territory through which the convoy will pass and in which the humanitarian assistance will be delivered given its full approval to the principle and modalities of an armed escort? Remember that should this approval be withdrawn, the situation must be reassessed and negotiations must take place once again.
- Is the escort intended to provide protection against bandits and common criminals in a situation of general law-and-order breakdown? Remember that there should be no risk of confrontation between the escort and the actual parties to the conflict or organized armed groups that control part of the area through which the humanitarian convoy has to travel.

Finally, the working group proposed criteria for deciding on the composition and behaviour of the armed group should a member of the movement decide to employ an armed escort for its humanitarian operations after having gone through the foregoing checklist. The armed escort should be seen as a preventive measure, its main feature being its deterrent effect. The escort could be provided by either a reputable private company, the police, or military personnel. The working group added that members of the escort must not be movement staff, must not be allowed to display the emblem, and must travel in vehicles that are identifiably different from those of the Red Cross and Red Crescent and that are not marked with the emblem. Other issues addressed by the working group included the kinds of weapons that could be used and under what conditions; weapons were to be used in self-defence, and with full respect for the principle of proportionality.

The Montreux Document

As highlighted by the working group, whether the member of the Red Cross/ Red Crescent Movement chooses to use regular armed forces, the police, or a private company for security purposes, a host of problems is foreseeable. Whereas utilizing police and military personnel gives rise to obvious issues of perception, the hiring of private contractors may muddy the waters even more, especially given the choice of companies available. Considerations such as the company's track history, training, and employees' background become that much more important. How can one be sure that the prospective company is aboveboard and comes with a clean slate and an irreproachable reputation? A simple tender and bid process for the armed escort contract may be insufficient to distinguish the reputable companies from the questionable ones.

The greater presence of private contractors in zones of armed conflicts at the turn of the twenty-first century as well as the negative publicity a number of these companies received following a spate of unsavoury incidents in Iraq led to calls for greater regulation and accountability of the private security industry. An initiative launched cooperatively by the government of Switzerland and the ICRC led to the publication on 17 September 2008 of the *Montreux Document on Pertinent International Legal Obligations and Good Practices for States Related to Operations of Private Military and Security Companies during Armed Conflict.*[14] The document was developed with the participation of government experts from Afghanistan, Angola, Australia, Austria, Canada, China, France, Germany, Iraq, Poland, Sierra Leone, South Africa, Sweden, Switzerland, the United Kingdom, Ukraine, and the United States in meetings convened in January and November 2006, November 2007, and April and September 2008. A number of representatives from civil society, NGOs, and the private military and security industry were consulted as part of the process.

In addition to recalling state obligations under IHL by specifying that private contractors are bound to respect IHL and human rights law imposed upon them by national law, as well as other applicable national law such as criminal law, tax law, immigration law, labour law, and specific regulations on private military or security services, the *Montreux Document* elaborates upon a number of good practices that states should take into account before hiring or before allowing private contractors to operate in conflict zones. Suggested criteria include:

II. Procedure for the selection and contracting of PMSCs

2. To assess the capacity of the PMSC to carry out its activities in conformity with relevant national law, international humanitarian law and international human rights law, taking into account the inherent risk associated with the services to be performed, for instance by:

a) acquiring information relating to the principal services the PMSC has provided in the past;

  b) obtaining references from clients for whom the PMSC has previ-
     ously provided similar services to those the Contracting State is
     seeking to acquire;
  c) acquiring information relating to the PMSC's ownership structure
     and conducting background checks on the PMSC and its superior
     personnel, taking into account relations with subcontractors, sub-
     sidiary corporations and ventures.

...

 4. To ensure transparency and supervision in the selection and con-
    tracting of PMSCs. Relevant mechanisms may include:

  a) public disclosure of PMSC contracting regulations, practices and
     processes;
  b) public disclosure of general information about specific contracts,
     if necessary redacted to address national security, privacy and
     commercial confidentiality requirements;
  c) publication of an overview of incident reports or complaints, and
     sanctions taken where misconduct has been proven; if necessary
     redacted to address national security, privacy and commercial
     confidentiality requirements;
  d) oversight by parliamentary bodies, including through annual re-
     ports or notification of particular contracts to such bodies.

III. Criteria for the selection of PMSCs

 5. To adopt criteria that include quality indicators relevant to ensuring
    respect for relevant national law, international humanitarian law and
    human rights law, as set out in good practices 6 to 13. Contracting
    States should consider ensuring that lowest price not be the only cri-
    terion for the selection of PMSCs.
 6. To take into account, within available means, the past conduct of the
    PMSC and its personnel, which includes ensuring that the PMSC has:

  a) no reliably attested record of involvement in serious crime (in-
     cluding organised crime, violent crime, sexual offences, violations
     of international humanitarian law, bribery and corruption) and,
     insofar as the PMSC or its personnel had engaged in past unlawful
     conduct, has appropriately remedied such conduct, including by
     effectively cooperating with official authorities, taking disciplin-
     ary measures against those involved, and, where appropriate and

consistent with findings of wrongdoing, providing individuals injured by their conduct with appropriate reparation;

b) conducted comprehensive inquiries within applicable law regarding the extent to which any of its personnel, particularly those
who are required to carry weapons as part of their duties, have a
reliably attested record of not having been involved in serious
crime or have not been dishonourably discharged from armed or
security forces;

c) not previously been rejected from a contract due to misconduct of
the PMSC or its personnel.

...

10. To take into account that the PMSC's personnel are sufficiently
trained, both prior to any deployment and on an ongoing basis, to
respect relevant national law, international humanitarian law and human rights law; and to establish goals to facilitate uniformity and
standardisation of training requirements. Training could include
general and task- and context-specific topics, preparing personnel
for performance under the specific contract and in the specific environment, such as:

a) rules on the use of force and firearms;

b) international humanitarian law and human rights law;

c) religious, gender, and cultural issues, and respect for the local
population;

d) handling complaints by the civilian population, in particular by
transmitting them to the appropriate authority;

e) measures against bribery, corruption, and other crimes.

Contracting States consider continuously reassessing the level of
training by, for example, requiring regular reporting on the part of
PMSCs.

...

12. To take into account the PMSC's internal organisation and regulations, such as:

a) the existence and implementation of policies relating to international humanitarian law and human rights law, especially on
the use of force and firearms, as well as policies against bribery,
corruption, and other crimes.

As can be seen, many of the proposed criteria and procedures focus on the steps that should be taken to make certain that the private contractors operate in full compliance with national law, IHL, and international human rights law. Of course, any compliance will depend on the strength of the domestic law in the countries of registration of the companies, in the countries in which they operate, and in those of the citizenship of the employees and of the contractor. In addition to the legal framework, the *Montreux Document* implicitly recognizes that there is a need for an effective information-sharing system whereby details of the various PSCs, including references for past services rendered as well as particulars of corporate structure and names of subsidiaries and subcontractors, are readily available. There are also moves by certain states and the industry itself for industry self-regulation and the adoption of national as well as an international code of conduct. Of course, any efforts aimed at improving the private industry's capacity to provide effective security services in full compliance with the law and without risks to the beneficiaries of humanitarian assistance should be encouraged.

It should be noted that the *Montreux Document* makes a number of recommendations regarding relevant national laws and regulations. Many of the recommendations reflect pre-existing state obligations under IHL and international human rights law that require state implementation. Likewise, the effectiveness of the vetting procedures and best practices highlighted in the document to improve the conduct and accountability of companies might necessitate translation into domestic regulatory frameworks and industry codes of conduct. Nevertheless, the advisory nature of the *Montreux Document,* read in conjunction with the criteria suggested by the working group (discussed above), form a useful point of departure for humanitarian organizations as they consider whether to hire private armed security.

Conclusion

Short-term gain versus long-term risks to an organization's activities in the region need to be carefully weighed before the organization hires armed escort services. Access to victims is usually predicated on trust, acceptance, and the perception by the parties to the conflict of the neutrality and independence of the humanitarian organization. Dialogue with the parties to the conflict as well as with the beneficiaries has been shown to serve humanitarianism well, reducing misunderstandings and misconceptions among the various actors. For the ICRC, introducing armed escorts into the equation risks undoing the good work of countless delegates who have reached out to belligerents and beneficiaries alike to convey and explain the organization's mandate and humanitarian endeavours.

Coupled with the dialogue are the recognition of the emblem, the protective value that it provides, and the reflexive respect that it engenders. In conflicts, the emblem remains universally recognized as a symbol of humanitarian activities carried out in a neutral, impartial, and independent manner. Association of the emblem with armed security escorts will undoubtedly erode this image, possibly creating doubt in the minds of the beneficiaries and parties to the conflict as to the meaning and representation of the emblem. It goes without saying that in conflict areas where violence prevails over the rule of law, the sight of armed escorts, and the possible threat that they connote, will distract from the purely humanitarian message that the emblem seeks to convey.

Finally, in terms of regulation of the private security industry, the more transparent a system is, with effective accountability mechanisms, the easier it will be for humanitarian organizations that intend to resort to armed security escorts to make an informed decision about which company to hire, thereby minimizing the risk of hiring a disreputable firm. This alone, however, may not be sufficient to affect positively the perception of the beneficiaries and parties to the conflict, who will not necessarily have access to the same information. In their eyes, a private arms carrier remains just that in the theatre of hostilities, and is unlikely to be seen as an aid worker.

NOTES

1 The views and opinions expressed in this paper are those of the author alone and do not necessarily reflect those of the International Committee of the Red Cross.

2 At the time of writing, the *Geneva Conventions* have been universally ratified and 164 States have ratified Additional Protocol I, 168 Additional Protocol II, and 40 Additional Protocol III.

3 For instance, arts. 9, 9, 9, and 10 of the four *Geneva Conventions*, respectively, and art. 81(1) of Additional Protocol I provide that "the present Convention constitute[s] no obstacle to the humanitarian activities which the International Committee of the Red Cross ... may, subject to the consent of the Parties to the conflict concerned, undertake for the protection of the wounded and sick, medical personnel and chaplains, and for their relief." Article 3(2) common to the four *Geneva Conventions* states: "An impartial humanitarian body, such as the International Committee of the Red Cross, may offer its services to the Parties to the conflict." Article 126 of the *Third Geneva Convention* and arts. 76 and 143 of the *Fourth Geneva Convention* recognize that the ICRC has permission to go to all places where protected persons

may be, in particular those deprived of liberty, have access to all premises occupied by them, interview them without witnesses, and have full liberty to select the places of visit as well as the duration and frequency of the visits.

4 The Statutes of the International Red Cross and Red Crescent Movement were adopted by the 25th International Conference of the Red Cross at Geneva in October 1986 and amended by the 26th International Conference of the Red Cross at Geneva in December 1995.

5 Abby Stoddard, Adele Harmer, and Victoria DiDomenico, "Private Security Contracting in Humanitarian Operations," HPG (Humanitarian Policy Group) Policy Brief 33 (2009), online: Overseas Development Institute <http://www.odi.org.uk/resources/>.

6 "Report on the Use of Armed Protection for Humanitarian Assistance" (Extract from Working Paper, ICRC and International Federation, Council of Delegates, Geneva, 1-2 December 1995), online: ICRC <http://www.icrc.org/>.

7 *Ibid.*

8 *Ibid.*

9 Mani Sheik, Maria Isabel Gutierrez, Paul Bolton, Paul Spiegel, Michel Thieren, and Gilbert Burnham, "Deaths among Humanitarian Workers" (2000) 321 British Medical Journal 166, online: British Medical Journal <http://www.bmj.com/>.

10 *Ibid.* at 5.

11 *Ibid.*

12 *Ibid.*

13 *Ibid.*

14 *The Montreux Document on Pertinent International Legal Obligations and Good Practices for States Related to Operations of Private Military and Security Companies during Armed Conflict* (Montreux: Government of Switzerland, 2008), online: ICRC <http://www.icrc.org/web/>.

Obligations of Private Military and Security Companies under International Humanitarian Law

FRED SCHREIER

Since the early 1990s, ever more functions traditionally performed by the armed forces and security apparatuses of states have been contracted out to private military and private security companies – profit-driven private business entities that provide military and/or security services, irrespective of how they describe themselves. There is no internationally agreed definition of what constitutes a private military company or a private security company (PMSCs), but one may be starting to crystallize for private security companies with the finalization of the *Montreux Document* in September 2008[1] and the even more recent signing of the International Code of Conduct for Private Security Service Providers (ICoC).[2] Whereas the bulk of the outsourced contracts initially involved logistical and other support tasks, recent years have witnessed a significant growth in the involvement of PMSCs in security and military functions in situations of armed conflict. This involvement includes the protection of persons, objects, convoys, and critical infrastructure; maintenance and operation of information technology, communications, reconnaissance, surveillance, and various weapons systems; risk assessment; intelligence collection and analysis; the detention and interrogation of suspects and prisoners; technical advice and provision of training to armed forces and security forces; combat service support and combat support; and sometimes even direct participation in combat operations.

The visible presence of contractors in Iraq since 2003 and now in Afghanistan has drawn much public attention to PMSCs. With a large number of companies operating in a corporate industry worth US$100 billion,[3] PMSCs appear to be here to stay. Proof of this is found in the fact that the United States Armed Forces can no longer function effectively or sustain themselves without contractor support. The scope of contractor integration is reflected in military doctrine. In describing "contractors as a force-multiplier," US Army Field Manual 3-100.21 explains that "contractor support ... should be understood [as] more than just logistics; it spans the spectrum of combat support (CS) and combat service support (CSS) functions[,] traditional goods and service support, [and] may include interpreter, communications, infrastructure, and other non-logistic-related support. It also has applicability to the full range of Army operations, to include offense, defense, stability, and support within all types of military actions from small-scale contingencies to major theater of wars."[4] In Iraq, the US government employs – directly and indirectly through subcontracts – more contractors than military personnel, for example, some 265,000 contract personnel in the second quarter of the 2008 fiscal year.[5] Although the numbers are striking, few of these contractors are armed, some 55 percent are Iraqis, about 30 percent are third-country nationals (TCN), and only 15 percent are Americans.[6]

States, however, are not the only clients of PMSCs. This developing industry also provides a growing variety of services to other actors in situations of armed conflict, such as international and regional intergovernmental organizations, NGOs, multinational corporations operating in the extracting sector, as well as individuals. They also fulfill tasks in support of humanitarian assistance, disaster relief operations, reconstruction, and state building.[7] The term "humanitarian theatre of operations" falls into this context, and can be understood as a theatre in which a humanitarian action is taking place. Humanitarian action refers to the intervention in domestic affairs of another state by a variety of means. It can include a whole range of actions, from diplomatic protests, sanctions, and intervention short of war, to military invasion and occupation occurring over an indeterminate period of time. For the military, it can also take the form of stability operations.[8] The aim of humanitarian action is to provide victims of conflict with a measure of protection, to bring them aid, to initiate a dialogue with the belligerents, to institute rehabilitative projects that have a stabilizing influence on communities, and to bring order back to people's lives. These aims are all based on the realization that people's lives must return to normal before long-term stability can be achieved.

The engagement of PMSCs in this area raises a multitude of legal, political, and practical questions. It is often asserted that there is a vacuum in the law when it comes to the engagement and operations of PMSCs. In situations of armed conflict, however – which is the case in a humanitarian theatre of operations where humanitarian actions take place – there is indeed a body of law that regulates both the activities of PMSCs and their staff and the obligations of states.

In this chapter, I examine the key legal issues raised by PMSCs operating in situations of armed conflict. After addressing the status of PMSC staff under international humanitarian law (IHL),[9] I examine the obligations of PMSCs and their personnel, whether employed directly or under contract, including employees, managers, and directors. The obligations of states that hire PMSCs are then outlined; these states include those that directly engage the services of PMSCs, including PMSCs that subcontract to other companies. Following this, I address the obligations of the states of nationality of the companies, the states in whose territory they operate, and the role all other states play in promoting respect for IHL. If the state where the PMSC is incorporated is not the one of its principal place of management, then the state where the PMSC has its principal headquarters or place of management is considered the home state.

The Status of the Staff of PMSCs under IHL

The foundation of IHL rests upon the distinction between combatants and civilians. Given that IHL was formed long before the advent of PMSCs and without the intention of embracing the privatization of warfare, private contractors were clearly not considered by the drafters of IHL when they afforded protection to civilians from the effects of hostilities. Nevertheless, the application of IHL to private contractors is less problematic than the application of human rights law (HRL).[10] This is due to the unusual feature of IHL that, unlike most rules of international law, enables it to bind not only the state and its organs but also the individual.[11] IHL thus addresses all persons involved in situations of armed conflict with the aim of defining their status with regard to the conflict and the legal consequences thereof. More specifically, it distinguishes between the rights, privileges, and immunities of combatants and non-combatants, that is, those taking part in the hostilities and the civilians who normally remain outside all fighting. Hence, there is no *de jure* gap in law when it comes to private contractors and IHL.

Essentially, IHL applies only in times of *armed conflict,* including occupation, and not to internal political violence. Only states can be parties to the *Geneva Conventions,* and international armed conflicts can be fought either between states or between a state and an armed group that is associated to a determined degree with another state. Among the activities of armed groups covered by the law of international armed conflicts are all hostilities directed against the armed forces or the territory of one state by forces representing another state or acting *de facto* under the direction or control of that other state.[12] Ultimately, IHL is not concerned with the lawfulness or legitimacy of PMSCs *per se,* nor with their engagement by states to perform particular activities. Rather, it regulates the behaviour and comportment of such companies if they are operating in situations of armed conflict. This is consistent with the approach adopted by IHL more generally. IHL does not address the lawfulness of resorting to armed force but instead regulates *how* hostilities are conducted. Neither does IHL address the legitimacy of organized armed groups, instead regulating *how* these groups must fight.

Since IHL does not regulate the status of *legal* persons, the companies proper have neither status nor obligations under IHL. On the other hand, their employees do – even though these are not specifically mentioned in any treaty. There is, however, no simple answer applicable to all employees of PMSCs with regard to status, as it depends on the nature of any relationship they may have with a state and on the types of activities they carry out. Thus, status is something that must be determined on a case-by-case basis, particularly according to the nature and circumstances of the function in which PMSCs are involved. IHL contains criteria for determining this status as well as clear obligations and rights.

For the purposes of IHL, the central question, with immediate practical consequences for the persons involved, is: are they combatants or are they civilians? If they are combatants, then they have the right to take part in hostilities and may also be targeted at all times. If captured, they are entitled to prisoner-of-war status and cannot be prosecuted for having participated in hostilities.[13] Conversely, if they are civilians, they may not be attacked so long as they do not participate directly in hostilities. Should they participate directly in hostilities, they not only lose immunity from attack during such participation but also become "unprivileged belligerents." As such, in the event of capture they are not entitled to prisoner-of-war status and can be tried for having participated in hostilities, even if they did not commit any violations of IHL.[14]

Of the four categories of possible combatants,[15] two are relevant for classifying the staff of PMSCs:

- members of the armed forces of a state party to an armed conflict, or members of militias or volunteer corps forming part of such forces[16]
- members of other militias and of other volunteer corps, including those of organized resistance movements, belonging to a state party to an armed conflict, provided that such militias or corps fulfill all of the following conditions: 1) they are commanded by a person responsible for his/her subordinates; 2) they have a fixed distinctive sign recognizable at a distance; 3) they carry arms openly; and 4) they conduct their operations in accordance with the laws and customs of war.[17]

IHL clearly classifies members of the armed forces of a state as combatants. Article 43(2) of Protocol I, Additional to the *Geneva Conventions* of 1949 (Protocol I) stipulates: "Members of the armed forces of a party to a conflict ... are combatants, that is to say, they have the right to participate directly in hostilities." The armed forces of a party to the conflict consist of all organized armed forces, groups, and units that are under a command responsible to that party for the conduct of its subordinates. The party may also incorporate paramilitary or armed law enforcement agencies into its armed forces, which are then to be seen as combatants. The very hiring of PMSC staff by a given state is the clearest indicator that these people should be considered "members of the armed forces" of the state concerned. It is the state's prerogative that armed forces, and only companies hired by, or acting on behalf of, a state party to an international armed conflict, be capable of meeting the requirements of the *Third Geneva Convention* of 1949. As some of the most thorough analyses of the problem confirm, however, "it is difficult to imagine private contractors qualifying as formal members of the armed forces to a party regardless of the duties they perform."[18] If specific contracts do not incorporate private contractors into the armed forces of a party to an international conflict, they cannot be regarded as lawful combatants within the meaning of IHL. This conclusion finds support in the fact that neither the companies nor their employees have claimed combatant status, and at least some contracts between the US government and PMSCs specifically indicate that the contractors concerned are to be considered non-combatants.[19]

As stated earlier, article 4A(2) of the *Third Geneva Convention* recognizes the existence of persons not formally incorporated within the military who may be entitled to combatant status due to the nature and actions of their respective group. For this to be the case, a group must fulfill the four conditions set out in the second category of combatants: those of being commanded by a person responsible for his/her subordinates; of having a fixed distinctive sign recognizable at a distance; of carrying arms openly; and of conducting their operations in accordance with the laws and customs of war. These four requirements must *all* be met by the group as a whole – which is rarely the case with PMSCs. Thus, the most authoritative analyses come to the conclusion that only a small minority of PMSCs are likely to satisfy these requirements. Given that the logic of IHL classifies every person as either a combatant or a civilian, if PMSC employees are not combatants, they are civilians. Since the discourse appears to go against giving PMSC employees the status of combatants, it is imperative to consider the ramifications of such persons having the status of civilians.[20] There also appears to be consensus among states on the topic.[21]

Article 4A(4) of the *Third Geneva Convention* establishes another exception to the principle that only combatants are entitled to prisoner-of-war status:

> Persons who accompany the armed forces without actually being members thereof, such as civilian members of military aircraft crews, war correspondents, supply contractors, members of labor units or of services responsible for the welfare of the armed forces, provided that they have received authorization from the armed forces which they accompany, who shall provide them for that purpose with an identity card similar to the annexed model.

The legal position of persons falling within this category is clear: they are neither members of the armed forces nor combatants, but they are entitled to prisoner-of-war status if captured. As the enumeration in the article is not meant to be exhaustive, it may also be applicable to other persons, such as private contractors.[22] Clearly some contractors may fall under the notion of "persons accompanying the armed forces." Private contractors who do not carry out any military activities but focus on keeping the armed forces functioning – for example, by delivering food, building roads, or providing services for facilities – can be categorized as persons accompanying the armed forces. A prerequisite for the status is that the state hiring their services grants them the status of "persons accompanying the armed forces." It is noteworthy that the examples in Article 4A(4) of the *Third Geneva*

Convention do not involve the use of force and therefore should be considered to cover only private contractors performing support functions without military relevance. Thus, any use of force by persons who accompany the armed forces must be strictly limited to self-defence. Private contractors who work independently from the armed forces or those engaged in providing security to private persons or companies are clearly not accompanying armed forces.

On 17 September 2008, seventeen states[23] finalized the *Montreux Document on Pertinent International Legal Obligations and Good Practices for States Related to Operations of Private Military and Security Companies during Armed Conflict.* It was the first international document to detail international law as it applies to the activities of PMSCs in relation to armed conflict. As a whole, the *Montreux Document* gives expression to the consensus that international law, particularly IHL and HRL, does have a bearing on PMSCs, and that there is no legal vacuum for their activities. The result of an initiative launched jointly by Switzerland and the International Committee of the Red Cross (ICRC), and developed on the basis of four intergovernmental meetings between January 2006 and September 2008 that brought together various experts from government, industry, civil society, and human rights organizations, the *Montreux Document* is now an official document of the United Nations and is available in six languages.[24] It is divided into two parts. Part I recalls pertinent international legal obligations of PMSCs, while Part II contains a list of good practices drawn largely from existing practices of states not only directly with regard to PMSCs but also from existing regulations for arms and armed services. The compilation of good practices is designed to assist states in fulfilling their obligations under international law through a series of national measures. The Geneva Centre for the Democratic Control of Armed Forces (DCAF) participated in all the meetings and contributed to the *Montreux Document,*[25] and the following section highlights the international legal obligations as contained in it.

The Obligations of PMSCs and Their Personnel

In the same way they are obliged to comply with criminal law, tax law, immigration law, labour law, and specific regulations on private military or private security services, PMSCs are obliged to comply with IHL and HRL imposed upon them by national law. The personnel of PMSCs are obliged to respect, in particular, the criminal law of the state in which they operate, and, as far as applicable, the law of the state of their nationality.

The Personnel of PMSCs

- are obliged to comply with applicable IHL, regardless of their status, whether combatants, civilians accompanying armed forces, or "ordinary" civilians
- are protected as civilians under IHL, unless they are incorporated into the regular armed forces of a state or are members of organized armed forces, groups, or units under a command responsible to the state
- are entitled to prisoner-of-war status in international armed conflict if they are persons accompanying the armed forces meeting the requirements of Article 4A(4) of the *Third Geneva Convention*
- are compelled to comply with a state's obligations under human rights law to the extent that they exercise governmental authority
- may face individual criminal responsibility for any serious violations they commit or have ordered to be committed; hence, they are subject to prosecution if they commit acts recognized as crimes under applicable national or international law.

Superiors of PMSC personnel – governmental officials, whether they are military commanders or civilian superiors, directors, or managers of PMSCs – may be liable for crimes under international law committed by PMSC personnel under their effective authority and control. Superior responsibility is not engaged solely by virtue of a contract but instead as a result of the failure of superiors to properly exercise control in accordance with the rules of international law. The responsibility of superiors for grave breaches of IHL is expressly recognized in Article 86(2) of Protocol I.

Pertinent International Legal Obligations Relating to PMSCs

Existing international legal obligations of states regarding PMSCs are drawn from IHL, HRL, and customary international law. Each state is responsible for complying with the obligations it has undertaken pursuant to international agreements, subject to any reservations, understandings, and declarations made, and to customary international law. Although the universal ratification of the *Geneva Conventions* means that all states are bound by consistent rules of IHL, ambiguity persists with respect to the application of HRL to PMSCs. First, there is the preliminary question of whether PMSCs and private individuals have obligations under HRL. Second, there is the problem of which HRL and which corresponding obligations may apply. Perhaps providing some clarity on this matter, the International Code of

Conduct for Private Security Service Providers (ICoC) sets out clear HRL-based standards for the provision of private security service providers. As of December 2011, over 250 private security companies from more than 45 countries had signed the ICoC.

The Obligations of Contracting States

IHL does not prohibit states from hiring PMSCs to perform certain activities. If the contracting states are occupying powers, they have an obligation to take all measures in their power to restore and ensure, as far as possible, public order and safety, and to exercise vigilance in preventing violations of IHL and HRL.

Contracting states have an obligation not to contract PMSCs to carry out activities that IHL explicitly assigns to a state agent or authority, such as exercising the power of the responsible officer over prisoner-of-war camps or places of internment of civilians in accordance with the *Geneva Conventions.*

Contracting states have an obligation, within their power, to ensure respect for IHL by PMSCs they contract, particularly to:

- ensure that PMSCs and their personnel are aware of their obligations and are trained accordingly
- avoid encouraging or assisting in any violations of IHL by personnel of PMSCs and to take appropriate measures to prevent such violations
- take measures to suppress violations of IHL committed by the personnel of PMSCs through appropriate means, such as military regulations, administrative orders, and other regulatory measures, as well as administrative, disciplinary, or judicial sanctions, as appropriate.

Contracting states must implement their obligations under international HRL, including adopting such legislative and other measures as may be necessary to give effect to these obligations. To this end, they have the obligation, in specific circumstances, to take appropriate measures to prevent, investigate, and provide effective remedies for relevant misconduct of PMSCs and their personnel.

Contracting states have an obligation to enact any legislation necessary to provide effective penal sanctions for persons committing, or ordering the commission of, grave breaches of the *Geneva Conventions* and, where applicable, Protocol I. Moreover, they have an obligation to search for persons alleged to have committed, or to have ordered to be committed, such grave breaches, and to bring such persons, regardless of their nationality, before their own courts. They may also, if they prefer, and in accordance with the provisions of their own legislation, hand such persons over for trial to another state concerned, provided the state in question has made out a *prima facie* case, or to an international tribunal.

Contracting states have an obligation to investigate and, as required by international law or otherwise as appropriate, prosecute, extradite, or surrender persons suspected of having committed other crimes, such as torture or hostage taking. Such prosecutions are to be carried out in accordance with international law providing for fair trial, mindful that sanctions must be commensurate with the gravity of the crime.

Although entering into contractual relations does not automatically engage the responsibility of states, where violations of IHL, HRL, or other rules of international law committed by PMSCs or their personnel are attributable to contracting states, the latter are responsible. This is particularly so if the PMSCs are:

- incorporated by the state into its regular armed forces in accordance with its domestic legislation
- members of organized armed forces, groups, or units under a command responsible to the state
- empowered to exercise elements of governmental authority, and if they are acting in that capacity (are formally authorized by law or regulation to carry out functions normally conducted by organs of the state)
- in fact acting on the instructions of the state (the state has specifically instructed the private actor's conduct) or under its direction or control (actual exercise of effective control by the state over a private actor's conduct).

Contracting states have an obligation to provide reparations for violations of IHL and HRL caused by wrongful conduct of the personnel of PMSCs when such conduct is attributable to the contracting state in accordance with customary international law of state responsibility.

The Obligations of Territorial States, Home States, and All Other States

Territorial States

- have an obligation, within their power, to ensure respect for IHL by PMSCs operating on their territory, in particular to: (1) disseminate, as widely as possible, the text of the *Geneva Conventions* and other relevant norms of IHL among PMSCs and their personnel; (2) avoid encouraging or assisting in any violations of IHL by personnel of PMSCs, and take appropriate measures to prevent such violations; (3) take measures to suppress violations of IHL committed by the personnel of PMSCs through appropriate means, such as military regulations, administrative orders, and other regulatory measures, as well as administrative, disciplinary, or judicial sanctions.

- are responsible for implementing their obligations under international HRL, including adopting such legislative and other measures as may be necessary to give effect to these obligations. To this end, they have the obligation, in specific circumstances, to take appropriate measures to prevent, investigate, and provide effective remedies for relevant misconduct of PMSCs and their personnel.

- have an obligation to enact any legislation necessary to provide effective penal sanctions for persons committing, or ordering the commission of, grave breaches of the *Geneva Conventions* and, where applicable, Protocol I. Moreover, they have an obligation to search for persons alleged to have committed, or to have ordered to be committed, grave breaches and bring such persons, regardless of their nationality, before their own courts. They may also, if they prefer, and in accordance with the provisions of their own legislation, hand such persons over for trial to another state, provided that the state concerned has made out a *prima facie* case, or to an international criminal tribunal.

- have an obligation to investigate and, as required by international law or otherwise as appropriate, prosecute, extradite, or surrender persons suspected of having committed other crimes, such as torture or hostage taking. Such prosecutions are to be carried out in accordance with international law providing for fair trial, mindful that sanctions must be commensurate with the gravity of the crime.

In situations of occupation, the obligations of territorial states are limited to areas in which they are able to exercise effective control.

Home States

- have the obligation, within their power, to ensure respect for IHL by PMSCs of their nationality, in particular to: (1) disseminate, as widely as possible, the text of the *Geneva Conventions* and other relevant norms of IHL among PMSCs and their personnel; (2) avoid encouraging or assisting in any violations of IHL by personnel of PMSCs, and take appropriate measures to prevent such violations; (3) take measures to suppress violations of IHL committed by the personnel of PMSCs through appropriate means, such as administrative or other regulatory measures as well as administrative, disciplinary, or judicial sanctions.

- are responsible for implementing their obligations under international HRL, including adopting such legislative and other measures as may be necessary to give effect to these obligations. To this end, they have the obligation, in specific circumstances, to take appropriate measures to prevent, investigate, and provide effective remedies for relevant misconduct of PMSCs and their personnel.
- have an obligation to enact any legislation necessary to provide effective penal sanctions for persons committing, or ordering the commission of, grave breaches of the *Geneva Conventions* and, where applicable, Protocol I. Moreover, they have an obligation to search for persons alleged to have committed, or to have ordered to be committed, grave breaches and to bring such persons, regardless of their nationality, before their own courts. They may also, if they prefer, and in accordance with the provisions of their own legislation, hand such persons over for trial to another state, provided the state concerned has made out a *prima facie* case, or to an international criminal tribunal.
- also have an obligation to investigate and, as required by international law or otherwise as appropriate, prosecute, extradite, or surrender persons suspected of having committed other crimes, such as torture or hostage taking. Such prosecutions are to be carried out in accordance with international law providing for fair trial, mindful that sanctions be commensurate with the gravity of the crime.

All Other States

- have an obligation, within their power, to ensure respect for IHL. This implies that they have an obligation to refrain from encouraging or assisting in violations of IHL by any party to an armed conflict.
- are responsible for implementing their obligations under international HRL, including adopting such legislative and other measures as may be necessary to give effect to these obligations.
- have an obligation to enact any legislation necessary to provide effective penal sanctions for persons committing, or ordering the commission of,

grave breaches of the *Geneva Conventions* and, where applicable, Protocol I. Moreover, they have an obligation to search for persons alleged to have committed, or to have ordered to be committed, grave breaches and bring such persons, regardless of their nationality, before their own courts. They may also, if they prefer, and in accordance with the provisions of their own legislation, hand such persons over for trial to another state, provided that the state in question has made out a *prima facie* case, or to an international criminal tribunal.

- have an obligation to investigate and, as required by international law, or otherwise as appropriate, prosecute, extradite, or surrender persons suspected of having committed other crimes, such as torture or hostage taking. Such prosecutions are to be carried out in accordance with international law providing for fair trial, mindful that sanctions must be commensurate with the gravity of the crime.

The *Montreux Document* is a major step forward in clarifying state legal obligations for PMSCs under IHL. Turning to the question of human rights responsibilities of private security companies, the International Code of Conduct for Private Security Service Providers attempts to provide greater clarity on this.

The International Code of Conduct for Private Security Service Providers

In response to industry demands for international private security service provider standards *with teeth,* the Swiss government has launched another initiative to develop an International Code of Conduct for Private Security Service Providers (ICoC), which would articulate clear standards for private security service providers based on international human rights law, as well as to develop an independent oversight and compliance mechanism to provide effective sanctions when the ICoC is breached, and remedies to victims. Developed through a multi-stakeholder approach involving private security companies, states, and civil society, the ICoC was finalized and signed by participating companies in November 2010. The ICoC uses the vehicle of the contract in order to impose human rights–compliant standards *directly on the companies themselves, regardless of where they are operating.* As of this writing, over 250 companies from more than 45 countries have signed the ICoC. Currently, the ICoC is in an institution-building phase, with a multi-stakeholder steering committee leading development of the operational framework for the oversight institution. This framework is

expected to be completed by mid-2012, with the institution beginning operations shortly thereafter.[26]

NOTES

1 The *Montreux Document on Private Military and Security Companies* (PMSCs) was
   the first statement of the international obligations of states toward PMSCs operating
   in situations of armed conflict, as well as a listing of good practices for states regarding PMSCs. As of November 2011, thirty-seven states have endorsed the document. For further information, please visit <www.eda.admin.ch/psc>.

2 On 9 November 2010, fifty-eight companies signed the International Code of
   Conduct for Private Security Service Providers (ICoC). The ICoC defines private
   security companies as those companies whose business activities include "guarding
   and protection of persons and objects, such as convoys, facilities, designated sites,
   property or other places (whether armed or unarmed), or any other activity for
   which the Personnel of Companies are required to carry or operate a weapon in
   the performance of their duties." The ICoC is available online at <http://www.icoc-
   psp.org/>.

3 See *Report of the Third Meeting of Experts on Traditional and New Forms of
   Mercenary Activity*, UN ESCOR, 61st Sess., UN Doc. E/CN.4/2005/23 (2005) at
   para. 12.

4 *Contractors on the Battlefield*, Field Manual 3-100.21 (Washington, DC: US
   Department of the Army, 2003), online: United States Army <http://www.osc.army.
   mil/> at 1-1.

5 *Contractors' Support of U.S. Operations in Iraq* (Washington, DC: Congressional
   Budget Office, 2008), online: Congressional Budget Office <http://www.cbo.gov/>.

6 In *reconstruction*, the Department of Defense (DOD) employs 25,000, and the State
   Department (State) and the Agency for International Development (USAID) 79,100,
   mostly Iraqis, who assist in the rebuilding of infrastructure, from oil fields to roads
   and schools. In *logistics and base support*, DOD employs 139,000 and State employs
   1,300, of whom 24 percent are Americans, 27 percent Iraqis, and 49 percent third-
   country nationals (TCN). Most of the US personnel are used as electricians, maintenance specialists, and truck drivers, and to keep materiel flowing and bases
   running. Iraqis and TCNs from Sri Lanka, the Philippines, Bangladesh, and other
   countries perform a wide range of functions, with the majority of them working in
   dining facilities. As for *interpreters*, DOD employs 6,600 and State 100, consisting of
   a mix of Americans, TCNs, and Iraqis. As for *advisors and others*, DOD employs
   2,000 and State 2,200, most of whom are Americans, along with some TCNs. In *security*, excluding bodyguards, DOD employs 6,300 and State 1,500. Most are TCNs
   but some are Iraqi, with most protecting fixed facilities inside major bases. As *bodyguards*, DOD employs 700 and State 1,300, all either US or UK nationals and most
   coming from a handful of specialized companies such as DynCorp International,
   Triple Canopy, Aegis Security, and Blackwater USA (renamed "xe Services LLC" in
   February 2009). Engaged in personal security details, these have attracted the most
   attention and engendered the greatest controversy.

7　In the humanitarian community, the term "state building" is usually preferred to "nation building." State building can be seen as the use of military force to underpin a process of democratization, and comprises phenomena such as occupation, peacekeeping, peace enforcement, stabilization, and reconstruction.

8　The term "stability operations" is an inexact concept. It can be all-encompassing or exclusionary, depending on its usage. See *Operations,* Field Manual 3-0 (Washington, DC: US Department of the Army, 2008), online: United States Army <http://downloads.army.mil/> at 3-12, which describes stability operations as "encompass[ing] various military missions, tasks, and activities conducted outside the United States in coordination with other instruments of national power to maintain or re-establish a safe and secure environment, provide essential governmental services, emergency infrastructure reconstruction, and humanitarian relief. Stability operations can be conducted in support of a host-nation or interim government or as part of an occupation when no government exists. Stability operations involve both coercive and constructive military actions. They help to establish a safe and secure environment and facilitate reconciliation among local or regional adversaries. Stability operations can also help establish political, legal, social, and economic institutions and support the transition to legitimate local governance. Stability operations must maintain the initiative by pursuing objectives that resolve the causes of instability. *Stability operations cannot succeed if they only react to enemy initiatives*" [emphasis added; internal references omitted].

9　International humanitarian law is largely codified in treaties, in particular the four *Geneva Conventions* of 1949 and the two Additional Protocols of 1977. The conventions and protocols establish a strict distinction between international and non-international armed conflicts, with the latter being governed by less detailed and less protective rules.

10　See Katja Creutz, *Transnational Privatised Security and the International Protection of Human Rights,* Research Reports 19/2006 (Helsinki: Erik Castrén Institute, 2006).

11　Christopher Greenwood, "Historical Development and Legal Basis," in Dieter Fleck, ed., *The Handbook of Humanitarian Law in Armed Conflict* (Oxford: Oxford University Press, 1995) 1.

12　See International Criminal Tribunal for the former Yugoslavia (ICTY), *Prosecutor v. Tadić,* Appeal Judgment, IT-94-1-A (15 July 1999), online: UNHCR <http://www.unhcr.org/refworld/> at paras. 116-44.

13　*Protocol Additional to the Geneva Conventions of 12 August 1949, and Relating to the Protection of Victims of International Armed Conflicts (Protocol I),* 8 June 1977, 1125 U.N.T.S. 3 (entered into force 7 December 1978) at art. 43(2) [API].

14　Knut Dörmann, "The Legal Situation of 'Unlawful/Unprivileged' Combatants" (2003) 85 Int'l Rev. Red Cross 45.

15　API, *supra* note 13 at art. 50(1).

16　*Convention Relative to the Treatment of Prisoners of War,* Geneva, 12 August 1949, 75 R.T.N.U. 135 at art. 4A(1) [GCIII].

17　*Ibid.* at art. 4A(2). The two other categories of combatants listed in arts. 4A(3) and (6) are members of regular armed forces who profess allegiance to a government or authority not recognized by the detaining power and participants in a *levée en masse*, respectively.

18 Michael N. Schmitt, "Humanitarian Law and Direct Participation in Hostilities by Private Contractors or Civilian Employees" (2005) 5 Chicago J. Int'l L. 511. See also Emanuela-Chiara Gillard, "Business Goes to War: Private Military/Security Companies and International Humanitarian Law" (2006) 863 Int'l Rev. Red Cross 525; and Lindsey Cameron, "Private Military Companies: Their Status under International Humanitarian Law and Its Impact on Their Regulation" (2006) 863 Int'l Rev. Red Cross 573.

19 US government contracts with Titan and CACI expressly state that the contractors are non-combatants.

20 See Cameron, *supra* note 18 at 587.

21 See, *e.g.*, "Contractor Personnel Authorized to Accompany the U.S. Armed Forces," United States Department of Defense Instruction Number 3020.41 (3 October 2005) at s. 6.1.5; and "Guidance for Determining Workforce Mix," United States Department of Defense Instruction Number 1100.22 (7 September 2006).

22 Jean S. Pictet, *The Geneva Conventions of 12 August 1949 Commentary: III Geneva Convention Relative to the Treatment of Prisoners of War* (Geneva: ICRC, 1960) at 64.

23 Afghanistan, Angola, Australia, Austria, Canada, China, France, Germany, Iraq, Poland, Sierra Leone, South Africa, Sweden, Switzerland, the United Kingdom, Ukraine, and the United Sates.

24 UN Doc. A/63/467-S/2008/636 in English, French, Chinese, Russian, Spanish, and Arabic.

25 DCAF is now in the same intergovernmental framework contributing to a code of conduct for PMSCs.

26 For the latest news and information on the ICoC, please visit its website at <www.icoc-psp.org>.

PART 3

THE "HUMANITARIAN SPACE" DEBATE

10 "Humanitarian Space" in Search of a New Home (Limited) Guidance from International Law

SYLVAIN BEAUCHAMP

The complexity of today's humanitarian and other international assistance provided to civilians around the world in the contexts of emergency, rehabilitation, and development is phenomenal. During the twentieth century, the conceptual paradigms surrounding the delivery of international aid saw an expansion from humanitarian relief proper to rehabilitation and development. From cases of armed conflict to natural and technological disasters, the provision of aid moved from being almost solely the purview of independent humanitarian/charitable organizations and non-governmental organizations (NGOs) to increasingly involving political and military actors and intergovernmental agencies. Alongside these changes, unimpeded humanitarian access to victims has now given way to a situation where the security of humanitarian personnel is increasingly at risk due to the many impediments placed by states and non-state actors on international aid of all forms. From the perspective of international NGOs, there is unquestionably a correlation between the increasing politicization of humanitarian aid and the decreasing security of relief personnel. It is certainly this politicization that prompted NGOs to develop the notion of "humanitarian space" in the 1990s.

The very meaning of the notion of humanitarian space is profoundly unclear, however. In Rony Brauman's vision of the "space for humanitarian action,"[1] which through time became humanitarian space, NGOs need a "space of freedom in which we are free to evaluate needs, free to monitor the distribution and use of relief goods, and free to have a dialogue with the people."[2] The freedom referred to in this definition applies to all actors, both donors and recipients of international aid, and it implies that there should be no political interference in the delivery of humanitarian aid by NGOs. For its part, the United Nations Office for the Coordination of Humanitarian Affairs (OCHA) glossary of humanitarian terms of 2008 defines the "humanitarian operating environment" as a "key element for humanitarian agencies and organizations when they deploy, [which] consists of establishing and maintaining a conducive humanitarian operating environment, sometimes referred to as 'humanitarian space.'"[3] Indeed, as further developed below, the UN views humanitarian space as a sphere within which UN-led (and coordinated) humanitarian aid activities are provided in a secure and unimpeded manner. For this reason, the numerous calls for the expansion of humanitarian space made by UN agencies are mostly directed towards governments and non-state actors that are active in the country where international aid is being delivered, rather than towards pursuit of the broader aim of decreasing the politicization of international aid, including on the part of donor countries. In this sense, the UN's conception of the "shrinking of humanitarian space" refers to the margin of manoeuvre that UN-coordinated organizations have in delivering humanitarian aid, whereas NGOs include in this notion the increased politicization of international aid generally, including by intergovernmental agencies such as the UN.

Moreover, although the notion of humanitarian space was originally limited to humanitarian assistance proper in the 1990s (namely, emergency assistance in times of war or disaster), this notion is also being used today by NGOs involved in rehabilitation work and more long-term international development. Important aid organizations are increasingly involved in the distribution of humanitarian aid and in carrying out rehabilitation and development work in the same country (for example, Afghanistan, Iraq, Sri Lanka, Sudan, and so on). The broadening of these organizations' mandates can certainly account for the change in the notion of humanitarian space from being focused on the nature of the assistance provided, which was originally the case, to the nature of the actor involved in international work.

The meaning and contours of this humanitarian space are therefore anything but clear. Leaving aside the complex policy questions raised by the humanitarian space debate, I focus in this chapter on the extent to which public international law can be used to delineate the discussion. In order to do this, I review the historical origins of the debate, and examine more carefully key areas of public international law that are relevant to the humanitarian space. I conclude by arguing that a new approach, centred on the victims, is now needed. In this regard, draft treaty principles are included to initiate a wider discussion.

Historical Origins of the Humanitarian Space Debate

Today's debate on the meaning and use of humanitarian space has been informed by several milestones in recent history. This section briefly reviews four important factors that have shaped today's debate: (1) the change in the focus of humanitarian aid from military to civilian beneficiaries; (2) the institutionalization of international disaster relief; (3) the institutionalization of international development; and (4) the changing role of military actors.

Humanitarian Aid: Change in Focus from Military to Civilians

Domestic charitable activities in favour of those affected by natural and manmade disasters may be traced back centuries in one form or another,[4] but it was only in the late nineteenth century, with the creation of the International Committee of the Red Cross (ICRC) and national Red Cross societies in 1863 and the adoption of the 1864 *Geneva Convention for the Amelioration of the Condition of the Wounded in Armies in the Field,* that the notion of international humanitarian assistance (or aid) began to appear in an institutionalized manner. At that time, wartime relief consisted exclusively of what is today known as "humanitarian assistance," namely, "relief operations to save and preserve life in emergencies or their immediate aftermath."[5] As shown by the language of the resolution that created the International Red Cross and Red Crescent Movement, the national Red Cross committees were initially designed to provide emergency assistance to the armies to which they were attached ("their respective armies"), and were acting under military command when deployed on the battlefield.[6] This framework was only natural at that time, since the vast majority of the direct casualties of war were military personnel, as described in 1862 by Henry Dunant in *Un souvenir de Solférino.* Naturally, the notion of humanitarian space was a non-issue then.

In time, armed forces developed their own medical units, which are entitled to, and do, use the red cross and red crescent emblems. Red Cross entities increasingly, and eventually almost exclusively, focused on providing humanitarian assistance to civilian victims of wars.[7] Indeed, as subsequent historical developments progressively reversed the proportion of military versus civilian deaths from that prevailing in the nineteenth century to the situation today, when it is commonly estimated that approximately 80 percent of all casualties of war are non-combatants,[8] independent humanitarian relief organizations were almost naturally drawn to focus their aid on civilians. It was the same increasing proportion of civilian casualties that, after reaching the astounding figures of the Second World War – 47.2 million civilian deaths, or 65 percent of all casualties – finally led to the adoption by the international community of the *Fourth Geneva Convention* of 1949 on the protection of the civilian population,[9] and to the emergence of modern international human rights law with the 1948 *Universal Declaration of Human Rights* (UDHR).[10] Naturally, humanitarian relief agencies had begun providing assistance to the civilian population and civilians caught in wars long before the adoption of these instruments, but these postwar legal developments – or at least the *Fourth Geneva Convention* – imposed strong legal obligations upon states to provide and to allow the provision of humanitarian assistance to civilians who were victims of armed conflicts. From the perspective of public international law, the *Fourth Geneva Convention* is therefore the first legal foundation of some form of humanitarian space, as will be shown below.

Institutionalization of International Disaster Relief

Besides the normative development of providing international legal protection to civilians in wartime and peacetime, and the change in the beneficiaries of the international aid provided by charitable organizations, the second half of the twentieth century also saw a sharp increase in the number of actors that seek to provide humanitarian assistance to civilians. Relief organizations also began to focus significantly on natural disasters from the 1960s onward, especially through the work of the International Federation of Red Cross and Red Crescent Societies (IFRC) and the UN. Regarding the division of labour between the various actors involved in international disaster relief at that time, it is noteworthy that, in its first resolution on international disaster relief, the UN General Assembly noted its "readiness to be at the disposal of international NGOs concerned with emergency relief to assist them in pursuing the question of co-ordination."[11] In 1965, the position of the UN was therefore to merely make its agencies available to already existing relief organizations, particularly the Red Cross/Red Crescent Movement. In contrast, the UN's philosophy today is that international NGOs be coordinated by the UN, as discussed below, with respect to integrated missions. These changes played a significant role in shaping today's humanitarian space debate, mainly with respect to *who* delivers humanitarian aid but also concerning *how* humanitarian aid is delivered. Regarding the latter, it is important to mention the landmark adoption in 1995 of the Code of Conduct for the International Red Cross and Red Crescent Movement and NGOs in Disaster Relief.[12]

Institutionalization of International Development Aid

Another aspect crucial to understanding the humanitarian space debate is the emergence of the notion of international development as a separate idea in the postwar era, especially during the decolonization period.[13] International development has allowed the involvement of state and state-controlled/influenced actors in the delivery of aid to civilians, mainly through the work of the UN, the Bretton Woods institutions, and other intergovernmental bodies.[14] Today, many thousands of institutions – some of which are linked to states while others are independent – are involved in international development work all over the world and focus their efforts on various pillars, such as human rights, poverty reduction, the rule of law, education, the condition of women, elections, and so on.

The distinction between humanitarian assistance (whether wartime or disaster-related), rehabilitation work, and international development is a pivotal variable regarding the "who" and the "how" of the humanitarian space equation, introduced above. Through their proliferation and professionalization after 1945, international NGOs refined the conceptual foundations of humanitarian assistance as applicable to both armed conflicts and disasters, based on the principles of humanity, impartiality, independence, and non-discrimination.[15] NGOs further postulated that humanitarian assistance must remain devoid of any and all politicization in order to respond solely to the humanitarian needs of the victims.[16] As will be seen in greater detail in the next section, these principles of humanitarian assistance find their origin in international humanitarian law and Red Cross law. They were, however, never imported as legal principles into the field of international development, in which traditional "humanitarian" organizations, such as the Red Cross/Red Crescent Movement, CARE International, and others, found themselves increasingly involved. Concurrently, international development institutions and states became more and more involved in war-affected and disaster-affected countries during and after the period of decolonization. The need for the conceptual blending of the two fields – emergency relief and development – was expressed in 1991 by the UN General Assembly, which stated: "There is a clear relationship between emergency, rehabilitation and development. In order to ensure a smooth transition from relief to rehabilitation and development, emergency assistance should be provided in ways that will be supportive of recovery and long-term development. Thus, emergency measures should be seen as a step towards long-term development."[17]

This continuum of international aid – emergency, rehabilitation, development – is crucial to understanding the humanitarian space debate. Instead of attempting to foster the emergence of international legal principles for international development work in order, *inter alia*, to replicate key humanitarian principles in this field, NGOs that became also involved in development work have tried from the 1990s onwards to protect their own sphere of action, especially from political and military interference, based on principles of action that had been developed for humanitarian assistance proper. This is what was referred to at the beginning of this chapter as a change in focus from "activities" to "institutions" in the humanitarian space debate.

This chapter does not allow for extensive analysis on the lack of specific legal normativity in international development assistance, which is ultimately governed by public international law, as indicated below. It must be underscored, however, that the legal imbalance regarding *how* and *by whom* humanitarian aid and international development work should be conducted occupies a significant part of the current humanitarian space dispute in which organizations involved in both humanitarian aid and development are caught. As Cornish pointedly observed:

> Unfortunately by questioning the politicisation of aid and the notion of shared goals (commonly ascribed) amongst all 3D [defence, diplomacy, and development] actors, humanitarians are now seen as obstructionist and antiquated by the political and military communities. Multi-mandate organizations are caught in this paradox, as entities committed both to providing relief (according to independent humanitarian principles) and carrying out development programming which can be seen as supporting the political interests of host governments and/or of donor governments.[18]

The Changing Role of Military Actors

The contemporary debate about humanitarian space is also informed by the international military interventions of the twentieth century and by fundamental changes in the nature of warfare in general. These have resulted, among other things, in increasing overlaps between the functions of militaries and those that were traditionally the domain of NGOs. The first notable step in this direction was the involvement of domestic military forces in international "humanitarian missions," which were gradually systematized and organized from 1956 onward under the aegis of peacekeeping and peace enforcement missions under the UN Charter. Originally consisting of the monitoring of ceasefire agreements or other similar tasks by military personnel under the UN with the consent of the host state,[19] post–Cold War UN peacekeeping missions received increasingly robust mandates and crystallized into modern peace enforcement. Of great significance was the addition of humanitarian components to peace enforcement mandates, mainly to protect the delivery of humanitarian aid to populations in need while supporting the work of the UN and other humanitarian agencies.[20]

The trend towards inclusion of humanitarian components in multinational peace enforcement missions was further strengthened during the 1990s, particularly in the cases of Somalia[21] and Rwanda.[22] Eventually, this led to the concept of UN integrated missions, which was further refined in 2000 by the *Report of the Panel on United Nations Peace Operations,* also known as the Brahimi Report.[23] The principal goal of the proposed Integrated Mission Task Forces (IMTFs) was to coordinate the activities of complex UN missions[24] in the field of "political analysis, military operations, civilian police, electoral assistance, human rights, development, humanitarian assistance, refugees and displaced persons, public information, logistics, finance and personnel recruitment, among others."[25] Today, the United Nations Stabilization Mission in Haiti (MINUSTAH) and the United Nations Organization Mission in the Democratic Republic of the Congo (MONUC) are prime examples of such integrated missions.[26]

From the perspective of independent humanitarian agencies and NGOs, humanitarian aid in the context of integrated missions has been reduced to merely one component of the UN rehabilitation and development efforts. As such, humanitarian aid faces serious risks of being used and instrumentalized to achieve the political (and possibly military) goals of the mission at the peril of humanitarian principles. It is therefore not surprising that the UNOCHA defines "humanitarian operating environment" without making any reference to the independence of humanitarian assistance, as recalled by Daniel Thürer.[27] It is partly for this reason, and in order to safeguard its own independence of action, that the ICRC does not wish to participate fully in UN integrated missions.[28]

This is not to say that the notion of humanitarian space is not an important aspect of integrated missions from the perspective of the UN. Indeed, in
a 2005 report entitled *Humanitarian Response Review* led by Jan Egeland,
an independent commission observed:

> The UN Integrated Mission model does not take adequately into account
> humanitarian concerns and represents a challenge for a more inclusive hu-
> manitarian system. In that sense and as a minimum requirement to be met,
> when Integrated Missions are established, it is essential that the DSRSG
> [Deputy Special Representative of the Secretary General] for Humanitarian
> Affairs and Development be empowered to *ensure that humanitarian space
> is preserved* and the humanitarian principles of independence, impartiality
> and neutrality are consistently upheld. For the humanitarians, the challen-
> ges revolve around creating and protecting the necessary humanitarian
> space *and preserving the principles of humanitarian imperatives in a polit-
> ically charged environment* [emphasis added].[29]

As indicated in the introduction of this chapter, however, the numerous
calls for the safeguarding of humanitarian space[30] made by the UN are addressed to governments that are the recipients of the assistance, and are not
meant to protect NGOs from international politics and developmental doctrines and interference. In other words, the UN's notion of humanitarian
space is as a sphere of UN-coordinated humanitarian assistance activities,
rather than the recognition that NGOs have the right to be free from political interference from the UN or other intergovernmental agencies.

Regarding international disaster relief, the Egeland report led to the creation of "clusters" of humanitarian actors acting under the direction of lead
agencies with the goal of increasing aid coordination. The fact that the
International Federation of Red Cross and Red Crescent Societies was
chosen as the lead agency for emergency shelter relief in natural disasters
was a positive step for the proponents of non-politicized humanitarian action. Extending the invitation to NGOs increased their input and participation in the cluster mechanism and was also positive. On the other hand,
all the other cluster leads are UN agencies,[31] and much remains to be seen in
terms of implementation of the reform as a whole. This is so especially regarding the coordination of humanitarian assistance in armed conflicts and
regarding the relationship between UN agencies and NGOs. In any event, it
is certain that, as recognized by the UN Secretary-General in 2007, the
"drive towards integration often raises concerns over conflicting mandates,

in particular in the area of humanitarian space and neutrality, which have yet to be adequately or consistently addressed."[32]

At roughly the same time as the UN's move towards integrated missions (from 2000 onward), military and political actors began regarding the provision of assistance to civilians as a component of the "Three Block War" through a domestic rather than international approach to military action. This notion was advanced by US Marine General Charles Krulak in 1999 to describe how, in the same mission, soldiers may be required to conduct full-scale military actions, peacekeeping operations, and humanitarian relief.[33] In this concept of a Three Block War, military "humanitarian" relief operations would, *inter alia,* focus on gathering intelligence in order to increase the security of the soldiers and thereby facilitate the fulfillment of the military mission, rather than being guided solely by humanitarian principles. From the perspective of independent humanitarian agencies, the notion of Three Block War is comparable to the more recent Canadian approach referred to as "3D" (defence, diplomacy, and development).[34] Such an approach articulates foreign actions in war-affected countries in a coordinated manner, thereby instrumentalizing each of the components to pursue a broader goal that is rooted more in politicized – and often military-led – development than humanitarian assistance proper.[35] Both the Three Block War and 3D doctrines take place within the wider, controversial framework of humanitarian interventions, which was conceptualized in the notion of the "Responsibility to Protect" in late 2001.[36] Similarly, both doctrines subsume humanitarian and development aid provided by international NGOs within the wider political agenda of peacebuilding, often in the name of aid coordination. This has a direct bearing on the humanitarian space debate and, for many actors, constitutes the debate's very heart.

It is in this complex international environment that the humanitarian space debate rages. The debate occurs within a spectrum that includes two extremities: at one end, the view that humanitarian aid should be solely guided by humanitarian considerations and delivered by "humanitarian" organizations; and at the other end, the postulate that, in order to achieve peace and conflict prevention, humanitarian aid must be integrated into a holistic political and military approach linked to peacebuilding and development. As alluded to, not only is this debate about which actors should be involved in international aid but it also concerns the manner in which international aid is delivered. The debate transcends humanitarian assistance proper and applies to both rehabilitation and development aid. In the context of this shift in focus from activities to actors, NGOs maintain that the increased politicization of the international aid continuum results in a decrease of security for international NGOs because they are now increasingly associated with politicized actors.

This chapter does not pretend to offer ready solutions to the very complex policy issues at stake.[37] Rather, the next section will focus on rules and principles of public international law that help to delineate the legal contours of the humanitarian space debate. It will seek to determine whether the very notion of humanitarian space is in any way supported by public international law, and it will also explore the legal elements of two main aspects of the humanitarian space debate: *who* may be involved in humanitarian assistance, and *how* it may be provided. As will be seen, states must respect a certain form of humanitarian space for the benefit of "impartial humanitarian organizations" – albeit of an uncertain content – in armed conflicts and other situations. Conversely, aside from the application of international human rights law, "hard law" is mostly silent outside situations of armed conflict and natural disasters, and yields to "soft law" rules.

Humanitarian Aid and International Law: Who and How?

Despite the ever-increasing and often very positive influence of international civil society on the development and implementation of public international law, the latter remains a state-centred body of law, which directly binds, first and foremost, state actors.[38] The most relevant fields of public international law that come into play with respect to the humanitarian space question, and which are examined in the present section, are IHL, Red Cross law, United Nations law, and international human rights law (IHRL). As seen below, each of these fields can be used to delineate a portion of the legal contours of a certain form of humanitarian space.

International Humanitarian Law

IHL applies in situations of international and non-international armed conflicts. Under this body of law, it is the parties to the conflict that have the duty to provide humanitarian aid to civilians and the civilian population under their power.[39] The source of such an obligation varies depending on whether an armed conflict is a military occupation, another form of international armed conflict, or a non-international armed conflict.

In situations of military occupation, this obligation first arose from Article 43 of the 1907 *Hague Convention IV*,[40] which provides that the occupying power (the state) "shall take all the measures in his power to restore, and ensure, as far as possible, public order and safety, while respecting, unless absolutely prevented, the laws in force in the country." It is hard to deny that, in case of need, providing humanitarian assistance will be necessary to ensure the safety of the population under occupation. This obligation to provide humanitarian assistance during military occupation was further developed with more specificity in Article 55 of the *Fourth Geneva Convention* of 1949. It provides that "[t]o the fullest extent of the means available to it, the Occupying Power has the duty of ensuring the food and medical supplies of the population"; this was extended to clothing, bedding, means of shelter, and other supplies essential to the survival of the civilian population with the adoption in 1977 of Protocol I, Additional to the *Geneva Conventions* of 1949 (Protocol I).[41]

For international armed conflicts other than military occupation, Protocol I also specifies that relief actions "shall be undertaken" when the civilian population is not adequately provided with supplies essential to its survival.[42] Although this language is somewhat ambiguous, the bearers of this legal obligation can only be the states that are parties to an international conflict covered by Protocol I. This obliges states to either deliver the aid themselves or, should they be unable, allow other actors to provide surrogate assistance.

With respect to non-international armed conflicts in general, the obligation to provide humanitarian relief to the population is not explicitly contained in Common Article 3 of the *Geneva Conventions*, but it has been convincingly argued that this obligation forms part of the principle of humane treatment that is applicable to this type of armed conflict.[43] With respect to non-international armed conflicts where Protocol II, Additional to the *Geneva Conventions* of 1949 (Protocol II) is applicable, Article 18 provides that impartial relief actions "shall be undertaken" if the civilian population is suffering undue hardship owing to a lack of the supplies essential to its survival. As specified in the authoritative ICRC *Commentary* on this provision, "[s]uch external aid is complementary; it is only provided when the responsible authorities can no longer meet the basic necessities of the civilian population whose survival is in jeopardy."[44]

Therefore, not only is there an obligation (albeit not an absolute one) for states involved in international and non-international armed conflicts to provide humanitarian assistance to civilians in their power but this obligation is accompanied by a *right* to do so. Consequently, for the purpose of the "who" component of the humanitarian space debate, IHL cannot be used as a basis for arguing that military and other political actors are prohibited from delivering humanitarian relief or carrying out related activities. This field of public international law says exactly the opposite.

Nevertheless, states must discharge this obligation in accordance with the fundamental IHL principles of humane treatment and "without any adverse distinction based, in particular, on race, religion, or political opinion."[45] This significantly impacts the "how" element of the humanitarian space debate. Protocol I specifies that the relief provided must also be "humanitarian and impartial in character."[46] This was later confirmed by the International Court of Justice, which specified that genuine humanitarian aid must comply with the Red Cross principles of humanity, impartiality, and non-discrimination; aid that failed to comply with these principles would be considered tantamount to unlawful intervention in the recipient state's domestic affairs.[47] It follows that any distribution of humanitarian aid by military actors that is conditioned, for example, on the provision of military "intelligence" by the recipients, or is conducted for any reason other than purely humanitarian considerations and in a discriminatory manner, is a breach of international humanitarian law and of the principle of non-intervention found in public international law.

In addition, since this obligation to distribute humanitarian assistance in an impartial manner rests upon parties to the conflict and High Contracting Parties to the *Geneva Conventions* as a whole, these parties also have the obligation to ensure that the agents they choose to implement it comply with the principle. In circumstances where a given state knows or should know that its military forces have distributed humanitarian assistance in a discriminatory manner or for reasons based on considerations other than the needs of the victims, it has a legal obligation not to entrust humanitarian functions to that part of the state apparatus. IHL would be similarly breached if a given state were to direct humanitarian organizations to provide their aid in a way contrary to the principle of impartiality, for example, by subjecting funds allocated to NGOs in such a manner. This legal protection against the politicization – and enforced politicization – of humanitarian action is a crucial component of the legal contours of humanitarian space.

Interestingly, this right to ensure that the population is provided with supplies essential to its survival is not exclusive to states pursuant to IHL. Indeed, the general principle is that the ICRC and other impartial humanitarian organizations are also granted such a right under IHL. Pursuant to Common Article 9/9/9/10 of the *Geneva Conventions*, "[t]he provisions of the present Convention constitute no obstacle to the humanitarian activities which the International Committee of the Red Cross or any other impartial humanitarian organization *may, subject to the consent of the Parties* to the conflict concerned, undertake for the protection of civilian persons and for their relief" (emphasis added).

In situations of non-international armed conflicts, IHL similarly provides that "an impartial humanitarian body, such as the International Committee of the Red Cross, may offer its services to the parties to the conflict."[48] This right of impartial relief organizations to humanitarian initiative is also an important aspect of the concept of humanitarian space.

Although humanitarian organizations possess the right to offer their services in international and non-international armed conflicts, this does not necessarily mean that the parties to the conflict have the corresponding obligation to accept such offers of services. In fact, it follows from the above-quoted article that the right vested in impartial humanitarian organizations did not carry a general obligation to the same extent as for states upon adoption of the 1949 *Geneva Conventions*. Nevertheless, and already in 1949, this general principle contained exceptions that, in some cases, prevailed over the general principle as a matter of *lex specialis*. This was the case in situations of military occupation, where Article 63 of the *Fourth Geneva Convention* specified that relief organizations in occupied territories "shall" be allowed to pursue their activities in accordance with "the Red Cross principles," subject to "temporary and exceptional measures imposed for urgent reasons of security." Making this even clearer, the *Fourth Geneva Convention* also stated:

> If the whole or part of the population of an occupied territory is inadequately supplied, the Occupying Power shall agree to relief schemes on behalf of the said population ... Such schemes, which may be undertaken either by States or by impartial humanitarian organizations such as the International Committee of the Red Cross, shall consist, in particular, of the provision of consignments of foodstuffs, medical supplies and clothing.[49]

In situations of military occupation, the *Geneva Conventions* therefore provide a relatively wide space to those impartial humanitarian organizations that have offered their services, even obliging states themselves to guarantee the protection of the relief items.[50] This humanitarian space is not absolute, however. First, it is restricted to impartial humanitarian organizations, specifically those that pursue their activities in accordance with the

Red Cross principles.[51] Other types of organizations do not belong to this humanitarian space created by the *Geneva Conventions* for situations of military occupation. Second, the parties to the conflict always retain a certain "right of control," that is, a right to search the relief consignments, to regulate their passage, and to ensure that they are to be used by the population in need.[52] This is the case even where they are obliged to accept impartial humanitarian assistance provided by NGOs.

Outside the context of military occupation, the requirement that humanitarian relief activities be agreed upon by states pursuant to Common Article 9/9/9/10 of the four *Geneva Conventions* was significantly softened by international practice during the second half of the twentieth century. The departure point of this evolution was the development of the positive right that civilians have to receive the relief consignments sent to them. Although such a right to receive humanitarian assistance is still debated by a minority of scholars,[53] it is clear to this author that, under Article 23 of the *Fourth Geneva Convention,* parties to a conflict have a general obligation to allow the free passage of all consignments of medical and hospital supplies.[54] This embryo of the right to receive humanitarian relief in situations of international armed conflict was strengthened by Article 70 of Protocol I, which specifies that impartial and humanitarian relief actions "shall" be undertaken if the civilian population is not adequately provided with supplies essential to its survival, although subject to the consent of the concerned parties to the conflict. This right is also available in non-international armed conflicts pursuant to Article 18(2) of Protocol II. Furthermore, in all instances, it was agreed by the states that drafted the Additional Protocols of 1977 that a "Party refusing its agreement [to impartial relief activities] must do so for valid reasons, not for arbitrary or capricious ones."[55] Therefore, regardless of whether a party is in a position to comply with its own obligation to provide humanitarian assistance to the population, IHL stipulates that states have the parallel obligation to implement the civilian population's right to receive humanitarian relief that is indispensable to its survival. This includes allowing impartial relief organizations to conduct humanitarian activities in favour of this population under certain conditions. Nevertheless, only impartial *and* humanitarian organizations can be part of this humanitarian space, whether in the context of international or non-international armed conflicts.[56]

With the passage of time and the increasing role of impartial humanitarian organizations in armed conflicts after 1977, the obligation to allow the passage of relief supplies continued to be strengthened. In an ICRC study carried out in 2004, this obligation was found to be part of customary international humanitarian law, with the specification that the possibility for states to refuse the passage of humanitarian relief must not be exercised arbitrarily.[57] The study further confirmed that, during both international and non-international armed conflicts, "[i]f it is established that a civilian population is threatened with starvation and a humanitarian organization which provides relief on an impartial and non-discriminatory basis is able to remedy the situation, a party is obliged to give consent."[58] Such a legal obligation was also recently confirmed by the International Court of Justice. The court decided, in the context of an international armed conflict in August 2008, that both the Russian Federation and Georgia were under a legal obligation to "facilitate, and refrain from placing any impediment to, humanitarian assistance in support of the rights to which the local population are entitled under the International Convention on the Elimination of All Forms of Racial Discrimination."[59] In addition, the *Rome Statute of the International Criminal Court* recognizes that "wilfully impeding relief supplies as provided for under the Geneva Conventions" is a war crime that can be prosecuted before the court.[60] Furthermore, when calculated to bring about the destruction of a part of the population, the intentional deprivation of humanitarian assistance amounts to a crime against humanity.[61] In circumstances where civilians are threatened with starvation, the possibility for territorial states – and other parties to the conflict – to withhold consent to the provision of humanitarian aid by impartial humanitarian organizations does not exist. I submit that this is also the case in circumstances where other basic needs of civilians are not adequately met, that is, even in the absence of possible starvation.

A final component of the humanitarian space concept covered by IHL is the obligation of states to ensure the respect and protection of relief personnel, as expressly provided under Article 71 of Protocol I,[62] and as recently identified as forming part of customary international law.[63] In addition, UN relief personnel and peacekeepers who do not take part in a peace enforcement mission under Chapter VII of the UN Charter are further protected by the 1994 *Convention on the Safety of United Nations and Associated Personnel* as well as by customary international law.

In summary, IHL does provide support for impartial humanitarian action not conducted by states during armed conflicts, but it also contains important limitations. In particular, states that are parties to armed conflicts always retain a right of control concerning the nature and destination of the assistance. In addition, impartial humanitarian organizations must comply with the security requirements of the party in whose territory they are carrying out their activities.[64] Perhaps more important, the assistance provided by NGOs, like that provided by states, must be both humanitarian and impartial in order to benefit from the protection afforded by IHL. I submit that these requirements are also applicable to non-international armed conflicts by analogy. Provided that the foregoing conditions are met, impartial and humanitarian actors enjoy a legal protection against the enforced politicization of humanitarian activities by state actors.

Finally, states must not only respect this humanitarian space but also equally ensure its effective existence on the ground as a result of their obligation to "ensure the respect" for IHL.[65] This includes the obligation of states that are parties to an international or non-international armed conflict[66] to actively monitor the unfolding of the conflict to ensure that the IHL-based humanitarian space is observed; to give necessary orders for the same purpose; to monitor the execution of the orders; and to resort to penal measures to enforce IHL if applicable.[67] For their part, states that are not parties to an armed conflict have, at the very least, the obligation to exert diplomatic pressure to ensure respect for the IHL-based humanitarian space, particularly for the protection against the enforced politicization of international aid.[68]

Red Cross Law

The first set of norms adopted to guide humanitarian action in disaster situations are the Fundamental Principles of the Red Cross and Red Crescent proclaimed by the Twentieth International Conference of the Red Cross held in Vienna in 1965. These principles, incorporated into the Statutes of the International Red Cross and Red Crescent Movement in 1986, are the principles of humanity, impartiality, neutrality, independence, voluntary service, unity, and universality. The principles are applicable in all situations, including within and outside of international and non-international armed conflicts.

These principles are legally binding not only on the components of the Red Cross and Red Crescent Movement but also upon states through their incorporation into treaty law,[69] as is the case in situations of military occupation, as indicated above.[70] Given their incorporation into the statutes of the movement, these principles are also binding upon the states party to the

Geneva Conventions. The manner in which the principles are binding is explained by Bugnion:

> [I]n accepting the Movement's new Statutes, the States party to the Geneva Conventions explicitly undertook to cooperate with the Movement's components in accordance with the Conventions, the Statutes and the resolutions of the International Conference.[71]
>
> ...
>
> Given the mandatory force of the principles for members of the Movement and their place in "Red Cross law" on the one hand, and the participation of governments in the adoption of the principles on the other, it is obvious that, quite apart from any treaty obligation, *States are bound to allow Red Cross and Red Crescent bodies to act in accordance with the principles and to insist on this right being respected. If this were not the case, government support for the adoption of the principles would be meaningless* [emphasis added].[72]

It follows that states are also bound by the declaration that international disaster relief must be conducted by the Red Cross and Red Crescent Movement in accordance with the Fundamental Principles,[73] and are therefore obliged to avoid politicizing international disaster relief. Under Red Cross law, such a legal obligation is, however, valid only with respect to the International Red Cross and Red Crescent Movement, and does not extend to other NGOs for the purpose of the humanitarian space debate.

The principles of humanity and impartiality also constitute important components of the 1995 Code of Conduct for the International Red Cross and Red Crescent Movement and NGOs in Disaster Relief, which has so far been signed by 462 NGOs as well as a significant number of states, including Canada.[74] These principles certainly play a role in tracing the contours of the international humanitarian space. The Sphere Project also developed a charter that expresses the same ideas as the code of conduct and is applicable during both disasters and armed conflicts.[75] Although not legally binding upon states, these codes of conduct nonetheless constitute very important best practices (or "soft law") that, from a conceptual point of view, inform the content of humanitarian space.[76]

Finally, one should take note of the ambitious and much-needed project launched in 2001 by the International Federation of Red Cross and Red

Crescent Societies on "international disaster response laws,"[77] which "seeks to address how legal frameworks at the international, regional and national levels, can best address the operational challenges in international disaster relief operations carried out by States, international organisations, NGOs, military forces and private companies."[78] The outcome of this project will be very important to further refining the borders of humanitarian space in disaster relief operations.

For the purpose of the humanitarian space debate, Red Cross law therefore serves two functions. First, it obliges states to respect and ensure that the Red Cross principles are upheld in natural disaster situations. The fact that humanity and impartiality form part of the Red Cross principles confirms that the legal protection against the politicization and enforced politicization of humanitarian relief that was found to ensue from IHL also applies in disaster situations. Second, the Red Cross code of conduct serves as a reference in terms of how non-governmental and state institutions jointly view the principles that must guide international disaster relief, which includes their mutual interaction.

United Nations Law

Elements of humanitarian space can also be found in UN resolutions adopted by both the General Assembly and the Security Council. For example, the influence of the 1965 Fundamental Principles of the Red Cross is seen in Resolution 2816 entitled *Assistance in Cases of Natural Disaster and Other Disaster Situations*, adopted in 1971 at the General Assembly's Twenty-Sixth Session. This resolution dealt with disaster-related humanitarian assistance and established a Disaster Relief Co-ordinator. Interestingly, this resolution – which is not legally binding on state members – leaves the impression that the relationship prevailing at the time between UN agencies and international NGOs was at arm's length. This is supported by the Disaster Relief Co-ordinator's express task to "co-ordinate United Nations assistance with assistance given by intergovernmental and NGOs, in particular by the International Red Cross."[79]

This arrangement, however, was reversed in 1991 when the UN General Assembly established the Office for the Coordination of Humanitarian Affairs, on the premise that "[t]he United Nations has a central and unique role to play in providing leadership and coordinating the efforts of the international community to support the affected countries [in international disaster relief]."[80] Although this seriously affects the independence of NGOs in humanitarian relief, the resolution nevertheless reinforces the principle that "humanitarian assistance must be provided in accordance with the principles of humanity, neutrality and impartiality."[81] The resolution thus constitutes an important normative benchmark for state-led humanitarianism, whether inside or outside the context of armed conflicts.[82] Since the same resolution, however, emphasizes that "emergency assistance must be provided in ways that will be supportive of recovery and long-term development," it somewhat diminishes the importance of the principle of impartiality. Despite the fact that the resolution is not legally binding upon state members, it has produced very concrete effects on the ground and has led to the development of the concept of integrated missions. Additionally, as noted earlier, it has helped strengthen the UN's leadership role in coordinating humanitarian assistance, including the assistance provided by NGOs.

Apart from elements of institutional independence for NGOs that may or may not characterize humanitarian space from the perspective of the UN, the General Assembly and the Security Council have condemned impediments to humanitarian relief actions on numerous occasions,[83] regardless of whether the relief was provided by states or NGOs, and have reiterated the obligation to grant civilians access to relief supplies.[84] The Security Council's Revised Aide-Mémoire on the Protection of Civilians in Armed Conflict of January 2009 also recalls the "prohibition against wilfully impeding relief supplies as provided for under international humanitarian law," and "the responsibility of parties to armed conflict to respect, protect and meet the basic needs of civilian populations within their effective control."[85] In this regard, it must be recalled that UN Security Council decisions are binding upon members of the UN pursuant to the UN Charter[86] and take precedence over other international obligations of member states.[87] Despite the observation made earlier in this chapter that, for the UN, the humanitarian space is in fact its own space in which it coordinates the actions of NGOs, the foregoing resolutions on unimpeded humanitarian access and the obligation to provide assistance to victims benefit all "humanitarian and United Nations personnel."[88] This reinforces humanitarian space as traditionally conceived by independent humanitarian actors.

As mentioned above, UN law also contains foundational references to humanitarian space in terms of *how* humanitarian aid should be provided. In particular, the General Assembly adopted the principle in Resolution 46/182 of 1991 that "[h]umanitarian assistance [of the United Nations System] must be provided in accordance with the principles of humanity,

neutrality and impartiality."[89] Although these three principles are not defined in the resolution, there is no reason to believe that they should be
interpreted differently from the Red Cross principles.

International Human Rights Law

The connection between the humanitarian space debate and IHRL has seldom been made.[90] This is largely explained by the fact that the debate started within the context of armed conflicts, where IHL is the *lex specialis* and
of primary – though not exclusive – relevance.[91] Yet, the question of *how*
development aid should comply with human rights norms and standards
has been explored in depth under the umbrella of the "rights-based approach to development" during the past decade.[92] Canada has even created
an international first by enshrining the link between human rights and development in its domestic legal system.[93] The argument, which I share, that
international development assistance must be provided in compliance with
IHRL has important repercussions for humanitarian space, as will be seen
below. In addition, IHRL provides an important normative framework within which, arguably, all types of international aid must be provided and distributed by states, regardless of whether the relief in question qualifies as
emergency, rehabilitation, or development assistance. This directly impacts
the content of humanitarian space.

Similar to the IHL principle of impartiality, the main principle in this
respect is that every type of international aid must be provided without
discrimination. This is the result of the combination of the principle of non-
discrimination and the rights to life and to food,[94] all of which are non-
derogable.[95] When one admits, as does the Committee on Economic, Social
and Cultural Rights and other authors,[96] that the human right to food (and
to life) conceptually implies that the state on whose territory populations in
need are located is obliged to give consent, and not to place impediments,
to impartial humanitarian actions offered by states or by independent humanitarian actors to address this human right in a surrogate manner, this
obligation must be complied with without discrimination by that state as a
result of the right to non-discrimination resulting, *inter alia,* from the 1966
International Covenant on Civil and Political Rights and the 1966 *International Covenant on Economic, Social and Cultural Rights.*[97]

IHRL also sets parameters regarding the "who" component of the humanitarian space debate. For the territorial state on whose territory humanitarian aid, recovery assistance, or development assistance is being provided,
there exists an international legal obligation to allow other actors to focus

on the fulfillment and implementation of rights, and to refrain from placing any discriminatory impediments on such work. As noted above, this was confirmed by the International Court of Justice with respect to the conflict between the Russian Federation and Georgia in August 2008.[98] Under the doctrine of positive obligations,[99] a legal consequence of this decision is that the right to non-discrimination provides that actors whose programs and projects focus on the fulfillment of human rights in a non-discriminatory manner must be given the necessary space by the state on whose territory their work is conducted.

Other states, including those implementing or sponsoring programs and projects seeking to provide humanitarian aid, rehabilitation assistance, or development aid on the territory of another state, are also under a legal obligation to comply with the right to non-discrimination. This results from the assisting states' own human rights obligations and also apply when any of the assisting states' components exercise public powers normally reserved for the territorial state, with the latter's consent, at its invitation, or with its acquiescence.[100] In addition, it may be argued that, in the conduct of their international relations, states must not induce other states to violate IHRL by supporting, in particular, the politicization of any form of international aid or any other discriminatory form of aid. This flows, in particular, from UN General Assembly Resolution 2625 of 24 October 1970, which expressed customary international law by declaring that "States shall co-operate in the promotion of universal respect for, and observance of, human rights and fundamental freedoms for all, and in the elimination of all forms of racial discrimination and all forms of religious intolerance."[101]

Conclusion

As demonstrated in this chapter, the notion of humanitarian space is fluid. When the concept was originally developed in the early 1990s, humanitarian space was concerned with humanitarian assistance proper, and sought to maximize the victim's access to aid based on the principles of humanity and impartiality. With the passage of time, the proliferation of actors involved in the delivery of international aid, and these actors' working methods, the notion of humanitarian space has increasingly been used in different ways and for different purposes. Today, NGOs mainly use it to protect their independence of action in all aspects of their international work (emergency, rehabilitation, and development). From their perspective, the humanitarian space is really an "NGO space." For its part, the UN uses humanitarian space to assert its role as the natural coordinator of international aid, which must be done through a continuum in which humanitarian assistance is only a fragment that must generally answer to wider peacebuilding considerations, particularly in the context of integrated missions. Despite this difference, all actors agree that humanitarian space should protect them from attacks as they carry out their duties, which are performed with different degrees of politicization.

Although containing no specific definition or rule regarding humanitarian space as an identifiable concept, public international law is useful for highlighting some elements of this space, mainly with respect to *by whom* and *how* humanitarian assistance may be delivered. If it is provided within the context of armed conflicts, international humanitarian law requires that any and all humanitarian assistance to civilians, including relief, rehabilitation, and development assistance, must be provided in accordance with the principles of humanity and impartiality – that is, such aid must be given solely on the basis of humanitarian needs and without discrimination. While states involved in armed conflicts have the obligation, and therefore the right, to provide humanitarian relief to the population in their power, impartial and humanitarian NGOs also have a relative right to carry out humanitarian activities and to offer assistance. In such cases, they must be protected and allowed to act independently from any interference, including from the politicization of aid. In certain circumstances, offers of surrogate humanitarian assistance shall be accepted by states, but humanitarian assistance that does not comply with the principles of humanity and impartiality is excluded from the humanitarian space created by IHL. States also have the obligation to respect and to ensure respect for the IHL-based humanitarian space.

Outside the context of armed conflicts, the legal situation is more fragmented. Although states have an international legal obligation to respect and to refrain from politicizing the disaster relief activities of the Red Cross and Red Crescent Movement, NGOs outside the movement are not covered by this legal obligation. For its part, UN (soft) law mixes the "who" and the "how" of humanitarian aid, and tends to confuse rather than coordinate actors. This field, however, holds promise for increasingly focusing the humanitarian space debate on the victims, with affirmation of their right to receive adequate assistance. Like IHL and Red Cross law, UN soft law recognizes that humanitarian aid must be provided in accordance with the principles of humanity and impartiality, although this is restricted to agencies of the UN system. Finally, IHRL obliges states to abide by the principle of non-discrimination in providing any type of international aid, and to allow actors involved in the delivery of aid to conduct their work in accordance with this principle. In certain circumstances, this implies that states must take positive measures to ensure this component of the humanitarian space. IHRL also provides some degree of protection against the enforced politicization of aid by donor and assisting states.

In short, both states and other actors have the right to provide international aid to populations in distress, and the former even have the obligation to accept such aid in certain circumstances. Regardless of the type of aid involved, it must be provided in accordance with the principles of humanity and impartiality, regardless of whether it is furnished by states or other actors. Public international law cannot be used to entertain the idea that certain types of actors have a greater legitimacy than others in providing international aid.

Although it is recognized that the independence of humanitarian action must be protected with respect to NGOs, the traditional divides between humanitarian aid, rehabilitation, and international development cannot be applied rigidly in today's world. Public international law offers only a partial answer to the question of how and by whom international aid can be delivered, and it does so in a very fragmented manner. Moreover, the actor-focused conception of humanitarian space is inadequate in situations when international aid must be delivered in situations where armed conflicts and international disasters are mixed, and where such situations require humanitarian, rehabilitation, and development aid, such as in tsunami-affected Sri Lanka and Indonesia from December 2004 onward.

For these reasons, it is essential to refocus the humanitarian space debate on *victims* rather than actors, and to articulate in a more comprehensive manner their right to international aid within the parameters set by the principles of humanity and impartiality, within and outside the context of armed conflicts. Significant efforts in this direction have already been made, including the International Institute of Humanitarian Law's 1993 Guiding Principles on the Right to Humanitarian Assistance, which focused particularly on the necessity to avoid "any political bias" in humanitarian assistance.[102] The Sphere Project's Humanitarian Charter of 2004 is also an interesting example of widely recognized standards that apply in armed conflicts and disasters,[103] not to mention the Code of Conduct for the International Red Cross and Red Crescent Movement and NGOs in Disaster Relief. Draft principles to be taken into account in the negotiation of a treaty on humanitarian assistance in situations of natural disaster were also proposed in 1998 by Hardcastle and Chua.[104] More recently, states have adopted substantive donor coordination initiatives, including the 2005 *Paris Declaration on Aid Effectiveness*, which was later construed within a human rights framework in particular by the Organisation for Economic Co-operation and Development (OECD) Development Assistance Committee, of which Canada is a member.[105] Together with the state-developed *Good Humanitarian Donorship* launched in 2003,[106] which recognizes the primacy of human rights, humanitarian law, and humanitarian imperatives in humanitarian assistance proper, the foregoing initiatives not only show an important amount of convergence among scholars, practitioners, and like-minded states in putting the interest of victims at the forefront of the humanitarian space debate, but also demonstrate that such a necessity must be based on well-established legal rules and principles whose sources lie in different fields of public international law. Yet, positive international law still carries a normative differential – or at the very least a fragmented normativity – between humanitarian assistance, disaster relief, and development aid that does not reflect realities on the ground where all these types of assistance often overlap or take place simultaneously.[107] Besides presenting a challenge for aid recipients, this dichotomy between international normativity and practice seriously hardens the humanitarian space debate and confuses all actors.

The time is ripe to propose the adoption of an international treaty to codify rights and obligations that together form an international legal corpus governing the delivery and reception of international aid of all forms – humanitarian, relief, and development assistance – by peoples in need. The humanitarian space belongs to them, rather than to governmental or non-governmental aid actors. It is in this spirit that the following draft treaty principles are submitted for discussion.

Draft Treaty Principles on Humanitarian Space

1 The following definitions apply to the present principles:

   (a) "International aid" consists of financial and other resources provided by States and other actors in another country, with a view to fulfilling the basic needs of individuals or to reduce their vulnerability. This includes emergency, recovery, rehabilitation, and development aid.
   (b) The "principle of humanity" is based on the desire to prevent and alleviate human suffering wherever it may be found. Its purpose is to protect life and health and to ensure respect for the human being.

This principle promotes mutual understanding, friendship, cooperation, and lasting peace among all peoples.

(c) The "principle of impartiality" means that no discrimination shall be made as to nationality, race, religious beliefs, class, political opinions, or any other ground in providing international aid. Decisions must be based on the necessity to relieve the suffering of individuals, being guided solely by their needs, and to give priority to the most urgent cases of distress.

2 Everyone has the right to have his human rights and freedoms respected, protected, and fulfilled, without any adverse distinction of a discriminatory nature, by States and other actors that have the power to affect them. In particular, everyone has the right to life and to be provided with adequate food, health, clothing, and housing, which constitute basic needs for every individual.

3 The State within whose jurisdiction an individual is has the primary obligation to provide for his basic needs.

4 When a State is unable or unwilling, for reasons related to an armed conflict, a disaster, or any other reason, to provide for the basic needs of individuals within its jurisdiction, that State shall consent to surrogate international aid provided by States or other actors, provided that such aid is offered and effectively provided on the basis of the principles of humanity and impartiality. Allowing surrogate aid does not relieve the State from its primary obligation as per principle 3.

5 All States undertake to take all positive and prohibitive measures available to protect and facilitate the work of those who engage in activities related to international aid that are compliant with the present principles. No one shall place impediments to international aid that is compliant with the present principles.

6 Any international aid shall be provided in compliance with applicable rules of international human rights and humanitarian law, and in particular in accordance with the principles of humanity and impartiality. In case of conflict, the rule that is the most favourable to the recipients of international aid shall prevail.

7 Anyone who commits an act that is aimed at or that results in placing impediments to international aid, or participates in such an act, commits an international crime and shall be prosecuted by a domestic court or by an international tribunal. States recognize universal jurisdiction to prosecute such crimes.

8	States shall cooperate to ensure respect of the present principles to the fullest possible extent.

9	States undertake to entrust the monitoring of the present principles to an independent and neutral body to be designated or created especially for that purpose. -

NOTES

1	Ulrike von Pilar, "Humanitarian Space Under Siege – Some Remarks from an Aid Agency's Perspective" (Background paper prepared for the symposium Europe and Humanitarian Aid – What Future? Learning from Crisis, Bad Neuenahr, 22-23 April 1999) at 4, online: Médecins Sans Frontières <http://www.aerzte-ohne-grenzen.de/>.

2	See Johanna Grombach Wagner, "An IHL/ICRC Perspective on 'Humanitarian Space'" *Humanitarian Exchange Magazine* (December 2005), online: Humanitarian Practice Network <http://www.odihpn.org/>.

3	"Glossary UN-CMCoord" (17 September 2008), online: UNOCHA <http://ochaonline.un.org/>.

4	For an in-depth study of the origins and historical activities of international NGOs, see, *e.g.*, Philippe Ryfman, "Non-Governmental Organizations: An Indispensable Player of Humanitarian Aid" (2007) 89 Int'l Rev. Red Cross 21; see also Peter Walker and Daniel G. Maxwell, *Shaping the Humanitarian World* (London: Taylor and Francis, 2008).

5	European Union, *Council Regulation No 1257/96 of 20 June 1996 Concerning Humanitarian Aid*, Preamble at para. 5. Article 1 of the regulation further specifies that "humanitarian aid shall comprise assistance, relief and protection operations on a non-discriminatory basis to help people in third countries, particularly the most vulnerable among them, and as a priority those in developing countries, victims of natural disasters, manmade crises, such as wars and outbreaks of fighting, or exceptional situations or circumstances comparable to natural or man-made disasters. It shall do so for the time needed to meet the humanitarian requirements resulting from these different situations." For its part, the United Nations High Commissioner for Refugees (UNHCR) Glossary provides the following: "'Humanitarian assistance' refers to assistance provided by humanitarian organizations for humanitarian purposes (*i.e.*, non-political, non-commercial, and non-military purposes)." See "Master Glossary of Terms" (June 2006), online: UNHCR <http://www.unhcr.org/>.

6	See arts. 5 and 6 of the *Resolutions of the Geneva International Conference* (26-29 October 1863), online: ICRC <http://www.icrc.org/>.

7	The exception is with respect to prisoners of war and other persons detained in relation to the hostilities, in the favour of whom the ICRC conducts various types of humanitarian activities on the basis of international humanitarian law.

8	For data on casualties resulting from armed conflicts, see in particular the Uppsala Conflict Data Program, online: Uppsala Universitet <http://www.ucdp.uu.se/>.

9	This convention was hardly the first attempt to develop an internationally binding instrument to protect the civilian victims of wars. Already in 1923 the International

Committee of the Red Cross had proposed to the 21st International Conference of the Red Cross the *Projet d'une Convention internationale réglant la situation des civils tombés à la guerre et au pouvoir de l'ennemi.* See François Bugnion, *Le Comité international de la Croix-Rouge et la protection des victimes de la guerre* (Geneva: Comité International de la Croix-Rouge, 1994) at 141.

10 Adopted under the format of a simple declaration of the UN General Assembly, the *Universal Declaration of Human Rights,* GA Res. 217(III), UN GAOR, 3d Sess., Supp. No. 13, UN Doc. A/810 (1948), was not as such legally binding upon states. Today, however, it is acknowledged that the principles it proclaims are binding upon all states of the international community, either by way of rules of customary international law or general principles of law. On the general nature of the declaration, see, *inter alia,* Malcolm N. Shaw, *International Law,* 5th ed. (Cambridge: Cambridge University Press, 2003) at 260; Quoc Dinh Nguyen, Patrick Daillier, and Alain Pellet, *Droit international public,* 7th ed. (Paris: LGDJ, 2002) at 660; P.R. Ghandhi, "The Universal Declaration of Human Rights at Fifty Years" (1998) 41 German Yearbook of International Law 206.

11 See *Assistance in Cases of Natural Disasters,* GA Res. 2034(XX), UN GAOR, UN Doc. A/Res/2034(XX) (1965).

12 Annex VI to the resolutions of the 26th International Conference of the Red Cross and Red Crescent, Geneva (1995), online: International Federation of Red Cross and Red Crescent Societies <http://www.ifrc.org/>.

13 For an example of a historical appraisal of international development, see Uma Kothari, ed., *A Radical History of Development Studies: Individuals, Institutions and Ideologies* (London: Zed Books, 2005).

14 International development programs are also conducted by a number of countries on a bilateral basis.

15 See in particular the *Code of Conduct: Principles of Conduct for the International Red Cross and Red Crescent Movement and NGOs in Disaster Relief,* adopted by the 26th International Conference of the Red Cross and Red Crescent, Geneva, 3-7 December 1995. As of 23 November 2007, the Code of Conduct had been signed by 433 international NGOs, in addition to being applicable to the almost 190 components of the International Red Cross and Red Crescent Movement. See "Annex VI: The Code of Conduct for the International Red Cross and Red Crescent Movement and NGOs in Disaster Relief," online: ICRC <http://www.icrc.org/eng/>.

16 These concepts were expressed for the first time internationally in 1965 with the adoption of the Fundamental Principles of the Red Cross and Red Crescent by the 20th International Conference of the Red Cross held in Vienna. These principles are humanity, impartiality, neutrality, independence, voluntary service, unity, and universality.

17 *Strengthening of the Coordination of Humanitarian Emergency Assistance of the United Nations,* UN GAOR, Annex to GA Res. 46/182, UN Doc. A/RES/46/182, (1991) at para. 9.

18 See Stephen Cornish, "No Room for Humanitarianism in 3D Policies: Have Forcible Humanitarian Interventions and Integrated Approaches Lost Their Way?" (2007) 10 Journal of Military and Strategic Studies 1 at 3. Cornish's article also contains a very

useful and interesting review of the interactions between international military actors and international NGOs in recent history, including in Iraq, Sierra Leone, Somalia, and Rwanda.

19 See, *e.g.*, Security Council Resolution 340 (1973), which established the second United Nations Emergency Force in order to supervise the ceasefire between Egyptian and Israeli forces; online: United Nations <http://www.un.org/en/documents/>.

20 The first such case was Security Council Resolution 761 (1992), which authorized "the Secretary-General to deploy immediately additional elements of the United Nations Protection Force to ensure the security and functioning of Sarajevo airport and the delivery of humanitarian assistance in accordance with his report of 6 June 1992" in Sarajevo and other parts of Bosnia-Herzegovina (at para. 1); online: United Nations <http://www.un.org/en/documents/>.

21 In its Resolution 794 (1992), the Security Council authorized "the Secretary-General and Member States cooperating to implement the offer referred to in paragraph 8 above to use all necessary means to establish as soon as possible a secure environment for humanitarian relief operations in Somalia" (at para. 10); online: United Nations <http://www.un.org/en/documents/>.

22 Security Council Resolution 925 (1994) mandated the United Nations Assistance Mission for Rwanda (UNAMIR) to "(a) Contribute to the security and protection of displaced persons, refugees and civilians at risk in Rwanda, including through the establishment and maintenance, where feasible, of secure humanitarian areas; and (b) Provide security and support for the distribution of relief supplies and humanitarian relief operations" (at para. 4); online: United Nations <http://www.un.org/en/documents/>.

23 *Report of the Panel on United Nations Peace Operations*, UN Doc. A/55/305, S/2000/809 (21 August 2000), online: United Nations <http://www.un.org/en/documents/> [Brahimi Report]. For a historical account of integrated missions, see in particular Espen Barth Eide, Anja Therese Kaspersen, Randolph Kent, and Karen von Hippel, *Report on Integrated Missions: Practical Perspectives and Recommendations* (Oslo: Norwegian Institute of International Affairs, 2005) at 10-12, online: ReliefWeb <http://reliefweb.int/node/22250>.

24 The examples cited in the report are Sierra Leone (UNAMSIL), Kosovo (UNMIK), and East Timor (UNTAET). See Brahimi Report, *ibid.* at 34, para. 198.

25 *Ibid.*

26 As specified in UN Security Council Resolution 1542 (2004), the mandate of the MINUSTAH extends to securing and stabilizing the environment, strengthening the political process, and improving human rights; online: United Nations <http://www.un.org/en/documents/>.

27 Daniel Thürer, "Dunant's Pyramid: Thoughts on the 'Humanitarian Space'" (2007) 89 Int'l Rev. Red Cross 47 at 55.

28 For a full description of the position of the ICRC on integrated missions, see ICRC, Official Statement, "An ICRC Perspective on Integrated Missions" (delivered by ICRC Vice-President Jacques Forster, 31 May 2005), online: ICRC <http://www.icrc.org/>.

29 *Humanitarian Response Review: An Independent Report Commissioned by the United Nations Emergency Relief Coordinator and Under-Secretary-General for Humanitarian Affairs, Office for the Coordination of Humanitarian Affairs (OCHA)* (New York and Geneva: United Nations, 2005) at 51.

30 The safeguarding of humanitarian space was, for example, described as one of the outputs of the United Nations Assistance Mission in Iraq in a report from the UN Secretary-General: *Report of the Secretary-General, Estimates in Respect of Special Political Missions, Good Offices and Other Political Initiatives Authorized by the General Assembly and/or the Security Council, United Nations Assistance Mission for Iraq*, UN Doc. A/62/512/Add.5 (26 November 2007) at 11; see also the *Report of the Secretary-General on Children and Armed Conflict in Myanmar*, which called upon the government of Burma to respect humanitarian space: UN Doc. S/2007/666 (16 November 2007) at 9, para. 29, and at 10, para. 32, online: United Nations <http://unic.un.org/>.

31 See *The Global Cluster Leads, Cluster Approach*, online: UNOCHA <http://ocha.unog.ch/>.

32 *Triennial Comprehensive Policy Review of Operational Activities of the United Nations Development System – Report of the Secretary-General*, UN GAOR/ESC, UN Doc. A/62/73–E/2007/52 (11 May 2007) at 23, para. 97, online: United Nations <http://www.un.org/en/documents/>.

33 See Charles C. Krulak, "The Strategic Corporal: Leadership in the Three Block War" *Marines Magazine* (January 1999), online: Air University <http://www.au.af.mil/>.

34 The two notions – Three Block War and 3D – are conceptually different, however. The Three Block War expresses the changing nature of warfare from a military point of view, whereas the 3D approach seeks to engage various stakeholders within the state, through a "whole of government" approach to country engagement.

35 On the 3D doctrine and humanitarian space, see Cornish, *supra* note 18.

36 See *The Responsibility to Protect: Report of the International Commission on Intervention and State Sovereignty* (Ottawa: International Development Research Centre, 2001), online: The Responsibility to Protect <http://www.iciss-ciise.gc.ca/>. The notion of "responsibility to protect" was also endorsed by the UN General Assembly in the 2005 World Summit Outcome Document, UN Doc. A/60/L.1 (15 September 2005) at paras. 138-40, online: United Nations Information Service <http://www.unis.unvienna.org/>.

37 For an example of how the Red Cross and the Red Crescent Movement approaches humanitarian space from the angle of "neutral and independent military action," see the resources found in the ICRC website at <http://www.icrc.org/>.

38 On how public international law binds non-state actors, see, *inter alia*, Andrew Clapham, *Human Rights Obligations of Non-State Actors* (Oxford: Oxford University Press, 2006); and Philip Alston, ed., *Non-State Actors and Human Rights* (Oxford: Oxford University Press, 2005).

39 See, *e.g.*, Wagner, *supra* note 2; and Ruth Abril Stoffels, "Legal Regulation of Humanitarian Assistance in Armed Conflict: Achievements and Gaps" (2004) 855 Int'l Rev. Red Cross 515.

40 The Hague Regulations (*Convention [IV] Respecting the Laws and Customs of War on Land and Its Annex: Regulations Concerning the Laws and Customs of War on Land,* 1907, online: UNHCR <http://www.unhcr.org/refworld/>) are part of customary international law. As early as 1946, the International Military Tribunal for Germany at Nuremberg held that "[t]he rules of land warfare expressed in the [Hague] convention undoubtedly represented an advance over existing international law at the time of their adoption. But the convention expressly stated that it was an attempt 'to revise the general laws and customs of war,' which it thus recognized to be then existing, but by 1939 these rules laid down in the convention were recognized by all civilized nations, *and were regarded as being declaratory of the laws and customs of* war which are referred to in Article 6 (b) of the Charter" [emphasis added], *Opinion and Judgment of the International Military Tribunal for the Trial of German Major War Criminals* (1947) 41 A.J.I.L. 172 at 248-49.

41 See art. 69(1) of *Protocol Additional to the Geneva Conventions of 12 August 1949, and Relating to the Protection of Victims of International Armed Conflicts (Protocol I),* 8 June 1977, 1125 U.N.T.S. 3 (entered into force 7 December 1978) [API].

42 See API at art. 70(1).

43 See in particular Stoffels, who, citing Jean Pictet and Luigi Condorelli, recalls that "[i]n the case of internal conflicts, however, the existence of these duties and rights can be clearly deduced from Article 3 common to the four Geneva Conventions, in particular from the prohibition of violence to life and person": *supra* note 39 at 519. See also Wagner, *supra* note 2.

44 Yves Sandoz, Christophe Swinarski, and Bruno Zimmermann, eds., *Commentary on the Additional Protocols of 8 June 1977 to the Geneva Conventions of 12 August 1949* (Geneva: Martinus Nijhoff, 1987) at 1479, para. 4878.

45 Article 27 of the *Convention Relative to the Protection of Civilian Persons in Time of War,* 12 August 1949, 75 R.T.N.U. 287 [GCIV], online: ICRC <http://www.icrc.org/ihl.nsf/>. This requirement that humanitarian relief shall be made available "without any adverse distinction" is also specifically mentioned in art. 69(1) of API, *supra* note 41, which provides the obligation that states have to ensure the survival of the population under occupation, as well as within art. 70(1) of API.

46 API, *supra* note 41 at art. 70(1).

47 See *Military and Paramilitary Activities in and against Nicaragua (Nicaragua v. United States),* Merits, Judgment [1986] I.C.J. Rep. 14 at 114 [*Nicaragua*], where the International Court of Justice held at para. 242 that "[t]here can be no doubt that the provision of strictly humanitarian aid to persons or forces in another country, whatever their political affiliations or objectives, cannot be regarded as unlawful intervention, or as in any other way contrary to international law. The characteristics of such aid were indicated in the first and second of the fundamental principles declared by the Twentieth International Conference of the Red Cross, that 'The Red Cross, born of a desire to bring assistance without discrimination to the wounded on the battlefield, endeavours, in its international and national capacity, to prevent and alleviate human suffering wherever it may be found. Its purpose is to protect life and health and to ensure respect for the human being. It promotes mutual understanding, friendship, co-operation and lasting peace amongst all peoples' and that 'It

makes no discrimination as to nationality, race, religious beliefs, class or political opinions. It endeavours only to relieve suffering, giving priority to the most urgent cases of distress."'

48 Common Article 3 of the *Convention for the Amelioration of the Condition of the Wounded and Sick in Armed Forces in the Field*, Geneva, 12 August 1949, 75 R.T.N.U. 31 [GCI]; *Convention for the Amelioration of the Condition of Wounded, Sick and Shipwrecked Members of Armed Forces at Sea*, Geneva, 12 August 1949, 75 R.T.N.U. 85 [GCII]; *Convention Relative to the Treatment of Prisoners of War*, Geneva, 12 August 1949, 75 R.T.N.U. 135 [GCIII]; and GCIV, *supra* note 45. See also art. 18(1) of *Protocol Additional to the Geneva Conventions of 12 August 1949, and Relating to the Protection of Victims of Non-International Armed Conflicts (Protocol II)*, 8 June 1977, 1125 U.N.T.S. 609 (entered into force 7 December 1978) [APII].

49 GCIV, *supra* note 45 at art. 59(1).

50 *Ibid.* at art. 59(3).

51 This included the principles that had been embodied by the *Geneva Conventions* of 1864, 1906, 1929, and 1949, *i.e.*, humanity, impartiality, and neutrality.

52 GCIV, *supra* note 45 at art. 59(4).

53 See in particular Yoram Dinstein, "The Right to Humanitarian Assistance in Peacetime" (2000) 53 Naval War College Review 77, online: International Humanitarian Law Research Initiative <http://ihl.ihlresearch.org/>, who states that "[i]t is impossible to assert, at the present point, that a general right to humanitarian assistance has actually crystallized in positive international law."

54 For arguments in favour of a legal obligation for states to accept humanitarian assistance under IHL, see in particular Dietrich Schindler, "Humanitarian Assistance, Humanitarian Interference and International Law" in Ronald St. J. MacDonald, ed., *Essays in Honor of Wang Tieya* (London: Kluwer Academic Publishers, 1993) 689 at 696ff.

55 Sandoz *et al.*, *supra* note 44 at 819, para. 2805; see also Katja Luopajärvi, "Is There an Obligation on States to Accept International Humanitarian Assistance to Internationally Displaced Persons under International Law?" (2003) 15 Int'l J. Refugee L. 678 at 689-90.

56 See Common Article 9/9/9/10 of GCI, GCII, GCIII, and GCIV, *supra* note 48, and art. 18(2) of APII, *supra* note 48.

57 Jean-Marie Henckaerts and Louise Doswald-Beck, *Customary International Humanitarian Law. Volume I: Rules* (Cambridge: Cambridge University Press, 2005); see also Jean-Marie Henckaerts, "Study on Customary International Humanitarian Law: A Contribution to the Understanding and Respect for the Rule of Law in Armed Conflict" (2005) 87 Int'l Rev. Red Cross 175. In particular, Rule 55 of the study provides that "[t]he parties to the conflict must allow and facilitate rapid and unimpeded passage of humanitarian relief for civilians in need, which is impartial in character and conducted without any adverse distinction, subject to their right of control."

58 Henckaerts and Doswald-Beck, *ibid.* at 197. For the same opinion, see Joakim Dungel, "A Right to Humanitarian Assistance in Internal Armed Conflicts Respecting Sovereignty, Neutrality and Legitimacy: Practical Proposals to Practical Problems"

(2004) Journal of Humanitarian Assistance, online: <http://sites.tufts.edu/jha/archives/838>.

59 *Application of the International Convention on the Elimination of All Forms of Racial Discrimination (Georgia v. Russian Federation)*, Provisional Measures, Order of 15 October 2008, I.C.J. Reports (2008) at 42 [*Georgia v. Russian Federation*].

60 See United Nations Diplomatic Conference of Plenipotentiaries on the Establishment of an International Criminal Court, *Rome Statute of the International Criminal Court*, UN Doc. A/CONF.183/9 (17 July 1998) at art. 8(b)(xxv) [*Rome Statute*].

61 *Ibid.* at art. 7(2)(b).

62 On the protection of humanitarian personnel, see in particular Kate Mackintosh, "Beyond the Red Cross: The Protection of Independent Humanitarian Organizations and Their Staff in International Humanitarian Law" (2007) 89 Int'l Rev. Red Cross 113.

63 See Henckaerts and Doswald-Beck, *supra* note 57, Rule 31, which provides that "Humanitarian relief personnel must be respected and protected. [IAC/NIAC]."

64 API, *supra* note 41 at art. 71(4).

65 Article 1 common to the four *Geneva Conventions* provides that the "High Contracting Parties undertake to respect and to ensure respect for the present Convention in all circumstances."

66 In the *Nicaragua* case, the International Court of Justice confirmed that Common Article 1 is applicable in both international and non-international armed conflicts: *supra* note 47 at para. 220.

67 This obligation also extends to commanders in the field. This was confirmed in particular by the International Criminal Tribunal for the former Yugoslavia (ICTY) in the *Halilovic* case in the following terms: "The argument that a failure to punish a crime is a tacit acceptance of its commission is not without merit. The Trial Chamber recognises that a commander, as the person in possession of effective control over his subordinates is entrusted by international humanitarian law with the obligation *to ensure respect of its provisions.* The position of the commander exercising authority over his subordinates dictates on his part to take necessary and reasonable measures for the punishment of serious violations of international humanitarian law and a failure to act in this respect is considered so grave that international law imputes upon him responsibility for those crimes" [emphasis added]: ICTY, *Prosecutor v. Halilovic*, Trial Judgment, IT-01-48-T (16 November 2005) at para. 95.

68 See Luigi Condorelli and Laurence Boisson de Chazournes, "Quelques remarques à propos de l'obligation des États de 'respecter et faire respecter' le droit international humanitaire 'en toutes circonstances'" in Christophe Swinarski, ed., *Studies and Essays on International Humanitarian Law and Red Cross Principles in Honour of Jean Pictet* (Geneva: ICRC; The Hague: Martinus Nijhoff, 1984) 27. See also Umesh Palwankar, "Measures Available to States for Fulfilling their Obligation to Ensure Respect for International Humanitarian Law" (1994) 298 Int'l Rev. Red Cross 9 at 12-13, who argues that diplomatic pressures include "a) Vigorous and continuous protests lodged by as many Parties as possible with the ambassadors representing the State in question in their respective countries and, conversely, by the representatives of those Parties accredited to the government of the aforementioned State;

b) Public denunciation, by one or more Parties and/or by a particularly influential regional organization, of the violation of international humanitarian law; c) Diplomatic pressure on the author of the violation, through intermediaries; and d) Refer all to the International Fact-Finding Commission (Article 90, Additional Protocol I) by a State with regard to another State, both of which have accepted the competence of the Commission."

69 See François Bugnion, "Red Cross Law," (1995) 308 Int'l Rev. Red Cross 491.

70 See GCIV, *supra* note 45 at art. 63.

71 Bugnion, *supra* note 69 at 501.

72 *Ibid.* at 507.

73 See art. 6 of the Statutes of the International Red Cross and Red Crescent Movement, which were adopted by the 25th International Conference of the Red Cross at Geneva in October 1986 and amended by the 26th International Conference of the Red Cross and Red Crescent at Geneva in December 1995 and by the 29th International Conference of the Red Cross and Red Crescent at Geneva in June 2006.

74 See "Signatories of the Code of Conduct," online: IFRC <http://www.ifrc.org/>.

75 The Humanitarian Charter developed by the Sphere Project is available online: Sphere Project <http://www.sphereproject.org>.

76 On the importance of soft law in the international legal order, see in particular Georges Abi-Saab, "Eloge du 'droit assourdi': quelques réflexions sur le rôle de la *soft law* en droit international contemporain" in *Nouveaux itinéraires en droit : Hommage à François Rigaux*, Coll. Bibliothèque de la Faculté de Droit de l'Université catholique de Louvain (Bruxelles: Bruylant, 1993) 59.

77 For more information on the IDRL project, see <http://www.ifrc.org/idrl>. See also David Fischer, "Domestic Regulation of International Humanitarian Relief in Disasters and Armed Conflict: A Comparative Analysis" (2007) 89 Int'l Rev. Red Cross 345.

78 See "Disaster Management: International Disaster Response Laws, Rules and Principles Programme (IDRL)," online: IFRC <http://www.ifrc.org/>.

79 See para. 1(c) of the resolution.

80 See para. 12 of *Strengthening of the Coordination of Humanitarian Emergency Assistance of the United Nations*, GA Res. 182, UN GAOR, 78th Plenary Meeting, UN Doc. A/RES/46/182 (19 December 1991).

81 *Ibid.* at para. 2.

82 The UN General Assembly reaffirmed "the importance of the principles of neutrality, humanity and impartiality for the provision of humanitarian assistance" in Resolution 57/150 of 16 December 2002.

83 For example, with respect to the Democratic Republic of Congo, Security Council Resolution 1794 of 21 December 2007 reaffirmed "the obligation of all parties to comply fully with the relevant rules and principles of international humanitarian law relating to the protection of humanitarian and United Nations personnel, and also demand[ed] that all parties concerned grant immediate, full and unimpeded access by humanitarian personnel to all persons in need of assistance, as provided for in applicable international law." For its part, the General Assembly uses similar language. In the case of Afghanistan, it appealed in a resolution on 6 March 1998 (UN

Doc. A/RES/52/145), "to Member States and to the international community to provide, on a non-discriminatory basis, adequate humanitarian assistance to the people of Afghanistan and to the Afghan refugees in neighbouring countries, pending, and with a view to encouraging, their voluntary repatriation, and request[ed] all the parties in Afghanistan to lift the restrictions imposed on the international aid community and to allow the free transit of food and medical supplies to all populations of the country."

84 See, *e.g.*, Security Council Resolution 824 (1993) and General Assembly Resolution 55/2 (2000), in addition to General Assembly Resolution 52/145 (1998).

85 Statement by the President of the Security Council, UN SCOR, UN Doc. S/PRST/2009/1 (14 January 2009). Although this document does not constitute a "decision" for the purpose of art. 25 of the UN Charter, it nevertheless reflects the belief of the Security Council that the obligations listed therein are binding upon all UN members, *i.e.*, that they form part of customary international law.

86 See art. 25 of the UN Charter.

87 Article 103 of the UN Charter provides that "In the event of a conflict between the obligations of the Members of the United Nations under the present Charter and their obligations under any other international agreement, their obligations under the present Charter shall prevail."

88 See, *e.g.*, Security Council Resolution 1794 with respect to the Democratic Republic of Congo, *supra* note 83.

89 GA Res. 182, UN GAOR, 46th Sess., UN Doc. A/RES/46/182 (1991).

90 For the sake of ease, only universal – as opposed to regional – international human rights and mechanisms are addressed in the present section.

91 On the relationship between IHL and IHRL, see in particular Marco Sassòli, "Le droit international humanitaire, une *lex specialis* par rapport aux droits humains?" in Michel Hottelier, Andreas Auer, and Alexandre Flückiger, eds., *Les droits de l'homme et la constitution. Études en l'honneur du Professeur Giorgio Malinverni* (Zürich: Collection Genevoise, Schulthess, 2007) 375.

92 Philip Alston, Henry Steiner, and Ryan Goodman, *International Human Rights in Context – Law, Politics, Morals*, 3d ed. (Oxford: Oxford University Press, 2007) at 1433. For important works on human rights and development, see in particular Philip Alston and Mary Robinson, eds., *Human Rights and Development – Towards a Mutual Reinforcement* (Oxford: Oxford University Press, 2005); and Philippe Sands, "Treaty, Custom and the Cross-Fertilization of International Law" (1998) 1 Yale Human Rts. & Dev. L.J. 85. For a practical analysis of the rights-based approach to development, see, *e.g.*, Jakob Kirkemann Boesen and Tomas Martin, "Applying a Rights-Based Approach: An Inspirational Guide for Civil Society" (2007), online: Danish Institute for Human Rights <http://www.humanrights.dk/>, and *Integrating Human Rights into Development: Donor Approaches, Experiences and Challenges* (Paris: OECD Publishing, 2006).

93 See *Official Development Assistance Accountability Act*, S.C. 2008, c. 17, online: Canadian Legal Information Institute <http://www.canlii.org/>. The purpose of this act, as stated in s. 2(1), is to "ensure that all Canadian official development assistance abroad is provided with a central focus on poverty reduction and in a manner that is

consistent with Canadian values, Canadian foreign policy, the principles of the Paris Declaration on Aid Effectiveness of March 2, 2005, sustainable development and democracy promotion and that promotes international human rights standards."

94 Article 2 of the *Universal Declaration of Human Rights, supra* note 10, states that "[e]veryone is entitled to all the rights and freedoms set forth in this Declaration, without distinction of any kind, such as race, colour, sex, language, religion, political or other opinion, national or social origin, property, birth or other status." See also art. 2(1) of the 1966 *International Covenant on Civil and Political Rights,* New York, 16 December 1966, 999 U.N.T.S. 171 (entered into force 23 March 1976) [ICCPR].

95 On non-derogable human rights, see in particular Daniel Prémont, Christian Stenersen, and Isabelle Oseredczuk, eds., *Non-Derogable Rights and States of Emergency* (Brussels: Bruylant, 1996).

96 Committee on Economic, Social and Cultural Rights, *General Comment 12: The Right to Adequate Food (Art. 11),* UN ESC, 20th Sess., Agenda Item 7, UN Doc. E/C.12/1999/5 (12 May 1999) at para. 19. See also Katja Luopajärvi, *supra* note 55 at 692-93.

97 See ICCPR, *supra* note 94 at arts. 2, 3, and 26; and in particular *International Covenant on Economic, Social and Cultural Rights,* New York, 16 December 1966, 993 U.N.T.S. 3 (entered into force 3 January 1976) at art. 2(2) [ICESCR].

98 See *Georgia v. Russian Federation, supra* note 59. The court especially underscored the link between the obligation not to impede humanitarian assistance and the *International Convention on the Elimination of All Forms of Racial Discrimination,* New York, 7 March 1966, 660 U.N.T.S. 195 (entered into force 4 January 1969).

99 On positive human rights obligations, see, *e.g.,* Alastair Mowbray, *The Development of Positive Obligations Under the European Convention on Human Rights by the European Court of Human Rights* (Oxford: Hart Publishing, 2004). For a good summary of the distinction between positive and negative rights, see, *e.g.,* Tamar Ezer, "A Positive Right to Protection for Children" (2004) 7 Yale Human Rts. & Dev. L.J. 1 at 3-10. See also Silvia Borelli, "Positive Obligations of States and the Protection of Human Rights" (2006) 15 INTERRIGHTS Bulletin 101. Borelli in particular recalls the fact that the origin of the distinction between positive and negative obligations is found in the traditional divide between civil and political rights versus social, economic, and cultural rights.

100 For the extraterritorial application of human rights law, see, *e.g.,* the judgment of the International Court of Justice in *Legal Consequences of the Construction of a Wall in the Occupied Palestinian Territory,* Advisory Opinion, [2004] I.C.J. Reports 136 at paras. 108-13. For a critical view of the ICJ's opinion regarding the extraterritorial application of international human rights law, see in particular Michael J. Dennis, "Application of Human Rights Treaties Extraterritorially in Times of Armed Conflict and Military Occupation" (2005) 99 A.J.I.L. 119 at 122-37. The European Court of Human Rights also confirmed the approach that a particular state's international human rights obligations are applicable in occupied territories abroad. See European Court of Human Rights, *Loizidou v. Turkey, (Preliminary Objections),* Judgment of 23 March 1995 at para. 62. See also *Bankovic* case (*Vlastimir and Borka Bankovic and Others v. Belgium et al.,* Decision of 12 December 2001 at para. 71). For a recent

review of the case law applied by regional and human rights machinery, see in particular Virginia Mantouvalou, "Extending Judicial Control in International Law:
Human Rights Treaties and Extraterritoriality" (2009) 9 Int'l J.H.R. 147.

101 United Nations General Assembly Resolution 2625 (XXV) of 24 October 1970, entitled "Declaration on Principles of International Law Concerning Friendly Relations
and Cooperation among States in Accordance with the Charter of the United
Nations." Regarding the customary status of this resolution, the ICJ declared in the
Nicaragua case that "[t]he effect of consent to the text of such resolutions cannot be
understood as merely that of a 'reiteration or elucidation' of the treaty commitment
undertaken in the Charter. On the contrary, it may be understood as an acceptance
of the validity of the rule or set of rules declared by the resolution by themselves":
Nicaragua, supra note 47 at para. 188.

102 These principles were published as "Guiding Principles on the Right to Humanitarian
Assistance" (1993) 297 Int'l Rev. Red Cross 519.

103 The Sphere Project, *supra* note 75.

104 Rohan J. Hardcastle and Adrian T.L. Chua, "Humanitarian Assistance: Towards a
Right of Access to Victims of Natural Disasters" (1998) 325 Int'l Rev. Red Cross 589.

105 For additional information on the OECD's Development Assistance Committee, see
<http://www.oecd.org/>. For the particular linkages between the 2005 *Paris
Declaration on Aid Effectiveness* and the endorsement of a human rights framework
by DAC members, including Canada, see the DAC's *Action-Oriented Policy Paper on
Human Rights and Development*, DCD/DAC(2007)15/FINAL (Paris: OECD, 2007).
See also Marta Foresti, David Booth, and Tammie O'Neil, "Aid Effectiveness and
Human Rights: Strengthening the Implementation of the Paris Declaration" (2006),
online: Overseas Development Institute <http://www.odi.org.uk/resources/>.

106 See <http://www.goodhumanitariandonorship.org>.

107 For a review of the discussion on the linkages between relief, rehabilitation, and de-
velopment (LRRD), see, *e.g.*, Margie Buchanan-Smith and Paola Fabbri, "Linking
Relief, Rehabilitation and Development: A Review of the Debate" (2005), online:
Active Learning Network for Accountability and Performance in Humanitarian
Action <http://www.alnap.org/>.

11

Humanitarian Space and Stability Operations

MICHAEL KHAMBATTA

The goal of this chapter is to contribute to the discussion of how "humanitarian space" can be preserved in the evolving environment of counterinsurgency operations, primarily from a practitioner's point of view.[1] The impact of counterinsurgency operations, which often involve stability operations, on humanitarian space is complex. Although it is possible to identify areas where humanitarian space is shrinking, there are also areas where it is stable or actually increasing. Indeed, in certain cases humanitarian space can be shrinking in one part of a country while expanding in another. In each case, a full understanding of the context is needed in order to analyze the correlation between humanitarian space and counterinsurgency operations.

This chapter will look at the approach of the International Committee of the Red Cross (ICRC), which is based on the Red Cross and Red Crescent Movement's principles, and will argue that it is the long-standing adherence to these principles that has enabled the ICRC to remain active and to assist victims of conflict throughout the world. Although successful to a large degree, the ICRC nevertheless continues to face challenges in certain contexts. This chapter will explore these challenges and will conclude with a review of issues that arise in the context of substantial stability operations, which involve civilian capacities in support of political-military objectives. In particular, it will look at questions that arise as these tools are refined and made more effective.

The ICRC Approach

Humanitarian space is largely about acceptance. In an area of armed conflict, each humanitarian actor must be accepted individually, the process
beginning with the parties to the conflict. Without their acceptance, a humanitarian actor cannot be present on the ground and work with reasonable expectation of safety. It is a basic operating principle of the ICRC that
the armed actors in control of a particular territory must accept its presence. The ICRC relies on this acceptance for its security, and also often engages with elements of the civilian population that can influence the armed
groups. Significant effort is expended in engaging with those who can contribute to bringing about acceptance of the ICRC.

Thus, the creation of humanitarian space requires proactive effort by humanitarian actors in order for them to be accepted, at a minimum, by the
parties to the conflict. Other actors can facilitate or hamper these efforts,
but they cannot generate acceptance on their own. With this acceptance,
the ICRC hopes to gain access to those who are not participating in hostilities but are nevertheless affected by conflict and are in need of the organization's protection and assistance.

The ICRC has offices in eighty countries around the world and is active to
some degree in virtually every armed conflict, whether international or
non-international. This means that the ICRC must be coherent over time
and across contexts. Action in one context must be explainable in other
situations today and into the future. The increased availability of information as well as the speed at which it is shared requires the ICRC to be ever
more attentive to this coherence. The basis for the approach taken by the
ICRC and the Red Cross and Red Crescent Movement as a whole has been
to define seven principles for overall guidance of its activities. Of these, four
will be explored: Humanity, Neutrality, Impartiality, and Independence.[2]
These principles are the basis and reference for the ICRC in its attempts to
be accepted as a humanitarian actor with concrete activities on the ground.

Humanity

Humanity is the first principle of the Red Cross and Red Crescent Movement
and it is the basis of the Movement's activities. It is defined as follows:

> International Red Cross and Red Crescent Movement, born of a desire to
> bring assistance without discrimination to the wounded on the battlefield,
> endeavours, in its international and national capacity, to prevent and al-
> leviate human suffering wherever it may be found. Its purpose is to protect

life and health and to ensure respect for the human being. It promotes mutual understanding, friendship, cooperation and lasting peace amongst all peoples.[3]

This principle applies to all of the Movement's activities, including those of the National Societies and the International Federation of Red Cross and Red Crescent Societies, most of whose operations are largely peacetime ones. In the ICRC's case, its mission statement explains the focus on victims of conflict:

> The International Committee of the Red Cross (ICRC) is an impartial, neutral and independent organization whose exclusively humanitarian mission is to protect the lives and dignity of victims of armed conflict and other situations of violence and to provide them with assistance.
>
> The ICRC also endeavours to prevent suffering by promoting and strengthening humanitarian law and universal humanitarian principles.
>
> Established in 1863, the ICRC is at the origin of the Geneva Conventions and the International Red Cross and Red Crescent Movement. It directs and coordinates the international activities conducted by the Movement in armed conflicts and other situations of violence.[4]

The methods used by the ICRC to achieve this mission rest largely on the following three principles.

Neutrality

> In order to continue to enjoy the confidence of all, the Movement may not take sides in hostilities or engage at any time in controversies of a political, racial, religious or ideological nature.[5]

Neutrality is probably the most complex principle to convey and gain acceptance of. Throughout the ICRC's history, it has been faced with the challenge that parties to a conflict can view any other actor as either friendly or unfriendly. This was heightened in the post-9/11 period but is by no means a new phenomenon. The challenge for the ICRC and other neutral actors is to engage with parties to a conflict who face fundamental threats to the make-up of their state, their society, or even the basis of their power. In this context, they are asked, or even legally obliged, to accept and trust actors who, while not on their enemy's side, are also not on theirs. The acceptance of this role is a prerequisite for the acceptance of the ICRC itself. It is important not to underestimate the risk that parties to a conflict perceive in trusting the ICRC. From their perspective, the ICRC must constantly prove itself worthy of this trust. A measure of this is how quickly an ill-considered position or even a mistake by an individual staff member can damage the overall position of the ICRC in a given context. Even the smallest suspicion that is resolved can have lingering effects on such a relationship.

Neutrality is often viewed as either passive or non-involved. For states that are neutral in a conflict, this can mean the absence of any role. Conversely, the ICRC sees its Neutrality as a very active one. The purpose of Neutrality is to gain access to those affected and provide concrete assistance and protection. As indicated by the ICRC's Director of Operations at the Brookings Institution in Washington, DC, in November 2008:

> I always said to colleagues, there is no interest in a principle if you describe it by a negative. The Neutrality is interesting only and should be something that people feel connected to, if I can actually refer to the fact that in Darfur, in Iraq, in Afghanistan today, in the key conflict zones of today, it is actually something that allows us to reach people that we otherwise wouldn't be able to reach.[6]

Thus, from the ICRC perspective it is the acceptance of its neutral status by parties to a conflict that enables it to act in the field. This can include acting as a neutral intermediary on humanitarian issues, for example, by facilitating releases once the parties have agreed to them, as took place recently in Colombia, or by using its contacts with armed opposition channels to ensure that a vaccination campaign in Afghanistan was able to cover the entire country. As an overview of activities, the ICRC endeavours to use its Neutrality to:

- secure access to all potential victims of armed conflict or internal violence through contact with and safe passage clearance from all parties concerned
- alleviate the hardship and suffering of civilians caught up in conflict by, for example, enabling them to cross frontlines or to be supplied across frontlines with the goods needed for their survival
- obtain access to medical services for the wounded and sick without discrimination

- ensure medical care across frontlines by obtaining the security guarantees needed for health teams to deliver primary health care services in conflict areas
- request the parties to the conflict to authorize the exchange of family news across frontlines and borders, and, whenever appropriate, to authorize family reunifications
- facilitate contact between people deprived of their freedom and their families
- facilitate the release of people deprived of their freedom, and, where appropriate, their voluntary repatriation, transfer, or resettlement
- help families in their efforts to obtain clear information about their missing relatives, during and after the fighting.[7]

Impartiality
Whereas Neutrality characterizes the ICRC's approach and boundaries of action with the parties to the conflict, Impartiality is the framework for those who need the ICRC's help.

> It makes no discrimination as to nationality, race, religious beliefs, class or political opinions. It endeavours to relieve the suffering of individuals, being guided solely by their needs, and to give priority to the most urgent cases of distress.[8]

Although Impartiality usually attracts less controversy and discussion than Neutrality, a more limited amount of controversy nevertheless tends to arise during the implementation phase. Conceptually, it is easy to accept that the Red Cross and Red Crescent Movement should provide assistance to those who need it most. This concept becomes an issue, however, when needs are primarily linked to one side of a conflict. Logically, the ICRC puts its efforts where the needs are greatest. For observers, especially those at a distance, the perception can be created that the ICRC is helping only one side, with an obvious impact on the organization's perceived Neutrality. For the ICRC, this is a communications challenge – whether involving key interlocutors, arms carriers, or the wider public – and requires significant effort on the part of the organization in order to properly explain its activities. The ICRC often has a presence in conflicts that last for decades. In most conflicts, all parties will need humanitarian assistance of one kind or other at some point. The organization's rigorous respect for Impartiality over time often helps build respect for the concept, since it can demonstrate that it will help all those who meet the needs criteria.

Independence
This principle of Independence addresses the underlying tension of being part of an international movement dedicated to alleviating suffering while at the same time having national components that act as a public auxiliary of their state's government.

> The Movement is independent. The National Societies, while auxiliaries in the humanitarian services of their governments and subject to the laws of their respective countries, must always maintain their autonomy so that they may be able at all times to act in accordance with the principles of the Movement.[9]

Thus, this role must allow the National Societies as well as the ICRC to work in accordance with the Movement's principles, particularly those articulated above. For the purposes of this discussion, this principle reinforces those of Humanity, Neutrality, and Impartiality, even for a national society that is engaging with its own government that may be involved in an armed conflict.

Humanitarian Space
Maintaining the respect for humanitarian space is an ongoing challenge in any armed conflict. The ICRC has found that consistently observing its principles is one of the best ways to ensure access to areas where its assistance is needed most. Even with the strictest adherence to its principles, however, there are external factors that can restrict access. The ICRC's identity is linked to its principles and action, and this is usually well known to its immediate interlocutors. The wider civilian, military, or political community may, however, see the ICRC as a member of the "humanitarian community," or even more broadly as part of the "West." Actions affecting the overall confidence in the humanitarian community have an impact on the ICRC's ability to act and require significant efforts by the organization to preserve its reputation.

Three issues will be addressed below in the context of stability operations: (1) the confusion that can be created when similar activities are carried out by both humanitarian organizations and parties to the conflict,

(2) the impact of armed escorts, and (3) specific concerns for national Red Cross and Red Crescent societies.

Although maintaining the ICRC's identity in the minds of its interlocutors is a challenge in any context, particular challenges arise when one or more parties begin to use civilian means along with military forces to advance their political-military objectives. For the purposes of this chapter, I will use the term "stability operations."[10] The integration of civilian tools into military operations in order to achieve political-military objectives is likely to cause confusion in the eyes of affected civilians as well as the military opponent. The challenge for the ICRC is to ensure that its humanitarian activities are distinguishable from stability operations in the minds of armed actors and the civilian population.

Stability operations cover a full range of civilian governmental tasks and are carried out by military as well as civilian actors. These civilian governmental tasks go well beyond humanitarian activities, and include promoting the rule of law and economic growth. There are also situations where the ICRC and the civilian or military elements of a stability operation may be carrying out almost indistinguishable activities – the only real difference being the motivation behind the action. For example, in its role as a neutral humanitarian actor, the ICRC may be working to improve a municipal water system because it has been identified as an area of great need. In contrast, in a neighbouring city, a party to the conflict may be addressing a real need by restoring a municipal water system, but with the ultimate goal of winning the confidence, trust, and support of the civilian population.

There has been discussion within the humanitarian community as to whether parties to conflict should engage in so-called humanitarian activities. This is now largely beside the point. Stability operations are here to stay and humanitarian actors will need to adapt to them. For the ICRC, the challenge is to ensure that these very similar efforts do not create a perception in the minds of combatants or civilians that the ICRC is part of the political and military efforts of one side.

The communication approach taken by political and military actors is very important. If their message is that all humanitarian activity is part of overall political-military efforts, then organizations such as the ICRC will be associated with such an approach in the minds of interlocutors, armed actors, and civilians. In such cases, the ICRC will have to focus its communications on counteracting this impression. On the other hand, if a party to the conflict chooses to focus its communications upon its specific support activities, there is more space for humanitarian actors to explain their role to all sides with a view to gaining acceptance.

The second issue is the impact of humanitarians' use of armed escorts. Offers by parties to the conflict to provide armed escorts are common. Regardless of the circumstances, the use of armed escorts by humanitarian actors will inevitably create a perception that they are associated with that armed group. The ICRC view is that parties to the conflict must provide a secure environment, primarily for the civilian population but also for humanitarian actors to do their work. This includes a fairly frank discussion on the effective extent of the control exercised by the military actors involved.

Lastly, National Societies face specific challenges. National Red Cross or Red Crescent Societies in the country in question also work to maintain the humanitarian space they need in order to function. These National Societies are the primary partners of the ICRC in any action and they have the same obligations as the ICRC to respect the fundamental principles. As part of the community, they are often deeply affected by the conflict, and their capacity to assist can be hampered as resources become limited. The ICRC strives to support National Societies or even elements of National Societies that continue to work on behalf of victims. It should be noted that national society staff and volunteers often show great personal courage and can access areas where the ICRC cannot go. Finally, from the ICRC perspective, any association of the national society with the political-military objectives of a party to the conflict poses security risks to both the national society and the ICRC.

Trends

The United States is currently focusing on developing soft (or smart) power to support its stability operations as discussed above. It is the stated aim of the US government to improve the capacity of the civilian elements of its national power in order to foster support among the populations in areas where they engaged militarily, notably in Afghanistan and Iraq.[11] These conflicts have led to widespread research proposals with the goal of ensuring that the US government will be structured in such a way as to improve the effectiveness of its efforts. Much of the discussion surrounds the topic of the effective coordination and alignment of different government departments' efforts to achieve the national strategy.[12] The ICRC does not, and cannot, take an opinion on whether such tools are appropriate, as such an approach would violate the very Neutrality it is striving for. It must, however, work on the assumption that increased effort in this regard will lead to increased effectiveness. The question to be raised, then, is what this increased effectiveness could mean for the ICRC, which is striving to maintain its humanitarian space. What approaches will be needed in order to adapt to this evolution?

Although it could be concluded that this evolution only complicates the efforts of the ICRC, there has been improvement from the ICRC's perspective in at least one area. Based on interactions between ICRC Washington and the US military, there is an increasingly widespread understanding that associating the activities of NGOs with American political-military objectives poses a threat to organizations working in the field, which rely on acceptance by all parties for their security. While this is a trend in the right direction, it needs to be reinforced at every opportunity by military and governmental interlocutors. Comments that describe the activities of Provincial Reconstruction Teams (PRTs) in Afghanistan as "mainly humanitarian" continue to arise and should be discouraged.

A wide range of civil society actors, from local community organizations to large international NGOs and contractors, have been associated in various contexts with the political and military objectives of a party to a conflict. In cases where the military situation has intensified, such as Afghanistan, some of these organizations have been forced to cease their activities in certain areas once they determined that their presence was no longer secure. This kind of situation prompts the following question: Is their departure due to concerns that the enemy is gaining advantages such as intelligence gathering or is building support because the assistance is associated with a party to the conflict, or is it the activity itself that is perceived to be a threat? In the first case, an activity that may be unacceptable if carried out by those associated with one side may be acceptable if carried out in accordance with the ICRC approach. In the second case, where the activity itself is seen as a threat, even the ICRC approach will not work. This requires careful analysis of each situation on an ongoing basis. From an operational perspective, there are many areas where the ICRC is one of the few actors who are accepted by all sides, while there are areas where the ICRC is not fully accepted and thus cannot be present. This kind of analysis can usually be done only in close proximity to the context and with a strong network of contacts on the ground. Furthermore, dialogue and credible action have led to changes in armed actors' perceptions that opened up humanitarian space. Assumptions that certain parties to a conflict will not allow humanitarian actors to work should be fully tested before being accepted.

Questions for the Future

Rather than offering conclusions, I would like to point out some remaining questions. What is the impact on humanitarian space when there is an actor using a full range of effective civilian tools while largely respecting the role of the ICRC and similar organizations? There are no easy answers to this question. Rather, there are perhaps factors that will need to be taken into account. Assistance associated with parties to a conflict has already come under threat. Will it be attacked more systematically in the future? And what conclusions should be drawn from this? Will armed actors still accept the ICRC and similar organizations operating in humanitarian space? In contexts where parties to a conflict have significant autonomy and the civilian population has limited access to information, what steps will have to be taken to ensure that the humanitarian actors are not targeted due to misperceptions? The targeting of assistance by any party has been assumed to result from an absence of respect for neutral, impartial humanitarian action. Perhaps this analysis will have to place additional weight on whom the humanitarian actor is associated with. This kind of precision is difficult in an environment of incomplete information, so significant effort is needed if one is to make operational decisions on whether it is safe enough to work.

NOTES

1 The views expressed in this chapter are those of the author and do not necessarily represent the views of the International Committee of the Red Cross.

2 The three other principles – Voluntary Service, Unity, and Universality – lie beyond the scope of this chapter.

3 "The Fundamental Principles of the Red Cross and Red Crescent" (1996) at 2, online: ICRC <http://www.icrc.org/> ["Fundamental Principles"].

4 "The ICRC's Mission Statement" (19 June 2008), online: ICRC <http://www.icrc. org/>.

5 "Fundamental Principles," *supra* note 3 at 7.

6 The Brookings Institution, "The Future of Humanitarianism: A Conversation with the ICRC's Pierre Krähenbeühl," Washington, DC, 24 November 2008, online: The Brookings Institution <http://www.brookings.edu/>.

7 Internal ICRC documents prepared by the ICRC Communications Department dealing with armed forces.

8 "Fundamental Principles," *supra* note 3 at 4.

9 *Ibid.* at 9.

10 Terms such as "comprehensive approach," "interagency approach," and "whole of government approach" are also used.

11 "Hillary Rodham Clinton, Secretary of State, Remarks to Department Employees at Welcome Event, Washington, DC" (22 January 2009), online: US Department of State <http://www.state.gov/>.

12 See, *e.g.,* "Building Civilian Capacity for Complex Operations," National Defense University, Washington, DC, 19-20 November 2008.

12 The Implications for Women of a Shrinking Humanitarian Space

VALERIE OOSTERVELD

The implications for women of a shrinking "humanitarian space" are dire: more women at risk of gender-based and sexual violence, including in places that are meant to be safe; fewer women receiving the kind of assistance and protection they need in order to survive; and fewer women being able to contribute humanitarian assistance in the field where they are most needed.[1] This chapter begins by examining the negative effect on female recipients of humanitarian aid when the humanitarian space meant to be a safe haven instead becomes a place of sexual exploitation and abuse. It then explores how attacks or threats against humanitarian workers reduce women's access to humanitarian assistance and how these effects are compounded when the targeted workers are female. It underlines the manner in which these scenarios contribute to the narrowing of the humanitarian space available for women, both in perception and in reality. The notion of humanitarian space is compared with the experiences of women in courtrooms of international and internationalized criminal tribunals. The ultimate conclusion is that there are clearly many instances where humanitarian space, however defined, is constrained for women, leaving them even more vulnerable in difficult circumstances.

Humanitarian Space and Women

The meaning of humanitarian space appears to vary depending on the person or organization using the term. Chapter 10 identifies a lack of agreement on the definition of the term. In his analysis, Sylvain Beauchamp provides examples of how the understanding of humanitarian space differs between, for example, the International Committee of the Red Cross (ICRC), the United Nations (UN), and non-governmental organizations (NGOs).

The fluidity of the notion of humanitarian space was demonstrated on 14 January 2009 in the United Nations Security Council Presidential Statement on the protection of civilians in armed conflict. The statement underlined "the importance of safe and unhindered access of humanitarian personnel, and of the timely, safe and unhindered passage of essential relief goods, to provide assistance to civilians in armed conflict in accordance with applicable international law."[2] It also stressed "the importance of upholding and respecting the humanitarian principles of humanity, neutrality, impartiality and independence."[3] The Presidential Statement was accompanied by a revised Aide-Mémoire for the consideration of issues pertaining to the protection of civilians in armed conflict that contains a section on humanitarian access and the safety and security of humanitarian workers. It calls upon parties to armed conflict to "agree to and facilitate relief operations that are humanitarian and impartial in character[,] to allow and facilitate rapid and unimpeded passage of relief consignments, equipment and personnel" and to "respect and protect humanitarian workers and facilities."[4] Under this section, it also listed for consideration the need to "[m]andate United Nations peacekeeping and other relevant missions authorized by the Security Council, where appropriate and as requested, to facilitate the provision of humanitarian assistance" and to, "as requested and within capabilities, [create] the necessary security conditions for the provision of humanitarian assistance."[5]

The Presidential Statement and Aide-Mémoire echo the responsibilities of parties to armed conflict under international humanitarian law and provide potential mandate language for Security Council–authorized peacekeeping missions. The language is vague enough that it does not clearly separate – as Ulrike von Pilar would advocate – the responsibility of states and parties to the conflict for the creation of humanitarian space from the action to be undertaken in that space by humanitarian organizations.[6] The Presidential Statement and Aide-Mémoire illustrate how the concept of humanitarian space is currently indeterminate. In one sense, this lack of definition does not matter: women are at risk as a result of limitations on humanitarian space, however defined, and are at risk even within that space.

Women often comprise a large percentage of any internally displaced or refugee population,[7] which frequently translates into specific vulnerabilities.[8]

Already often marginalized due to gender-based discrimination within their societies,[9] as refugees or internally displaced persons (IDPs) women must deal with losing the protection of their homes, their government, and often their family structure, with the rigours of their journeys to hoped-for safety, with the stresses of life in camps or elsewhere, and with official harassment or indifference, poverty, and sexual abuse. Moreover, these must be dealt with while coping with new or continuing roles as breadwinners and physical protectors of their families, without the tools that may have been available before they were uprooted.[10] Due to their central role in the family unit and the absence of male heads of households as a result of armed conflict, women are often the family members who must seek assistance.[11] Restricted access to humanitarian space – for example, because of threats to humanitarian workers – results in limited accessibility for these women and their dependents to food, shelter, and other necessities of life, and threatens their physical security.

There are also risks for women within humanitarian space. In refugee and IDP camps, women are exposed to sexual exploitation and abuse, in part by the very individuals who are meant to provide humanitarian assistance. Moreover, such sexual exploitation and abuse can occur within, and in the vicinity of, United Nations peacekeeping missions. This violation of women by a range of actors blurs the line between humanitarian workers and military actors. It also means that female beneficiaries of humanitarian assistance may perceive their humanitarian space to be, and experience it as, narrower (both physically and socioculturally) than do other actors such as humanitarian workers, peacekeepers, donors, armed groups, communities, and states.

Women as Recipients of Humanitarian Assistance

Refugee and IDP camps are commonly considered humanitarian spaces. This section examines how women, as recipients of humanitarian assistance in such camps, are vulnerable to mistreatment from the camp population, members of the surrounding community, non-state armed groups or government forces, and even those meant to alleviate their situation.

While gender inequality and discrimination are the root causes of gender-based violence, including sexual violence, many factors present in refugee and IDP camps contribute to the increased vulnerability of women.[12] For example, there are sociocultural vulnerabilities such as the collapse of social and family support structures, a greater number of female-headed households with fewer resources, lack of work for both male and female family members, and increased domestic abuse.[13] There are also infrastructure-related vulnerabilities, such as poor camp design[14] resulting in overcrowded, multi-household dwellings or communal shelters, a shortage of appropriate sanitary facilities, a lack of well-protected women's quarters, long distances between tents and latrines, and insufficient lighting in camps.[15] Other risk factors include lack of camp security patrols or police protection, lack of United Nations or non-governmental presence in the camp, and gender-biased decisions resulting from predominantly male camp leadership.[16] Lack of access to food, clean water, cooking fuel, or money-generating activities within camps means that women must venture beyond them in order to cook and support their families.[17] These vulnerabilities increase the chances of women in refugee and IDP camps being subjected to sexual or gender-based violence as well as related serious physical injury, forced pregnancy, disease, death, and ostracism from their communities.[18]

A case in point of extreme vulnerability is that of women living in IDP camps in Darfur, Sudan. According to a UN report on the situation in Darfur:

> The majority of the victims of sexual violence documented by HROs [Human Rights Officers] are women and girls who live in camps for internally displaced persons (IDPs), some of which are guarded by forces allied with those responsible for the original displacement. Many of the incidents took place when victims went to collect firewood or grass or were travelling on the roads between major towns in Darfur. Many of the cases were gang-raped by groups of armed men who arrived on camels or horses. Collective rapes of a number of women and girls together were also common. The victims were almost always insulted and humiliated, often threatened with death, beaten and, in a few cases, killed. In the vast majority of cases where the perpetrators have been identified, they were either members of the Government armed forces, law enforcement agencies or pro-Government militia ... In [the] vast majority of cases victims and their representatives do not ordinarily approach the authorities, for fear of reprisals or because of the futility of reporting given the lack of redress for sexual violence. In cases where the victim has sought legal justice, HROs have observed that the authorities have failed to bring most perpetrators to justice, and in some cases their action has aggravated the situation and revictimized the rape survivor through humiliation and insensitive treatment.[19]

The Prosecutor of the International Criminal Court has classified these and other rapes occurring as a result of the conflict in Darfur as crimes against humanity.[20] The physical and psychological insecurity[21] created for women as a result of the high incidence of sexual violence in and around IDP camps in Darfur is compounded by reports that women "cannot voice their feelings of fear and frustration about the daily risks they face because of the danger of being arrested by [Sudan's] National Security Service[,] which has infiltrated almost every IDP camp."[22]

More generally, women's insecurity is made worse by lack of consistent attention to gender-based violence by those in charge of refugee and IDP camps and their international organizations, by confusion among camp staff about who is responsible for gender issues or the safety of women, and by poor routines for reporting and follow-up of cases of gender-based violence.[23] Odd Olsen and Kristen Scharffscher report that rape in refugee and IDP camps can be regarded as the ultimate result of organizational failures occurring during the early planning phase of these camps, beginning with the United Nations High Commissioner for Refugees (UNHCR) and extending to the implementation phase under international non-governmental organizations, their national-level affiliates, and the organization's camp staff and camp residents.[24] Poor reporting or feedback on gender-based violence sustains this cycle and further supports the original lack of attention to such violence. Thus, the ultimate result is the reinforcement of a narrowed humanitarian space for female beneficiaries of aid in refugee and IDP camps.[25] This chain of reinforcing failures has improved somewhat, with far more United Nations and institutional attention focused on gender-based violence in refugee and IDP camps as a result of improvements put into place following the revelation of sexual exploitation and abuse by humanitarian workers in 2002. Underreporting of gender-based violence – and therefore the sequence of reinforcing failures – remains an issue, however.[26]

This dilemma of shrinking humanitarian space becomes even more obvious with reports of sexual exploitation and abuse of refugee and internally displaced women by humanitarian personnel and UN peacekeepers.[27] Although such reports date back to at least the early 1990s, the situation remained largely unnoticed until a 2002 report substantially raised the profile of the issue within and outside the United Nations.[28] That February, a joint assessment by the UNHCR and Save the Children UK issued a shocking report detailing the nature and extent of sexual violence and exploitation of refugee, internally displaced, and returnee children in Guinea, Liberia, and Sierra Leone.[29] The report detailed how girls, largely between the ages of thirteen and eighteen years, were used for sexual services in exchange for money, food, and other basic necessities.[30] The girls found to be the most vulnerable were those separated from their parents, living with just one parent, living with extended family members, and living in child-headed households, as well as orphans or those in foster care.[31]

Implicated in this exploitation and abuse were sixty-seven men in positions of relative power and influence who either controlled access to goods and services or who had relative wealth or income: UN peacekeeping forces, UN agency staff, staff of international and local NGOs, and staff of government agencies responsible for humanitarian response.[32] The report indicated that most of the allegations involved male national staff working in areas with large established aid programs, who traded humanitarian commodities and services such as oil, bulgur wheat, tarpaulins or plastic sheeting, medicines, transport, ration cards, loans, educational courses, skills training, and other basic services for sex.[33] Agency workers with special responsibilities for children were allegedly using the resources meant to improve children's lives as an avenue of exploitation.[34] UN peacekeepers were reportedly asking girls to pose naked for pictures in exchange for food, as well as paying or trading items for sex.[35] Some girls who were sexually exploited contracted sexually transmitted diseases, became pregnant and sought abortions or became girl mothers, dropped out of school, and/or were ostracized.[36] The United Nations Office of Internal Oversight Services subsequently conducted its own investigation and, while acknowledging deficiencies in the camps that exposed young girls to sexual exploitation and abuse, concluded that it was incorrect to claim that such abuse was widespread.[37] The report did, however, uncover forty-three cases of potential sexual exploitation and substantiated ten of these cases.[38]

In 2003, more allegations surfaced concerning sexual exploitation and abuse of women in Nepal by humanitarian workers.[39] In 2004, allegations emerged of sexual exploitation and abuse of girls and young women by UN peacekeeping and related civilian personnel in the Democratic Republic of the Congo. An ensuing report outlined how this exploitation mostly involved the exchange of sex (or rather rape) for money (on average, between $1 and $3 per encounter), food, or jobs.[40] Similar allegations also surfaced with regard to peacekeeping operations in Burundi as well as other missions, including Haiti and Liberia.[41] In 2008, another study detailed sexual exploitation and abuse of children – especially orphaned girls and girls separated from their parents – by aid workers and peacekeepers in Southern Sudan, Côte d'Ivoire, and Haiti, including forced sex, sex in exchange for food, money, soap, or other items, verbal sexual abuse, and sexual assault (sexual touching or adult physical sexual displays to children).[42]

Regardless of which report one reads,[43] it is clear that, for the girls concerned, their families, and others,[44] the theoretical humanitarian space of the refugee or IDP camp, humanitarian office, or other places was not realized.[45] The humanitarian space was smaller for these women than it would have been absent this exploitation. The various reports and resulting extensive media coverage led to some welcome changes with the intent of reducing or eliminating sexual exploitation and abuse, thereby expanding the humanitarian space available for refugee and internally displaced women.

At the institutional level, the United Nations Inter-Agency Standing Committee Task Force on Sexual Exploitation and Abuse developed a plan of action for the entire UN system to prevent sexual exploitation and abuse in humanitarian crises.[46] The UNHCR and various non-governmental humanitarian groups implemented training on how to investigate allegations of sexual abuse and adopted or amended existing codes of conduct and policies explicitly prohibiting sexual exploitation and abuse of refugees or other persons of concern.[47] In October 2003, the Secretary-General issued a bulletin obliging UN agencies and their non-governmental partners to prevent and to investigate any suspected sexual exploitation and sexual abuse by humanitarian staff.[48] Standard codes of conduct were also adopted for peacekeeping personnel explicitly prohibiting sexual exploitation and abuse of the local population, especially women and children.[49]

The UN and NGOs also took steps to improve inter-agency coordination on the issue of sexual exploitation and abuse of refugees and IDPs, to provide better training to those working on refugee and IDP issues, and to introduce new mechanisms to encourage the reporting of abuses.[50] Even with these changes, significant underreporting of sexual exploitation and abuse on the part of victims and their families/communities continues. This underreporting is due to several factors: fear of losing access to humanitarian assistance, fear of being stigmatized, fear of negative economic impact on girls and their families, threats of retribution or retaliation, cultural acceptance or resignation to abuse within the community, lack of knowledge of how to report sexual exploitation or abuse, a feeling of powerlessness to report abuse, lack of effective legal services, and lack of faith in the response an allegation of sexual abuse will receive.[51]

Following the publication of an investigative report outlining a comprehensive strategy to eliminate future sexual exploitation and abuse in UN peacekeeping operations,[52] the Security Council has referred to the zero-tolerance policy on sexual exploitation and abuse in its resolutions mandating peacekeeping operations.[53] In a 2008 resolution on women, peace, and security, the Security Council requested "the Secretary-General and relevant United Nations agencies, *inter alia,* through consultation with women and women-led organizations as appropriate, to develop effective mechanisms for providing protection from violence, including in particular sexual violence, to women and girls in and around UN managed refugee and internally displaced persons camps."[54] Both the Security Council and the General Assembly have required the Secretary-General to report regularly on the zero-tolerance policy and the situation of women and children at risk of sexual exploitation and abuse in areas with UN operations.[55] This has not only helped to improve reporting within the UN on sexual exploitation and abuse matters but also provided some welcome transparency as to the extent of such incidents, even if still underreported.[56] Although not all of the recommendations in the comprehensive strategy to eliminate future sexual exploitation and abuse in UN peacekeeping operations have so far been implemented, more investigations of sexual exploitation and abuse by UN personnel are underway.[57]

At the operational level, helpful changes have been made to some refugee and IDP camps. For example, many women have been made aware of their rights not to be exploited in exchange for basic goods and services.[58] Camp design has been improved to add better lighting and to provide increased privacy for women in the use of latrines and communal wash areas.[59] In some camps, steps have been taken to provide solar cooking alternatives and income-generation possibilities to women in order to reduce or eliminate the need to venture outside camps.[60] Not all camps provide ideal levels of physical security for women, however, and there is still much room for improvement.

Another way in which humanitarian space is shrinking for female recipients of humanitarian assistance is demonstrated in cases where the recipients of aid come under attack as a result of the aid they have received. For example, Afghan girls attending schools built or maintained by aid agencies have been attacked at or on their way to school, or have had their schools burned down.[61] This is different from the scenarios outlined above, in which women and girls were exploited in exchange for their access to aid or as a result of vulnerabilities inherent in the refugee camp environment. This development "opens up a new and even more complex set of challenges, and agencies have often simply suspended programming" in response.[62]

All of these institutional and operational steps are helpful, but ongoing reports of gender-based violence against women in and around what would otherwise be considered humanitarian spaces indicates that more needs to be done to expand that specific shrinking space for women.

Implications for Women of Attacks on Humanitarian Workers

Attacks on humanitarian workers also shrink humanitarian space. Recently, the number of such attacks has risen sharply. An indication of the reason for concern can be seen in the numbers from 2008, when "260 humanitarian aid workers were killed, kidnapped or seriously injured in violent attacks."[63] The Humanitarian Policy Group notes that the rise in attacks is both absolute and relative: "The absolute number of attacks against aid workers has risen steeply over the past three years, with an annual average almost three times higher than the previous nine years" and "[r]elative rates of attacks per numbers of aid workers in the field have also increased – by 61%."[64] There has been a particular surge in kidnapping as a tactic of violence, with kidnappers being at least partly politically motivated.[65] The political targeting of aid workers is both associative and direct, "that is, aid organizations may be attacked because they are perceived as collaborators with the 'enemy,' be it a government, a rebel group or a foreign power; in other cases, the organization itself may be the primary target, attacked for its own actions or statements, or to prevent or punish the delivery of aid to a population."[66]

Violence against, and intimidation of, aid providers directly deprives affected populations of much-needed assistance and protection. If there is no safe corridor for the delivery of food and other supplies, the deliveries risk being curtailed or cut off. If workers cannot access the population they are attempting to help, then that population cannot benefit. One example having a clear impact upon women occurred in Sudan:

> In early 2008, the Government [of Sudan] denied access for forty days to humanitarian agencies assisting some 160,000 conflict-affected people, including an estimated 80,000 children in the northern part of Western Darfur. As a result, protection activities, including sexual and gender-based violence, human rights and child protection projects, were suspended.[67]

Somalia provides yet another example. Throughout 2006 to 2008, violence directed against aid workers in that country has substantially increased. As a result, the provision of aid has at times been withdrawn or suspended. The UN Office for the Coordination of Humanitarian Affairs

(OCHA) reported that in 2008 UN international staff present in Somalia fell by 41 percent, and NGO international staff presence dropped by 13 percent in south and central Somalia.[68] One NGO reported closing its surgical program that provided emergency trauma and obstetric care.[69] Withdrawal of such care clearly has a negative impact upon women and girls. The limiting or removal of aid obviously puts all who depend on it at risk, but also means that those most powerless – including women – are especially likely to suffer.

The targeting of humanitarian workers limits what they can do and where they can go, thereby affecting how they do their jobs. International humanitarian organizations have adapted to this reality by conducting more operations through local staff or through local partner organizations.[70] This remote form of management tends to result in more cautious programming, without the ability to assess emerging needs.[71] While there is little analysis of how remote management affects women, it can be seen intuitively that their vulnerability increases as international visibility of their situation decreases. Such vulnerability may arise from reduced access to food and other basic necessities for both women and their families, increased need to venture outside IDP and refugee camps, reduced physical protection, diminished ability to file complaints of sexual and gender-based violence, and decreased access to medical care.

There has been a recent revisiting of decisions to use more remote management as a response to insecurity. Over the past three years, many providers of humanitarian assistance have become more professional in addressing security needs with the goal of avoiding attacks against their workers as much as possible in order to be able to maintain a presence in the field. They have established more security-related posts at headquarters, regionally, and in the field; invested in security audits; established organizational security policies and procedures; and provided more security training to international and national staff, including those most at risk, such as drivers and guards.[72] The United Nations began a process of risk management aimed at allowing "UN and partner programs to continue operating in insecure contexts, rather than scaling back or evacuating."[73] Full institutionalization of that process has been set back by the 2007 bombing of United Nations buildings in Algiers, however.[74]

The presence of female humanitarian workers can improve the access of humanitarian organizations to female aid beneficiaries. In some communities, it is considered inappropriate for women to be in contact with men who are not part of their family.[75] Even in societies where this is not the case, women may not be willing to discuss taboo or intimate subjects (such as menstruation, health and hygiene problems, or sexual violence) with male humanitarian workers.[76] This may mean that aid is less accessible to women when it is provided solely by male humanitarian workers. In order to facilitate access of women to humanitarian organizations, many organizations provide female personnel (local and expatriate) and make an effort to locate and talk with women on field missions.[77] When these female humanitarian workers are targeted for killing, kidnapping, or intimidation, or when their supplies are stolen, the female beneficiaries of their assistance are likewise negatively affected. For example, on 11 March 2009 Canadian nurse Laura Archer and four others with Médecins Sans Frontières (MSF) were kidnapped in north Darfur, Sudan, but were later released.[78] The General Director of MSF-Belgium stated: "As a result of this kidnapping, MSF was forced to drastically reduce all medical projects across Darfur. We are incredibly saddened by this, particularly as in many areas we were the only healthcare provider."[79] This withdrawal undoubtedly meant a reduction in, or even elimination of, health care to internally displaced women and girls in those areas.[80]

Intimidation of humanitarian workers also extends to their efforts to publicize the plight of women caught in armed conflict. In May 2005, the MSF head of mission in Sudan, Paul Foreman, was arrested in Khartoum and charged with crimes against the state. Foreman was accused of publishing false reports, undermining society in Sudan, and spying.[81] Vincent Hoedt, the organization's regional coordinator in Darfur, was also arrested.[82] The arrests were linked to the publication of a report by MSF entitled "The Crushing Burden of Rape: Sexual Violence in Darfur," which detailed hundreds of rapes in the region.[83] The charges were ultimately dropped, after an intervention by the UN Special Representative of the Secretary-General with the government of Sudan.[84] The efforts of the Sudanese government to prevent the organization from publicizing the extent of rapes in Darfur, and so to hide the stories of the affected women, nevertheless remains a clear example of intimidation of humanitarian workers.

Mistreatment of humanitarian workers results in a shrinking humanitarian space for women. When programs are curtailed due to threats to humanitarian staff, female recipients of that aid are placed in a more vulnerable situation. As well, when female aid workers are directly targeted, the benefit they may bring – in the form of better access to refugee and IDP women in the field – is lost.

Women as Witnesses

This final section compares the shrinking humanitarian space described above to the "humanitarian space" found in the courtrooms of international and internationalized criminal justice tribunals such as the International Criminal Court, the International Criminal Tribunals for the former Yugoslavia and Rwanda and the Special Court for Sierra Leone.[85] While these courtrooms are not necessarily humanitarian spaces according to the understanding of the various actors identified earlier, it is nonetheless interesting to note that the experiences of women subject to shrinking humanitarian space is mirrored, to some extent, by the experience of women in international courtrooms. In both spaces, they have been subjected to denial (of access to aid, or the ability to fully tell their stories) or trauma. This disadvantages women receiving aid and victim-witnesses in courtrooms both in the present and in the future.

For female victims of international crimes, it can be empowering to be able to tell their stories about the individuals accused of at least part of their suffering.[86] Over time, international criminal tribunals have adopted extensive procedures to address the needs of, *inter alia,* female victims and witnesses who are assisting in the investigation of and/or testifying about sexual or gender-based violence. These include confidentiality measures such as the use of pseudonyms or closed sessions[87] and protection from re-traumatization.[88] Some measures extend to the post-trial stage in order to protect an individual from retribution for providing testimony. The victims and witnesses are assisted in a specially designated unit within each court, and are provided with access to counselling and support as well as medical care.[89] The counselling, support, and medical care include assistance specifically designed for those who have suffered gender-based violence.[90]

The gender-sensitive procedures and practices adopted by international criminal tribunals help to expand courtroom "humanitarian space" for women. They do so by providing places in which stories may be told in as safe a manner as possible. Sometimes this space is unduly constrained, however. The experience of female victims and witnesses at the Special Court for Sierra Leone during the *Fofana and Kondewa* trial (popularly referred to as the Civilian Defence Forces, or CDF, case) provides an example. In this case, the Prosecutor requested clarification from the Trial Chamber as to whether he could introduce evidence of gender-based violence to prove the crime against humanity of inhumane acts and the war crime of cruel treatment.[91] The Prosecutor's request was in line with the practice of other international criminal tribunals. Without adequate reasoning, a majority of the Trial Chamber rejected the Prosecutor's request.[92] As a result, seven female witnesses were forced to avoid mentioning any experience related to (or that *might* be related to) gender-based violence, while certain female witnesses were not permitted to testify at all.[93] The end result was that the trial record was either silent on gender-based violence or inaccurate due to the way in which the women who did testify were forced to tailor their stories. For instance, witness TF2-188 was originally supposed to testify that she had been raped by and forcibly married to the accused Kondewa, but was permitted to testify only about the killing of her mother. Thus, in the final trial judgment, the only story recorded is the one about her mother.[94]

As a result, and in direct contrast to other trial judgments of the Special Court for Sierra Leone, very little evidence of gender-based violence is included in the CDF judgment, despite the fact that serious gender-based violence did occur in CDF-controlled areas during the Sierra Leonean conflict. Although the Appeals Chamber admonished the majority Trial Chamber judges for their decisions in the CDF case, it could not undo the damage caused to the trial record by the silencing of the victims.[95] Michelle Staggs Kelsall and Shanee Stepakoff investigated the impact of this unjustified silencing on the female witnesses, reporting that many suffered from psychological distress.[96] In addition, this silencing meant that the testimony of certain women did not contribute to the tribunal's crucial truth-recording function.[97]

The CDF trial experience is not the only one of its kind. Victims and witnesses at the International Criminal Tribunals for the former Yugoslavia and Rwanda have also reported frustrations about, and negative repercussions from, their appearances before these tribunals.[98] This can be understood as a sort of constriction of "humanitarian space" for women with respect to these tribunals. The end result is that women's stories are ultimately erased from, or are fragmented within, the final story told by these tribunals about the conflict. This discourages other women from coming forward to the same or other tribunals. The elimination of these stories can also lead to the growth of myths in the future, such as a myth that no gender-based crimes were committed by one side or the other during a conflict. Ultimately, just as shrinking humanitarian space in the traditional sense disadvantages women both in the present and in the future, so too does the shrinkage of the international courtroom as a safe place.

Conclusion

The term "humanitarian space" does not have one commonly accepted meaning. The understanding of humanitarian space varies among a range of actors, such as the UN, the ICRC, non-governmental aid agencies, donors, and recipient states. Even so, this indeterminacy of meaning is not of consequence when one focuses upon the experiences of female aid beneficiaries. Furthermore, the various actors willing and able to take advantage of the increased vulnerability of women seeking safety – whether fellow refugees or internally displaced persons, armed groups, state security forces, UN peacekeepers, or humanitarian workers – means that, for female aid recipients, the line separating humanitarian space from militarized or unsafe space becomes blurred.

Threats to, or attacks on, humanitarian personnel often lead to the restriction or elimination of aid programs in given areas, such as Darfur. With the limitations that emerge following the withdrawal of humanitarian assistance, women are placed in an ever more vulnerable position in armed conflict situations. These vulnerabilities are compounded by the sexual exploitation and abuse of women in and around refugee and IDP camps. Although these camps are meant to be safe havens, this is not the experience of women who must trade sex for basic necessities in order for them and their families to survive. Clearly, shrinking humanitarian space has negative consequences for many women.

ACKNOWLEDGMENT
The author wishes to thank Katherine Ferreira for her helpful research assistance.

NOTES

1 This chapter uses the term "women" throughout, but it is also meant to reflect the realities of girls.
2 Statement by the President of the Security Council, UN SCOR, 6066th meeting, UN Doc. S/PRST/2009/1 (2009) at 2.
3 *Ibid.*
4 *Ibid.* at 7-8, s. C.
5 *Ibid.*
6 Ulrike von Pilar, "Humanitarian Space under Siege" (Background paper for the symposium "Europe and Humanitarian Aid – What Future? Learning from Crisis," 22-23 April 1999, Bad Neuenahr) at 4.
7 United Nations High Commissioner for Refugees, "Internally Displaced People: Questions & Answers" (1 November 2007) at 4, online: UNHCR <http://www.

unhcr.org/>; United Nations High Commissioner for Refugees, "Refugee Women" (25 April 2002), online: UNHCR <http://www.unhcr.org/>.

8 Hilde van Dijkhorst and Suzette Vonhof, *Gender and Humanitarian Aid: A Literature Review of Policy and Practice* (Wageningen, Netherlands: Wageningen Disaster Studies and Cordaid, 2005) at 7.

9 The International Labour Organization identifies women's subordination as a root cause of their vulnerability in disasters: International Labour Organization, *Crisis, Women and Other Gender Concerns* (Geneva: Selected Issues Papers of the Recovery and Reconstruction Department at the International Labour Office, 2002) at 7.

10 UNHCR, "Refugee Women," *supra* note 7; van Dijkhorst and Vonhof, *supra* note 8 at 7; International Committee of the Red Cross, *Women Facing War* (Geneva: ICRC, 2001) at 28.

11 International Committee of the Red Cross, *ibid.* at 40.

12 United Nations High Commissioner for Refugees, *Sexual and Gender-Based Violence against Refugees, Returnees and Internally Displaced Persons* (Geneva: UNHCR, 2003) at 21 [UNHCR, "Sexual and Gender-Based Violence"]. Olsen and Scharffscher helpfully observe that, in their experience in Sierra Leonean IDP camps, "our assumption is that these camps constitute a miniature version of the general society [in which women suffer gender-based discrimination on many levels], only with a more vulnerable sample of the population": Odd Einar Olsen and Kristin S. Scharffscher, "Rape in Refugee Camps as Organisational Failure" (2004) 8 Int'l J.H.R. 380.

13 Van Dijkhorst and Vonhof, *supra* note 8 at 12-13; UNHCR, "Sexual and Gender-Based Violence," *supra* note 12 at 22.

14 Olsen and Scharffscher state that sometimes there is a "significant distance – both organizational and geographical – between the engineers designing the refugee camps and the people working and living in them. We also found that the engineers were predominantly men, whereas the program managers, field workers and majority of residents were women": Olsen and Scharffscher, *supra* note 12 at 390.

15 Van Dijkhorst and Vonhof, *supra* note 8 at 14; UNHCR, "Sexual and Gender-Based Violence," *supra* note 12 at 22.

16 UNHCR, *ibid.* at 22.

17 *Ibid.*

18 United Nations Office of the High Commissioner for Human Rights, *Access to Justice for Victims of Sexual Violence: Report of the United Nations High Commissioner for Human Rights* (Geneva: OHCHR, 2005) at para. 17, online: UNHCR <http://www.unhcr.org/refworld/>.

19 *Ibid.* at paras. 20-21.

20 International Criminal Court, *Prosecutor v. Omar Hassan Ahmad Al Bashir,* Decision on the Prosecution's Application for a Warrant of Arrest against Omar Hassan Ahmad Al Bashir, ICC-02/05-01/09 (4 March 2009) at para. 107.

21 Olsen and Scharffscher note that Post-Traumatic Stress Disorder is common among rape survivors, including a reduced ability to function as provider and carer: Olsen and Scharffscher, *supra* note 12 at 379. It can be surmised that, in the context of Darfur and other armed conflicts, rape of refugee or internally displaced women potentially has effects not only on the targeted woman but also on her family and other dependents.

22 Women's Initiatives for Gender Justice, "Women's Voices" (March 2009), online: Women's Initiatives for Gender Justice <http://www.iccwomen.org/>.

23 Olsen and Scharffscher concluded in their study that a very low percentage of sexual violence ever reaches the attention of staff in charge of the camps, there was widespread confusion about who was responsible for gender issues or gender safety in camps, and there were poor reporting routines with respect to allegations of gender-based violence: Olsen and Scharffscher, *supra* note 12 at 380, 389, and 390.

24 *Ibid.* at 385 and 394.

25 *Ibid.* at 394.

26 Csáky reports in her 2008 study that beneficiaries of aid and emergency staff themselves "are confused by the many different reporting procedures specific to individual organizations": Corinna Csáky, *No One to Turn to: The Under-Reporting of Child Sexual Exploitation and Abuse by Aid Workers and Peacekeepers* (London: Save the Children UK, 2008) at 13. While she was referring to reporting of sexual exploitation and abuse by aid workers and peacekeepers, there is no reason to believe that the situation is markedly better with respect to reporting of abuse by others in the community.

27 Sexual exploitation and abuse by fellow refugees and IDPs, police, teachers, family, and community members often occur alongside abuse committed by aid workers and peacekeepers and other local and foreign staff associated with the international community: *ibid.* at 3 and 9.

28 Elizabeth Defeis, "UN Peacekeepers and Sexual Abuse and Exploitation: An End to Impunity" (2008) 7 Washington University Global Studies Law Review 186. See also United Nations Secretary-General, "Letter Dated 24 March 2005 from the Secretary-General to the President of the General Assembly," UN GAOR, 59th Sess., UN Doc. A/59/710 (2005) at para. 3 [Zeid Report].

29 United Nations High Commissioner for Refugees and Save the Children UK, *Note for Implementing and Operational Partners on Sexual Violence & Exploitation: The Experience of Refugee Children in Guinea, Liberia and Sierra Leone Based on Initial Findings and Recommendations from Assessment Mission (22 October–30 November 2001)* (Geneva: UNHCR and Save the Children UK, 2002).

30 *Ibid.* at 3. Note that there were reports of a few boys being similarly exploited by older women (at 3) and male sexual exploitation against boys may have taken place (at 14).

31 *Ibid.* at 4.

32 *Ibid.* at 2 and 4.

33 *Ibid.* at 4.

34 *Ibid.* at 4-5.

35 *Ibid.* at 6.

36 *Ibid.* at 10-12.

37 United Nations Secretary-General, "Investigation into Sexual Exploitation of Refugees by Aid Workers in West Africa: Note by the Secretary-General," UN GAOR, 57th Sess., UN Doc. A/57/465 (2002) at para. 42.

38 *Ibid.* at 4.

39 Human Rights Watch, *Trapped by Inequality: Bhutanese Refugee Women in Nepal* (New York: Human Rights Watch, 2003).

40 Zeid Report, *supra* note 28 at para. 6.
41 Security Council Report, "Update Report No. 3: Sexual Exploitation and Abuse by UN Peacekeeping Personnel" (20 February 2006), online: Security Council Report <http://www.securitycouncilreport.org/>.
42 Csáky, *supra* note 26 at 5-7.
43 It is recognized that some would not characterize the Zeid Report on sexual abuse by peacekeeping personnel as part of the humanitarian space debate. However, if the women and girls affected do not see a difference between the efforts of the UN Mission in the Democratic Republic of the Congo (MONUC) to create space to provide assistance and the efforts of humanitarian agencies to provide assistance, then arguably their perception of humanitarian space is that it is constrained or non-existent.
44 Others may include those who witnessed the sexual exploitation and abuse of girls, and children at risk of or who fear such abuse.
45 Although this chapter has explored the refugee and IDP camp as a theoretical humanitarian space, it should be noted that humanitarian space also extends to other places where refugees and IDPs live and access aid, such as cities, towns, and host families.
46 United Nations Secretary-General, *Comprehensive Report Prepared Pursuant to General Assembly Resolution 59/296 on Sexual Exploitation and Sexual Abuse, Including Policy Development, Implementation and Full Justification of Proposed Capacity on Personnel Conduct Issues*, UN GAOR, UN Doc. A/60/862 (2006) at para. 9 [UNSG, "Comprehensive Report"].
47 United Nations High Commissioner for Refugees, *Code of Conduct and Explanatory Notes* (Geneva: UNHCR, 2004). Under the seventh guiding principle, UNHCR employees pledge: "I will never request any service or favour from refugees or other persons of concern in return for protection or assistance. I will never engage in any exploitative relationships – sexual, emotional, financial or employment-related – with refugees or other persons of concern." See also Women's Commission for Refugee Women and Children, *Breaking the Code: Building Capacity to Investigate Sexual Abuse and Exploitation by Humanitarian Workers, Evaluating ICVA's Building Safer Organizations Project* (New York: Women's Commission for Refugee Women and Children, 2006) at 1.
48 United Nations Secretary-General, *Secretary-General's Bulletin on Special Measures for Protection from Sexual Exploitation and Sexual Abuse*, UN Doc. ST/SGB/2003/13 (2003). As Defeis notes: "Although initially only UN staff members were expressly bound by the prohibitions in the Secretary-General's 2003 Bulletin, these standards have been incorporated into the contracts, letters of engagement and undertakings of all personnel": *supra* note 28 at 195.
49 United Nations Conduct and Discipline Unit, "Ten Rules: Code of Personal Conduct for Blue Helmets," online: http://cdu.unlb.org/; and United Nations Conduct and Discipline Unit, "We Are United Nations Peacekeeping Personnel," online: <http://cdu.unlb.org/>.
50 Csáky, *supra* note 26 at 1 and 18.
51 *Ibid.* at 10-14.

52 Zeid Report, *supra* note 28.

53 *E.g.*, the Security Council extension of the mandate for MONUC: *The Situation Concerning the Democratic Republic of the Congo*, SC Res. 1856, UN SCOR, UN Doc. S/RES/1856 (2008). This resolution (at para. 15) "[t]akes note of the measures taken by MONUC to address instances of sexual exploitation and abuse and of the zero-tolerance policy, requests the Secretary-General to continue to fully investigate the allegations of sexual exploitation and violence by civilian and military personnel of MONUC, to take the appropriate measures set out in the Secretary-General's bulletin on special measures for protection from sexual exploitation and sexual abuse (ST/SGB/2003/13)."

54 SC Res. 1820, UN SCOR, UN Doc. S/RES/1820 (2008) at para. 10.

55 *E.g.*, UNSG, "Comprehensive Report," *supra* note 46.

56 *E.g.*, see United Nations Secretary-General, *Special Measures for Protection from Sexual Exploitation and Abuse*, UN GAOR, UN Doc. A/62/890 (2008), reporting on information provided by thirty-nine of forty-three UN entities (including the UNHCR) about allegations of sexual exploitation and abuse during 2007.

57 Defeis, *supra* note 28 at 197-99.

58 See United Nations High Commissioner for Refugees, *UNHCR Handbook for the Protection of Women and Girls* (Geneva: UNHCR, 2008) at chs. 2, 4, and 5 for an explanation of this rights approach [UNHCR, *Handbook for the Protection of Women and Girls*].

59 See UNHCR, "Sexual and Gender-Based Violence," *supra* note 12 at 42, and United Nations High Commissioner for Refugees, "Shedding New Light on Refugee Women's Safety in Bangladesh" (19 February 2009), online: UNHCR <http://www.unhcr.org/>.

60 Rhone Resch and Noah Kaye, "Giving Life with the Sun: Darfur Solar Cookers Project" (2007) 44 UN Chronicles, online: United Nations <http://www.un.org/>.

61 Abby Stoddard, Adele Harmer, and Victoria DiDomenico, "Providing Aid in Insecure Environments: 2009 Update," HPG (Humanitarian Policy Group) Policy Brief 34 (2009) at 9, online: Overseas Development Institute <http://www.odi.org.uk/resources/> [Stoddard *et al.*, "2009 Update"]. There are numerous media reports on the targeting of aid-funded Afghan girls' schools, including this one, illustrated with a picture of burned textbooks bearing the UNICEF logo: United Nations Children's Fund, "UNICEF Condemns Attacks on Schools in Afghanistan" (14 November 2008), online: UNICEF <http://www.unicef.org/>. Other reports describe acid or gas attacks on female Afghan students: "Acid Attack on Afghan Schoolgirls" (12 November 2008), online: BBC News <http://news.bbc.co.uk/>; Emma Graham-Harrison, "Attacks Threaten Gains to Afghan Girls' Education – UN" (20 May 2009), online: Reuters <http://www.reuters.com/>. The latter report indicates that UNICEF is asking local communities to contribute money or labour to the construction of girls' schools, "which cuts costs and encourages parents to protect the building."

62 Stoddard *et al.*, "2009 Update," *supra* note 61 at 9.

63 *Ibid.* at 2.

64 *Ibid.*

65 *Ibid.* at 4-5.

66 *Ibid.* at 5-6.

67 United Nations Secretary-General, *Report of the Secretary-General on Children and Armed Conflict in the Sudan*, UN SCOR, UN Doc. S/2009/84 (2009) at para. 46.

68 Stoddard *et al.*, "2009 Update," *supra* note 61 at 4 and 10.

69 *Ibid.* at 10.

70 Abby Stoddard, Adele Harmer, and Katherine Haver, "Providing Aid in Insecure Environments: Trends in Policy and Operations," HPG (Humanitarian Policy Group) Report 23 (2006) at 37, online: Overseas Development Institute <http://www.odi.org.uk/resources/>.

71 *Ibid.* at 42.

72 Stoddard *et al.*, "2009 Update," *supra* note 61 at 7.

73 *Ibid.* at 7.

74 *Ibid.*

75 International Committee of the Red Cross, *supra* note 10 at 40.

76 *Ibid.*

77 *Ibid.* at 41. See also UNHCR, *Handbook for the Protection of Women and Girls*, *supra* note 58 at 15 and 17.

78 Médecins Sans Frontières, "Kidnapped MSF staff Released in Darfur, Sudan" (14 March 2009), online: Médecins Sans Frontières <http://www.msf.org/>.

79 *Ibid.*

80 In another recent example that likely deprived the female population of access to female humanitarian workers, two female aid workers (Stéphanie Jodoin and Claire Dubois of Aide Médicale Internationale) were kidnapped in Darfur and held for more than three weeks in open-air captivity: Tu Thanh Ha, "Kidnappers Release Canadian, French Women" *Globe and Mail* (14 May 2009).

81 Médecins Sans Frontières, "MSF Shocked by Arrest of Head of Mission in Sudan – Charged with Crimes against the State" (31 May 2005), online: Médecins Sans Frontières <http://www.msf.org/> [MSF, "Shocked"].

82 Médecins Sans Frontières, "MSF Welcomes Dropping of Charges against Its Representatives in Sudan" (20 June 2005), online: Médecins Sans Frontières <http://www.msf.org/>.

83 MSF, "Shocked," *supra* note 81.

84 Office of the High Commissioner for Human Rights, *supra* note 18 at 3.

85 The term "international criminal tribunal" is used to refer to institutions such as the International Criminal Tribunals for the former Yugoslavia and Rwanda, and the International Criminal Court. The term "internationalized" criminal tribunals is used to describe tribunals that contain joint international and domestic aspects (such as having jurisdiction over a mix of international and domestic crimes, and/or a judiciary consisting of international and domestically chosen individuals) such as the Special Court for Sierra Leone and the Extraordinary Chambers in the Courts of Cambodia.

86 See Rebecca Horn, Simon Charters, and Saleem Vahidy, "Testifying in an International War Crimes Tribunal: The Experience of Witnesses in the Special Court for Sierra Leone" (2009) 3 International Journal of Transitional Justice 135. Henry indicates that there are four main motivations for victims who choose to serve as witnesses before the International Criminal Tribunal for the former Yugoslavia: to

speak for the dead, to tell the world the truth about what happened, to look for justice in the present, and to help prevent future war crimes from happening: Nicola
Henry, "Witness to Rape: The Limits and Potential of International War Crimes
Trials for Victims of Wartime Sexual Violence" (2009) 3 International Journal of
Transitional Justice 6n21. Henry also indicates that participation in war crimes trials
may provide some degree of satisfaction to victims not available in the non-legal
realm, while also questioning the therapeutic nature of criminal trials (*ibid.* at 5).

87 *E.g., Rome Statute of the International Criminal Court,* Rome, 17 July 1998, 2187
U.N.T.S. 3 (entered into force 1 July 2002) at art. 68(2) [*Rome Statute*]; Preparatory
Commission for the International Criminal Court, *Report of the Preparatory Com-
mission for the International Criminal Court, Finalized Rules of Procedure and
Evidence,* UN Doc. PCNICC/2000/1/Add.1 (2000) at rule 87 [*ICC Rules*].

88 *E.g., ICC Rules, ibid.* at rules 70, 71, and 72.

89 *E.g., ibid.* at rules 16-19 and Anne-Marie L.M. de Brouwer, *Supranational Criminal
Prosecution of Sexual Violence: The ICC and the Practice of the ICTY and the ICTR*
(Oxford: Intersentia, 2005) at 277.

90 *E.g., Rome Statute, supra* note 87 at art. 43(6); *ICC Rules, supra* note 87 at rules
16-19.

91 Special Court for Sierra Leone, Trial Chamber, *Prosecutor v. Sam Hinga Norman,
Moinina Fofana and Allieu Kondewa,* Reasoned Majority Decision on Prosecution
Motion for a Ruling on the Admissibility of Evidence, SCSL-04-14-T (24 May 2005)
at paras. 1-3, 5, and 9 [CDF 24 May 2005 Thompson Majority Decision]. The reason
for his request is linked to a series of motions decisions that preceded this one, in
which the Trial Chamber had denied his request to amend the indictment to include
crimes of sexual and gender-based violence. For a summary, see Valerie Oosterveld,
"The Special Court for Sierra Leone's Consideration of Gender-Based Violence:
Contributing to Transitional Justice?" (2009) 10 Human Rights Review 89.

92 Oral decision: Special Court for Sierra Leone, Trial Chamber, *Prosecutor v. Sam
Hinga Norman, Moinina Fofana and Allieu Kondewa,* Decision on the Urgent
Prosecution Motion Filed on the 15th of February 2005 for a Ruling on the
Admissibility of Evidence, SCSL-04-14-T (23 May 2005); written decision: CDF 24
May 2005 Thompson Majority Decision, *ibid.* at 154.

93 Sara Kendall and Michelle Staggs, *Silencing Sexual Violence: Recent Developments in
the CDF Case at the Special Court for Sierra Leone* (Berkeley: University of California
Berkeley War Crimes Studies Center, 2005), online: <http://violet.berkeley.edu/~
warcrime/>.

94 *Ibid.* at 2, 3 fn. 4, and 17 fn. 79; versus Special Court for Sierra Leone, Trial Chamber,
Prosecutor v. Moinina Fofana and Allieu Kondewa, Judgment, SCSL-04-14-A (2
August 2007) at para. 625.

95 Special Court for Sierra Leone, Appeals Chamber, *Prosecutor v. Alex Tamba Brima,
Brima Bazzy Kamara and Santigie Borbor Kanu,* Judgment, SCSL-04-16-A (22
February 2008) at paras. 441-451.

96 Michelle Staggs Kelsall and Shanee Stepakoff, "'When We Wanted to Talk about
Rape': Silencing Sexual Violence at the Special Court for Sierra Leone" (2007) 1
International Journal of Transitional Justice 372.

97 On the truth-recording function of international tribunals, see de Brouwer, *supra* note 89 at 231.

98 Binaifer Nowrojee, *"Your Justice Is Too Slow": Will the ICTR Fail Rwanda's Rape Victims?* (Geneva: United Nations Research Institute for Social Development, 2005) at 4; Henry, *supra* note 86 at 18.

13

Whither Humanitarian Space?
The Costs of Integrated Peacebuilding in Afghanistan

EMILY PADDON AND TAYLOR OWEN

Since its inception, the US and NATO intervention in Afghanistan has included an unprecedented mix of military, political, and development assistance. Combined, these efforts represent for many of the troop-contributing countries the first test of a new integrated approach to foreign policy in conflict regions: "Whole-of-Government," "3D" (Defence, Development, Diplomacy), or "Integrated Peacebuilding." This new doctrine responds to the increasingly prevalent view that development, governance, and security problems in failed and fragile states create a vicious cycle that demands comprehensive solutions and requires significant bureaucratic, conceptual, and operational restructuring. The doctrine has been recognized by many NATO members as the harbinger of a new era of intervention, and many have made substantial efforts to institutionalize its emerging practices and structures. The idea that the various components present in a peace operation should be better integrated has potential costs, however. In particular, the notion of "humanitarian space" has come into question as nongovernmental organizations (NGOs), now ubiquitous in Afghanistan, struggle to balance their relations with a range of armed actors and the local population.

As several authors in this volume have argued, traditionally the safe and effective delivery of humanitarian assistance in conflict by international NGOs has been contingent upon respect for certain key principles: *neutrality* (assistance must be provided without taking sides or engaging in hostilities), *impartiality* (assistance should be provided on the basis of need alone), *humanity* (all individuals are equal and human suffering should be addressed wherever it is found), and *independence* (assistance should not be connected to the parties directly involved in armed conflicts and those delivering assistance should have unencumbered operational independence).[1] These principles have regulated the behaviour of humanitarians and have been crucial, as many would argue, in creating and accessing the humanitarian space necessary for delivering assistance in the first place. The principles are strengthened further by the humanitarian imperative that suffering populations have a right to assistance without discrimination, which is affirmed in international humanitarian law (IHL).

Yet, despite these strong legal and ethical norms, the definition, permanency, and significance of the above principles have been deeply contested.[2] Over the last several decades, and particularly since the end of the Cold War, as the number and activities of NGOs have expanded, humanitarian actors have engaged in a process of self-identification and clarification of operational principles. Humanitarian actors are no longer a monolithic group.[3] Indeed, a wide range of NGOs in Afghanistan can be plotted on a spectrum, from those willing to operate in conflict zones, with government funding and military support, to those that will do so only independently, to those who will not engage at all. This spectrum is further complicated by the increasing prevalence of multi-mandated organizations that, depending on the context, are committed to providing relief, development assistance, and advocacy. Integration efforts in Afghanistan have further entrenched these differences and exacerbated what were more or less existing but dormant tensions, throwing the community as a whole into a crisis over the very meaning and purpose of humanitarianism.

This chapter examines the ways in which integration has affected humanitarians in Afghanistan. It draws on a series of interviews conducted from 2006 to 2008 as part of a larger project funded by the Canadian Department of Foreign Affairs and International Trade (DFAIT), and thus has a particular focus on the Canadian experience.[4] There are four sections. The first examines the conceptual origins of the integrationist approach in the post–Cold War era. The second traces the development of integration efforts in Afghanistan over the last fifteen years, with a focus on post-9/11 practices. The third section then explores the key challenges posed by integration for humanitarians working in Afghanistan. The chapter concludes with suggestions on how to potentially mitigate the negative effects of integration on humanitarians. Although this chapter focuses on one specific case of intervention, many of the same issues that the NGO community grapples with in the context of Afghanistan are visible elsewhere. Moreover, the experience of Afghanistan will almost certainly influence future thinking on military and humanitarian intervention, given the mission's high visibility, the extent and novelty of integration efforts (for example, the Provincial Reconstruction Team [PRT] model[5]), and the sheer number of NGOs involved in the country.

Conceptual Origins of Integration

The shift towards integrated approaches to conflict and humanitarian crises is rooted in several broad post–Cold War trends, particularly changing conceptualizations of security and a rethinking of state sovereignty.[6]

In the early 1990s, the geopolitical stability provided by the Cold War gave way to a new understanding of the causes of human vulnerability. An array of harms that had been marginalized due to the prioritization of macro threats during the Cold War were suddenly in view, and the nation state was often found to be unable or unwilling to protect citizens from these widespread vulnerabilities. This shift led to the challenging of the notion of traditional security by such concepts as cooperative, comprehensive, societal, collective, international, and human security.[7] Although all these concepts move away from a focus on interstate relations, human security takes the most dramatic step by making the referent object not the state, society, or community but the individual.

Such changes in the concept of security have been inextricably linked to changes to sovereignty leading in the 1990s to the so-called "new interventionism."[8] Where sovereignty was once sacrosanct, a state's right to keep others out increasingly came to depend on treating its own well. The "Responsibility to Protect" doctrine explicitly presented itself as a transition "from territorial security, and security through armaments, to security through human development with access to food and employment, and to environmental security."[9] The interrelationship between security and development came to the fore with the United Nations' High-Level Panel on Threats, Challenges and Change, which concluded that "development and security are inextricably linked."[10] Accordingly, the actions of intervening actors, including many humanitarian organizations, increasingly sought to address the underlying and long-term causes of conflict. The "relief-development continuum" became prevalent as divergent humanitarian actors, often working under the mandate of the same organization and in the same location, provided both emergency relief and longer-term development assistance. For many practitioners, coordination and integration seemed a logical approach given the complexity of these ambitious tasks and the proliferation of actors deployed across the continuum. Moreover, failure to adequately respond to several conflicts, most notably Rwanda, resulted in further calls to strengthen and deepen integration, as organizational isolation and its purported inability to meet expansive objectives were seen as a cause of institutional and operational weakness.

Following 9/11, the promotion of human security and military intervention in what were widely cast as failed, failing, and fragile states assumed a newfound strategic importance. In the context of the global War on Terror, underdevelopment came to be viewed as a potential "threat" and aid as an instrument of "soft" security, crucial for addressing the root causes of terrorism. As the *National Security Strategy of the United States* observed in 2002, "poverty, weak institutions, and corruption can make weak states vulnerable to terrorist networks and drug cartels within their borders."[11] Integrated approaches, combining military power, diplomacy, and development, became a necessary triad in the effort to stabilize fragile states, "win hearts and minds," and secure Western interests. Former US Secretary of State Colin Powell, extolling the virtues of government working with NGOs, stated in October 2001: "I am serious about making sure we have the best relationship with NGOs who are such a force multiplier for us, and such an important part of our combat team."[12] As many warned, however, the inherent risk in treating NGOs as "force multipliers" is that the humanitarian imperative will be subordinated to political interests and to the promotion of strategic, rather than humanitarian, objectives.

Both of these trends were given further momentum by the increasing emphasis that international institutions and Western democracies have placed on coordination and integration – what became known in the late 1990s as "joined up" government or governance. Since the 1970s, there has been a growing awareness that complex policy problems require action that cuts across departments and issue areas, thereby necessitating greater cooperation. Moreover, the expansion in perceived threats as well as the normative ambitions of international society at the end of the Cold War only served to further highlight what many saw as the need for comprehensive policies. Beginning in 1997 with the launch of several initiatives at both headquarters and in the field, the UN was one of many institutions to adopt a more integrated approach.[13] In New York, the initiatives consisted of a series of organizational reforms, including the creation of new integrated executive committees on peace and security, humanitarian affairs, development, and economic and social affairs, as well as a Secretary-General Management Group in charge of overseeing coordination within the UN. At the operational level, the 2000 *Report of the Panel on UN Peace Operations* and the 2005 World Summit, led to the establishment of Integrated Mission Task Forces[14] and the Peacebuilding Commission (PBC),[15] respectively.

Alongside a broadening definition of security, which increasingly encompassed relief and development concerns as well as visible institutional efforts to implement integrated policies at both the level of bureaucracy and in the field, many NGOs thought it important to reaffirm the inviolability of humanitarian principles. In 1995, the Red Cross Code of Conduct reiterated that assistance must be provided without engaging in hostilities or taking sides in conflict, stating that as humanitarians "[w]e will never knowingly – or through negligence – allow ourselves, or our employees, to be used to gather information of a political, military or economically sensitive nature for governments or other bodies that may serve purposes other than those which are strictly humanitarian, nor will we act as instruments of foreign policy of donor governments."[16] Similarly, since its launch in 1997, the Sphere Project has developed minimum standards in core areas of humanitarian assistance, aiming to improve the quality of assistance provided to people affected by disasters and to enhance the accountability of the humanitarian system in disaster response. Under both of these frameworks, as Stephen Cornish and Marit Glad note, assistance delivered in conjunction with government activities is not prohibited, so long as it is delivered impartially and based solely on need.[17]

Integration in Afghanistan

Efforts to coordinate humanitarian activity in Afghanistan were spearheaded by the UN and commenced in the mid-1990s during the period of Taliban control. According to Antonio Donini, the country's Office for the Coordination of Humanitarian Affairs (OCHA) director from 1999 to 2002, the development of the Strategic Framework was intended to bring coherence to the UN's political, assistance, and human rights objectives. Moreover, the Principled Common Programming initiative attempted to bring NGOs into the Strategic Framework and resulted to a certain degree in coordinated and joint assistance programming through the UN.[18] Despite this connection to the UN, as well as what were at times strained relations with the Taliban over controversial issues such as the education of women and girls, NGO activities were not overtly politicized and aid workers were afforded a considerable degree of access in delivering assistance.

The events of 9/11 renewed Afghanistan's strategic importance. The UN Assistance Mission in Afghanistan (UNAMA) was "established as the most 'integrated' mission to date."[19] OCHA was subsumed under the broader UNAMA umbrella; in the process, Donini notes, the humanitarian and human rights pillars lost much of their agency as they were beholden to the mission's political objectives, with many organizations uncritically supporting the fledgling government, and implicitly, the NATO intervention. Here, critics assert that the coalition and UN were too quick in classifying Afghanistan as a "post-conflict" state.[20] They argue that this premature designation served multiple purposes: it assisted in selling the intervention domestically, permitting the channelling of funds towards infrastructure and development, to which NGOs flocked, and it legitimized the nascent Afghan government.[21] As a result, NGOs that had previously maintained links with the Taliban to negotiate acceptance and secure access increasingly worked directly with the government and the UN as implementing partners in what was viewed as "development" work. Once the shaky foundations of the so-called peace became evident, NGOs struggled to distance themselves from the UN and the government of Afghanistan, both in the way they were perceived and operationally. This was made more difficult as funds were increasingly channelled through the Afghan government's National Priority Programmes.[22] In this context, the UN's coordinating role was weakened by the proliferation of other actors who appeared on the scene. Of these new actors, the Provincial Reconstruction Teams (PRTs) eventually came to represent the most novel manifestation of integration approaches, with donor governments channelling foreign aid directly through these entities.

The PRTs were first established by the United States in 2002 with the goal of bolstering support for Operation Enduring Freedom through a new localized reconstruction effort designed to "win hearts and minds." Aid, development, and reconstruction, conducted interchangeably and with military support, were viewed as critical in facilitating the acceptance of international military forces by the peoples of Afghanistan, in enabling the country's stabilization, and in ridding the country of terrorism. As US General Karl Eikenberry emphasized, "[w]here the road ends, the Taliban begins."[23] Since 2002, the PRT model has been adopted by the other members of the International Security Assistance Force (ISAF), including Canada, and, despite varying interpretations of their core mandate of "enabling reconstruction," all twenty-six PRTs now deployed represent a mix of civil and military operations. Moreover, there has been an accelerating "civilianization" of the PRTs over the last couple of years as donor countries have increased "civilian capacities to deliver on political and aid-related objectives, and have encouraged coordination with the activities of the Government of Afghanistan (GOA)" (confidential interview, 18 September 2008). The drive towards PRT integration has had a profound influence upon, and to a certain extent has also been driven by, changes in the bureaucratic structure and government communication strategies of troop-contributing countries, as departments (as diverse as Defence, Agriculture, Justice, and Development) that used to function independently are increasingly being asked to collaborate, both on the battlefield and at headquarters.

For Canada, the move towards integrated operations in Afghanistan has been central to the mission and has remained robust across three governments. In 2004, then Prime Minister Paul Martin explained: "[T]he three Ds means building public institutions that work and are accountable to the public for their actions, 'not just policing' but also government ministries, a system of laws, courts, Human Rights Commissions, schools, hospitals, energy and water and transportation systems."[24] The term "3D" has since fallen out of favour under the Conservative government, to be replaced by "Whole-of-Government." The substance, however, is the same. Peter MacKay, in his role as Minister of Foreign Affairs, has stated that "not just the Canadian Forces, but Canadian diplomats, development workers and experts in human rights, good governance, the rule of law and democracy building have all come together in common endeavour overseas to advance Canada's security ... a whole different approach is what is needed and is how we are proceeding."[25]

The findings of the Manley Panel, which was formed by Prime Minister Stephen Harper to assess the mission in Afghanistan, further pressed the notion that greater integration, at both the operational level in Afghanistan and the bureaucratic level at headquarters, was essential. Two central recommendations of the panel, that the mission in Afghanistan be coordinated by a new entity based in the Privy Council Office, and that the civilian component of the mission be significantly increased, were both immediately implemented. With respect to the latter, there has been a scaling up of civilian presence from six officials in 2006 to over seventy in 2008, and for the first time, a civilian – the Representative of Canada in Kandahar (ROCK) – was placed in charge of all operations in the province, a significant cultural shift in a mission that had from the start been military-led.

Implications of Integration for Humanitarian Actors

A central challenge of integration in Afghanistan is that conflating humanitarian action with the broader geopolitical agendas, from which NGOs have historically sought to distance themselves, politicizes humanitarian organizations and their activities. Seen this way, integration efforts have translated into three key areas of tension: the changing relationship between the military and NGOs, within the NGO community itself, and between NGOs and donor governments. These three areas are discussed below separately for the purpose of clarity, but in practice all three are inextricably linked.

Military and NGOs: The Security Dilemma

The international military forces deployed in Afghanistan have increasingly undertaken humanitarian activities themselves, through the employment of contractors as well as through local and international NGOs, all of which have come to form part of the coordinated strategy. In their effort to win hearts and minds and promote security as part of the broader stabilization strategy, several of the PRTs have undertaken "quick impacts projects" (QIPs) or "signature projects," such as the current Canadian Dahla Dam and school rehabilitation schemes. Concerned with short-term and visible gains, which are perceived as advantageous for force protection, these projects have often entailed the hiring of costly and often inexperienced implementing partners, including private contractors who fail to properly deliver on projects and further risk tarnishing the image of legitimate NGOs.[26] Moreover, these projects have been criticized as being self-serving, often of poor quality, and contradictory to both short-term relief based on need and traditional long-term development strategies. Afghan civilians are well accustomed to being assisted only when and where it suits broader geopolitical objectives; as a result, many have been suspicious of these short-term projects, citing their preference for long-term development strategies.[27]

Given the overtly political aims of the PRTs, principally the extension of the Afghan government's authority and the combating of terrorism, many NGOs assert that they are either tainted by association or adversely affected by the blurring of identities, leading to a loss of impartiality and neutrality regardless of whether they chose to collaborate with PRTs or the government. Accordingly, they argue that this compromise to their fundamental operating principles has impeded their access to vulnerable populations and has made them legitimate targets in the eyes of belligerents. This logic of NGOs wanting to distance themselves from PRT members has at times been counterintuitive, however, particularly for members of the military. In one instance, members of a prominent NGO reported that their compound was visited by members of the local PRT shortly following a raid by insurgents and "[w]hile such enquiries might seem normal to the military, who were compiling an incident report, it went against the NGO's security needs, in the context – having survived the incident, they had wanted to distance themselves from the PRT."[28]

Although the PRT model has been the focus of such criticisms, the blurring of identities resulting from a mix of military and humanitarian activities as well as the compromise of fundamental principles have been present from the inception of the campaign in Afghanistan. As US Senator John Warner noted on the night of the first military campaign: "This is the first time in contemporary military history where a military operation is being conducted against the government of a country, and simultaneously, with the troops carrying out the mission, other troops are trying to take care of the innocent victims who all too often are caught in harm's way."[29] Far from harmless benevolence, actions undertaken by the intervening coalition "to take care of the victims" – for example, the dispersion of cluster bombs that were the same colour and shape as food packets dropped in similar areas, and the deployment of Special Forces bearing arms but dressed in civilian clothes and transported in white unmarked caravans that traditionally had been the choice of NGOs and the UN – were in contravention of the principles of the *Geneva Conventions* and arguably had a profound and lasting impact on civilians and humanitarian organizations.[30]

Over time, the blurring of identities and the loss of humanitarian space has manifested itself in threats to the security of both NGO actors and the beneficiaries of their assistance. As security has worsened, NGOs have reconsidered how they go about providing assistance. Indeed, the security of NGO workers in Afghanistan has steadily declined since the initial invasion, with a pronounced deterioration in 2007-09. Violent attacks and threats of attack are increasingly politically motivated and afflict NGOs across the spectrum (such as those associated with PRTs, those who are implementing Afghan government programming, and those who are completely independent and emphasize their neutrality). Whereas in 2007, 61 percent of security incidents were attributed to criminals and 39 percent to political opposition groups, the ratio was reversed in 2008, with 65 percent of incidents believed to be the work of armed opposition groups.[31]

Moreover, who is considered a "legitimate target" by insurgents appears to have broadened to encompass the humanitarian community more widely. Raids against NGO offices to find "evidence" of links to international

military actors still occur, but are increasingly overshadowed by direct
wholesale targeting. A recent Overseas Development Institute report argued
that aid organizations in Afghanistan "are being attacked not just because
they are perceived to be cooperating with Western political actors, but because they are perceived as wholly a part of the Western agenda."[32] This represents a marked change from past practices, where "even just a few years
ago Afghan locals made distinctions between organizations, for instance
between agencies that were working with the coalition force's PRT and
agencies that were not."[33] These observations are supported by interviews
with specific NGOs that, like CARE, were previously able to strike deals
with the Taliban in which they were told that if they remained independently funded and separate from the PRTs, their continued security would
be guaranteed.[34] These assurances have become untenable given both the
proliferation of new armed actors and NGOs. The presence of new foreign
jihadists who do not have long-standing relationships with, or knowledge
of, the various NGOs operating in their vicinity has compromised NGO access. Furthermore, the crowding of the development marketplace with the
springing up of new organizations has made differentiation between the experienced and opportunistic NGOs all the more difficult. According to most
organizations working in the country, humanitarian space has all but evap-
orated in Afghanistan.

In this context, the ICRC stands out as the only exception. The organization is praised for having effectively carved out neutral operational space in
which to work, as well as a distinct and well-branded identity.[35] Several factors have potentially contributed to the ICRC's unique standing, including
"its mandate; its well-known emblem; an established presence in the Afghan
and cross-border context; and its ability to maintain its independence from
the armed forces and the GOA."[36] Given the role that the ICRC has safe-
guarded for itself, it comes as no surprise that as Médecins Sans Frontières
(MSF), an organization with a similar approach to core principles, has attempted to re-establish an operational capacity in the country, it has consulted extensively with the ICRC on how to adhere to humanitarian
principles in the current operational environment.[37]

The security repercussions of integration are not limited to NGO workers, and extend to the perceived and actual beneficiaries of assistance, development, and reconstruction activity. Accusations of having direct and
indirect ties to the military, the GOA, or NGOs can endanger civilians.
Members of PRTs have been criticized for being insensitive to these risks as
they interact with civilian populations and design reconstruction-related

programming. As one senior NGO official stated, referring to Canada's strategic objective to build more schools: "From my perspective, the presence of soldiers in the schools turns the schools into a military target and putting the school bag on the child, and sending her off into the street, increases her vulnerability as a target."[38] This view became a horrendously grim reality in December 2006, when a bicyclist suicide bomber attacked Canadian officials in Kandahar as they distributed candy, notebooks, and pens to a crowd of children near the district of Panjwayi. Twenty-four children were injured and four soldiers were killed.[39]

Beneficiaries are also indirectly affected by this deteriorating security situation for NGOs and the broader community. In the wake of attacks, many organizations cease operations, scale back, resort to remote management, or decide not to commence operations in the first place, leaving beneficiaries destitute.[40] As the country's security has deteriorated and attacks against civilians have escalated, access has decreased, with the United Nations High Commissioner for Refugees (UNHCR) estimating that it has reach into only 55 percent of the country and the Red Cross stating in 2008 that humanitarian access is the worst in twenty-seven years.[41] NGOs have tried to mitigate the lack of access by increasing remote management models of program implementation, a strategy that involves reducing the field role for international staff and relying primarily on local staff. This strategy is based on the unsubstantiated assertion that locals, by being less conspicuous than ex-patriots, minimize attacks targeted at Western NGOs. This strategy is both practically and ethically problematic.

Tensions within the NGO Community

In addition to presenting security challenges, integration has recast relations between NGOs operating in Afghanistan as organizations have adopted different approaches to funding and operational cooperation. The "defeat" of the Taliban in 2001 and the overwhelming availability of resources for relief and development prompted an influx of NGOs operating in the country. Although many of these organizations were reputable and established institutions, often with previous experience working in the country, the development marketplace was also flooded with unskilled entrepreneurial local and international entities, described by some Afghans as "briefcase NGOs" or "Come N' GOs."[42] These organizations often have little knowledge of or training in humanitarian ethics. Moreover, as donor funds have increasingly been channelled through the Afghan government and the PRTs, some NGOs have had little choice but to accept funding and act as implementing partners, thereby compromising their independence in order to reach beneficiaries. This has been the case particularly for smaller and local NGOs for whom direct donor and private funding is inconsistent, and who find the lighter reporting and monitoring procedures of the PRTs more manageable.

NGOs that are vehemently opposed to integration have increasingly distanced themselves from those that have, to varying degrees, been willing to coordinate with the Afghan government and PRTs. This has resulted in strained relations within the NGO community, making communication and intelligence sharing more difficult. Although the establishment of several NGO coordinating bodies has assisted to some extent with negotiation of this complex terrain, members recount how meetings are plagued by mutual suspicion, inconsistent attendance, and a reluctance to share information.[43] These tensions point to a deeper and more troubling lack of coherence among the humanitarian community, as aid workers increasingly disagree on the purpose and appropriate means of humanitarianism. It is therefore unsurprising, as Joanna Macrae argues, that humanitarianism "as a concept ... remains poorly understood within the wider development, security, and diplomatic arena."[44]

Tension between NGOs and Donors/Governments

Because both major aid donors and the governments of troop-contributing countries are preoccupied with the security benefits of assistance, many NGOs argue that the humanitarian ethic is being rendered subordinate to political aims. Such critics point to a number of trends that together have led to what they see as a politicization of aid and a blurring of lines between humanitarian relief, development, and politically driven reconstruction. For some NGOs, this has led to a complete separation from government-funded activities in Afghanistan or a refusal to operate in the country should private funding be unavailable.

Many in the development community have argued that the political priorities of donor nations have led to a prioritization of reconstruction and development seen as strategically useful, and to a sidelining of humanitarian relief. This has led, critics argue, to a concentration of funding in provinces that are politically and militarily important (*i.e.*, the volatile South) but not necessarily most in need of assistance. As Glad and Cornish note:

> USAID channels more than half of its budget to the four most insecure
> provinces ... Helmand province alone is the third largest recipient of USAID

funding in the world, and thus receives more aid dollars than many of the world's poorest countries. Similarly, the British government concentrates 25 percent of its development funds in Helmand, where its main forces are deployed. On the same note, Canada which had been allocating 25 percent of its aid to its military stronghold of Kandahar, has now undertaken to spend 50 percent of its ODA [official development assistance] in that province.[45]

This same impetus, some argue, drives aid to the PRTs, with significant consequences. A reliance on officials with little field and regional experience and poor resourcing deployed to work on assistance in the PRTs, for example, can lead to increased contracting out to questionable companies, ineffective programming, and the further subordination of aid projects to military objectives. NGOs are also under donor pressure to operate in regions where PRTs are located in order to complement PRT initiatives and further contribute to strategic objectives.

This tension between the humanitarian and the strategic imperative (need-based assistance and long-term development versus politically motivated aid and QIPs) is also visible *within* governmental development departments, such as the Canadian International Development Agency (CIDA) and the United Kingdom's Department for International Development (DFID). CIDA, for example, is involved in both politically driven reconstruction in support of specific mission objectives as well as long-term development projects. While both may be entirely appropriate, when conducted by a single organization there is a real risk of the different mandates becoming intermixed at the planning stages and consequently encountering a confused reception from the beneficiary population. This clearly raises questions about the long-term role of CIDA. Can CIDA be both an explicitly political actor and a responsible and arm's-length development donor? Can it do so in the same region of operation? And, most critically for the question of humanitarian space, how should CIDA separate these two very different functions in its dealings with the NGO community? These questions are central to the way in which humanitarian assistance is integrated into broader political objectives.

Conclusion

NGOs and international coordinating bodies, increasingly concerned by the effects integration is having on humanitarianism, have begun to develop policy frameworks for dealing with the issue at both a conceptual and a

practical level. The Guidelines for the Interaction and Coordination of
Humanitarian Actors and Military Actors in Afghanistan, better known as
the "Civ-Mil Coordination Guidelines," are a step in the right direction.[46]
These guidelines stress that "[a]ll humanitarian actors, military actors and
other security actors should at all times be respectful of international law
and Afghan laws, culture and customs," and that "[h]umanitarian assistance
must not be used for the purpose of political gain, relationship-building, or
winning hearts and minds." The guidelines were prepared and endorsed by
UNAMA, over one hundred NGOs, the Afghan government, and NATO-
ISAF in 2008. Efforts to regulate and monitor NGO behaviour according to
standards of conduct, including sensitivity to local social and cultural customs and norms, are also critical to ensuring the success of guidelines on
coordination. Donors have a significant role to play in ensuring that such
standards are developed and implemented. Moreover, as numerous NGOs
and Afghan officials have argued, the incorporation of Afghan perspectives
on humanitarian action at both the local and national levels must be central
to the development of programming and implementation. Furthermore, efforts should be made to broaden the paradigm away from Western aid with
the translation of humanitarian principles to the relevant context.

The reopening of an OCHA office to coordinate NGOs and negotiate access has been lauded by some as a step in the right direction. Given the UN's
track record in the country, however, and particularly its previous role in
supporting and strengthening the Afghan government, there is reason to be
cautious. Moreover, the ramping up of the counterinsurgency efforts with
the strengthening of US military forces not only underscores the need to
create clearer distinctions between the military and humanitarian aspects
of the international effort in Afghanistan but also underlines the importance
of differentiating and labelling types of humanitarian action (relief, development, and reconstruction). Alternative models where military and civilian
activities are clearly demarcated, with separate financial and administrative
control, should be explored.

Integration, in Afghanistan but also more broadly, has real costs for
NGOs as well as for the beneficiary communities they aim to assist. Many of
these implications have gone largely unnoticed as integration efforts deep-
ened over the last decade of international engagement in Afghanistan.
Although the situation for humanitarians in the country is likely to be ir-
reversible – the reclaiming of a completely neutral space for all humanitarian action an unrealistic goal – there are nonetheless potential reforms to

current and future practices that could make a difference, as long as policy makers and donors recognize this as the critical issue that it is.

NOTES

1 The origin of these principles is traceable to the International Committee of the Red Cross (ICRC). In addition to the aforementioned, the ICRC also holds universality, voluntary service, and unity as core principles. See David Forsythe, *The Humanitarians: The International Committee of the Red Cross* (Cambridge: Cambridge University Press, 2005).

2 "Humanitarian Space, Humanitarian Principles: Experiences from Iraq and Afghanistan" (A Foreign Policy and Brookings-Bern Project on Internal Displacement Event, 20 February 2009), online: The Brookings Institution <http://www.brookings.edu/>.

3 Examples of NGO typologies include Tony Vaux, "Humanitarian Trends and Dilemmas" (2006) 16 Development in Practice; Abby Stoddard, "Humanitarian NGOs: Challenges and Trends," HPG (Humanitarian Policy Group) Briefing 12 (2003), online: Overseas Development Institute <http://www.odi.org.uk/resources/>; and Daniel Thurer, "Dunant's Pyramid: Thoughts on Humanitarian Space" (2007) 89 Int'l Rev. Red Cross 47.

4 Interviews were conducted with a number of international NGOs operating in Afghanistan; government and military officials from the US, UK, and Canada; Afghan officials; and journalists covering the country. Written consent forms have been obtained by the authors for these anonymous interviews.

5 See, *e.g.*, Robert Perito, "Provincial Reconstruction Teams in Iraq" (March 2007), online: United States Institute of Peace <http://www.usip.org/>; and John Drolet "Provincial Reconstruction Teams: Afghanistan vs. Iraq – Should We Have a Standard Model?" USAWC Strategy Research Project (15 March 2006), online: Microlinks <http://www.microlinks.org/>.

6 For further reading on integration, see Larry Minear, "Informing the Integration Debate with Recent Experience" (2004) 18 Ethics and International Affairs 53; Espen Eide Barth, Anja Therese Kaspersen, Randolph Kent, and Karen von Hippel, *Report on Integrated Missions: Practical Perspectives and Recommendations, Independent Study for the Expanded UN ECHA Core Group* (New York: United Nations/ECHA, 2005); and Joanna Macrae, "Understanding Integration from Rwanda to Iraq" (2004) 18 Ethics and International Affairs 29 at 33.

7 John Baylis, "International Security in the Post–Cold War Era" in John Baylis and Steve Smith, eds., *The Globalization of World Politics*, 3d ed. (Oxford: Oxford University Press, 2009).

8 James Mayall, *The New Interventionism 1991-1994: United Nations Experience in Cambodia, Former Yugoslavia and Somalia* (Cambridge: Cambridge University Press, 1996).

9 ICISS, *The Responsibility to Protect: Report of the International Commission on Intervention and State Sovereignty* (Ottawa: International Development Research Centre, 2001) at 15.

10 High-Level Panel on Threats, Challenges, and Change, *A More Secure World: Our Shared Responsibility* (New York: United Nations, 2004) at viii.

11 *The National Security Strategy of the United States of America* (Washington, DC: White House, 2002), Foreword.

12 Secretary of State Colin Powell, speech delivered at the State Department on 26 October 2001.

13 See also Vernon Bogdanor, ed., *Joined-Up Government* (Oxford: Oxford University Press, 2005).

14 UN Doc. A/55/305–S/2000/809 at paras. 198-217.

15 GA Res. 180, UN GAOR, 60th Sess., Agenda items 46 and 120, UN Doc. A/RES/60/180 (2005), and SC Res. 1645, UN SCOR, UN Doc. S/RES/1645 (2005).

16 "The Code of Conduct for the International Red Cross and Red Crescent Movement and NGOs in Disaster Relief," Annex VI to the resolutions of the 26th International Conference of the Red Cross and Red Crescent, Geneva (1995), online: International Federation of Red Cross and Red Crescent Societies <http://www.ifrc.org/>.

17 Stephen Cornish and Marit Glad, *Civil-Military Relations: No Room for Humanitarianism in Comprehensive Approaches* (Flekkefjord, Norway: Den norske Atlanterhavskomité, Security Policy Library, 2008).

18 Antonio Donini, *Humanitarian Agenda 2015: Afghanistan Country Study* (Medford, MA: Feinstein International Center, 2006) at 28. Donini argues that while coordination in the area of assistance was achieved, there was little integration between the humanitarian and human rights pillar on the one hand, and the UN political pillar on the other.

19 *Ibid.* at 28.

20 Antonio Donini, "An Elusive Quest: Integration in Response to the Afghan Crisis" (2004) 18 Ethics and International Affairs 21.

21 *Ibid.* p. 26.

22 Currently, approximately 80 percent of NGO activities are tied to or channelled through government programs: Cornish and Glad, *supra* note 17 at 19.

23 Senator Jack Reed, "Iraq Trip Report" (17-18 January 2008) at 4, online: Jack Reed, US Senator for Rhode Island <http://www.reed.senate.gov/>.

24 "Address by Prime Minister Paul Martin on Occasion of His Visit to Washington, DC" (29 April 2004).

25 Peter Mackay, "Why We Are There: Canadian Leadership in Afghanistan – Address to the Members of the Canadian International Council" (Ottawa, 19 October 2006).

26 Sippi Azarbaijani-Moghaddam, Mirwais Wardak, Idrees Zaman, and Annabel Taylor, *Afghan Hearts, Afghan Minds: Exploring Afghan Perceptions of Civil-Military Relations* (European Network of NGOs in Afghanistan (ENNA) and the British and Irish Agencies Afghanistan Group (BAAG), 2008), online: ENNA News <http://www.ennanet.eu/>.

27 *Ibid.* at 13.

28 "Aid and Civil-Military Relations in Afghanistan," *supra* note 23.

29 Norman Solomon, "TV News: A Militarized Zone" *Media Beat* (8 October 2001), online: FAIR (Fairness and Accuracy in Reporting) <http://www.fair.org/media-beat/>.

30 These practices ceased after concerted lobbying of the US government by groups such as Interaction, a consortium of over 160 US NGOs based in Washington, DC. See Peter Slevin, "U.S. Troops Working Relief to Modify Clothing" *Washington Post* (21 April 2002) A22.

31 Afghanistan NGO Security Office, ANSO Quarterly Data, Report Q.4 (2008). Quoted in Abby Stoddard, Adele Harmer, and Victoria DiDomenico, "Providing Aid in Insecure Environments: 2009 Update," HPG (Humanitarian Policy Group) Policy Brief 34 (2009), online: Overseas Development Institute <http://www.odi.org.uk/resources/>. Incidents were classified as politically motivated based on a combination of the following factors: "1) first-hand determinations and evidence cited in the original incident report; 2) explicit statements and claims of responsibility by perpetrators; 3) tactics used (*e.g.*, bombs, suicide attacks, targeted IEDs, etc.); 4) political/military actors known to be the perpetrators; and 5) a high degree of deliberate violence without apparent economic motive (*i.e.*, aid workers killed or seriously injured with vehicles/facilities burned but not robbed)."

32 *Ibid.* at 6.

33 *Ibid.* at 6.

34 Confidential interviews in Ottawa, September 2008.

35 Workshop organized by authors, "Coordination and Collaboration in Peace Operations: Assessing Canada's Integrated Approach in Afghanistan" (12-13 November 2008), Rights and Democracy, Montreal Canada. This view of ICRC is corroborated by Stoddard *et al.*, *supra* note 31, and Azarbaijani-Moghaddam *et al.*, *supra* note 26.

36 Azarbaijani-Moghaddam *et al.*, *ibid.* at 34.

37 Confidential interview, February 2009. After having worked nearly without interruption alongside the most vulnerable Afghan people since 1980, MSF left the country following staff killings and threats. In the wake of the killings, the Taliban asserted that organizations like MSF work for US interests and were therefore targets for future attacks. See "Afghanistan: MSF Leaves Country Following Staff Killings and Threats" (16 December 2004), online: Médecins Sans Frontières <http://www.msf.org/>.

38 Confidential interview, 18 September 2008.

39 "Four NATO Soldiers Killed, 24 Children Hurt by Suicide Bomber" (18 September 2006), online: Afghanistan News Center <http://www.afghanistannewscenter.com/>.

40 Stoddard *et al.*, *supra* note 31 at 10. From 2006 to 2008, the Aid Worker Security Database (AWSD) estimates that 22 percent of security incidents against NGOs resulted in suspension, withdrawal, or relocations of activities.

41 Richard Norton-Taylor, "Afghanistan's Refugee Crisis 'Ignored'" *Guardian* (13 February 2008) online: Guardian <http://www.guardian.co.uk/>. Quoted in Cornish and Glad, *supra* note 17 at 16.

42 "Aid and Civil-Military Relations in Afghanistan," *supra* note 23 at 10. By November 2003, there were more than 1,600 NGOs registered with the Ministry of Planning, of which the majority were Afghan organizations. The largest programs, however, were and continue to be implemented by international or multinational NGOs.

43 The four main coordinating bodies are the Afghan NGOs Coordination Bureau (ANCB), Agency Coordinating Body for Afghan Relief (ACBAR), Islamic

Coordination Council (ICC), and South West Afghanistan and Baluchistan Association for Coordination (SWABAC). Of these, only ACBAR is formally linked to UNAMA.

44 Macrae, *supra* note 6 at 35.

45 Cornish and Glad, *supra* note 17 at 10.

46 The implementation of the guidelines will be monitored by a Civ-Mil Coordination Group, which meets every six months and is composed of representatives of NATO-ISAF, UN agencies, NGOs, and the Afghan government. See also Edwina Thompson, *Principled Pragmatism: NGO Engagement with Armed Actors* (Monrovia, CA: World Vision International, Humanitarian Emergency Affairs, 2008) for a broader framework for dealing with civil-military issues.

PART 4

ADDRESSING ENDEMIC URBAN VIOLENCE

14

Silent Wars in Our Cities
Alternatives to the Inadequacy of International Humanitarian Law to Protect Civilians during Endemic Urban Violence

CARLOS IVÁN FUENTES

According to the United Nations Human Settlements Programme (UN-HABITAT), Rio de Janeiro, Mexico City, Lima, and Caracas share a particular characteristic: the number of homicides in these cities is higher than the total number of homicides in the rest of their respective countries.[1] In the last five years, there were over twenty thousand gang-related murders in Guatemala.[2] In Brazil alone, more than a hundred people are killed by guns every day, over half of them in Rio de Janeiro.[3] Under these circumstances, it is not surprising to hear that cities are going through "silent wars." Cities have always experienced a degree of violence that radically differs from that of rural areas. This phenomenon is usually rationalized by pointing to the higher concentration of people in a relatively limited space.

While cities become larger and social problems become more complex, populations face levels of violence beyond what might be considered tolerable in times of peace (if violence is ever tolerable). These urban realities are regulated by applicable laws, but regular law enforcement activities and human rights approaches have failed to stop the suffering of innocent victims, the recruitment of children into gangs, and the rising death toll. Can international law help regulate these situations?

The question addressed in this chapter is whether, and to what extent, it is desirable to apply the standards of international humanitarian law (IHL) and/or regional human rights regimes to address urban violence.

I will argue that IHL has too many shortcomings to properly address the complex situations found in cities. Although some aspects of urban violence can be regulated in a manner similar to how IHL regulates armed conflict, the logic of this body of law does not permit an analogous application of its general standards and principles in cases of urban violence. Furthermore, the general lack of compliance and enforcement mechanisms in IHL would ultimately leave us with a useless framework. On the other hand, relying on regional human rights systems to address situations of urban violence (either enforcing IHL or promoting its own standards) would be efficient in promoting compliance only on the part of the state, leaving violent non-state actors largely untouched. Even if one argues that these obligations could be extended to non-state actors, it is evident that urban violence is caused by both groups and individuals that might not have the capacity or the interest to comply with these obligations. In sum, this chapter challenges the limits of international law in dealing with the regulation of urban violence. International law could become a plausible alternative solution, however, when it comes to preventing and addressing the systemic poverty that is a contributing factor to urban violence.

As big as the problem might be, the regulation of the means and methods of urban violence would certainly be counterproductive. Applying the legal framework of IHL to situations of urban violence would mean that society has passively accepted the insolubility of this issue. States and the international community must address urban violence, but instead of trying to regulate the way in which urban violence is carried out, they should seek policy solutions that address the systemic problems that cause this violence.

Understanding Urban Violence

"Urban violence" is a broad term that encapsulates many different types of violent behaviour. An essential feature is that it occurs within densely populated areas, most notably in the so-called slums or poverty belts that surround many cities. It is particularly rampant in cities experiencing rapid growth.

Each city experiences violence in a different way. The intent here is not to generalize the situation to the point that the phenomenon seems homogeneous, or to present a self-created narrative of the problem. It is necessary, however, to identify the common denominator of this violence in order to address it properly, and to base the following analysis on diverse economic, demographic, and sociological studies of the subject.[4]

The kind of violence that is witnessed in urban areas can generally be classified into four distinct but interrelated types: (1) institutional forms of violence (when the perpetrator is the state or vigilante groups); (2) violence of an economic nature (broadly economically motivated crimes performed by individuals or organized criminal groups); (3) social violence (domestic or sexual violence, and occasional quarrels); and (4) socioeconomic forms of violence (gangs, street children, ethnic violence).[5] Urban violence is manifested through a different set of criminal activities, including murder, physical and psychological abuse, intimidation, armed robbery, petty theft, kidnapping, drug trafficking, and so on.[6] Urban violence can be part of organized activities by groups with apparent stability (such as gangs), rivalry among those groups, incidental acts performed by groups or individuals, or the violent outbreak of mass gatherings turning into riots.

Before beginning a discussion of how to regulate interactions in situations of urban violence, it is necessary to outline the legal framework that generally covers situations of urban violence, and the role of humanitarian actors in this framework.

The types of violence that occur within cities are usually addressed through national criminal laws. Damage to life and property is treated initially from a criminal perspective. This includes the substantive laws, which criminalize both the modalities of violence and certain activities related to the violence, and the procedural laws used to prosecute those crimes. Many countries also criminalize the formation of a joint criminal enterprise or a gang, independent of the crimes they commit. It must be noted that, thanks to the action of the international community, most countries have adopted special systems of juvenile justice that work under different procedural rules and often impose lesser sentences than regular criminal courts. The legal response from the criminal system occurs *post facto,* and works on a long-term concept of prevention.

When state agents such as the police carry out the violence, their actions are first dealt with in the realm of administrative and disciplinary regimes. The response of the legal system has more to do with the measurement of the consequences versus the objective, taking into account the circumstances in which state agents performed the violent act. Theoretically, if violent actions go beyond the necessary response, the individual criminal responsibility of the state actor may be triggered under the same circumstances as for normal citizens. Nevertheless, the level of impunity in these situations is extremely high.

In some cases, human rights law might become the applicable legal framework, either as manifested in national constitutional guarantees or as appeals to international courts and human rights bodies. Whereas the national approach depends on the existence of a functional constitutional system, the international approach remains limited to cases where the violent actions were performed directly by state agents or by private individuals with the support, encouragement, or authorization of the state.

The International Committee of the Red Cross (ICRC) has a long tradition of promoting the principles of humanity in situations of urban violence that do not amount to a non-international armed conflict.[7] This comes from the organization's mandate to "take any humanitarian initiative which comes within its role as a specifically neutral and independent institution and intermediary."[8] The 2007 International Conference of the Red Cross and Red Crescent focused on "four great challenges facing the world today which affect the individual and specifically the most vulnerable."[9] Among the enumerated challenges was "violence, in particular in urban settings."[10] The declaration adopted by the conference recognized the magnitude of the problem and stated:

> Violence in urban areas poses a particular challenge, where problems are often aggravated by rapidly growing populations, poverty and economic inequalities, unemployment, social exclusion and marginalization, insufficient public security and services, and the easy availability of drugs and weapons.
>
> We acknowledge that States are responsible for providing safety and ensuring adequate care and support for the victims of violence, to the extent feasible, and for the creation of policies and legal frameworks which aim at prevention and mitigation of violence. Such policies and frameworks may also need to address cases of urban armed violence between organized groups.[11]

While reinforcing the ICRC's commitment to work with states in the prevention and reduction of urban violence, this declaration places the responsibility for creating a proper legal framework in the hands of states.

The Inadequacy of International Humanitarian Law in Addressing Urban Violence

IHL is a broad field of law. The presence and nature of an armed conflict determine which laws apply. Conflicts can be international or non-international in nature. The former refers to conflicts between states and, under particular circumstances, conflicts between states and certain non-state actors.[12] Non-international conflicts are those between one or more non-state actors against the armed forces of a state. Since urban violence occurs within a city, and never between state-like entities, it is necessary to focus on the branch of law that actually includes the possibility of non-state actors, that is, the law of non-international armed conflicts. Accordingly, the primary focus is upon Common Article 3 of the *Geneva Conventions* of 1949; Protocol II, Additional to the *Geneva Conventions* of 1949 (Protocol II); and customary international humanitarian law (CIHL, or simply customary IHL) as applicable to non-international armed conflicts. While Protocol II is inapplicable to "situations of internal disturbances and tensions, such as riots, isolated and sporadic acts of violence and other acts of a similar nature, as not being armed conflicts," the following analysis considers whether IHL *should* apply to such situations.[13]

As mentioned earlier, urban violence encompasses a fairly large spectrum of violent activities, which also have diverse and particular manifestations. Some types of violence, such as domestic abuse, simply cannot be covered by IHL because of the particular relations between the people involved. In the same sense, IHL deals with particular relations that might resemble some types of urban violence. In other words, this branch of law tries to regulate the actions of individuals as it relates to the exercise of military and humanitarian activities during a conflict between two or more armed parties. The broadness of the definition of "parties to the conflict" in Common Article 3 will help accommodate many actors in urban violence. Protocol II is more restrictive, however, with respect to what constitutes "organized armed groups," establishing that they must act "under responsible command, [and] exercise such control over a part of its territory as to enable them to carry out sustained and concerted military operations."[14] This high threshold of application can hardly be met in situations of urban violence (some might say that this is so even in certain internal armed conflicts[15]), but Protocol II will nevertheless be used as a guide to distinguish groups that can meet this definition and be regulated under the laws of non-international armed conflicts.

In situations of urban violence, it is possible to identify three types of groups that, to a certain extent, resemble the minimum requirements established in Protocol II for its application:

- *State security services.* This includes the police or other government-based security agencies. Since they are governmental institutions, security services operate under responsible command and exercise the jurisdiction of the state. As the government officials in charge of maintaining the security in the country, they are authorized to carry weapons.

- *Private security services and vigilante groups.* The levels of violence in certain cities have led to widespread use of private security contractors. These entities possess a command structure and are contracted to protect certain areas of private property through the use of weapons. The situation of vigilante groups is less clear, because they often react to particular threats and do not seek territorial control.
- *Criminal organizations and gangs.* Broadly defined as any type of joint criminal enterprise with some level of permanence, they perpetrate violence as a means of furthering their illegal activities. These activities include drug trafficking, human trafficking, prostitution networks, and so on. In addition to the economic component, gangs also have social cohesion and share some kind of identity (often ethnic) that triggers a search for territorial control.

These three types of groups will form the basis for the analysis in the next section. The selected IHL norms will be applied to interactions that could occur between the groups.

Just as IHL is not concerned with the right to wage war,[16] the scope of this study must ignore the various reasons that give rise to urban violence and focus on the phenomenon itself.

Having established the focus of this section, I will now move to answer the main question: Why is IHL inadequate for addressing situations of urban violence? In my view, this question can be approached by resolving two subordinate questions. First, can the existing rules of IHL, particularly the laws addressing internal armed conflicts, be applied to urban violence? Second, is there room to create within the general framework of IHL a body of law covering internal violence? This approach will be strictly theoretical and will look at the bases of the system to see whether such a creation is feasible.

Possible Subjects of Interest in the Law of Internal Armed Conflicts
The body of law regarding non-international armed conflicts is considerably smaller than the body of law dedicated to international wars. This is mostly due to the fact that states have less motivation to regulate the sorts of conflicts that might affect their own integrity. Nevertheless, despite its relatively smaller breadth, it would be impractical to contrast and compare

every single article of Protocol II with the violent experiences found in urban settings.

Instead, I will focus on four particular subjects that *prima facie* appear to bring interesting ideas to the regulation of urban violence. For each subject, I will briefly review the applicable law of internal armed conflict and will try to apply its logic to situations of urban violence. The goal of this subsection is to analyze whether the rules of IHL as applicable to non-international armed conflicts can be used analogously in cases of urban violence.

Protection of Civilians

In any conflict, the well-being of civilians is one of the principal concerns of humanitarian actors. IHL provides a vast body of rules concerning the protection of those "[p]ersons taking no active part in the hostilities."[17] The general rules regarding the protection of civilians in internal armed conflicts establish that civilians cannot be the object of an attack, either directly against them[18] or indirectly through attacks of an indiscriminate nature.[19] Additionally, civilians should be affected as little as possible during an attack against a legitimate military objective.[20] When thinking about situations of urban violence, it seems logical and desirable to afford a high level of protection to those individuals that are not participating in intergroup violence, and to protect regular individuals from the institutional violence of the state or vigilante groups.

The application of the law of non-international armed conflicts presents an inherent shortcoming, however: the question of how a civilian is to be identified and distinguished from the combatants. Customary IHL applicable to non-international armed conflicts establishes that "[c]ivilians are persons who are not members of the armed forces,"[21] but it is acknowledged that there is no clear state practice on the qualification of members of armed opposition groups as either civilians or combatants.[22] The ambiguity of customary law and the total silence of Protocol II on the issue render the protection of civilians in such conflicts quite complicated. It has been argued that the whole principle of distinction is totally unsuited for internal armed conflicts and needs to be reconceptualized for it to be operative.[23]

While the protection of persons not taking a direct part in situations of urban violence is desirable, the issue of identification is troubling. More specifically, although it would be quite easy to identify the police forces operating in a given city, persons participating in criminal groups are rarely identifiable. This is the case since wearing uniforms and carrying visible

weapons are not typically compatible with their interest in pursuing criminal activities. The ICRC has acknowledged that in non-international armed
conflicts, the obligation of state forces to wear identifiable uniforms can
give a considerable advantage to armed opposition groups.[24] Similarly, affording a different threshold of protection to the non-uniformed population would not make a difference, since police forces are under human rights
obligations not to violate the rights to life and personal integrity of the
population.[25]

As a general rule of IHL, a civilian loses his or her protection "for such
time as they take a direct part in hostilities."[26] This does not take into account, however, how to identify those persons who are engaging in direct
violence and those who are acting in self-defence.

Paragraph 1 of Common Article 3 and Articles 4(2) and 6(2) of Protocol
II establish the minimum protection afforded to individuals who do not take
part in combat (civilians) or who have ceased to be involved in hostilities
(for example, those who have become wounded or sick or have been captured). This includes a general prohibition against performing acts of violence to the life, health, and physical integrity of a person; outrages upon
personal dignity; pillaging; taking hostages; and penal prosecutions without
procedural guarantees. When transposing this protection to situations of
urban violence, all of the above acts are generally prohibited by national
criminal systems (when committed by civilians) and human rights law
(when committed by the state or its agents). In this sense, the protection of
civilians can hardly be addressed as an absence of law. The only difference
that the application of IHL would make is that vigilante groups, criminal
groups, and gangs could "legally" (or "non-illegally") perform acts of violence on each other and on police forces. This would ultimately transform
the *de facto* battlegrounds in cities into *de jure* wars.

Emergency Medical Services and Humanitarian Action

Fast and reliable emergency medical services are a necessity in any city. In
slums, however, territorial disputes or other situations commonly endanger
access to medical care. This is very similar to what occurs in times of war,
when humanitarian action is always dangerous and is limited by the accessibility of the battle zone.

IHL has responded to this challenge by establishing legal obligations for
belligerents to provide medical care without discrimination[27] and to allow
humanitarian actors access to the field.[28] In the case of non-international
armed conflicts, Protocol II establishes that all wounded and sick "shall be

treated humanely and shall receive to the fullest extent practicable and with the least possible delay, the medical care and attention required by their condition."[29] Customary IHL also contemplates the obligations to allow and facilitate civilian access to humanitarian relief[30] and to ensure freedom of movement of impartial humanitarian relief personnel.[31]

Through respect and reinforcement of its neutrality, the ICRC has ensured its capacity to deliver humanitarian relief to both civilians and combatants in countless conflicts.[32] It has also played a role in providing humanitarian aid in situations of urban violence,[33] as in the current dynamics of Cité-Soleil, Haiti.[34]

The IHL approach has limits, however, when confronted with the realities of urban violence. As big as criminal organizations and gangs might be, it would be quite unreasonable to impose on them an obligation to have their own medical personnel. Gangs and other criminal groups would have no incentive to have their own medical staff and first aid equipment unless the medical services of the state were not available to their members, but if a state were to choose to exclude the provision of medical aid to criminal organizations, this would constitute adverse treatment and discrimination, which are forbidden by both IHL and international human rights law (IHRL).[35]

Regulating humanitarian actors and their access to the vulnerable is something quite different. It is difficult to imagine a situation where urban criminal groups and gangs would block the action of neutral humanitarian aid agencies. More than a legal obligation, it is a dictate of human conscience that sick and wounded people should be given proper medical care. This might be one of those rare cases where "if it goes without saying, does it always go better when you say it?"[36]

For the purposes of urban violence, the application of IHL rules regarding prompt medical care for the wounded and sick would simply be unrealistic. Such rules require a minimum level of medical aid that cannot be satisfied unless the parties have their own medical staff and supplies. And spelling out a duty to allow humanitarian actors in the cities would be redundant, since IHRL already imposes an obligation upon the state to ensure that "primary health care, that is, essential health care [is] made available to all individuals and families in the community."[37]

Respect for Children and Protection against Their Recruitment
One of the most complicated features of urban violence is that most of its actors and victims are minors. The type of violence that urban children suffer, and their level of participation in the violence, differs radically from city

to city, but the problem mostly turns on social vulnerability and encouragement by adults to carry out illegal activities (drug abuse, petty robbery). In
countries such as El Salvador and Guatemala, children are both perpetrators and victims of the violence due to the increasing phenomena of the
maras, or gangs. Meanwhile, in countries such as Colombia and Brazil, the
problem consists of institutional violence against street children, which may
or may not be related to gang activity.

The law of internal armed conflict has created a small but important set
of rules regarding the involvement of children both as combatants and as
possible victims. Protocol II establishes that "children who have not attained
the age of fifteen years shall neither be recruited in the armed forces or
groups nor be allowed to take part in hostilities."[38] It also extends certain
rights, such as access to education and family life,[39] which remain valid even
if the child has engaged in combat.[40] Customary IHL also provides protection from sexual violence and access to food and medical care.[41] Although
the minimum age for recruitment and participation in combat remains fifteen years,[42] the *opinio juris* and practice of states is evolving towards rais-
ing the minimum age to eighteen. It is particularly important that in the
*Optional Protocol to the Convention on the Rights of the Child on the In-
volvement of Children in Armed Conflict,* states bound themselves not to
recruit any person under the age of eighteen,[43] and in cases where children
join the army before that age, states have committed to take all necessary
measures to keep them away from direct hostilities.[44] Moreover, the same
optional protocol establishes a general prohibition for non-state armed
groups to recruit persons under the age of eighteen years.[45]

Regarding the situation of child civilians caught in urban centres with
high levels of violence, the rights accorded by IHL do not substantially differ
from those already established in IHRL. Given that the most comprehensive
instrument dealing with human rights of children to date is the *Convention
on the Rights of the Child,* and that this instrument has almost universal
ratification,[46] it is evident that the problem is not one of absence of law. The
situation of child soldiers nevertheless reveals a lower threshold of protection in IHL than IHRL, since children are considered soldiers under IHL
and thus legitimate objects of an attack for "such time as they take a direct
part in hostilities."[47]

All the same, an area in which IHL can likely make the best contribution
towards the issue of urban violence is that of the recruitment of children.
The existing international prohibition on the participation of minors in
combat and the prohibition on the recruitment by armed opposition groups

of persons under the age of eighteen in non-international armed conflicts can be used as the basis for a general prohibition and criminalization of the practice. It must be noted, however, that in international criminal law the "war crime of using, conscripting and enlisting children"[48] applies the limit of fifteen years, as provided under customary international law.[49] The successfully prosecuted cases in the Special Court for Sierra Leone[50] and the forthcoming trial of Thomas Lubanga Dyilo at the International Criminal Court[51] are based on this standard.

Even if IHL rules for child recruitment were assumed to be applicable to gangs and other criminal organizations, certain aspects of IHL's general framework would make them very difficult to adapt to urban violence. Initially, armed opposition groups perceive IHL as a legal restraint, that is, these groups are not conducting themselves illegally so long as they comply with the laws of non-international armed conflicts and human rights. Imposing a framework in which only child recruitment in gangs and other criminal groups would be illegal would have to necessarily condone other types of joint criminal enterprises and consider them to be not (as) illegal. In addition, such a framework presupposes that there is an interest on the part of gangs and other criminal groups not to include children in their activities.

Gangs are in themselves a phenomenon linked to youth, and criminal organizations often rely on children to commit economic and violent crimes.[52] It would be naïve to request these groups to follow legal means, against their own interests, in pursuing an illegal end. Finally, opposition groups often violate the laws of war because of the asymmetry in the conflict. Since the state is bound to comply with IHL, these groups see the violation of international law as a way to compensate for the disadvantages in the battlefield. On this particular issue, even before the optional protocol on child recruitment was finalized, agreements with armed opposition groups to stop child recruitment were continuously violated.[53]

Protected Persons and Objects

Besides the generic protection of civilians, the law of internal armed conflicts provides for the protection of particular persons who perform important humanitarian roles in the field. It also provides for the protection of objects and places that are used to perform these functions or that carry a significant value.

In a non-international armed conflict, protected persons include all medical and religious personnel of the armed forces,[54] humanitarian relief personnel,[55] personnel in peacekeeping missions,[56] and journalists.[57] The protected objects include medical units and transports;[58] any transport or unit caring the distinctive emblems of the red cross, red crescent, and red lion and sun on a white background,[59] or any combinations of symbols featuring the red crystal;[60] places of worship;[61] and buildings dedicated to religion, art, science, education, or charitable purposes and historic monuments.[62]

Unquestionably, the aforementioned persons can be endangered by episodes of violence in an urban area. There have certainly been cases where members of peacekeeping operations have lost their lives due to urban violence. But, as was the case with civilians, to afford them protection also means legitimizing violence directed at other targets. In any case, the life and well-being of any person in the city is legally protected by the regular laws of the state. Although it would be desirable to afford some higher level of protection to these people, it simply does not make sense in an urban setting.

The protection of places could be an area of interest where urban violence is concerned. Establishing that hospitals, schools, and places of worship (to say the least) are outside the realm of violence would arguably have a positive impact on the lives of citizens. Places of worship have traditionally been seen as neutral and off limits to attack, and there is a general belief that it is forbidden to carry weapons in schools and hospitals. An analogous application of IHL, however, would imply that violence in other places is not forbidden, and thus have counterproductive results.

In short, affording special protection in IHL makes sense because there is some degree of violence that can legally be carried out on non-protected people and places. Meanwhile, in urban settings, the fundamental premise is that violence against any person or any place is illegal. The idea of a protected person loses validity if the general premise is that nobody should be killed or wounded, hence IHL is completely unsuitable for situations of urban violence.

Beyond the Law of Internal Armed Conflicts

The previous subsection analyzed four areas of IHL that appear to be analogously applicable to situations of urban violence, and found that none would actually change the situation in general or benefit the victims of this violence.

Analogous application does not exhaust the issue. A point has been made that the law of non-international armed conflicts was indeed an evolution of the law of international conflicts. Now I wish to explore whether it is possible to bring about an evolution that brings internal disturbances within the system of IHL.

As I begin approaching the possibility of creating a branch of IHL for internal violence, some general issues related to the structure and conceptualization of this body of law begin to reveal certain theoretical incompatibilities. This subsection will explore the structure of the system in general, and how situations of urban violence are so specialized that they would complicate the creation of a regime for IHL to regulate.

The Nature and Rationale of IHL

Although there are various idealized views regarding the origins of IHL, it would be most accurate to say that the body of the laws of war was born out of the interest of states in preventing the unnecessary waste of human lives. Compliance with the rules of IHL was sustained largely out of reciprocity (that is, states would limit their means and methods of warfare only as a way of ensuring that opposing parties would do the same). Thus, until the twentieth century, a breach of the laws of war was punished by a similar breach by the opposing party to the conflict. It must be said that although pillage and destruction of property have long been features of war, until recent times civilian populations have rarely been the objects of military attack.

The underlying rationale for IHL becomes relevant in the discussion of urban violence because of the interest of the belligerent parties in having previously established limits to military action respected during the conflict. Urban violence is in itself an accumulation of illegal activities directed by individuals or a group towards other individuals or groups. In order to set limits on illegitimate actions between the perpetrators and on their actions towards non-participants, it would be necessary to accept and acknowledge that a certain level and perhaps certain methods of violent behaviour are acceptable.

In this sense, how can the state ban private violence and regulate it at the same time? It is possible to envisage a framework where violent activities would be regarded as less illegal or even "non-illegal" if performed between actors in an urban conflict, but this raises many philosophical issues regarding state power and the function of law. Weber stated that an entity could be considered a state if "its administrative staff successfully upholds a claim to the monopoly of the legitimate use of physical force in the enforcement of its order."[63] Structuring a framework where legal – or at least non-illegal – forms of violence can be performed by entities other than the state would result in the legitimization of the authority of non-state actors in a given space.

IHL, Actors, and Compliance

Traditional IHL reflects the realities of the nineteenth and early twentieth centuries, that is, war between states. Besides the consideration of what is a just or an unjust war, the authority of states to carry out war was hardly contested – it came with the territory. With the explosion of intrastate conflicts, the legal regime normally accorded to international wars was applied to certain types of non-international conflicts. Simultaneously, a particular regime was created for conflicts of a pure non-international nature. Protocol II expanded the content of Common Article 3 and adapted the minimum possible norms of international conflicts to conflicts where only one of the parties is formally a state.

In non-international armed conflicts, IHL is perceived by armed opposition groups as imposing legal restraints and substantial obligations,[64] including a wide range of prohibitions and an obligation to respect humanity in general. There are no rights, but there is recognition of their status and a presumption of non-illegality while complying with the restraints and obligations.

This adaptation has proven highly ineffective as Protocol II did not envisage mechanisms of enforcement beyond the existing structures in IHL.[65] Thus, in cases of non-international armed conflict, reciprocity becomes a one-way street. That is, while the state is forced to respect the rules due to its international commitments, dissident armed forces commonly break them or use the asymmetry of the conflict to invoke military necessity.[66] For instance, the simple issue of identifying who is a "legitimate" actor in non-international conflicts has revolved around the fact that sometimes the use of uniforms is simply impossible or quite counterproductive.

All of these considerations reveal that the regulatory system of IHL was primarily created to work between states. The continuous difficulty in promoting compliance among non-state actors is indicative of this shortcoming.[67] Applying the principles of this body of law, which lacks efficient enforcement mechanisms, to create a regime for organizations that willingly operate outside the law is simply illogical.

Looking for Alternatives: International Human Rights Law

As has been recognized throughout this chapter, human rights law does not lose its validity during a situation of urban violence. Even when states formally declare a state of emergency, the catalogue of rights that can actually be suspended is short, and the conditions to sustain the suspension are very strict. International courts have stated that the application of IHL does not absolutely suspend the application of human rights law.[68]

In this section, I will explore the possibility of applying IHRL to situations of urban violence as a way to escape the inefficiency of the current paradigm. This includes both recognizing the responsibility of the state in addressing the phenomenon of urban violence and exploring the possibility of assigning human rights obligations to non-state actors. Beyond that, I will also argue for the use of other human rights obligations (those derived from economic and social rights) as a way to address the causes of urban violence.

Responsibility of the State and the Jurisprudence of the Inter-American System for the Protection of Human Rights

In this subsection, I will briefly address the jurisprudence of the Inter-American Court of Human Rights (IACtHR) in relation to three points for the purpose of shedding some light on the topic of this chapter:

- the practice and jurisprudence of the Inter-American Court of Human Rights (IACtHR) and the Inter-American Commission of Human Rights (IACHR) on the relation between IHL and IHRL
- the jurisprudence on state responsibility for the action of urban militias
- the opinion of the IACtHR regarding violence inflicted by state officials on street children.

International Humanitarian Law and Human Rights Law

The Inter-American System of Human Rights has considered on several occasions the relationship between IHL and IHRL. The Inter-American Commission of Human Rights, which has greater liberty to apply other treaties to its recommendations and reports, has emphasized that it is "during situations of internal armed conflict that these two branches of international law most converge and reinforce each other."[69] Moreover, the commission has always asserted its powers to interpret the *American Convention on Human Rights* using the rules of IHL.[70]

Although its views have evolved over time, the Inter-American Court of Human Rights has been more cautious when addressing this relationship. In the *Case of Las Palmeras (Colombia)*, the court argued for the full application of Common Article 3 to the facts of the case.[71] Back then, the court accepted that its material field of jurisdiction was delimited by the *American Convention,* and that other treaties could be included only as a matter of interpretation.[72] In the 2004 decision on preliminary exceptions in the *Case of the Serrano-Cruz Sisters (El Salvador),* the court insisted on its capacity to use IHL in order to give content to the articles of the *American Convention,*[73] and discussed the complementary relationship between IHL and IHRL.[74] For the decision on the merits in that case, however, the court avoided using the *Geneva Conventions* or its protocols as interpretation tools.

More recently, in the *Case of Vargas-Areco (Paraguay),* the court was faced with the execution of a fifteen-year-old soldier attempting to desert from his duty. Although the child was killed before the state of Paraguay accepted the contentious jurisdiction of the court, a public acknowledgment of international liability made by Paraguay opened the door for the court to comment on issues beyond its material jurisdiction. Citing multiple international instruments, the court found that there is a trend to increase the age of recruitment to eighteen;[75] given the international commitments already expressed by Paraguay, the court ordered the state to adopt in its national laws the mandates of the *Optional Protocol to the Convention on the Rights of the Child on the Involvement of Children in Armed Conflicts.*

State Responsibility and Urban Militias

When reviewing the jurisprudence of the IACtHR, it is not difficult to find cases where the government itself did not perform the actions that violated the *American Convention.* The use of paramilitary groups has been particularly relevant in the internal conflicts of Colombia and Guatemala.[76] The cases regarding the situation in these countries are not entirely relevant for our purposes because they indeed happened in the framework of a conflict and not in urban areas, but it will be useful to keep in mind the repeated decisions of the court regarding the extension of the responsibility of the state. In short, for the state to be responsible for the action of such entities, "it is enough to prove that there has been support or tolerance by public authorities in the infringement of the rights embodied in the Convention, or omissions that enabled these violations to take place."[77]

Having said that, the IACtHR has dealt with a case where a vigilante patrol performed acts of urban violence in Guatemala City. In the *Case of Paniagua Morales et al. (Guatemala),* also known as the *Case of the "White Van,"* a group of public officials kidnapped, tortured, and killed a significant number of people in the street, sometimes during daytime, using a white van. Although the court did not find that these actions were part of a generalized policy of the government, it emphasized that "the sole requirement is to demonstrate that the State authorities supported or tolerated infringement of the rights recognized in the Convention."[78]

In this sense, the state is as responsible as the entities that perform such acts of urban violence if the state tolerates it. One important aspect of *Paniagua Morales* is that even though the perpetrators were stopped by the police and taken to trial, the judicial system was unable to act because of coercion and acts of violence against the judges.

The Street Children Case

The *Case of Villagrán Morales et al. (Guatemala)*, also known as the *Case of the "Street Children,"*[79] is considered a paradigmatic case of the IACtHR regarding the rights of children. This case is particularly important in the framework of this chapter because it deals with the torture and summary execution of five males, three of them children, in the slums of Guatemala City by members of the national police corps. It is important to note that the court found that "in Guatemala, at the time the events occurred, there was a common pattern of illegal acts perpetrated by State security agents against 'street children'; this practice included threats, arrests, cruel, inhuman and degrading treatment and homicides as a measure to counter juvenile delinquency and vagrancy."[80]

Besides the evident violations of the right to life, personal integrity, and personal liberty, the court also found a violation of Article 19 (rights of the child) under the *American Convention on Human Rights* in connection with the *Convention on the Rights of the Child*:

> In the light of Article 19 of the American Convention, the Court wishes to record the particular gravity of the fact that a State Party to this Convention can be charged with having applied or tolerated a systematic practice of violence against at-risk children in its territory. When States violate the rights of at-risk children, such as "street children," in this way, it makes them victims of a double aggression. First, such States do not prevent them from living in misery, thus depriving them of the minimum conditions for a dignified life and preventing them from the "full and harmonious development of their personality," even though every child has the right to harbor a project of life that should be tended and encouraged by the public authorities so that it may develop this project for its personal benefit and that of the society to which it belongs. Second, they violate their physical, mental and moral integrity and even their lives.[81]

The interpretation of violence against street children as a systematic violation of both their right to life in the wider sense and their right to a dignified or decent life ("minimum living conditions that are compatible with the dignity of the human person and of not creating conditions that hinder or impede it"[82]) must be understood as a call for a more general appreciation of the problem of street children. In other words, addressing the responsibility of the state for the direct act of violence leaves the causes of the problem unsolved. The disproportionate response of the police agencies should be addressed only as the final element of a long chain of state omissions. This point is further addressed in the conclusion to this chapter.

Assigning Obligations to Non-State Actors

The jurisprudence of the Inter-American system is useful for finding the state responsible for the violence perpetrated by its organs and other entities linked to it. This leaves aside other possible perpetrators, however, precisely those acting outside the framework of the law.

Human rights law, as it is currently understood, is a body of law that binds states to respect the rights of individuals. As such, its rules on responsibility are strictly applicable to states. There is growing recognition, however, that the content of this body of law must be respected by other entities beyond the state.[83] The idea is that even if non-state actors are not subjects of international law in the strict sense, they must also respect the above rights given that their range of power and the activities they perform affect the lives of individuals.

Having said all this, the discourse on the expansion of IHRL's realm of application focuses more on international organizations, international corporations, and armed opposition groups. All of these examples are based on the logic that these groups have a certain degree of organization that might not only be misused but that, if organized correctly, can actually promote a decent level of living for the people in their realm of power. Also, it is in their best interest to actually respect and promote human rights.

But when thinking about urban violence, we are again confronted with the fact that it is highly unorganized. Moreover, in the cases of gangs or criminal groups, there is simply no interest in respecting human rights. For groups that expect to be permanently carrying out criminal activities without influencing the political setting, any type of regulation of their activities is counterproductive.

Towards Systemic Solutions: Social and Economic Rights

Since the adoption of the *International Covenant on Economic, Social and Cultural Rights*,[84] the promise of full compliance has been delayed using many arguments, such as their non-justiciability. The existence of limited supervision mechanisms at the international level was matched by the unwillingness of national courts to enforce the rights. Nevertheless, recent developments in national courts and the adoption of supervision mechanisms in Europe[85] have encouraged the creation of more mechanisms at the international level.

It is particularly important to mention that the *Optional Protocol to the International Covenant on Economic, Social and Cultural Rights*, which allows the UN Committee on Economic, Social and Cultural Rights to hear individual communications, was finally adopted in December 2008.[86] Although the road for its entry into force will be long, it provides hope in the search for long-term solutions to urban violence. Using a socioeconomic rights perspective, we must be able to address the underlying problems that cause urban violence instead of trying to regulate it or simply address its consequences. Sustainable solutions to employment, housing, access to food and water, and the alleviation of poverty in general are the only ways to address unorganized criminality and children's participation in organized crime. Other forms of organized crime do not necessarily respond to poverty, but take advantage of it to take greater control of urban areas and their population.

Conclusion

After reviewing the particular provisions of the law of non-international armed conflicts, the general principles that establish the bases of IHL, and the case law of the Inter-American System of Human Rights, it is my conclusion that the application of IHL to situations of urban violence is both dangerous and undesirable.

The comparison between the provisions of Common Article 3, Protocol II, and relevant parts of customary IHL has shown that the selected issues are not better regulated by IHL. On the contrary, adopting such a stance would open the door to the acceptance of violent behaviours between criminal groups.

Review of the principles of IHL showed that any creation of a new legal regime for urban violence based on the aforementioned laws would be absolutely impractical and even counterproductive. The violence that urban centres have witnessed over the last decades should not be addressed as an insoluble fact but as a systemic problem. Formally regulating violence legitimizes the violence itself and the groups that perpetrate it. In this particular case, regulating violence instead of combating it would end up perpetuating the misery in the slums and promoting lawlessness in cities.

Finally, the jurisprudence of the Inter-American System demonstrates the mixed results of the internationalization of local problems. Although victims have indeed received many forms of reparations and the state has often accepted its responsibility either directly or indirectly, this does not reflect an amelioration of the social and economic problems that cause the violence. Placing human rights obligations on non-state actors is redundant, given the fact that they are already obliged by criminal law to respect the lives of individuals.

For all these reasons, I agree with the report of the Secretary-General of the United Nations regarding the consultation process on "fundamental standards of humanity":

> [T]here are no evident substantive legal gaps in the protection of individuals in situations of internal violence. There is also broad-based agreement that there is no need for new standards. Nevertheless, situations of internal violence and non-international armed conflicts, including situations where there is a need to ensure accountability of non-State actors, pose particular challenges to securing practical respect for human rights and international humanitarian law.[87]

Having said that, I believe that international law can play an important role in the promotion of long-term solutions. Indeed, cities will benefit from the involvement of the international community in the promotion of social standards, the sustainability of development policies, the struggle against transnational crime, and the implementation of anti-criminal policies. Violence, however, will not be reduced by its straightforward regulation.

NOTES

1 United Nations Human Settlements Programme (UN-HABITAT), *Global Report on Human Settlements 2007: Enhancing Urban Safety and Security* (London: Earthscan, 2007) at 55.
2 *Ibid.* at 14.
3 *Ibid.* at 13.

4 Including: UN-HABITAT, *supra* note 1; Foreign Affairs and International Trade Canada (DFAIT), *Freedom from Fear in Urban Spaces*, online: Human Security Gateway <http://www.humansecuritygateway.com/>; *Human Security for an Urban Century*, online: Human Security Gateway <http://www.humansecuritygateway.com/>.
5 Caroline O.N. Moser and Cathy McIlwaine, *Encounters with Violence in Latin America: Urban Poor Perceptions from Colombia and Guatemala* (New York: Routledge, 2004) at 5.
6 *Ibid.*
7 Marion Harroff-Tavel, "Action Taken by the International Committee of the Red Cross in Situations of Internal Violence" (1993) 294 Int'l Rev. Red Cross 195; Jean-Philippe Lavoyer, "Refugees and Internally Displaced Persons: International Humanitarian Law and the Role of the ICRC" (1995) 305 Int'l Rev. Red Cross 162.
8 "Statutes of the International Committee of the Red Cross" at art. 4(2), online: ICRC <http://www.icrc.org/>.
9 "Together for Humanity, 30th International Conference of the Red Cross and Red Crescent, 26-30 November 2007," Doc. 30IC/07/R1/Declaration at 1, online: ICRC <http://www.icrc.org/>.
10 *Ibid.*
11 *Ibid.* at 3.
12 Protocol I establishes that conflicts in which one of the parties consists of peoples "fighting against colonial domination and alien occupation and against racist regimes in the exercise of their right of self-determination" are to be considered International Armed Conflicts: *Protocol Additional to the Geneva Conventions of 12 August 1949, and Relating to the Protection of Victims of International Armed Conflicts (Protocol I)*, 8 June 1977, 1125 U.N.T.S. 3 (entered into force 7 December 1978) at art. 1(4) [API].
13 *Protocol Additional to the Geneva Conventions of 12 August 1949, and Relating to the Protection of Victims of Non-International Armed Conflicts (Protocol II)*, 8 June 1977, 1125 U.N.T.S. 609 (entered into force 7 December 1978) at art. 1(2) [APII].
14 *Ibid.* at art. 1(1).
15 Laura Perna, *The Formation of the Treaty Law of Non-International Armed Conflicts* (Leiden: Martinus Nijhoff, 2006) at 103-5.
16 With the exception of the qualification on whether an internal armed conflict can be considered as an international one according to Protocol I: API, *supra* note 12 at art. 1(4).
17 *Convention for the Amelioration of the Condition of the Wounded and Sick in Armed Forces in the Field*, Geneva, 12 August 1949, 75 R.T.N.U. 31 at art. 3. (Evidently, the reader can look for the same content in any of the other three *Geneva Conventions* of 1949.)
18 APII, *supra* note 13 at art. 4(1); Jean-Marie Henckaerts and Louise Doswald-Beck, *Customary International Humanitarian Law. Volume I: Rules* (Cambridge: Cambridge University Press, 2005) at 3 (Rule 1).
19 *Ibid.* at 37-45 (Rules 11-13).
20 *Ibid.* at 46-55 (Rules 14 and 15).
21 *Ibid.* at 17 (Rule 5).

22 *Ibid.* at 19.
23 See Jann K. Kleffner, "From 'Belligerents' to 'Fighters' and Civilians Directly Participating in Hostilities – on the Principle of Distinction in Non-International Armed Conflicts One Hundred Years after the Second Hague Peace Conference" (2007) 54 Nethl. Int'l L. Rev. 315; see also Stefan Oeter, "Comment: Is the Principle of Distinction Outdated?" in Wolf Heintschel von Heinegg and Volker Epping, eds., *International Humanitarian Law Facing New Challenges: Symposium in Honor of Knut Ipsen* (Berlin: Springer, 2007).
24 Henckaerts and Doswald-Beck, *supra* note 18 at 21.
25 *American Convention on Human Rights,* San Jose, Costa Rica, 22 November 1969, O.A.S. Treaty Series No. 36, 1144 U.N.T.S. 123 (entered into force 18 July 1978) at arts. 4, 5, and 7 [*American Convention*].
26 APII, *supra* note 13 at art. 13(3).
27 *Ibid.* at art. 9; Henckaerts and Doswald-Beck, *supra* note 18 at 396-403 (Rules 109-10).
28 APII, *supra* note 13 at art. 18; Henckaerts and Doswald-Beck, *ibid.* at 193-202 (Rules 55-56).
29 APII, *ibid.* at arts. 7(2) and 5(1)(a).
30 Henckaerts and Doswald-Beck, *supra* note 18 at 193 (Rule 55).
31 *Ibid.* at 200 (Rule 56).
32 See Harroff-Tavel, *supra* note 7.
33 "The capacity of the ICRC to implement programmes to prevent violence in mainly urban areas in places like Brazil, El Salvador, Guatemala, Honduras, Jamaica or Haiti is limited. While by no means indifferent to the humanitarian needs of people affected by this type of violence, the ICRC is aware that the limitations on action in such situations probably require a much more integrated and comprehensive approach than it is able to adopt within the bounds of its mandate": "American States: Protection of Persons in Situations of Internal Disturbances and Tensions" (Address by the ICRC at the special meeting of the Committee on Juridical and Political Affairs of the Organization of American States on current issues in international humanitarian law, Washington, DC, 2 February 2006).
34 Didier Revol, "Hoping for Change in Haiti's Cité-Soleil" *Red Cross Red Crescent* (February 2006), online: International Red Cross and Red Crescent Movement <http://www.redcross.int/>.
35 APII, *supra* note 13 at art. 2(2); Henckaerts and Doswald-Beck, *supra* note 18 at 193 (Rule 55).
36 R.A. Macdonald, *Lessons of Everyday Law/Le droit du quotidien* (Montreal and Kingston: McGill-Queen's University Press, 2002) at 33.
37 *Additional Protocol to the American Convention on Human Rights in the Area of Economic, Social and Cultural Rights (Protocol of San Salvador),* 17 November 1988, O.A.S. Treaty Series No. 69, 28 I.L.M. 156 (entered into force 16 November 1999) at art. 10(2)(a); a similar obligation can be found in the universal system, which is described as creating the "conditions which would assure to all medical service and medical attention in the event of sickness": *International Covenant on Economic, Social and Cultural Rights,* New York, 16 December 1966, 993 U.N.T.S. 3 (entered into force 3 January 1976) at art. 12(2)(d).

38 APII, *supra* note 13 at art. 4(3)(c).

39 *Ibid.* at arts. 4(3)(a), (b), and (e).

40 *Ibid.* at art. 4(3)(d).

41 Henckaerts and Doswald-Beck, *supra* note 18 at 481 (Rule 135).

42 *Ibid.* at 484 (Rule 135).

43 *Optional Protocol to the Convention on the Rights of the Child on the Involvement of Children in Armed Conflicts*, New York, 25 May 2000, 2173 U.N.T.S. 222, 39 I.L.M. 1285 (entered into force 12 February 2002) at art. 2.

44 *Ibid.* at art. 1.

45 *Ibid.* at art. 4.

46 It has not been ratified by the United States and Somalia, and an exception exists for Kosovo given its recent declaration of independence.

47 APII, *supra* note 13 at art. 13(3).

48 *Rome Statute of the International Criminal Court*, Rome, 17 July 1998, 2187 U.N.T.S. 3 (entered into force 1 July 2002) at arts. 8(2)(b)(xxvi) and 8(2)(e)(vii).

49 International Criminal Court, Assembly of State Parties, First session, *Elements of Crimes*, ICC-ASP/1/3 (2002) at arts. 8(2)(b)(xxvi) and 8(2)(e)(vii).

50 Special Court for Sierra Leone, Trial Chamber I, *Prosecutor v. Fofana and Kondewa (CDF Case)*, Judgment, SCSL-04-14-T (2 August 2007) at paras. 182-99; Special Court for Sierra Leone, Trial Chamber II, *Prosecutor v. Brima, Kamara and Kanu (AFRC Case)*, Judgment, SCSL-04-16-T (20 June 2007) at paras. 727-28.

51 For the documents on this case, see online: International Criminal Court <http://www.icc-cpi.int/cases/RDC/c0106/c0106_doc.html>.

52 UN-HABITAT, *supra* note 1 at 64.

53 Stuart Maslen, "The Use of Children as Soldiers: The Right to Kill and Be Killed?" (1998) 6 Int'l J. Child. Rts. 445 at 449.

54 APII, *supra* note 13 at art. 9; Henckaerts and Doswald-Beck, *supra* note 18 at 79-86 and 88-91 (Rules 25 and 27).

55 Henckaerts and Doswald-Beck, *ibid.* at 105-9 (Rule 31).

56 *Ibid.* at 112-14 (Rule 33).

57 *Ibid.* at 115-18 (Rule 34).

58 APII, *supra* note 13 at art. 11; Henckaerts and Doswald-Beck, *ibid.* at 109-11 (Rule 32).

59 APII, *ibid.* at art. 12; Henckaerts and Doswald-Beck, *ibid.* at 102-4 (Rule 30).

60 *Protocol Additional to the Geneva Conventions 12 August 1949, and Relating to the Adoption of an Additional Distinctive Emblem (Protocol III)*, 8 December 2005, 2404 U.N.T.S. 261 (entered into force 14 January 2007) [APIII].

61 APII, *supra* note 13 at art. 16.

62 Henckaerts and Doswald-Beck, *supra* note 18 at 127-35 (Rules 38-40).

63 Max Weber, *The Theory of Social and Economic Organization* (New York: Free Press, 1997) at 154.

64 Cf. Lisbeth Zegveld, *Accountability of Armed Opposition Groups in International Law* (Cambridge: Cambridge University Press, 2002).

65 Georges Abi-Saab, "Les Protocoles Additionnels, 15 ans après," in Jean-François Flauss, ed., *Les nouvelles frontières du droit international humanitaire* (Brussels: Bruylant, 2003) 17 at 27.

66   René Provost, *International Human Rights and Humanitarian Law* (Cambridge: Cambridge University Press, 2005) at 161.
67   See M. Cherif Bassiouni, "The New Wars and the Crisis of Compliance with the Law of Armed Conflict by Non-State Actors" (2008) 98 J. Crim. L. & Criminology 711.
68   *Legality of the Threat or Use of Nuclear Weapons Case*, Advisory Opinion, [1996] I.C.J. Rep. 226 at para. 25 (reprinted in 35 I.L.M. 809).
69   *Juan Carlos Abella v. Argentina (La Tablada)* (1997), Inter-Am. Comm. H.R. No.24/98 at para. 160.
70   See René Provost, "El Uso del Derecho Internacional Humanitario por la Comision Interamericana de Derechos Humanos: Hacia un Derecho Humanitario Regional?" in *Jornadas de derecho internacional: 11 al 14 de diciembre de 2001, Ciudad de México, Estados Unidos Mexicanos* (Washington, DC: OEA, 2002); *American Convention on Human Rights*, San Jose, Costa Rica, 22 November 1969, O.A.S. Treaty Series No. 36, 1144 U.N.T.S. 123 (entered into force 18 July 1978) [*American Convention*].
71   *Case of Las Palmeras (Colombia)* (2000), Inter-Am. Ct. H.R. (Ser. C) No. 67 at para. 29.
72   *Ibid.* at para. 33.
73   *Case of the Serrano-Cruz Sisters (El Salvador)* (2004), Inter-Am. Ct. H.R. (Ser. C) No. 118 at para. 119.
74   *Ibid.* at para. 116.
75   *Case of Vargas-Areco (Paraguay)* (2006), Inter-Am. Ct. H.R. (Ser. C) No. 155 at para. 122.
76   For example: *Case of Blake (Guatemala)* (1998), Inter-Am. Ct. H.R. (Ser. C) No. 36; *Case of the 19 Tradesmen (Colombia)* (2004), Inter-Am. Ct. H.R. (Ser. C) No. 109.
77   *Case of the "Mapiripán Massacre" (Colombia)* (2005), Inter-Am. Ct. H.R. (Ser. C) No. 134, at para. 110.
78   *Case of Paniagua-Morales et al. (the "White Van") (Guatemala)* (1998), Inter-Am. Ct. H.R. (Ser. C) No. 37 at para. 91.
79   *Case of Villagrán Morales et al. ("Street Children") (Guatemala)* (1999), Inter-Am. Ct. H.R. (Ser. C) No. 63.
80   *Ibid.* at para. 79.
81   *Ibid.* at para. 191.
82   *Case of the Yakye Axa Indigenous Community (Paraguay)* (2005), Inter-Am. Ct. H.R. (Ser. C) No. 125 at para. 162.
83   See especially Andrew Clapham, *Human Rights Obligations of Non-State Actors* (Oxford: Oxford University Press, 2006) at 28.
84   *International Covenant on Economic, Social and Cultural Rights, supra* note 37.
85   See Carlos Iván Fuentes, "Protegiendo el Derecho a la Salud en el Sistema Interamericano de Derechos Humanos" (2006) 22 Am. U. Int'l L. Rev. 7.
86   GA Res. 63/117, UN GAOR, 63d Sess., Agenda item 58, UN Doc. A/RES/63/117 (10 December 2008).
87   *Fundamental Standards of Humanity: Report of the Secretary-General Submitted Pursuant to Commission Resolution 2000/69*, UN ESCOR, 57th Sess., Annex, Agenda item 17, UN Doc. E/CN.4/2001/91 (2001) at para. 6.

15

Rethinking Stabilization and Humanitarian Action in "Fragile Cities"

ROBERT MUGGAH AND OLIVER JÜTERSONKE

The Western world's current preoccupation with so-called ungoverned spaces can be traced back to the colonial epoch, if not before. Debates over unstable states and cities and how to contain and regulate them are once again assuming growing importance in certain policy and academic circles.[1] There are many reasons for this, including growing anxiety over rapid and unregulated urbanization and its implications for the erosion of governance and the onset of war. Concepts such as "fragility" and "stabilization" reflect a renewed commitment by most wealthy countries to reassert the primacy and reach of the state. They also signal how certain governments are attempting to reconcile complex integrated interventions to guarantee order while ensuring that the humanitarian space is maintained in areas of disorder.

This chapter considers the nascent lexicon of fragility and stabilization and its subsequent absorption into the security and development policy arenas. Crucially, it highlights how such concepts are positioned in relation to national (as opposed to subnational or metropolitan) priorities. It then critically assesses the implications of such concepts for humanitarian action in urban settings, specifically emerging efforts by the International Committee of the Red Cross (ICRC) to engage in chronically violent but ostensibly "non-war" contexts such as Rio de Janeiro, Brazil. In emphasizing the spatial and social features of subnational actors and orders, this chapter signals the potential of "resilience" in shaping civilian security and safety. Indeed, an accounting of resilience allows for a more nuanced reading of how formal and informal urban institutions can adapt and transform even in the midst of acute fragility.

The Onset of Fragility

The notion of fragility as a means of describing characteristics of state vulnerability emerged in popular development and security policy discourse during the late 1990s and early 2000s.[2] It represents, in certain ways, the latest iteration of a security paradigm that emerged during the years following the end of the Cold War.[3] The emergent paradigm was itself shaped by the centrality of human rights and concepts such as human security, civilian protection, and the responsibilities of states to protect and guarantee the basic rights of individuals residing in their territories, themes discussed elsewhere in this volume.[4]

This human-centred security agenda was, and to some extent remains, closely aligned with another strategic objective of states, namely, good governance and, more broadly, state building. International donor interest in fragility can also be directly linked to the growing discomfort of multilateral and bilateral agencies and humanitarian organizations with the absence of legitimate governmental or state institutions in areas where they operate. In such environments, it is commonly argued, populations are potentially at increased risk due to a lack of public authority and control. Ungoverned spaces are thus characterized by a variety of non-state actors vying for power and by acts of brutality, intimidation, and corruption by the state's security services.

A host of security and development institutions such as the North Atlantic Treaty Organization (NATO), the World Bank, and the Organisation for Economic Co-operation and Development (OECD) have fielded an array of terms to describe fragility. A shortlist might include "weak," "failing," "failed," and "collapsed" states.[5] These categories can be located on a continuum – with weakness and failing contingent on the degree to which a state (or comparable territorial unit) is capable of fulfilling its essential functions of providing security, welfare, and representation.[6] Where public and private institutions have completely surrendered this capability – whether due to external intervention, civil war, mismanagement, or natural disaster – the state is commonly described as having failed or collapsed altogether.

A corollary argument is that stability and order must be restored in one way or another. As such, the discourse and practice of good (enough) governance promotion can be regarded as the international (and domestic) community's effort to re-establish a "governance" state. The aspiration of creating progressive liberal democratic states in the Western model from poor and disorderly fragile states speaks to deeply rooted ideologies, assumptions, and interests within the aid and security communities.[7] While the argument summarized above is seldom made explicit in policy statements or documents, it nonetheless underpins the governance debate and encourages scholars such as Martti Koskenniemi to speak of a "new moral internationalism."[8]

A veritable industry has sprung up around the twin concepts of fragility and stabilization.[9] North American think tanks and government ministries and departments – including Canada's Department of Foreign Affairs and International Trade (DFAIT) and the Canadian International Development Agency (CIDA) – soon established early warning systems and indices to classify the extent of "fragility" and estimate the likelihood of a state's "going over the brink."[10] Although the challenges associated with ascribing numerical values and variables to complex and subtle dynamics were acknowledged by social scientists, these were routinely brushed aside in the rush to rank and prioritize the dangerousness of recipient states.[11]

A central assumption guiding many of these efforts was the conviction that it could be objectively knowable (or empirically observable) whether a state was "well governed" and, more controversially, that claims to statehood were in some way dependent on the verdict of such deliberations. It is useful to note that debates on fragility were shaped not just by geostrategic and liberal internationalist priorities but also by practical challenges and realities on the ground facing development and humanitarian agencies. Concerned with maintaining adequate space in which to administer assistance, bottom-up processes of policy formulation and programming helped steer debates away from the normatively loaded concepts of "collapse," "failure," and even "conflict" to the more politically neutral concept of "fragility."[12]

Notwithstanding the World Bank estimate of some forty to sixty fragile states home to more than 1.2 billion people,[13] there is surprisingly little consensus about what exactly fragility means. There does appear to be some agreement on its basic parameters, however, with the United Kingdom's Department for International Development (DFID) defining fragile situations as "those where governments cannot or will not deliver core functions to the majority of its people, including the poor."[14] Meanwhile, countries such as France have opted not to issue a definition at all, despite its creation of a fragility index.[15] In much the same way as human security, the concept

is deliberately vague even as it offers a roadmap for interventions that eschew conflict prevention in favour of containment, regulation, and the provision of security and relief aid.

Ultimately, the fragility concept applies a functional understanding of the
state. According to the OECD's Development Assistance Committee
(OECD-DAC),[16] for example, fragile states suffer from "deficits in governance" and lack the "capacity or willingness" as well as the legitimacy to exe-
cute basic and inclusive service provision functions. This diagnosis is
essentially identical with those of the "failing state" discourse. The only important difference is that "fragility" appears to apply to a wider spectrum of
contexts and offers more open-ended opportunities for engagement, with
(perhaps more worrisome) no clear exit strategy. Crucially, fragility does
not apply exclusively to the state. The OECD-DAC broadened the optic to
include "fragile states and situations," indicating that transnational and sub-
state units can also be construed as ungoverned spaces and, potentially, "the
most dangerous security threats" to international and national order.[17]

Due to rapidly escalating rates of urbanization, fragile and ungoverned
spaces are increasingly being identified within densely populated urban
and peri-urban areas, including slums and shantytowns. The referent of
fragility, then, is shifting. It is no longer confined exclusively to the state
but also includes supposedly chronically violent and ungovernable cities in
which public authorities have lost control, are unable to deliver basic public services, and cannot fulfill their function of providing security, welfare,
and representation.

The supposed threats generated by fragile cities are finding resonance
among social scientists, especially military strategists. For example, John
Rapley claims that mega slums constitute the new frontier of armed violence and sources of insecurity,[18] while Richard Norton argues that these
so-called feral cities are "natural havens for a variety of hostile non-state
actors" and may pose "security threats on a scale hitherto not encountered."[19]
Notwithstanding an important, if nascent, counter-argument that such
areas often provide new and informal forms of service and provision, the
political and ideological commitment to restoring state and metropolitan
order remains dominant.

Even though alarm bells are being sounded over the real and imagined
threats presented by fragile cities, surprisingly little is actually known
about them. The extent to which cities that have experienced protracted
fragility and insecurity are able to cope, adapt, and rebound from massive
shocks is seldom considered. The manner in which informal institutions in

chronically violent cities such as Rio de Janeiro, Port-au-Prince, Beirut, Kingston, or Johannesburg are capable of reproducing alternative service functions is also poorly understood. And although urban violence and its effects are of mounting concern to parliamentarians, mayors, urban planners, and civil society organizations in major cities and municipalities around the world,[20] the basic assumption about a positive correlation between city size or population density and rates of violence is highly contentious. Instead, there is evidence that urban violence is itself highly heterogeneous, multi-causal, and spatially uneven.[21] Nevertheless, policies aimed at tackling such violence frequently target symptoms and overlook the underlying factors shaping its emergence and severity, as well as the origins, motivations, and means of "violence entrepreneurs."[22]

Crucially, urban fragility is both a result of and a catalyst for transformations in state and metropolitan governance and, more prosaically, spatial organization.[23] In many cities of the global South, for example, certain slum neighbourhoods and shantytowns have assumed the character of forbidden gang and crime zones beyond the control of public security forces. Insecurity in these areas is of course relative, with some areas within these slums being considered more dangerous to residents than others. Yet many middle- and upper-class residents may feel compelled to build (higher) walls and elaborate (more sophisticated) security systems to shield themselves, giving rise to a Manichean landscape of "safe" gated communities and "violent" slums.

Real and perceived violence reinforce each other to create what Tunde Agbola has aptly termed an "architecture of fear."[24] The result is a progressive fragmentation of public space, a breakdown of social cohesion through the generation of new forms of spatial segregation and social discrimination, and potentially more violence. Urban violence must thus be understood as intricately linked to the structural dynamics of urban agglomeration, as well as to the competing interests of – and power relations between – social groups.[25] City disorder need not imply, however, that urban spaces are unable to cope with such challenges and ultimately transform. To the contrary, the "resilience" of cities is a crucial feature that is often overlooked, and one from which important lessons can be drawn for humanitarian action.

Enter Stabilization Operations
Part and parcel of this recent focus on fragility is the emphasis on stability, and on the discourses, practices, and outcomes of so-called stabilization.[26] As Mark Duffield observes, "just as the fragile state has in policy discourse

replaced the failed state, the idea of 'conflict' having held the ring for most of the 1990s, is now being replaced by 'instability.'"[27] While the term "fragility" allows for a potentially more banal and all-encompassing view of the challenges faced in supposedly ungovernable areas, the notion of instability ensures that chronic levels of violence and disorder that may not constitute "conflict" as such are being captured by the logic of intervention. And dealing with instability has catalyzed a set of rhetorical and operational commitments by intervening governments that are in stark contrast to the way humanitarian interventions were portrayed in the 1990s.

Although actively pursued by many governments in the past decade, there are in fact many iterations of stabilization, ranging from muscular military operations to restore order to the wholesale social engineering of societies.[28] As a result, the benchmarks and metrics of stabilization are routinely left deliberately vague and abstract. Even so, unifying features of these stabilization efforts are that they reinforce a security-first approach and that they privilege short-term interventions that win hearts and minds. In this way, stabilization is cast as a means of bridging the so-called relief-development gap. It is also purposefully conceived as a political exercise that embraces the possibility of military intervention and ultimately reconstruction and state building. But make no mistake: stabilization is not development.[29] Stabilization investments are premised on addressing strategic *means*, not developmental *ends*, whether these are described as basic needs, building human capacity, or restoring human dignity.

Unsurprisingly, stabilization has undergone a steady process of bureaucratization since its sanctioning by multilateral and bilateral agencies less than a decade ago. Examples of its emergence include, *inter alia*, the UN Stabilization Mission in Haiti (MINUSTAH) and the US government's Haiti Stabilization Initiative, and the International Stabilisation Force (ISF) in Timor-Leste. The language of stabilization also signals a shift away from traditional social technologies such as conflict prevention and peacebuilding towards more technocratic categories such as "efficiency gains," "service delivery," and "state-society bargaining." In framing documents such as the OECD's Principles for Good International Engagement in Fragile States and Situations,[30] for example, stabilization is described in technocratic terms that emphasize "effective, legitimate and resilient" state administrations, and programmatic interventions that are "concerted, sustained and focused on building the relationship between state and society."[31] "Solutions" for promoting stabilization are focused on redressing endogenous disequilibria within fragile states, including inherent weaknesses in the domestic political process, the flagrant disjuncture of expectations between citizens and the state, and the collapse of the social contract.

In practice, stabilization explicitly builds on comprehensive and multi-sector approaches, exemplified by the UN's concept of the "integrated mission" since the early 1990s. Recent iterations of the "integrated" model feature a combination of so-called soft, medium, and hard interventions that simultaneously seek to draw on military, diplomatic, development, and humanitarian levers. Vertical (headquarters-field) and horizontal (inter-departmental and inter-agency) coordination is considered to be of particular importance. Taken together, then, stabilization intends to prevent disorder and fragility, not just through muscular coercive interventions but also through the reconstitution and reinforcement of local policing and security provision capacities, investment in community capacities to resist insecurity and instability, the promotion of financial systems that allow for rapid dispersal of aid, and the integration of all these activities with reconstruction.[32]

Attaining such integration in practice is invariably a tricky affair. Different government departments and agencies exhibit varying understandings of basic concepts such as fragility and stabilization. Moreover, executive decision making is more likely to reinforce bureaucratic silos and discrete sector-specific interests than overcome them. Although calls for "whole-of-government" and "whole-of-system" approaches are commonplace,[33] different sectors continue to harbour distinct administrative structures and procedures that in turn configure incentives and organizational behaviour. Integration is thus often restricted to inter-agency working groups, tentative moves towards joint funding pools, task force mechanisms to promote inter-agency collaboration and joint deployment, and, in certain instances, stabilization and reconstruction operations, notably the Provincial Reconstruction Teams (PRTs) in Afghanistan. Crucially, however, such initiatives tend to not only blur the distinction between military and civilian activities but also risk potentially undermining humanitarian protection or assistance.[34]

The mounting interest in fragility and stabilization in states coincides with growing awareness that cities are a new and important arena of engagement. For example, a cursory review of military doctrine emerging from US, UK, and Canadian defence establishments suggests that (fragile) urban settings are fast assuming a more prominent role as sites for engagement with multi-mandate and multi-dimensional interventions.[35] Indeed, stabilization is connected fundamentally to strategic thinking on counterinsurgency and – as in Kabul and Port-au-Prince – is indeed synonymous with it. Strategies to regulate and contain violence and restore order increasingly revolve around the stabilization of dangerous slums, urban peripheries, and ungoverned spaces that may harbour insurgents, terrorists, or organized criminals. Owing to the fact that cities – especially capitals – are politically symbolic, economic engines, and home to increasingly high proportions of a country's population, stabilizing the city is increasingly high on the list of priorities. As some military commentators are wont to say, "as the city goes, so goes the state."

Despite its growing prominence in development and military circles, the fragile city has yet to elicit a similar level of interest from the humanitarian sector. Nevertheless, from the perspective of humanitarian actors, the role of the city, as well as the emerging multilateral strategies for dealing with disorder within them, is likely to generate far-reaching consequences. It should be recalled that although much humanitarian protection and relief focuses on alleviating the suffering of affected populations in rural and marginal areas, some of the great humanitarian tragedies of the last two decades are named after cities, from Srebrenica and Grozny to Goma, Kigali, and Fallujah. Humanitarian agencies – including the ICRC, the International Federation of Red Cross and Red Crescent Societies (IFRC), Médecins Sans Frontières (MSF), and a host of others – are being forced to grapple with the reality of urban fragility. They are also contending with the onset of stabilization operations that explicitly fuse military and civilian activities as one, and that potentially have profound implications for humanitarian space and the way humanitarian actors conduct their activities.[36]

The Changing Face of Humanitarian Action: The Case of Rio de Janeiro

The role and place of politics in humanitarianism is at the heart of current debates over whether or not the humanitarian space is being undermined by integrated approaches and stabilization missions. Stabilization explicitly couples military and civilian actors with relief and development work. Meanwhile, humanitarian action is reserved to relief agencies and a narrow mandate premised on impartial, neutral, and needs-driven aid. As such, as Michael Barnett and Thomas Weiss have argued, humanitarianism is precariously situated between a politics of solidarity and a politics of governance:

Humanitarian workers traditionally saw themselves as apolitical insofar as they defied the dominant systems of power and were in solidarity with the victims ... As they become increasingly implicated in governance structures, they find themselves in growing collaboration with those whose influence they once resisted. Such a development means that humanitarianism's "politics" are now more visible, and the relationship between humanitarianism and power is now more complex.[37]

There are major divisions within the humanitarian community on how to engage with stabilization. For example, there is a distinction between Dunantists, who emphasize the importance of maintaining autonomy and ensuring principled stances on neutrality and impartiality, and Wilsonians, who welcome a renewed focus on so-called root causes and rights-based interventions while adopting a more pragmatic approach and acknowledging the possibility of aligning themselves with "good" political objectives.[38] In this political-versus-apolitical dichotomy, others distinguish between humanitarian actors that seek to influence incentive structures of, and constraints on, local actors, and those that more narrowly work within the parameters of an existing situation.[39] Whatever the taxonomy deployed, it seems clear that something of a third way is being generated for humanitarian work, in terms of both the types of non-conflict settings that humanitarian actors are engaged in and the way this work can be reconciled with the integrated approaches increasingly favoured by the security and development community.

Nowhere are these tensions clearer than in recent attempts by major international humanitarian agencies to grapple with protection and violence reduction in urban areas. Recent efforts by the ICRC in contexts such as Bogota, Port-au-Prince, and Rio de Janeiro are a case in point. Seized by the issue of responding to urban violence in non-war settings, the ICRC began to explore possible entry points for expanding its work into such new and precarious environments. Following early experimentation in Haiti around 2005 and 2006,[40] a specialized working group was established in Geneva. Through it, experienced ICRC delegates were brought together to gauge potential forms of engagement and reflect on the kinds of practices that might be replicated in various scenarios.[41] A pilot was established in Rio de Janeiro beginning in 2008 with a five-year mandate. The aim was to explore options for engaging in protection and violence reduction in some of the city's more notorious slums, or *favelas.* Although the head of operations for Latin America likened operations in Rio de Janeiro to the ICRC's work in Baghdad, its approach cannot be described as "business as usual." On the contrary, it represents somewhat of a watershed for the future direction and strategy of one of the world's premier humanitarian agencies.

Conventional approaches adopted by the Brazilian government to "stabilizing" Rio de Janeiro's slums used to rely on heavy-handed military-style "pacification" operations undertaken by special branches of the country's federal and state-level military police. In extreme cases, the Brazilian armed forces have been involved in cordoning off gang- and militia-affected areas and "reoccupying" them, often making deeply symbolic gestures such as planting the national flag in areas liberated from narco-traffickers. Since 2008, however, Rio de Janeiro state authorities together with the mayor's office pursued a genuinely integrated "stabilization" strategy. On the one hand, it embeds police in communities; on the other, it pursues social interventions with community members to marginalize competitors to public order. While Brazil is not affected by a war in the normative sense, the ICRC determined that the agency could play a constructive role in humanizing stabilization efforts. Following controversial discussions with the national and metropolitan authorities in Rio de Janeiro, the ICRC launched a diagnostic exercise to identify areas and groups facing acute needs, institutional capacities, and locally appropriate intervention strategies.

Although not necessarily described as such by ICRC personnel, the agency is investing in enhancing the resilience of chronically affected areas of violence-plagued favelas. The road has been neither straightforward nor problem-free, however. A primary challenge facing the ICRC delegation in Brazil was that of ensuring support from local public authorities and non-governmental agencies. Accordingly, the ICRC began negotiating with police representatives to explore ways of extending protection to vulnerable civilians. At first wary that the ICRC was seeking to "protect the drug traffickers" – claims often made by governments fighting insurgents in war zones – the police eventually relented and accepted the concept of "negotiated access" for specific protection activities. Similar negotiations were undertaken with the national Red Cross association, which had previously not engaged in the favelas and initially expressed a reluctance to do so.

Between 2007 and 2008, the ICRC began to articulate a sensitive strategy for working in situations of urban violence. The intervention focused on seven selected favelas spread about Rio de Janeiro that exhibited different manifestations of urban violence – whether involving narco-traffickers, criminal gangs, militia, or others. Intending it from the beginning to serve as a pilot project, the ICRC purposefully began an incremental process of engagement premised on establishing trust and demonstrating effects. First, it recruited and trained a cadre of volunteers from the selected favelas in order to inculcate the ethics and values of the agency. Likewise, in order to ensure their legitimacy and to multiply their efforts, the agency established a network of implementing partners from among non-governmental associations located within affected favelas. Interventions were then designed with the intention of explicitly winning hearts and minds and building confidence rather than meeting specific material outputs or outcomes.

Specifically, at the physical entrance of specific favelas, the agency and the national Red Cross, together with its partners, began offering first aid training and limited treatment for violence-related injuries. Through a gradual process of building trust, representatives of the ICRC were able to eventually penetrate the interior and begin a process of interaction with previously hesitant residents. There, local grievances – including concerns with respect to the "heavy-handed" operations carried out by the Brazilian military police – could be confidentially reported back to the responsible authorities. Moreover, notes and letters could be passed between residents of favelas and others on the outside. These modest efforts have been accompanied by initiatives to promote special services for single mothers, safer schools, and activities targeting adolescent boys who may be susceptible to gang recruitment.

Although the Rio de Janeiro initiative has been underway for only a short period, some telling lessons are emerging. At the outset, there is recognition that many of the social technologies mobilized by ICRC in so-called war zones can, with some alterations, be exported to non-war areas to positive effect. This is because some characteristics of conflict-affected areas are analogous to those found in violence-afflicted urban slums and shantytowns. Another lesson concerns the importance of harnessing local expertise and capacity. The ICRC has deliberately altered its approach from a centralized strategy determined from above to one that consciously builds on localized networks and realities. But there are also important cautions. For example, partly because of the limited visibility afforded to the ICRC in favelas, but also because of the highly complex social morphology of urban violence in these areas, any intervention must proceed with extreme care.[42] What is more, "classic" areas of engagement for the ICRC – including direct negotiated access with leaders of armed groups or work with prison populations – are often difficult to entertain at this stage.[43] Nonetheless, modest interventions such as those currently underway in Rio de Janeiro are a potential bellwether. If successful, they could presage a radical transformation in the direction and nature of humanitarian action and even stabilization. They would represent the amplification of the lens of humanitarian actors, and a conscious expansion of how such entities understand and engage in complex environments where civilians face the daily risk of violence.

Conclusion

Since urban violence regularly features in news headlines, it suffers from what Marion Harroff-Tavel describes as "hyper mediatisation."[44] This implies an exaggeration of empirically observed acts of violence and a subsequent inflation of the perceived security threats. A modest jump in homicides in a given city can result in a wave of anxiety among the population, even if statistics reveal that rates of violence are actually declining. Even so, owing to unrelenting urbanization trends and the compression of social dynamics into dense urban spaces, it is obvious that cities will increasingly be the site of both chronic and acute forms of violence. These will range from low-level racketeering and petty crime to urban warfare and all-out conflict. Responses to urban violence will vary across time and space, with stabilization being one approach among many. The emerging "stabilization-and-reconstruction" agenda that is increasingly applied to fragile urban settings is arguably an even greater challenge to orthodox humanitarian principles and practice in the city than it is outside it.

This chapter reminds proponents of stabilization of the inherent heterogeneity, dynamism, and complexities of urban spaces and institutions, especially those affected by chronic violence. Just as aid recipients cannot be seen by humanitarian agencies as "passive" beneficiaries of aid but rather as active participants, so too cities and their institutions express unique and innovative forms of resilience to external and internal stress, including to fragility and external stabilization efforts. Urban resilience constitutes an ongoing process of coping and adaptation of territorially bounded units (that is, a city's formal and informal social, political, and economic institutions and its inhabitants) with regard to endogenous and exogenous shocks, whether the violence and disorder that lead to foreign intervention of one sort or another, or the social upheaval and strain caused by the intervention itself.[45]

Cities – particularly fragile cities – are not a *terra nullius* on which either stabilization or humanitarian action can be readily grafted. Indeed, there is presently a considerable knowledge gap about how fragile cities cope over time and how their fragility can be addressed. Despite substantial investment in understanding the resilience of the comparatively wealthier cities of North America and Western Europe, surprisingly little is known about how lower- and middle-income cities, institutions, and actors manage serious shocks, including the onset of violence. The consideration of urban resilience in situations of chronic violence draws attention to a particular scale of analysis among donors, and also to critical gaps and silences in development thinking. This focus is also much needed: cities are growing rapidly and often unsustainably around the world. As de-industrializing processes persist and unemployment escalates, these metropolitan areas are exposed to new forms of insecurity, crisis, and shock. Meanwhile, multilateral and bilateral agencies are struggling to engage above and below the state. They are also increasingly resorting to private forms of delivery to "harden" potential targets.

Of course, declaring that humanitarian action should engage with urban resilience does not in itself offer ways of doing this, although the ICRC's recent experiences in Rio de Janeiro should soon yield its first tentative conclusions. But the message, at least, is that cities and their institutions are not passive, dependency-prone establishments but rather active enablers of urban governance and sites of considerable dynamism and social engagement. Focusing on resilience, then, entails locating ways of strengthening and reinforcing both formal and informal institutions, while also recognizing the trade-offs between such activities and the principles and mandates of humanitarian actors. Supporting resilience requires acknowledging the primacy of continuity, and thus also the centrality of history and political processes in mediating adaptation to stress over time. Recognizing that cities and their institutions routinely cope with instability and shocks is a first step in preparing humanitarian action for the many urban challenges of the coming decades.

ACKNOWLEDGMENTS
The authors would like to thank the organizers and participants of the international humanitarian conference "On the Edges of Conflict," held at the Liu Institute for Global Issues in Vancouver, Canada, 29-31 March 2009, for their comments and suggestions on an earlier version of this chapter. The authors are also grateful for the important input of various ICRC delegates and personnel in Brazil, Colombia, Haiti, and Switzerland. Finally, the authors would like to give credit to the International Development Research Centre (IDRC) for its support to the Humanitarian Action in Situations Other than War (HASOW) initiative.

NOTES

1 For a summary of these debates, see Robert Muggah, "Stabilising Fragile States and the Humanitarian Space" in Mats Berdal and Achim Wennmann, eds., *Ending Wars and Consolidating Peace* (London: International Institute for Strategic Studies; Routledge, 2010) ["Stabilising Fragile States"]. See also the special issue of the journal *Disasters*, edited by Sarah Collinson, Samir Elharawy, and Robert Muggah, "States of Fragility: Stabilisation and Its Implications for Humanitarian Action" (2010).

2 See, *e.g.*, World Bank, *World Development Report: Conflict, Security and Development* (Washington, DC: World Bank, 2011).

3 See, *e.g.*, Robert Muggah, "States of Fragility" (2009), online: The Mark <http://www.themarknews.com/>.

4 These are also themes, ironically, now actively dismissed by the Canadian government. See Taylor Owen, "The Government's Newspeak" (2009), online: The Mark <http://www.themarknews.com/>.

5 As such, fragility encompasses failed and weak states, "neo-patrimonial" and clientelistic countries, "warlord" states, and "quasi" (or semi-independent) states.

6 See the overview of various definitions of fragility and state weakness in the development literature and in the comparative politics literature under "Chapter 1 – Understanding Fragile States" at the Governance and Social Development Resource Centre, online at <http://www.gsdrc.org/>. Also Robert Muggah and Timothy Sisk, *Governance for Peace* (New York: UNDP, 2011).

7 See Roland Paris, *At War's End: Building Peace after Civil Conflict* (Cambridge: Cambridge University Press, 2004).

8 Martti Koskenniemi, "Legitimacy, Rights, and Ideology: Notes towards a Critique of the New Moral Internationalism" (2003) 7 Associations 349.

9 See Muggah, "Stabilising Fragile States," *supra* note 1 at 33-52.

10 Foreign Policy and the Fund for Peace, "The Failed States Index" *Foreign Policy* (July/August 2005) at 56-65. See also United Nations Development Programme, *User's Guide to Measuring Fragility* (Oslo: UNDP, 2009).

11 See Keith Krause and Oliver Jütersonke, "Seeking Out the State: Fragile States and International Governance" (2007) 42 Politorbis 5, online: Switzerland Federal Department of Foreign Affairs <http://www.eda.admin.ch/politorbis>.

12 See Jennifer Miliken and Keith Krause, "State Failure, State Collapse and State Reconstruction: Concepts, Lessons and Strategies" (2002) 33 Development and Change Special Edition 753.

13 World Bank, *supra* note 2.

14 Department for International Development, *Why We Need to Work More Effectively in Fragile States* (London: DFID, 2005) at 7.

15 France, *Document de travail: agir en faveur des acteurs et des sociétés fragile* (Paris: Agence française de développement, département de recherche, 2005).

16 Organisation for Economic Co-operation and Development, *Service Delivery in Fragile Situations: Key Concepts, Findings and Lessons* (2008), online: OECD <http://www.oecd.org/>.

17 See, *inter alia,* United States Agency for International Development, *Fragile States Strategy* (Washington, DC: USAID, 2005); "START: Stabilization and Reconstruction

Task Force," Foreign Affairs and International Trade Canada (2008), online: DFAIT <http://www.international.gc.ca/>; and the UK's "Stabilisation Unit," online: Stabilisation Unit <http://www.stabilisationunit.gov.uk/>.

18 John Rapley, "The New Middle Ages" (2006) 85 Foreign Affairs 95.

19 Richard Norton, "Feral Cities" (2003) 56 Naval War College Review 97 at 105.

20 See United Nations Human Settlements Programme (UN-HABITAT), *Global Report on Human Settlements 2007: Enhancing Urban Safety and Security* (London: Earthscan, 2007).

21 See Small Arms Survey, *Small Arms Survey 2007: Guns and the City* (Cambridge: Cambridge University Press, 2007); also Geneva Declaration, *The Global Burden of Armed Violence* (Geneva: Geneva Declaration and Small Arms Survey, 2008).

22 Robert Muggah, ed., *Security and Post-Conflict Reconstruction: Dealing with Fighters in the Aftermath of War* (New York: Routledge, 2009).

23 Caroline Moser and Dennis Rodgers, "Change, Violence and Insecurity in Non-Conflict Situations," Working Paper 245 (March 2005), online: Overseas Development Institute <http://www.odi.org.uk/>.

24 Tunde Agbola, *Architecture of Fear: Urban Design and Construction Response to Urban Violence in Lagos, Nigeria* (Ibadan: African Book Publishers, 1997).

25 Dennis Rodgers, "Urban Violence Is Not (Necessarily) a Way of Life: Towards a Political Economy of Conflict in Cities" (2010), United Nations University – World Institute for Development Economics Research (UNU-WIDER) Working Paper No. 2010/20, online: <http://www.wider.unu.edu/publications/>.

26 Of course, the notion of stabilization is not a new one. Notably, stabilization programs have been regular phenomena for decades, but they were of a purely macro-economic nature, and did not entail an ostensible security component. See, *e.g.*, Chapter 16 of this book.

27 Mark Duffield, "Global Civil War: The Non-Insured, International Containment and Post-Interventionary Society" (2008) 21 Journal of Refugee Studies 145 at 161.

28 See Sarah Collinson, Samir Elharawy, and Robert Muggah, "States of Fragility: Stabilisation and Its Implications for Humanitarian Action," Humanitarian Policy Group (HPG) Working Paper (2010), online: Overseas Development Institute <http://www.odi.org.uk/>, for a review of differentiated approaches to stabilization in Afghanistan, Colombia, Haiti, Somalia, Sri Lanka, Sudan, and Timor-Leste.

29 See Muggah, "Stabilising Fragile States," *supra* note 1.

30 Organisation for Economic Co-operation and Development, "The Principles for Good International Engagement in Fragile States and Situations" (2007), online: OECD <http://www.oecd.org/>.

31 See Organisation for Economic Co-operation and Development, *Concepts and Dilemmas of State Building in Fragile Situations: From Fragility to Resilience* (2008), online: OECD <http://www.oecd.org/>.

32 See Robert Muggah and Nat J. Colletta, "Post-Conflict Security Promotion" (2009) 9 Conflict, Security and Development 425. See also Cristina Caan, "Post-Conflict Stabilization and Reconstruction: What Have We Learned from Iraq and Afghanistan" (2005), United States Institute of Peace (USIP) Peace Brief, online: <http://www.usip.org/publications/>.

33 Note also the evolution from defence, development, and diplomatic (3Ds) approaches to ones that emphasizes coordination, coherence, and complementarity (3Cs). See Cristina Hoyos and Robert Muggah, "Can Coherent, Coordinated and Complementary Approaches to Dealing with Fragile States Yield Better Outcomes?" (2009) 45 Politorbis 53, online: Switzerland Federal Department of Foreign Affairs <http://www.eda.admin.ch/politorbis>.

34 See Stephen Cornish, "No Room for Humanitarianism in 3D Policies: Have Forcible Humanitarian Interventions and Integrated Approaches Lost Their Way?" (2007) 10 Journal of Military and Strategic Studies 1, online: <http://www.jmss.org/>.

35 See, *e.g.*, United States Joint Forces Command, *The Joint Operating Environment (J.O.E.)* (2010), online: <http://www.fas.org/>; United Kingdom Department for International Development, *Eliminating World Poverty: Building Our Common Future* (2009), online: <http://reliefweb.int/node/24824>; confirmed by conversations between the authors and defence specialists and military liaison officers in Canada, France, the United States, and the United Kingdom.

36 See Collinson *et al.*, *supra* note 1 at 34.

37 Michael Barnett and Thomas G. Weiss, "Humanitarianism: A Brief History of the Present" in Michael Barnett and Thomas G. Weiss, eds., *Humanitarianism in Question: Politics, Power, Ethics* (Ithaca, NY: Cornell University Press, 2008) 1 at 38.

38 See Abby Stoddard, "Humanitarian NGOs: Challenges and Trends," HPG (Humanitarian Policy Group) Briefing 12 (2003), online: Overseas Development Institute <http://www.odi.org.uk/resources/>.

39 Michael Barnett and Jack Snyder, "The Grand Strategies of Humanitarianism" in Michael Barnett and Thomas G. Weiss, eds., *supra* note 37, 143 at 146.

40 This article focuses primarily on the case of the ICRC in Rio de Janeiro. For a review of ICRC activities in Port-au-Prince since 2005, see Robert Muggah, "The Effects of Stabilisation on Humanitarian Action in Haiti" (2010) 34 Disasters S444.

41 With guidance from ICRC delegates, the agency recognized it would need an innovative and flexible group of delegates to take the process forward. Indeed, the group would require new skills different from those traditionally privileged by the organization.

42 Indeed, ICRC's presence in Brazil, let alone the slums of Rio de Janeiro, is highly contentious. Added to the routine threats presented by violence entrepreneurs in favelas and their environs are dangers from other, unexpected quarters. With the city due to host the FIFA World Cup in 2014 and Olympic games in 2016, senior policy makers are keen to ensure that the country presents a "clean" image to the outside world. Economists forecast earnings of over US$70 billion for the Olympics alone. The presence of the ICRC represents, to some, a blight and a potential deterrent to the windfall gains that might result from official selection.

43 Importantly, the ICRC has determined that more proactive efforts to liaise directly with gang leaders and to engage in extensive prison visitations are premature. While fundamentally connected to violence prevention and reduction, they are also extremely high-risk and ICRC delegates concede that their level of knowledge of community dynamics is insufficient at this stage.

44 Marion Harroff-Tavel, "Violence armée et action humanitaire en milieu urbain" (24 July 2008), online: ICRC <http://www.icrc.org/>.

45 This application of "resilience" draws upon many other analyses using the concept, often in conjunction with urban settings and/or regional environments. Most of these definitions rest on the common understanding of resilience as the ability to tolerate a given "shock" and sustain usual behaviour. The notion of "adaptability" is also a key component for many conceptualizations of resilience, as it is often argued that flexible systems will be able to better adjust to unexpected shocks in order to continue functioning. See P. Berkes and C. Folke, eds., *Linking Social and Ecological Systems: Management Practices and Social Mechanisms for Building Resilience* (Cambridge: Cambridge University Press, 1998). For a recent exploration of some issues related to the study of resilience, see Melissa Leach, ed., "Re-framing Resilience: A Symposium Report," STEPS Working Paper 13 (Brighton: STEPS Centre, 2008).

16

Stabilization and Humanitarian Action in Haiti

ROBERT MUGGAH

Stabilization missions that combine defence, diplomacy, and development are gaining traction in post-conflict and fragile states and cities.[1] Notwithstanding donor preoccupation with fragility, the discourse, practice, and outcomes of stabilization – even narrowly conceived in terms of reducing violence and restoring basic security – remain under-conceptualized. Moreover, the implications of stabilization and stability operations for humanitarian action, including relief agency impartiality, neutrality, and access, have yet to be adequately considered. This chapter reviews the evolution of stabilization activities after Haiti's descent into extreme violence in 2004 and their implications for humanitarian action more generally. It does not focus extensively on the period following the devastating earthquake of January 2010.[2]

This chapter documents the experiences of three distinct stabilization initiatives advanced by a wide assortment of multilateral and bilateral agencies active in Haiti before and immediately after the 2010 natural disaster. Although differing subtly in form and content, these efforts were all broadly conceived within a security-first perspective. Stabilization is thus intended to restore and reinforce the capacity of the state to provide legitimate security. Specifically, such efforts are expected to bring about the conditions for the rule of law (justice and due process, legitimate policing, penal services, and so on) to take hold and, ultimately, for development to proceed. In order to shed light on the practice of stabilization, this chapter specifies key differences in how stabilization is operationally expressed – particularly by the United Nations, the United States, and a constellation of ostensibly middle-power donors such as Canada, Norway, and Brazil.

Overall, stabilization appears to have generated tentative but nonetheless important (temporally specific) returns in security and safety. These gains can be measured in relation to real and perceived reductions in the incidence of victimization and improvements in other metrics of safety and security. Although still precarious, stabilization has also created spaces for certain forms of socioeconomic development. The news is not all positive, however. In the absence of a rapid and meaningful scaling up of legitimate policing authority throughout Haiti and its capital, Port-au-Prince, superficial gains were and continue to be heavily dependent on continued (UN) Brazilian-led peacekeeping presence.[3] In contrast to other settings such as Iraq and Afghanistan, humanitarian agencies operating in Haiti between 2004 and 2009, while initially uncertain how to engage with proponents of stabilization, gradually adopted a pragmatic approach to collaboration.[4]

Reviewing Stabilization in Haiti

Haiti is alternately categorized as fragile, failing, and failed in international security and development circles.[5] The deepening of collective violence in 2000 and 2004 that led to the ousting of former president Jean-Bertrand Aristide was attributed to a host of external and internal factors, including historically embedded patterns of political behaviour among the country's elites, geopolitical influence, and chronic failures of governance and service delivery.[6] From 2007 onward, however, the country was (re)cast by some international actors as a priority concern in the Western hemisphere.[7] Despite a renewal of interest and engagement in wider private sector and development opportunities in the country in 2008 and 2009, donors were preoccupied with securing borders, containing so-called unregulated migration, preventing narcotics trafficking and arms flows, and controlling gang-related and organized criminal violence. Before and after the devastating earthquake of 2010, most observers agreed that the probability of "external" events affecting an already acutely vulnerable population – from the global financial crisis and attendant escalation in food prices to massive hurricanes and storms – would ensure that Haiti is trapped in a chronic humanitarian crisis.

The recipient of considerable inflows of overseas development assistance for decades, Haiti saw twenty-first century investments converging progressively on security promotion, stabilization, recovery, and reconstruction.

This marked a departure from the 1980s and 1990s, when aid was concentrated alternately on the promotion of "good governance" and institutional reform or on supporting non-governmental organizations (NGOs).[8] In the wake of successive UN missions since 1991, the UN adopted its first genuinely "integrated" peace support operation in 2004 – the UN Stabilization Mission in Haiti (MINUSTAH). In this way, it aimed to merge peacekeeping activities more clearly with civilian activities in the delivery of core services and ultimately the "exit" of peacekeepers from the country.[9] Despite major challenges and episodes of violence, security and safety on the ground appear to have steadily improved, particularly since 2007.

A major emphasis of international action in Haiti has been, and continues to be, on containing and, more recently, reducing armed violence through support for community security in urban centres.[10] Such programs have become increasingly prominent in the wake of coercive actions pursued by MINUSTAH peacekeepers between 2004 and 2006 in key urban slums, notably Cité Soleil and Bel Air.[11] While variously defined, violence appears to have diminished substantially in areas targeted by these community security interventions. Randomized household surveys of nine hundred families undertaken in 2009 detected significant reductions in key indicators of armed violence – physical assaults, sexual assaults, and homicide – since the launch of specific initiatives (see Figures 16.1, 16.2, and 16.3[12]). Statistical correlations require further testing and refinement, but empirical findings suggest an undeniable association.[13]

As discussed at length below, the humanitarian sector initially kept its distance from stabilization interventions. For example, humanitarian agencies such as the International Committee of the Red Cross (ICRC) and Médecins Sans Frontières (MSF) operated more or less autonomously and according to strict internal standard operating procedures, establishing a presence through the provision and maintenance of hospitals/trauma wards, targeted relief assistance, and specific mandated activities. Meanwhile, together with the Haitian National Police (HNP), MINUSTAH and a range of development agencies gradually consolidated their activities in areas "seized" or recovered from local gangs between 2007 and 2009.[14] Specifically, the ICRC and MSF began reducing certain protection-oriented activities in these areas on the grounds that safety had been restored. At the same time, MINUSTAH and a number of humanitarian agencies progressively expanded and strengthened their cooperation.

With development activities assuming a higher priority from 2007 to 2009,[15] bilateral donors such as the US, Canada, and Norway actively sought

FIGURE 16.1

Reduction in the number of physical assaults in urban slums in Haiti, January 2004 to August 2009

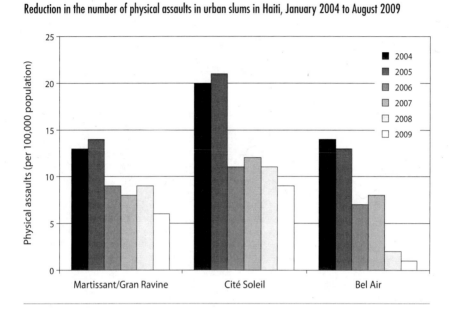

FIGURE 16.2

Reduction in the number of sexual assaults in urban slums in Haiti, January 2004 to August 2009

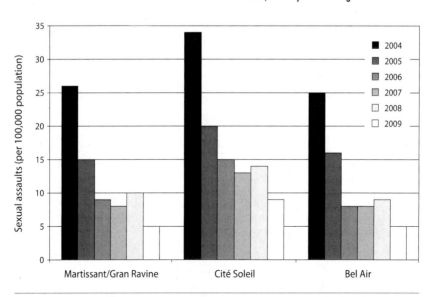

FIGURE 16.3

Reduction in the number of murders in urban slums in Haiti, January 2004 to August 2009

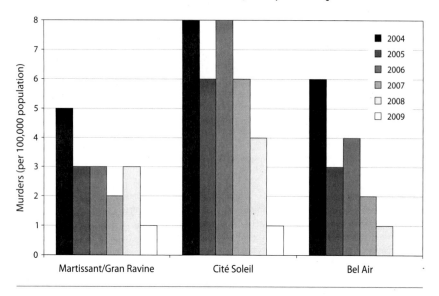

to reinforce stabilization and development in Haiti. They launched unilateral interventions (US) or supported UN and NGO-led activities (Canada and Norway). These interventions were expected to enhance the capacity of the Haitian state – especially its public institutions and service providers – to restore its monopoly over the legitimate use of force. What distinguishes the current stabilization agenda from earlier efforts to promote security are several key characteristics:

- clear definition as short-term (two to three years), emphasizing security promotion and police presence, not necessarily development
- joint operations with military and police actors and development agencies to win hearts and minds
- municipal and neighbourhood-oriented schemes emphasizing "inclusive community decision-making."

Although they have certain similarities in discourse, the practice and outcomes of such actions are, in fact, more different than widely appreciated.

UN Approach: The Stick and Carrot

MINUSTAH itself embodies the normative and political determination of UN member states and donor agency efforts to promote stability and reduce violence in order to restore order/governance and development. Discursively, a series of UN Security Council and General Assembly resolutions highlight the expectations of member states that stabilization would ensure the basic conditions for security and development to take hold on the ground. Programmatically, the UN approach to stabilization combined enforcement-led activities administered by UN "Blue Helmets" with community-led conflict prevention and the restoration of social cohesion and infrastructure. Since the beginning, however, there was a notable institutional separation between MINUSTAH peacekeepers on the one hand and MINUSTAH civilian and United Nations Development Programme (UNDP)–led interventions on the other, even with the existence of a moderate level of communication between personnel.[16]

Despite the wider emphasis of the UN system on stabilization, its constituent parts pursued separate, if parallel, tracks. With respect to UN peacekeepers, the Brazilian-led force sought to establish territorial control and to consolidate its hold through the establishment of a tangible presence in "priority" or "red" zones. Its emphasis was on repressive operations where necessary, physical confrontation and disarmament, and, more recently, joint patrols with HNP counterparts.[17] As for UN civilian and UNDP actors, their efforts were divided into two analogous initiatives – the Community Violence Reduction (CVR) program and the now-defunct Community Security Programme (CSP). The former consisted of a reformed "integrated" Disarmament, Demobilization and Reintegration (DDR) program formerly managed by MINUSTAH and the UNDP, and continues to operate in twelve areas throughout the country.[18] Meanwhile, the CSP included activities undertaken by the UNDP in nine areas,[19] although the project was terminated prematurely by the national authorities.[20]

Despite the important (and controversial) gains of UN peacekeeping activities, these civilian-led stabilization interventions achieved mixed returns. For example, although lauded by some host and bilateral government officials, UN personnel, and NGOs for enhancing stability in the short term, UN peacekeepers were also heavily criticized. Instead of reducing the presence and activities of gangs, muscular operations in peri-urban areas may have unintentionally dispersed and radicalized them.[21] Others contend that the military had considerable prestige and cachet among the local population – an observation supported by survey evidence.[22] As under-standing of the dynamics of gang structures grew – including the "bazes" (bases) and affiliated actors[23] – there was a growing consensus that their corresponding levels of influence were vastly diminished in 2009 compared with 2007.

Other challenges to UN stabilization efforts were more institutional and bureaucratic than substantive. For example, attempts to achieve an integrat-ed approach collapsed on several occasions – described by some insiders as an "amicable divorce."[24] One reason for this was related to the many admin-istrative and organizational challenges associated with "integration" as a UN-wide project more generally. For example, in 2009 the UN Country Team (UNCT) consisted of fourteen separate agencies, funds, and pro-grams.[25] And although the Deputy Special Representative of the Secretary-General/Resident Coordinator/Humanitarian Coordinator (DSRSG/RC/HC) served then as now as the permanent link between MINUSTAH and the rest of the mission, the position was frequently overwhelmed.[26] Nevertheless, MINUSTAH's CVR program appeared to be making important headway in the twelve areas where it was operating before the 2010 earthquake.[27]

The US Approach: Fast and Furious

Meanwhile, alongside other activities, the US government launched the Haiti Stabilization Initiative (HSI) in 2007.[28] The HSI was designed with support from the Defense Department and the State Department's Office of the Coordinator for Reconstruction and Stabilization (S/CRS). Together with guidance from the US Army Corps of Engineers, the HSI was expected to be implemented by the US Agency for International Development (USAID), the International Organization for Migration (IOM), and the pri-vate security company (PSC) DynCorp International and serve as a model for future stabilization efforts in Haiti and more widely.[29] The HSI initially focused on a large neighbourhood widely regarded as affected by systemic and chronic violence – Cité Soleil. This neighbourhood of some 300,000 residents was long marked out as a centre of acute criminal and political violence, transitory migration, and moribund infrastructure. Importantly, the HSI was deliberately undertaken in areas that MINUSTAH peace-keepers had largely cleared of gangs. According to key informants on the ground, the presence and authority of gangs was greatly diminished com-pared with 2004-06. Crucially, the HSI also emphasized an approach that did not directly engage with gangs or related structures themselves, distin-guishing it from UN and other approaches, described below.

The HSI, with the IOM and DynCorp as implementing partners, committed over US$20 million over two years to a combination of "bricks-and-mortar" operations and community-driven social welfare projects.[30] The initiative adopted a two-pronged approach to security promotion. First, it emphasized large-scale infrastructure activities such as roadbuilding and the construction of a central police station and modest police posts.[31] Second, it promoted development interventions – activities explicitly intended to win the hearts and minds of residents and undermine the legitimacy and authority of gangs – including literally hundreds of small-scale development projects. Importantly, the HSI was designed not so much to promote development as an *end*[32] but rather to use aid instrumentally as a *means* of opening the door for international and national agencies to consolidate activities. The Achilles' heel of the program, however, was always its transition or exit strategy.[33] The overall success of the US approach depended on whether the police – specifically, the HNP – would be capable of sustaining security gains, a reality that had not materialized before the 2010 earthquake.[34]

Nevertheless, the HSI advanced several straightforward objectives, many of which were achieved during its short lifespan. These included the generation of the necessary security conditions to enhance police presence and reduce UN peacekeeping presence in volatile areas, and the marginalization of spoilers through community actions (through so-called community forums, a social technology borrowed from the MINUSTAH Community Violence Reduction program). According to USAID, indicators of success included a reduction in threats from gangs, a reduction in the use of security forces for political repression, enhanced performance of security forces, strengthening of subordination of communities to legitimate government authority, enhanced public confidence in security forces, and consent for MINUSTAH.[35] Secondary impacts – from improved socioeconomic conditions to increased access to justice – were considered less central to overall success.[36] In this way, the HSI deviated from more conventional development practice. For example, HSI applied certain forms of conditionality to Cité Soleil neighbourhoods where gang activity persisted or threatened the outcomes of funded interventions – in some cases withholding assistance or ending projects to induce compliance. Observers close to the process claimed that some of these actions generated meaningful results and lasting changes in behaviour, though this is now impossible to test.

It is useful to highlight certain distinguishing features of HSI compared with other stabilization approaches. For one, the program explicitly avoided the option to "negotiate" or "engage" directly with gangs and criminal actors – preferring instead to focus on undermining their source of legitimacy and enhancing the credibility of the municipal structures and the police in re-covered "under-governed spaces." Specifically, then, it sought to establish a permanent police presence in Cité Soleil through rebuilding of physical infrastructure and training of the HNP and equipping of police stations, al-though it did not include provisions for recurring expenditures for police services or equipment. Finally, HSI identified and funded medium-scale projects with residents in Cité Soleil to offer them alternatives to gang rule, and sought to promote enhanced community/police relations[37] and com-munity policing.[38]

Although its benefits are heavily publicized, the overall outcome of the US approach to stabilization was mixed. Indeed, to the United States' credit, the intervention featured a clear theory of change and a robust surveillance mechanism to track outcomes over time. On the one hand, violence ap-peared to have been reduced in key catchment areas and the construction of a major road promised to transform formal and informal market trading. Since the expectation was to reduce violence to levels comparable with those in other areas of the country – that is, to normalize and "contain" crime – it appears that the intervention at least partially fulfilled expecta-tions. The extent to which police presence was enhanced and development resumed in a fundamental sense was harder to ascertain in late 2009, how-ever. Some donor informants claimed that dividends were limited due to the more unilateral approach and noted a subsequent "pushback" from the na-tional and municipal authorities, who were allegedly more wary of American interventionism.

The "Others": From the Ground Up

When it came to security promotion, bilateral donors such as Canada, Norway, and, to some extent, Brazil[39] appeared to support both multilateral interventions emphasizing justice and police reform and more voluntary and community-oriented projects on the ground. Although these activities were often characterized as "stabilization," their shape and character re-vealed important differences from alternatives discussed above. Indeed, middle-power donors frequently invested in a range of "soft" stabilization activities such as "conflict mitigation," "civic mediation," and "community development," even if they were also inclined to support the state's capacity to deliver security through improved policing, customs, penal services, and justice reform. One example of their alternative approach to stabilization

was the "integrated violence reduction program" launched in early 2007 by
a Brazilian NGO, Viva Rio, in the heart of Port-au-Prince.

The program integrated security with development activities in the most
practical way. Specifically, it combined direct gang mediation with rain harvesting, water collection and distribution, sanitation and hygiene activities,
solid waste and sewer management, education for at-risk youth, women's
health promotion, and recreation activities. The initiative was funded by
Canada's Stabilization and Reconstruction Team (START), the Canadian
International Development Agency (CIDA), the Norwegian Ministry of
Foreign Affairs, and Norwegian Church Aid (NCA), and was supported by
the Brazilian government and some funds from the MINUSTAH CVR program.[40] In contrast to externally implemented UN or US activities that
sought to engineer new mechanisms, the program purposely harnessed
existing actors, institutions, and sources of legitimacy. Program implement-
ers negotiated directly with individual *bazes* in selected neighbourhoods –
including community and gang leadership. Although this approach offered
an important entry point into community structures, some critics argued
that it could also unintentionally reinforce informal and possibly illegitimate actors and activities. The intended and unintended consequences of this
approach were recently assessed.[41]

Physically based in Bel Air – with a catchment of ninety thousand residents – the program blended thick theoretical, evidence-based, and cultural
understanding with a flexible incremental approach on the ground. For example, on the basis of a major census and intensive ethnographic studies,
the program-implementing agency, Viva Rio, brokered a peace accord between more than a dozen different gang-affected zones and negotiated
lotteries and bursaries in exchange for reductions in homicidal violence
between 2007 and 2009.[42] Crucially, Viva Rio was able to engage communities early on in an informal way, establishing formal and informal relations
with MINUSTAH and the HNP, which were more directly involved in stabilization. Instead of marginalizing gangs, they explicitly brought *les bazes* into
an iterative process of negotiation, dialogue, and ultimately self-regulation.
Likewise, Viva Rio consciously drew MINUSTAH peacekeepers into the
process, complementing their activities with training in community rela-
tions/outreach and encouraging a "softer," less coercive approach.

Like the UN and US approaches, the "other" approach deliberately located its interventions within a security-first model, recognizing that a
community's development potential is most usefully tapped after real and
perceived violence is diminished. Unlike the UN and US approaches,

however, the latter blended development interventions directly into the program rather than leaving them to other municipal actors or NGOs who were expected to assume responsibilities after real and perceived security was restored. Viva Rio promoted the development of a multi-pronged water management system that entailed the introduction of water kiosks in underserviced areas, rainwater harvesting in primary schools, and the strengthening of municipal (piped/kiosk) water delivery. Other ostensibly developmental activities included educational activities in schools (including vocational education), recreational and sporting alternatives ("soccer diplomacy"), and concerts with Haiti's wildly popular rara and hip-hop music bands. Despite some important gains, however, there were also clear challenges associated with transferring or embedding activities into what were frayed and predominantly illegitimate public institutions.

The "other" approach offers an example of south-south social technology transfer – with experiences from gang-affected urban slums/favelas in Rio being adapted and transferred to the Haitian context. While endorsing many of the same objectives as the UN and US activities – including reductions in real and perceived violence, reinforcement of the gains made by MINUSTAH, and more legitimate and accountable policing – it exemplified an adaptive and opportunistic approach to security promotion.[43] It sought to reinforce, in many ways, alternative nodes of legitimacy and authority through investment in local institutions.[44] Moreover, budgeted at a total of US$4.5 million (between 2006 and 2009), it offered a low-cost alternative to the US and UN. It is critical to note, however, that Bel Air was at the time a comparatively more stable social and economic environment than Cité Soleil, even if violence rates were still reportedly higher than the national average.[45]

Implications of Stabilization for Humanitarian Action

The humanitarian community operating in Haiti between 2004 and 2009 observed the emergence of multiple stabilization agendas with indifference and, in some cases, apprehension. Although instinctively suspicious of repressive activities such as those supported by MINUSTAH, attitudes softened over time – especially among civilian UN agencies, NGOs, the ICRC, and Médecins Sans Frontières.[46] It should be recalled that there were many actors engaged in various ways in the humanitarian and development enterprise in Haiti both before and after the earthquake. Besides the fourteen UN agencies that comprised the UN Country Team, there were literally thousands of NGOs and non-registered community-based organizations operating throughout the country in 2009. All of these actors confronted various guises of "instability" – from acute violence to hurricanes and floods. It is important to note that while the perceptions and attitudes of the humanitarian community towards stabilization may have shifted over the past decade, they are by no means homogeneous.

While difficult to generalize, humanitarian agencies harboured a complex love/hate relationship with the security sector, including MINUSTAH, the HNP, and private security companies. Due to their diversity and competing mandates, it is perhaps unsurprising that attitudes and operating procedures are heterogeneous. Indeed, such tensions are hardly unique to Haiti: persistent divisions in agency approaches to civil/military engagement in Haiti are analogous to those elsewhere, including Afghanistan, Sudan, or the Democratic Republic of Congo (DRC).[47] Put simply, on one side were the Dunantists – including the ICRC and MSF – who in theory opposed "integration" with political and military actors and maintained their autonomy and principled, albeit pragmatic, approach.[48] On the other side were the more Wilsonian NGOs – Oxfam, CARE, and Concern – who appeared to adopt more divergent approaches that entailed tentative yet closer forms of cooperation with military and policing actors, MINUSTAH or otherwise.

Across the humanitarian sector, however, attitudes towards engagement with proponents of stabilization began to warm appreciably between 2007 and 2009. With the exception of the ICRC and MSF, most relief agencies acknowledged that they had virtually no capacity to operate effectively in urban and rural areas affected by systemic violence between 2004 and 2005. Likewise, virtually all agencies agreed that from 2007 to 2009, collective violence diminished even as other forms of violence (such as sexual and gender-based) became more visible.[49] That MINUSTAH, and to a lesser extent the HNP, regained the humanitarian space through force is widely recognized as a critical if controversial achievement. Most prominent humanitarian and development NGOs observed that although they might have been able to access certain areas, they would never have been capable of doing so as quickly or on an equivalent scale without aggressive intervention and stabilization. In other words, humanitarian agencies acknowledged that the security sector regained spaces previously inaccessible to them.

The case of MSF reveals how civil/military relations changed between 2004 and 2009. Specifically, between 2004 and 2007 there was virtually no

contact between MINUSTAH and MSF. In fact, MSF established directives
to deliberately reduce formal and informal exchange between its personnel
and peacekeepers and police. This was considered an especially sensitive
area since MSF was operating in Cité Soleil, where MINUSTAH was active,
with many civilians killed and arrested.[50] Indeed, certain MSF hospitals
were the site of considerable violence between 2004 and 2005. Beginning
in 2008, however, the MSF/MINUSTAH relationship steadily improved. In
the wake of massive floods in August and September that year, for example,
MSF was provided with UN air transport and used MINUSTAH bases for
coordination. Personal relations between commanders, officers, and senior
MSF staff warmed manifestly, due largely to personalities rather than more
fundamental internal institutional adaptations.

The ICRC approach, while sharing similarities with that of MSF, hints at
how civil/military relations may be stronger than publicly assumed. Much
like the US approach discussed above, the ICRC conceived of Haiti as a "laboratory" for new engagement in urban areas affected by armed gangs.
Beginning in 2006 and 2007, for example, the agency explicitly linked its
prison outreach activities (with detained gang leaders) to mediation and access activities, the location of field hospitals, and the strengthening of water
provision in Cité Soleil.[51] From late 2008 to 2009, the ICRC also began
reducing direct actions, supporting instead the Haitian National Red Cross
in neighbouring slums such as Martissant. Meanwhile, an expansion of
operations was planned for 2010 (before the earthquake), including the
establishment of a functioning ambulance service and health posts in Bel
Air, another urban slum.

Overall, the ICRC found that it encountered comparatively few challenges associated with the stabilization agenda. Indeed, it observed that
stabilization expanded rather than closed the humanitarian space. More
provocatively, ICRC officials observed that the objectives of both
MINUSTAH and the ICRC between 2004 and 2009 were more unified
than widely believed. In practical terms, although collaboration with ongoing stabilization activities (UN, US, or the others) was limited until 2007,
it expanded dramatically in 2008. For example, the US and the ICRC worked
together to resolve practical issues in Cité Soleil such as the expansion of
water supplies and provision of electricity. Indeed, the ICRC signalled a
readiness to work more closely with the UN and the US. To many outsiders,
the ICRC often appears to adopt a high level of autonomy and independence from other agencies. In reality, however, it routinely works closely
with most proponents of stabilization, including military actors. It is also

possible, perhaps probable, that Haiti represents a special case where tight civil/military integration was more feasible than elsewhere.[52]

Notwithstanding the experiences of the ICRC and MSF, there appeared to be some concern that supporters of stabilization were insufficiently apprised of humanitarian mandates, even if this was changing by late 2009. Many MINUSTAH military actors were described by humanitarian NGOs as lacking a clear understanding of the value or requirements of humanitarian space. In some cases, humanitarian agencies resented their "forced" integration – the blending of relief, development, and security promotion agendas – as expressed by the UN or other multilateral and bilateral agencies. Some NGOs found that MINUSTAH and policing actors (as well as certain bilateral agencies) applied considerable pressure, including on humanitarian agencies, to adopt a more assertive political agenda and become involved in "civilian" activities in the wake of military operations. Meanwhile, non-UN agencies feared being co-opted by the UN or perceived by civilians as its appendages.[53] Indeed, some complained that MINUSTAH effectively superimposed a host of new "civilian" activities on what was already being undertaken by the UNCT and NGOs.[54]

Conclusion
Although the discourse of stabilization is frequently invoked by a wide variety of government and non-governmental actors, its practice and outcomes exhibit a high degree of variation. More important for the purposes of this chapter, the case of Haiti offers an example where "stabilization" – although aggressively pursued and widely criticized – generated a meaningful reduction in both real and perceived violence. It should be recalled, however, that the effectiveness of stabilization is likely to be heavily contingent on sustained MINUSTAH peacekeeping and police presence. Not surprisingly, given the natural disaster, as of 2010 there was no clear peacekeeping strategy without the military. The restoration of a legitimate physical police presence, much less community policing, appears to be a far-off goal.

Nevertheless, while the evidence is still preliminary, Haiti offers a case where stabilization did not severely compromise humanitarian action. To the contrary, despite initial reluctance to engage with UN peacekeepers, both humanitarian and development actors gradually came to welcome stabilization. Although some humanitarian agencies engaged with military actors less than others, most adopted pragmatic strategies while seeking not to compromise their mandates or standard operating procedures. Likewise, exogenous shocks – including major hurricanes in August and September

2008 – appeared to hasten greater integration between military and humanitarian actors, suggesting that the reality of stabilization is being accepted by most on the ground. The extent to which the earthquake of January 2010 has changed all of this remains to be seen.

NOTES

1 See Sarah Collinson, Samir Elhawary, and Robert Muggah, "States of Fragility: Stabilization and Its Implications for Humanitarian Action," Humanitarian Policy Group (HPG) Working Paper (July 2010), online: Overseas Development Institute <http://www.odi.org.uk/resources/> ["States of Fragility 1"], and Sarah Collinson, Samir Elhawary, and Robert Muggah "States of Fragility: Stabilisation and Its Implications for Humanitarian Action," (2010) 34 Disasters (special edition) 275 ["States of Fragility 2"].

2 For more on post-earthquake dynamics, see Athena R. Kolbe, Royce A. Hutson, Harry Shannon, Eileen Trzcinski, Bart Miles, Naomi Levitz, Marie Puccio, Leah James, Jean Roger Noel, and Robert Muggah, "Mortality, Crime and Access to Basic Needs before and after the Haiti Earthquake" (2010) 26 Medicine, Conflict and Survival 281. Also see Robert Muggah, "The Effects of Stabilisation on Humanitarian Action in Haiti" (2010) 34 Disasters S444; and Robert Muggah and Athena R. Kolbe, "The Tricky Science of Counting the Dead in Haiti" Los Angeles Times (22 July 2011); and Robert Muggah, "Appraising Security from the Bottom Up in Haiti" Embassy (2 November 2011).

3 For a review of police activities in Haiti before and following the natural disaster, consult Robert Muggah and Athena R. Kolbe, "Securing the State: Haiti before and after the Earthquake" in Small Arms Survey 2011 (Cambridge: Cambridge University Press, 2011).

4 For a review of stabilization activities in Afghanistan, see Stuart Gordon, "The United Kingdom's Stabilisation Model and Afghanistan: The Impact on Humanitarian Actors" (2010) 34 Disasters 368.

5 See, e.g., Robert Muggah, "The Perils of Changing Donor Priorities in Fragile States: The Case of Haiti" in Jennifer Welsh and Ngaire Woods, eds., Exporting Good Governance: Temptations and Challenges in Canada's Aid Program (Waterloo, ON: Wilfrid Laurier University Press, 2007).

6 See, e.g., Collinson et al., "States of Fragility 2," supra note 1, for a treatment of the political economy of state building in Haiti. The article finds that failures in stabilization and state building are routinely attributed to Haitians rather than to the contradictions generated by geopolitical manipulation and flawed prescriptions mandated from above.

7 In 2008, the UN appointed former US president Bill Clinton as a Special Representative of the Secretary-General. Likewise, prominent financiers and academics such as George Soros, Paul Collier, Jeffery Sachs, and Paul Farmer have all invested in Haiti. See, e.g., "Haiti: Poverty Reduction Strategy Paper," IMF Country Report No. 08/115 (March 2008), online: International Monetary Fund <http://www.imf.

org/>. See also Paul Collier, "Haiti's Rise From the Rubble: The Quest to Recover from Disaster," *Foreign Affairs* (September/October 2011).

8   See Muggah, "The Perils of Changing Donor Priorities," *supra* note 5.

9   In order to support these efforts, a number of multilateral and bilateral agencies invested in recruitment, training, and deployment of police; prison reform; and control of water/land borders, while simultaneously restoring state institutions and lessening corruption through rule-of-law programs and investment in penal and criminal law reform.

10 See Nat J. Colletta and Robert Muggah, "Rethinking Post-War Security Promotion" (2009) 7 Journal of Security Sector Management 1, online: Center for Security Sector Management <http://www.ssronline.org/jofssm/>.

11 See Athena R. Kolbe and Royce A. Hutson, "Human Rights Abuse and Other Criminal Violations in Port-au-Prince, Haiti: A Random Survey of Households" (2006) 368 *The Lancet* 864; and Peter Hallward, *Damming the Flood: Haiti, Aristide and the Politics of Containment* (Brooklyn, NY: Verso, 2008).

12 Source (Figures 16.1, 16.2, and 16.3): Kolbe *et al.,* "Mortality, Crime and Access to Basic Needs," *supra* note 2.

13 See, for example, ibid.

14 For example, MINUSTAH and the UNDP launched an ill-fated DDR program in 2005 that stalled by 2006. Both MINUSTAH and the UNDP then separately launched "community violence reduction" programs from 2007 onward. MINUSTAH's program continues in twelve regions of the country and emphasizes community forums to identify local solutions to violence. The UNDP's intervention was shut down in 2008 due to disputes with the government and internal disarray.

15 An exception is humanitarian assistance targeting "disaster-affected" areas in the north of the country, as occurred during August and September 2008.

16 See, *e.g.,* R. Muggah, "Great Expectations: (Dis)integrated DDR in Sudan and Haiti" (2007) 37 Humanitarian Exchange Magazine, online: Humanitarian Practice Network <http://www.odihpn.org/>.

17 Haiti's armed forces were dissolved by Aristide in 1995, a source of continued discontent among veterans. See Robert Muggah, *Securing Haiti's Transition: Reviewing Human Insecurity and the Prospects for Disarmament, Demobilization, and Reintegration,* Occasional Paper 14 (Geneva: Small Arms Survey, 2005).

18 These activities combine community forums (representative mechanisms designed to develop inclusive projects intended to reduce violence) and close collaboration with a national institution, the National Commission on DDR (CNDDR).

19 The program included violence reduction action plans designed through a participatory community-based diagnostic, and socioeconomic projects intended to jumpstart local development.

20 The UNDP subsequently put together a proposal for US$7 million from the Millennium Development Goals Fund, together with IOM, the United Nations Population Fund (UNFPA), the United Nations Educational, Scientific and Cultural Organization (UNESCO), the United Nations Children's Emergency Fund (UNICEF), and others to pursue a similar program in five "rural" areas.

21 For examples of similar processes – the so-called *"mano dura"* policies and practices of anti-gang activities in Central America – consult Oliver Jütersonke, Robert Muggah, and Dennis Rodgers, "Gangs, Urban Violence, and Security Interventions in Central America" (2009) 40 Security Dialogue 373.

22 A major household survey tracking perceptions of the security sector in Haiti was conducted in 2005 and 2006 by Athena R. Kolbe and Dr. Royce A. Hutson. It found that attitudes towards MINUSTAH were comparatively negative. A more recent assessment by Kolbe *et al.* undertaken in 2009 found that resident attitudes had become more favourable, especially in areas most affected by MINUSTAH operations: Athena R. Kolbe, *Household Survey of Insecurity in Port-au-Prince: Preliminary Findings* (Geneva: Small Arms Survey/University of Michigan, 2009).

23 See, *e.g.*, Robert Muggah, "Stabilization from Above and Below: The Case of Port-au-Prince," in Mats Berdal and Dominik Zaum, eds., *Power after Peace: The Political Economy of Post-Conflict Statebuilding* (New York: Routledge, 2012).

24 See, *e.g.*, Muggah, "Great Expectations," *supra* note 16.

25 The fourteen are the World Food Programme (WFP), UNICEF, UNFPA, UNDP, United Nations Development Fund for Women (UNIFEM), United Nations Office for Project Services (UNOPS), UNESCO, Food and Agriculture Organization of the United Nations (FAO), World Health Organization–Pan American Health Organization (WHO-PAHO), International Fund for Agricultural Development (IFAD), United Nations Office for the Coordination of Humanitarian Affairs (UNOCHA), Joint United Nations Programme on HIV/AIDS (UNAIDS), the World Bank, and IOM.

26 The DSRSG/RC/HC manages MINUSTAH's Humanitarian and Development pillar, and assumes responsibility for such portfolios as Community Violence Reduction initiatives (CVR Section), HIV-AIDS, gender, child protection, support to the electoral process, and humanitarian affairs (including OCHA). The DSRSG/RC/HC's office is staffed with an advisor for strategic planning, a partnership and donor relations officer, a coordination officer, and a humanitarian affairs officer. The DSRSG/RC/HC's office helps ensure ongoing and close coordination between MINUSTAH and agencies, funds, and programs through joint strategic meetings held between MINUSTAH section heads and the UNCT, along with thematic working groups such as the humanitarian forum, allowing for the permanent exchange of information and joint analysis and strategies.

27 See, *e.g.*, routine CVR monthly reports issued by the MINUSTAH/Department of Peacekeeping Operations (DPKO) section in Port-au-Prince.

28 In early 2007, a member of the Active Component of the Civilian Response Corps (CRC-A) deployed to Haiti with the interagency HSI team. The CRC-A member supported the Embassy in Port-au-Prince to create an administrative and logistics plan and budget for a new seven-person office that would coordinate the HSI with the Haitian government, the UN, and ongoing US bilateral development programs. The CRC-A member worked with the embassy management sections to get their input and to ensure their buy-in to the plan while keeping the Bureau of Western Hemisphere Affairs and the Washington-based offices of USAID informed of the progress of the HSI support platform. See "Haiti" under "Where We Work," online:

Office of the Coordinator for Reconstruction and Stabilization <http://www.state.gov/s/crs/where/index.htm>.

29 This new initiative is funded through a transfer authority from the Department of Defense. Section 1207 of the 2006 *National Defense Authorization Act* allows the transfer of funds to the Department of State for reconstruction and stabilization activities.

30 A review of the HSI was produced by David C. Becker and Robert Grossman-Vermaas, "Metrics for the Haiti Stabilization Initiative" (2011) 2 Prism 145, online: <http://www.ndu.edu/>.

31 A visit was undertaken to the principal police station (formerly a covered market) in Cité Soleil in November 2009. Site visits throughout Cité Soleil also revealed a considerable expansion of primary and secondary tarmac coverage. Similar types of operations were also pursued in Afghanistan and Iraq over the past five years, to positive effect.

32 HSI initiatives are expected to be undertaken in parallel with other USAID and development programs.

33 It should be noted that HSI personnel preferred the concept of "transition" to "exit." According to key informants, "transition" was gauged by the extent of police presence and real/perceived reductions in violence.

34 The last graduating class from the academy included 300 officers in 2007, but most were deployed to an area of interest to the Commissioner. Fewer than 30 officers are in Cité Soleil, although USAID hopes to see this increased to 130 by the end of 2009 and to 200 soon after.

35 See, *e.g.*, USAID, "Haiti Stabilization Initiative: MPICE Data Analysis Phase II, Draft" (5 November 2008); USAID, "MPICE Phase II: Survey Results: Cité Soleil, Haiti. Draft" (10 November 2008); USAID, "Measuring Progress in Conflict Environments (MPICE) for the Haiti Stabilization Initiative (HSI), Presentation of Baseline Assessment" (May 2008). For more information, consult "The MPICE Metrics Framework and the Haiti Stabilization Initiative," online: <http://www.usip.org/>.

36 Metrics included a reduction in "social disintegration," population displacement, and demographic pressures, and an increase in access to basic needs and related social services. See "Haiti Stabilization Initiative: MPICE Data Analysis Phase II," *ibid.*

37 Specifically, a rule of law program that will support the Ministry of Justice in establishing a permanent judicial presence in Cité Soleil. Under the program, justice officials and community leaders will receive training and equipment to better serve the local community.

38 Its proponents also expected to introduce community policing doctrine before phasing out the program, although the 2010 earthquake undermined these efforts.

39 See, *e.g.*, Robert Muggah and Iona Szabó de Carvalho, "Brazil's "Southern Effect" in Fragile Countries" *Open Democracy* (19 November 2009), online: Open Democracy <http://www.opendemocracy.net/>, for a review of Brazil's approach to fragile states.

40 CVR provided Viva Rio with funding for the "*tambou de la pay*" (low-violence merit-based scholarship program) in 2008. In 2009, it provided US$300,000 for labour-

intensive projects and a water cistern – a process mobilized through the CVR community forum.

41 For example, the Small Arms Survey fielded a large multi-disciplinary team to examine intended and unintended consequences. See Helen Moestue and Robert Muggah, *Social Integration, ergo, Stabilization: Assessing Viva Rio's Security and Development Programme in Port-Au-Prince* (Rio de Janeiro: CIDA Canada, MFA START Canada, MFA NCA Norway, 2009).

42 It is important to note that the "population" received direct benefits from the lotteries in 2007. As of 2008, however, gang leaders were also entitled to receive benefits from the monthly lotteries, an issue that has raised some concern among local NGOs and observers.

43 Viva Rio has also been criticized for being too flexible and close to the military. For example, it encouraged summer camps for children in MINUSTAH bases. This generated criticism from UNICEF, which claimed that this was a high-risk activity.

44 For example, the rainwater harvesting systems are installed in and managed by the schools and the health program is carried out in the schools. Viva Rio coordinates closely with the mayor's office on different issues and has a close collaboration with the public water utility company – CAMEP – and lately with Ministry of Public Works on solid waste management. This collaboration also has elements of informal or formal capacity building.

45 Rates of violence have dropped dramatically in Haiti since 2007: Kolbe, *Household Survey of Insecurity, supra* note 22. Even so, there appears to be a widespread perception that violence is higher than the regional average. This does not appear to be borne out by the limited evidence available. See, *e.g.*, Reed Lindsay, "Eyeing Tourism, Haiti Battles Its Violent Reputation" *Christian Science Monitor* (20 June 2008), online: Christian Science Monitor <http://www.csmonitor.com/>.

46 A range of debates have taken place since at least 2004 within various coordination platforms – including the United Nations Inter-Agency Standing Committee – and between agency directors and high-level personnel.

47 Collinson *et al.*, "States of Fragility 1," *supra* note 1.

48 MSF recently finished an internal audit of procedures and operations in order to review the conduct of both international and national personnel. Based on the charter of MSF, the agency must treat people without discrimination, pay staff no more than the agency decides, ensure no relations with national staff, maintain impartiality, and maintain distance from religious/political agendas. More practically, soldiers cannot enter centres with guns (armouries are set up outside), no military or policing actors can enter an MSF car, no military escorts are permitted, no flights on military planes or cars are permitted, and so on. These rules can generate a range of practical challenges; for example, in principle MSF cannot use USAID plastic sheeting or MINUSTAH helicopters during emergencies.

49 Although estimates vary, a recent survey detected an annual homicide rate of some 14-15 per 100,000 in key slums of Port-au-Prince, among the lowest rates in Latin America.

50 The relationship between MSF and MINUSTAH reached a low point when MSF denounced the Sri Lankan peacekeeping contingent for pedophilia, which resulted in the removal of more than a hundred soldiers.

51 Specifically, ICRC worked to reinstall local water boards in Cité Soleil – collecting funds at key water distribution points, thereby providing local resources for the national water authority to make routine repairs. Similar activities have been under-way since 2007 in Rio de Janeiro, where operations are opening up in favelas. See, for example, Robert Muggah and Albert Walter Souza Mulli, "Rio Tries Counter-insurgency" (2012) 111 Current History 62, and Chapter 15, this volume.

52 For example, the US Drug Enforcement Administration (DEA) is constructing a centre and the ICRC is supporting the design and development of related facilities.

53 There is a long history of NGOs being wary of the UN. NGOs believe that the UN seeks to act as the primary intermediary between states and NGOs.

54 For example, MINUSTAH, which is responsible for coordinating humanitarian ac-tors, duplicated OCHA. Duplication of activities was (and, according to some, re-mains) a major concern for the humanitarian sector.

17

Violence against Children in Urban Settings
Private Hurt, Public Manifestations

GURVINDER SINGH AND JUDI FAIRHOLM

We are displaced children
We are children who have been used by armed groups
We are orphans
We are street children
We are girls who sell our bodies to survive
We are children who have to work
We are children who can't go to school
We are children with disabilities
We are detained children
We are girls who have been raped
We are children taking care of our brothers and sisters
We are children without a childhood
We live in violence

– *Young people, ages 15-19 (*"Will You Listen?" Young Voices
  from Conflict Zones, *United Nations, 2007)*

Violence is a global problem that affects children in all settings, including urban environments. This chapter highlights the linkages between the public manifestations of violence, including gang and street-related violence, and the violence that occurs in private settings, such as homes. It also provides a context to the situation of violence against children in urban settings; definitions of different forms of violence; an overview of the scale of the problem; linkages between violence in public and private domains; and steps in a comprehensive approach to address violence against children in urban settings.

Violence against Children in Urban Settings: Context

As of 2005 (and for the first time in history) over 50 percent of the world's population lived in urban areas, with the numbers continuing to grow, especially in locations like Sub-Saharan Africa (nearly 6 percent urban growth a year) and Asia (3-4 percent a year).[1] One in three city dwellers – nearly a billion people – live in slums.[2] As the planet urbanizes, the social, cultural, political, and economic factors that both bind and wedge apart different communities and populations continue to shape the lives of individuals. In far too many urban environments, this has resulted in pockets of relevant prosperity, security, and calm, contrasted with expanding zones of insecurity that make the most vulnerable, such as children, even more vulnerable.

At its international conference in 2007, the Red Cross and Red Crescent Movement of 186 national societies and their governments declared violence, particularly in urban settings, a "Great Humanitarian Challenge" that affects all people in the world, especially children and youth: "Violence in urban areas poses a particular challenge, where problems are often aggravated by rapidly growing populations, poverty and economic inequalities, unemployment, social exclusion and marginalization, insufficient public security and services, and the easy availability of drugs and weapons."[3] Urban violence is a unique form of violence, as by definition it is based in a setting where all types of violence occur. These settings are both public and private and include homes, schools, institutions, workplaces, streets, and communities. Children become the victims, perpetrators, and witnesses of violent acts, and what happens in private settings subsequently spills over into the public domain.

Definition and Types of Violence

In the World Health Organization (WHO) 2002 *World Report on Violence and Health,* violence is defined as "the intentional use of physical force or power, threatened or actual, against oneself, another person, or against a group or community, that either results in or has a high likelihood of resulting in injury, death, psychological harm, maldevelopment, or deprivation."[4]

FIGURE 17.1

World Health Organization typology of violence

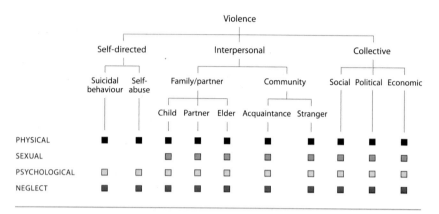

Within the WHO typology (Figure 17.1[5]), violence is addressed under three subtypes: self-directed violence, interpersonal violence, and collective violence. Although each one is unique, they share many similar qualities.

Worldwide, 54 percent of violence-related deaths are from suicide, 35 percent from interpersonal violence, and 11 percent from collective violence.[6] There is growing recognition that each type of violence is linked to other forms of violence; where there is a significant prevalence of one type, the risk of the others escalating increases.[7] A clear example is the prevalence of youth involvement in gangs where violence in the whole society is pervasive due to conflict or social, political, or economic tensions.[8]

Children, defined by the United Nations *Convention on the Rights of the Child*[9] as those under eighteen years of age, are at the highest risk of violence.[10] In every space in their lives – public or private – children risk being beaten, sexually assaulted, tortured, neglected, maimed, bought and sold, and killed. Some young people are more vulnerable than others: disabled children, orphaned or unaccompanied children, indigenous children, ethnic minority children, street children, those in institutions and detention, refugee and displaced children, and those living in communities where inequality, unemployment, and poverty are highly concentrated.[11]

The *World Report on Violence against Children*[12] states that emotional, physical, and sexual violence is rampant against children: 133 to 275 million children witnessed violence between their parents/caregivers on a frequent basis; 150 million girls (14 percent of the world's child population) and 73 million boys (7 percent of the world's child population) experienced sexual abuse. At any one time, an estimated 1.8 million children are being sexually exploited for profit across the world,[13] and 1.2 million children trafficked every year.[14] Each week, more than twenty thousand images of sexual torture of children are posted on the Internet.[15]

Only 2.4 percent of the world's children are protected from physical violence in all settings,[16] whereas 25-50 percent of children reported severe and frequent physical abuse.[17] In some countries, 97 percent of students revealed that they had been physically punished at school.[18] The violence often ends in death, with fifteen- to seventeen-year-old males most likely to be killed, followed by infants.[19] This toll of young males' lives is manifested in collective violence: at any given time, 250,000 children are used as combatants in armed conflicts.[20]

Linkages between Public and Private Forms of Violence

Many children have long struggled to survive in unforgiving urban settings, especially environments that are going through dramatic growth or transitions. While urban environments have never been easy for children, those living on the streets of cities have become a defining fixture of the urban scene from the nineteenth century onward, sparking continuing calls for remedy and social reform.[21]

This situation has become even more urgent in the modern context, where cities and towns are now home to approximately half of the world's children; more than one billion people under the age of eighteen years live in urban settings, many of them in slums or poverty belts.[22] Research is beginning to show clear links between urbanization and elevated risks of violence for children – as victims, perpetrators, and observers.[23]

A common and recognized form of urban violence against children stems from gangs and criminal organizations. Children are recruited by and exploited into gangs that may engage in a wide array of criminal activities and violence. They are drawn into a world of drugs, guns, and crime[24] along with other children, youth, and young adults in order to find a way to survive, belong, release their anger, and defend themselves.

Although the situation of children in gangs is alarming, the overwhelming focus on only this one part of urban violence highlights misconceptions about the risk for children in cities. Specifically, gang violence is only one part of a much larger phenomenon of violence against children that occurs in homes, schools, institutions, and workplaces within cities – places where violence is hidden, closed to the outside world, and kept secret. Gang violence is a visible, public culmination of violence that begins in the private sphere and that shapes children's lives. In order to understand public manifestations of violence, the violence that occurs in private spaces, such as child abuse in homes and bullying in schools, must be examined and recognized as root causes that fuel a trajectory towards gangs and life on the street.

Addressing the Larger Issues; Moving beyond Symptoms

When only the public dimensions of violence against children are recognized, violence is seen in a vacuum; the factors that shape, nurture, or diminish children are neglected. This poses serious limitations as it prevents a full understanding of children's vulnerabilities and registers only manifestations; the focus becomes the symptom rather than the cause. In such a scenario, children are seen as problems, delinquents, and something to be feared and controlled rather than protected, understood, and rehabilitated. To see children's vulnerability in its full context, it is critical to recognize that violence is a result of a complex interplay of variables between individual children, their families, communities, and societies. Each of the variables is tied together with others, cumulatively increasing the vulnerability of children to violence. The ecological model[25] is useful in helping to highlight the complex linkages between different levels of violence at the individual, relationship, community, and societal/cultural levels (Figure 17.2[26]).

Individual Level

There is mounting and compelling evidence indicating that the experience of children between the ages of zero and six years can significantly shape their health and success across their lifespan.[27] Research reveals that when children are victims of violence at an early age, there can be dramatic consequences that may in turn sharply increase their propensity to act out in harmful ways or become vulnerable to further violence. For instance, violence against young children has been shown to leave a "genetic imprint" that reduces the children's ability, as they grow into adulthood, to cope with stress in the same effective way as children who have not been abused.[28] Similarly, children affected by Fetal Alcohol Spectrum Disorder (FASD) – a variety of physical and cognitive birth impairments caused by alcohol consumption during pregnancy – can suffer its corrosive effects across their

FIGURE 17.2

The Ecological Model

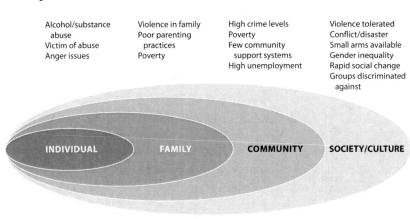

Alcohol/substance abuse	Violence in family	High crime levels	Violence tolerated
Victim of abuse	Poor parenting	Poverty	Conflict/disaster
Anger issues	practices	Few community	Small arms available
	Poverty	support systems	Gender inequality
		High unemployment	Rapid social change
			Groups discriminated against

INDIVIDUAL   FAMILY   COMMUNITY   SOCIETY/CULTURE

entire lives: difficulties in managing emotions and anger, low empathy or remorse, limited understanding of consequences, and use of violence against themselves or others.[29]

Not only is alcohol associated with prenatal injury to a child but its effects can be multiple and profound in increasing the child's risk of becoming the victim or the perpetrator of violence at any age. Children who are victims of violence have been shown to be 103 percent more likely to become alcoholics and 192 percent more likely to become addicted to drugs.[30] In turn, while alcohol and substance abuse are not themselves the cause of violence, their damaging influence on decision making, self-control, and the ability to confuse perceptions and communication can more readily lead to interpersonal violence.[31]

For children, the risk of violence – physical, sexual, psychological, or neglect – occurring in their homes and other private areas is far greater than in public spaces.[32] The resulting impact of low self-esteem, anger, helplessness, and powerlessness subsequently makes them vulnerable to gang recruitment and life on the street. Children who are physically or sexually abused in homes are more likely to run away from home or join gangs.[33] Once living on the street or once part of a gang, their risk for further violence escalates, intensifies, and becomes more visible.[34]

Relationship/Family Level

Harsh physical punishment or victimization of children in the home has been identified as a contributing factor to engagement in youth gangs.[35] It is in the home that children learn through exposure and experience that violence is acceptable. They learn that there are few, if any, consequences for violence, and that it is okay to harm someone who is small, weak, and dependent – someone who is vulnerable.

The socioeconomic status of a family has also been associated with potential violence. Studies from the United States, Peru, and Brazil have shown that the prevalence of self-reported assault and robbery among youths from low socioeconomic classes is about twice that among youth from high socioeconomic levels.[36] The linkages point to a pattern of low incomes and elevated violence, although, clearly, families at higher socioeconomic levels are also capable of maltreating their young.

Peers are another essential factor in sculpting the resilience or risk of violence among youth in urban settings. For example, bullying has been linked to notorious school shootings in North America since the 1990s.[37] While clear linkages between bullying and recruitment into gangs have yet to be shown in detail, the data nevertheless underscore that bullying behaviours can help put youth who are bullies on a trajectory towards physical violence.[38] In addition, having friends who are involved in violent or delinquent behaviours increases the risk for violence among youth.[39] This becomes more potent when drugs and alcohol are involved.

Community Level

Aside from individual and family factors, the communities in which children live have a significant influence on their risk of involvement in violence. One of the most significant community factors is poverty: it creates a climate where violence is fed by both hopelessness and helplessness. Approximately 50 percent of the world's children (one billion) live in poverty.[40]

In general, research shows that boys living in urban areas are more likely to be involved in violent behaviour than those living in rural areas.[41] Within urban settings, children living in pockets with high levels of crime or high levels of poverty and violence are more likely to be involved in violent behaviour than those living in other neighbourhoods.[42] Furthermore, when poverty is radicalized and ghettoized, stigmatization of specific groups can trigger more violence.

Other factors that drag children towards violence in cities are gangs, guns, and drugs. Where these elements mix, the risk of violence against and by children is amplified. Where all three are present, studies have shown that homicides committed by children increase.[43] In Brazil, for instance, drug dealing has been shown to be responsible for a large proportion of homicides, conflicts, and injuries caused by children.[44]

Societal/Cultural Level

The final factors in shaping the risk of urban violence against children are social and cultural variables. Where a society has undergone a traumatic "shock" induced by economic, political, environmental, and/or conflict-related stresses, the risk of violence against children can increase. The ensuing deficit of social support systems, of security and law, and of labour can result in poverty, in a shortfall of human security, and in a lack of dependable social or economic options. Not only does the risk of violence against children increase in the immediate aftermath of a crisis but it can resonate in the long term. Specifically, the risk of children being subject to violence in their homes at the hands of parents and caregivers during and after emergencies has been shown to substantially increase and thereby reinforce risk factors for anti-social and self-harming behaviours in the future.[45]

Cities in transition can also create unsafe landscapes for children. In Algeria, a study found that "rapid demographic growth and accelerating urbanization together created conditions, including unemployment and grossly inadequate housing, which in turn led to extreme frustration, anger and pent-up tensions among youths. Young people, as a result, were more likely to turn to petty crime and violence, particularly under the influence of peers."[46]

Underlying and reinforcing other social factors that drive violence in urban landscapes are cultural norms that foster violence. The sexual exploitation of children crystallizes cultural acceptance of violence against children; children are moved from rural areas to urban settings and beyond in order to become commodities that are bought and sold, used and abused. Approximately one million children with an average age of fourteen years are forced into the sex trade every year, with some starting as early as nine years.[47]

When the individual, relationship, community, and societal factors co-exist, the vulnerability of children to public urban violence is heightened. In the private spaces they have learned about alienation, low self-esteem, anger, unfairness, disrespect, powerlessness, helplessness, aloneness, and hopelessness. The public space offers them a channel for all their hurts. The agonizing hurt against children is complex, yet it can be prevented.

Comprehensive, evidence-based approaches can help reduce the risk of the hurt occurring in the first place.

Comprehensive Prevention: Starting Early and Acting Holistically

A common reaction to violence is to address the symptoms – the loud, visible, visceral manifestations that individuals can see on their streets, in their school grounds, and in their shopping centres. Yet youth clearly define what they need in order to prevent violence:

> "We're not being heard or believed"
> "Adults don't know how to help us"
> "Nobody asks us if we have experienced violence"
> "Control is taken away from us"
> "We need at least one person we can trust"
> "We need safe environments"[48]

An effective response includes listening to these voices and addressing violence at all levels of vulnerability – individual, family, community, societal/cultural – through comprehensive approaches that target all ages, actors, and agencies. Fundamental to any approach to preventing violence against children in urban settings are local child protection laws and the UN *Convention on the Rights of the Child* (UNCRC).[49] Since 1989, the UNCRC "has been ratified by more countries than any other human rights treaty in history."[50] It is the only international convention dedicated in its entirety to the specific needs of children, and includes articles on the prevention of and protection from violence (19, 27, 34, 36, and 39). Fundamental to the convention is "that in all actions concerning children, the best interests of the child shall be a primary consideration."[51] The convention incorporates a comprehensive approach that accounts for children as whole beings and encompasses children's civil, social, economic, political, and cultural rights in all settings, regardless of whether they are considered private or public.

Building on the UNCRC, numerous cities, governments, networks, and agencies are working to address urban violence with respect to children. While the approaches vary, there is increasing recognition that comprehensive multi-pronged models that focus on prevention and that address individuals, families, communities, and society are necessary.

The World Health Organization outlines ten "best buys" for preventing violence that encompass all settings, including urban environments:[52]

- increase safe, stable, and nurturing relationships between children and their parents
- reduce availability and misuse of alcohol
- reduce access to lethal means
- improve life skills and enhance opportunities for children and youth
- promote gender equality and empowerment of women
- change cultural norms that support violence
- improve criminal justice systems
- improve social welfare systems
- reduce social distance between conflicting groups
- reduce economic inequality and concentrated poverty.

A similar approach has been proposed by the Commonwealth of Massachusetts. In a report on urban violence,[53] it encourages leaders, government bodies, and communities to establish:

- mentorship for all children, especially the most vulnerable
- mandated comprehensive violence and bullying prevention programs from kindergarten to grade twelve
- truancy prevention programming (keep kids in school)
- violence peer councils in every community
- treatment for children exposed to violence
- job training and development for youth
- law enforcement initiatives
- accountability and re-entry support for offenders
- substance abuse treatment for all
- reduced access to and possession of illegal firearms.

Since 1984, the Canadian Red Cross has been working on violence prevention through its RespectED program. Through partnerships with communities, the program aims to prevent violence and protect children. The Canadian Red Cross' *Ten Steps to Creating Safe Environments for Children and Youth: A Risk Management Road Map to Prevent Violence and Abuse* guides organizations in proactively setting up environments where children will be safe and protected.[54]

Conclusion

Violence against children in urban settings can be prevented. Too many children are left to fend for themselves on city streets or are recruited into urban gangs. These public manifestations of violence are deeply intertwined with violence in hidden and private spheres such as homes. Although violence in homes is often kept secret, its consequences cannot be contained and its effects bleed into the streets, schools, and public squares of cities. What children learn and see in homes defines how they behave and respond in public.

In order to address and prevent violence in urban settings – whether public or private – comprehensive approaches that are founded on the *Convention on the Rights of the Child* are essential. Children must be supported at the individual, family, community, and societal/cultural levels. Through concerted effort, violence can be prevented.

> We want our rights to be respected
> We want justice and to be safe from violence
> We want safe spaces
> We want to learn
> We want to be healthy
> We want jobs and a means to survive
> We want to participate
> We just want to be children[55]

NOTES

1 Eduardo Lopez Moreno and Rasna Warah, "The State of the World's Cities Report 2006/7: Urban and Slum Trends in the 21st Century" (2006) 43 UN Chronicle 24, online: United Nations <http://www.un.org/>.
2 *Ibid.*
3 "Violence, in Particular Urban Settings" (Declaration, International Federation of Red Cross and Red Crescent Societies, 30th International Conference, 2007), online: IFRC <http://www.ifrc.org/>.
4 Etienne Krug, Linda Dahlbert, James Mercy, Anthony Zwi, and Rafael Lozano, eds., *World Report on Violence and Health* (Geneva: World Health Organization, 2002).
5 Source: *Ibid.*
6 Alexander Butchart, "Violence: An Introduction" (IFRC Global Strategy Meeting, Geneva, World Health Organization Department of Injuries and Violence Prevention, 15-17 December 2008).
7 David Brown, Alexander Butchart, Alison Harvey, Kidist Bartolomeos, David Meddings, and Laura Sminkey, *Third Milestones of a Global Campaign for Violence Prevention Report 2007: Scaling Up* (Geneva: World Health Organization, 2007), online: <http://whqlibdoc.who.int/publications/2007>.

8 Paulo Sérgio Pinheiro, *World Report on Violence against Children* (Geneva: United Nations, 2006), online: Violence Against Children: United Nations Secretary-General's Study <http://www.unviolencestudy.org/>.

9 *Convention on the Rights of the Child*, 20 November 1989, 1577 U.N.T.S. 3 (entered into force 2 September 1990).

10 Rachel Hodgkin and Peter Newell, *Implementation Handbook for the Convention on the Rights of the Child* (New York: UNICEF, 2002) at 1.

11 Pinheiro, *supra* note 8.

12 *Ibid.*

13 *The Small Hands of Slavery: Modern Day Child Slavery* (London: Save the Children UK, 2007), online: Child Rights Information Network <http://www.crin.org/>.

14 *Every Child Counts: New Global Estimates on Child Labour* (Geneva: International Labour Organization, 2002), online: International Labour Organization <http://www.ilo.org/>.

15 Emma Renold, Susan J. Creighton, Chris Atkinson, and John Carr, *Images of Abuse: A Review of the Evidence on Child Pornography* (London: National Society for the Prevention of Cruelty to Children, 2003).

16 *Ibid.*

17 *The World Health Report 2002: Reducing Risk, Promoting Healthy Life* (Geneva: World Health Organization, 2002), online: World Health Organization <http://www.who.int/>.

18 *Ibid.*

19 *Ibid.*

20 Graça Machel, *The Impact of War on Children* (Vancouver: UBC Press, 2001).

21 Pinheiro, *supra* note 8.

22 Eliana Riggio, "Child-Friendly Cities: Good Governance and the Best Interests of the Child" (2002) 14 Environment and Urbanization 45; *Children's Rights: A Second Chance* (London: Save the Children UK, 2001), online: <http://www.savethechildren.net/>.

23 Suzanne T. Ortega, Jay Corzine, Cathleen Burnett, and Tracey Poyer, "Modernization, Age Structure, and Regional Context: A Cross-National Study of Crime" (1992) 12 Sociological Spectrum 257.

24 *Human Security for an Urban Century: Local Challenges, Global Perspectives* (humansecurity-cities.org, 2007), online: European Urban Knowledge Network <http://www.eukn.org/>.

25 James Garbarino, "The Human Ecology of Child Maltreatment: A Conceptual Model for Research" (1977) 39 Journal of Marriage and the Family 721; James Garbarino, *Children and Families in the Social Environment*, 2d ed. (New York: Walter de Gruyter, 1992); Krug *et al.*, *supra* note 4.

26 Source: Krug *et al.*, *ibid.*

27 Clyde Hertzman, Lori G. Irwin, Michelle Jenkins, and Jill Houbé, "Executive Summaries of Evidence Papers" (Healthy Child BC Forum, 8-9 November 2004), online: Human Early Learning Partnership <http://www.earlylearning.ubc.ca/>.

28 Patrick O. McGowan *et al.*, "Epigenetic Regulation of the Glucocorticoid Receptor in Human Brain Associates with Childhood Abuse" (2009) 12 Nature Neuroscience 342.

29 *It Takes a Community: Framework for the First Nations and Inuit Fetal Alcohol Syndrome and Fetal Alcohol Effects Initiative* (Health Canada, 1997), online: Health Canada <http://www.hc-sc.gc.ca/>.

30 National Safety Council, *Family Safety and Health* (Winter 2002-03).

31 Mark D. Totten, *Guys, Gangs, and Girlfriend Abuse* (Toronto: Broadview Press, 2000).

32 Pinheiro, *supra* note 8.

33 Thomas de Benítez, *State of the World's Street Children: Violence* (London: Consortium of Street Children, 2007), online: Consortium of Street Children <http://www.streetchildren.org.uk/>; Krug *et al.*, *supra* note 4.

34 Loveleen Kacker, Srinivas Varadan, and Pravesh Kumar, *Study on Child Abuse: India 2007* (New Delhi: Ministry of Women and Child Development, 2007), online: Ministry of Women and Child Development <http://wcd.nic.in/>; A. Reza, E.G. Krug, and J.A. Mercy, "Epidemiology of Violent Deaths in the World" (2001) 7 Injury Prevention 104.

35 Krug *et al. supra* note 4.

36 Delbert D. Elliott, David Huizinga, and Scott Menard, *Multiple Problem Youth: Delinquency, Substance Use, and Mental Health Problems* (New York: Springer-Verlag, 1989); A. Perales and C. Sogi, "Conductas violentas en adolescentes: identificación de factores de riesgo para diseño de programa preventivo" [Violent behaviour among adolescents: identifying risk factors to design prevention programs] in C. Pimentel Sevilla, ed., *Violencia, familia y niñez en los sectores urbanos pobres* [Violence, the family and childhood in poor urban sectors] (Lima: Cecosam, 1995); R.J. Gianini, J. Litvoc, and J.E. Neto, "Agressão física e classe social" [Physical violence and social class] (1999) 33 Revista de Saúde Pública 180.

37 Pinheiro, *supra* note 8.

38 *Ibid.*

39 Perales and Sogi, *supra* note 36.

40 Anup Shah, "Causes of Poverty" (2007), online: Global Issues <http://www.global-issues.org/>.

41 David Farrington and Rolf Loeber, "Major Aims of this Book" in David Farrington and Rolf Loeber, eds., *Serious and Violent Juvenile Offenders: Risk Factors and Successful Interventions* (Thousand Oaks, CA: Sage, 1998); Perales and Sogi, *supra* note 36; Elliott *et al. supra* note 36.

42 Farrington and Loeber, *ibid.*; Perales and Sogi, *ibid.*

43 J.D. Hawkins *et al.*, "A Review of Predictors of Youth Violence" in Farrington and Loeber, *Serious and Violent Juvenile Offenders*, *supra* note 41; Farrington and Loeber, "Major Aims of This Book," *supra* note 41.

44 Maria Cecília de Souza Minayo, *Fala, galera: juventude, violência e cidadania* [What's up, gang: youth, violence and citizenship] (Rio de Janeiro: Garamond, 1999).

45 Thom Curtis, Brent C. Miller, and E. Helen Berry, "Changes in Reports and Incidence of Child Abuse Following Natural Disasters" (2000) 24 Child Abuse and Neglect

1151; Heather T. Keenan, Stephen W. Marshall, Mary Alice Nocera, and Desmond K. Runyan, "Increased Incidence of Inflicted Traumatic Brain Injury in Children after a Natural Disaster" (2004) 26 American Journal of Preventive Medicine 189.

46 Pinheiro, *supra* note 8.

47 Cherry Kingsley and Melanie Mark, *Sacred Lives: Canadian Aboriginal Children and Youth Speak Out about Sexual Exploitation* (Toronto: Save the Children, 2001).

48 Michael Ungar, Ken Barter, Sheri McConnell, Leslie M. Tutty, and Judi Fairholm, "Patterns of Abuse Disclosure among Youth" (2009) 8 Qualitative Social Work 341.

49 *Convention on the Rights of the Child, supra* note 9.

50 *Rights of the Child: Protection and the United Nations Convention on the Rights of the Child* (Ottawa: Canadian Coalition for the Rights of Children, 2002), online: Canadian Coalition for the Rights of Children <http://rightsofchildren.ca/>.

51 Malcolm N. Shaw, *International Law* (New York: Cambridge University Press, 2003).

52 Alexander Butchart, David Brown, Andrew Wilson, and Christopher Mikton, *Preventing Violence and Reducing Its Impact: How Development Agencies Can Help* (Geneva: World Health Organization, 2008), online: World Health Organization <http://whqlibdoc.who.int/>.

53 Commonwealth of Massachusetts, Governor's Anti-Crime Council, Urban Violence Subcommittee, *Urban Violence in the Commonwealth: Prevention, Intervention and Rehabilitation* (2008), online: Commonwealth of Massachusetts <http://www.mass.gov/>.

54 J. Fairholm, G. Singh, and S. Smith, *Ten Steps to Creating Safe Environments for Children and Youth: A Risk Management Road Map to Prevent Violence and Abuse* (2008), online: Canadian Red Cross <http://www.redcross.ca/>.

55 Vidar Ekehaug and Chernor Bah, *"Will You Listen?" Young Voices from Conflict Zones* (2007), online: United Nations <http://www.un.org/children/>.

Conclusion

BENJAMIN PERRIN

Traditionalist or classical approaches to international humanitarian law have become outmoded in many complex security situations, and have frequently failed to deliver on their objectives of mitigating unnecessary suffering and protecting civilians and civilian objects during armed conflict. Gone are the days when armed conflict was contested between relatively evenly matched professional armies of sovereigns, under the command of gentleman generals – if such a romanticized view of war ever truly existed. The archetypical armed conflict of the early twenty-first century is asymmetrical and protracted, fought by an array of armed groups on both physical and political battlefields, and causes disproportionate suffering and death to civilians, most notably women and children. Restoring peace and security in these divided societies requires democratic development and respect for the rule of law.

A tectonic shift in the identity and scope of actors involved in contemporary armed conflicts has taken place in recent decades. As a result, laws designed to address international armed conflict between states are the most advanced, but such conflicts are becoming less frequent in proportion to non-international armed conflicts that encompass a new range of players that are involved in perpetuating widespread violence for various reasons. So too has the number of non-state armed groups that are active in individual conflicts increased.[1] At the same time, the forms of systematic violence that are of concern to the international community as a whole have expanded beyond situations of armed conflict to encompass endemic urban violence. A growing body of international human rights law has also justified the increasing global focus on both the harm caused by criminal organizations and the response by national governments and law enforcement agencies. The internationalization of the regulation of violence has thus expanded beyond interstate and intrastate conflict to include other forms of systematic violence.

Law that is known, and agreed to, and that has an enforcement mechanism is more likely to be respected than law that is unclear, unilaterally imposed, and without a means of ensuring compliance. In many instances, each of these elements is problematic in contemporary armed conflicts and post-conflict environments. Attempting to enhance compliance with humanitarian law by state and non-state actors that see little prospect of its independent enforcement has rekindled calls for greater emphasis on the concept of reciprocity as a means of ensuring proper conduct. Recourse to reciprocity in this way has been questioned on both empirical and ethical grounds, however. Engaging non-state armed groups directly to secure their commitment on key standards, developing a "culture of compliance," and fostering ownership of international humanitarian law standards were all alternatives proposed in this volume to address violations perpetrated by non-state armed groups. It was also generally agreed, however, that some non-state armed groups would simply have no interest in respecting international humanitarian law, and there could be serious ethical problems with validating such entities, and affording them greater political weight, through meetings and negotiations. These discussions opened some new research questions for future consideration, including: What is the effectiveness of alternative approaches to enhancing compliance by non-state armed groups with international humanitarian law? What criteria should guide the decision to engage a non-state armed group in a program to enhance compliance with international humanitarian law, and under what terms and conditions?

As non-state actors have multiplied in their scope and activities, new questions have been raised with respect to threshold issues concerning the status and obligations of non-state actors under international law (including international human rights law, international humanitarian law, and international criminal law). A number of these concerns were examined in detail and some preliminary answers were vetted. For example, regardless of the advisability of the practice, there was some agreement on the proposition that humanitarian personnel and objects do not legally lose or have their protected status as civilians suspended if they resort to defensive armed protection by private military and security contractors, unless and until such time as they take acts hostile to one of the parties to the conflict. Importantly, legitimate self-defence against an imminent unlawful attack by a party to the conflict should not be considered as directly participating in hostilities.

Numerous contributors to this book have emphasized the need to re-focus global efforts on the protection of civilian populations from the often generational impact of armed conflict and violence, rather than focusing exclusively on the actors perpetuating harm or others seeking to provide relief and assistance. For example, the debate regarding the concept of "humanitarian space" frequently reaches a dead-end, with humanitarian organizations insisting that aid delivery be exclusively civilian in character (respecting core principles of neutrality, independence, and impartiality), while modern counterinsurgency doctrines view the delivery of aid and development by uniformed military and affiliated entities as a means of achieving peace and security. Even when humanitarian space is supposedly in place (as it has been traditionally conceived), it has not been very effective in protecting women and children from sexual abuse and violence.

One of the major themes that emerged in this collection was the sharp division within the humanitarian movement with respect to strict adherence to traditional humanitarian principles and how they are impacted by practices such as the hiring of armed private military and security companies for defensive armed protection, as well as collaboration with integrated missions or stability operations. International humanitarian law, unfortunately, does not provide clear-cut answers to some of the most problematic aspects of this reality on the ground. On the one hand, state armed forces are obliged to provide such aid, but on the other, there is a need for non-discriminatory delivery of assistance and for providing humanitarian access to aid that is neutral, independent, and impartial. It is hoped that a sharper focus on civilians as the beneficiaries of humanitarian aid and protected status from attack will provide an alternative paradigm for considering the challenges of delivering such aid in the midst of a complex environment.

More significant in the lives of those affected by armed conflict than the law in the books is practice in the field, however. There was a great deal of interest among practitioners in promoting external mechanisms to better promote humanitarian principles, including the use of external monitoring for the small arms trade, and the use of direct engagement with non-state armed groups to focus on key subject areas such as anti-personnel land-mines and the use of child soldiers. Such interdisciplinary and multisector approaches to meeting the original objectives of international humanitarian law are continuing to develop. Diverse initiatives to directly engage non-state armed groups, private military and security contractors, and humanitarian organizations in improving respect for international humanitarian law have significant potential to improve the lives of civilians caught up in situations of armed conflict.

Addressing endemic urban violence through alternative legal regimes and policies was viewed as necessary, particularly given that international humanitarian law largely contains principles that legitimize violence (e.g., proportionality, collateral damage) and could do more harm than good in seeking to address the problem of urban violence. Instead, alternative approaches address the root causes of the problem of urban violence, for example, by enhancing training and monitoring of use of force by law enforcement, and through greater use of stabilization programs to foster resilience in communities.

Several points of disagreement between contributors to this book are also apparent. Notably, the use of "stabilization missions" to achieve positive outcomes was found by some to be a problematic fusion of military, humanitarian, and development activities, whereas others found that such missions have been able to achieve impressive results for beneficiaries, as in Haiti before the devastating earthquake of 2010. Likewise, there are sharp divisions on the use of private military and security contractors to achieve meaningful increased long-term access to humanitarian assistance. The multiple, complex factors that are apparent in the various case studies considered in this book suggest the need for greater research and debate involving both scholars and practitioners.

In closing, these findings suggest that those concerned with regulating contemporary armed conflict and achieving more positive humanitarian outcomes for civilians during armed conflict should be engaged to a greater extent in a consideration of humanitarian *law, policy,* and *practice* and the complex interrelationship between these concepts as a way forward. Considering them in isolation is unlikely to achieve success beyond isolated instances. The rationale for considering law, policy, and practice together is both practically relevant from a realist perspective as well as morally necessary if the objectives of humanitarian law are to be respected, beyond mere admonitions to the parties to the conflict. Pragmatically, this approach also involves the multiplicity of actors whose positions and actions need to be considered, rather than just the narrower range of actors that international law traditionally limits itself to, arguably to the disadvantage of those it is designed to protect.

NOTES

1 See, *e.g.*, Lotta Harbom, Erik Melander, and Peter Wallensteen, "Dyadic Dimensions of Armed Conflict, 1946-2007" (2008) 45 Journal of Peace Research 697.

Contributors

Andrew Bearpark is Director General, British Association of Private Security Companies (BAPSC). Prior to taking up his position at the BAPSC, Mr. Bearpark served as Director of Operations and Infrastructure for the Coalition Provisional Authority (CPA) in Iraq. From 2000 to 2003, he served as Deputy Special Representative of the Secretary-General (DSRSG) in charge of the European Union Pillar of the United Nations Mission in Kosovo (UNMIK) and was responsible for overseeing the province's reconstruction and economic development. From 1998 until his appointment in Kosovo, Mr. Bearpark was based in Sarajevo, where he served as Deputy High Representative in the Office of the High Representative (OHR), and was responsible for the Reconstruction and Return Task Force, a grouping of international organizations facilitating minority return in Bosnia-Herzegovina. Before taking up his positions in Bosnia and Kosovo, Mr. Bearpark held a series of senior positions with Her Majesty's Government, including Head of the Information and Emergency Aid Departments of the Overseas Development Administration (ODA). Prior to this, he founded and managed a public relations consultancy. From 1986 to 1989, he served as Private Secretary to Prime Minister Margaret Thatcher, and later served as Chief of Staff to Lady Thatcher during her initial period after leaving office. Mr. Bearpark began his career in public service in 1973 with the Overseas Development Administration, running a number of bilateral development programs in Asia and Africa.

Sylvain Beauchamp, a member of the Quebec Bar, is a practising lawyer in the field of labour law, with the firm Melançon, Marceau, Grenier and Sciortino (http://www.mmgs.qc.ca), based in Montreal. Mr. Beauchamp was formerly a Senior Policy Advisor for the organization Rights and Democracy, based in Montreal. He worked in Geneva and Zurich from 1998 to 2002 as Senior Staff Attorney for the Claims Resolution Tribunal for Dormant Accounts in Switzerland, and as an attorney specializing in international arbitration for a Geneva-based law firm from 2002 to 2004. Between 2004 and 2006, Mr. Beauchamp worked in Hebron in the West Bank as a delegate for the International Committee of the Red Cross. He also acted as Senior International Humanitarian Law Advisor for the Canadian Red Cross. Mr. Beauchamp holds an LL.M. and a PhD in international law from the Graduate Institute of International Studies (GIIS) in Geneva, and regularly lectures in the field of international law in universities in Quebec. Since 1999, he has been associated with the Jean-Pictet Competition in international humanitarian law, in particular as a regular member of the jury and as a member of the competition committee.

Pascal Bongard has been working with Geneva Call since 2000. He currently holds the positions of Programme Director for Africa and Policy Advisor. Before joining Geneva Call, he worked with the Swiss Federal Department of Foreign Affairs in Berne and with the United Nations High Commissioner for Refugees in eastern Ethiopia. He studied history at the University of Fribourg and holds Master's degrees in international relations from the Graduate Institute of International Studies in Geneva and in politics from the London School of Economics and Political Science. He authored several articles and reports on Geneva Call's experience, including *Engaging Armed Non-State Actors in a Landmine Ban: The Geneva Call Progress Report (2000-2007).*

Elisabeth Decrey Warner, president and co-founder of Geneva Call, is a physiotherapist, politician, and human rights advocate. For over twenty-five years, she has worked with various NGOs on issues relating to refugees, torture, and landmines. Her work was officially recognized in 2005 when she was nominated for Switzerland as one of the 1000 Women for the Nobel Peace Prize, and in 2006 she was awarded the International Society for Human Rights Prize. Ms. Decrey Warner was a Member of the Parliament of the Republic and Canton of Geneva for twelve years before being elected as its President in 2000. For several years, she was a member of the Board of the Interdisciplinary Programme in Humanitarian Action of the University of Geneva and of the Board of the Graduate Institute of Development Studies in Geneva. She is currently a member of the Advisory Board of the Geneva Centre for the Democratic Control of Armed Forces (DCAF).

Judi Fairholm is Director of the Canadian Red Cross program, RespectED: Violence & Abuse Prevention. She spearheaded the growth of RespectED from a grassroots initiative to a national award-winning program to prevent child/youth abuse, neglect, bullying, harassment, and interpersonal violence. In 2002, she received a Queen Elizabeth II Golden Jubilee Medal for her tireless work, and in 2007 the Florence Nightingale Medal – the highest international honour awarded by the International Committee of the Red Cross for nurses – for her contribution to child and youth safety. Since 2000, she has worked on international projects in Turkey, Sri Lanka, India, Guyana, Benin, Chad, Indonesia, Liberia, Australia, Panama, and with the IFRC Zones. Ms. Fairholm's role as educator, writer, consultant, and mentor, both nationally and internationally, has provided her with a wide skills/ knowledge base and global perspective. Her cross-cultural experience and collaborative and development skills have enhanced her work with youth, educators, health and welfare professionals, Aboriginal organizations, justice professionals, and sport and recreational organizations. In addition to her leadership of RespectED, she has worked closely with the Secretariat of the International Federation of Red Cross and Red Crescent Societies on a Global Strategy on Violence Prevention and Mitigation, a strategy that is integrated into the Federation's work until 2020.

Carlos Iván Fuentes obtained his Law and Political Sciences degree (*summa cum laude*) from the Universidad Católica Santa María La Antigua (Panama City, Panama) in 2005. In the same year, he was granted the certification to practice law in Panama. He received his LL.M. from McGill University in 2007. During his Master's studies, he worked as a legal researcher for the Special Court for Sierra Leone Clinic at McGill University and received American University's 2006 Human Rights Award (Spanish) for his essay "Protegiendo el Derecho a la Salud en el Sistema Interamericano de Derechos Humanos." Before returning to McGill to pursue his doctoral studies, Carlos Iván briefly worked for the US-based consulting firm Casals and Associates, Inc., as a legal advisor and as a grant manager in USAID's Central America Transparency and Accountability Program. He was also a seasonal lecturer on philosophy of law at the Universidad Latina de Panamá.

Carlos Iván is currently an O'Brien Fellow at the Centre for Human Rights and Legal Pluralism at McGill. He is a member of the Reading Committee of the *Revue québécoise de droit international*, the American Society of International Law, and the Centro de Iniciativas Democraticas (CIDEM), a Panamanian NGO dedicated to the promotion of human rights and democracy. He currently works as an Associate Legal Officer at the Treaty Section of the Office of Legal Affairs, United Nations. The views expressed in his contribution are his own and do not necessarily reflect the views of the United Nations.

Oliver Jütersonke is Head of Research of the Centre on Conflict, Development and Peacebuilding (CCDP) at the Graduate Institute of International and Development Studies in Geneva. He teaches Epistemology and Methods for the Graduate Institute's Master in International Affairs (MIA) program, as well as graduate-level seminars and diplomatic training sessions on peacebuilding, urban violence, and the responsibility to protect. Since 2007, he has also been a postdoctoral research fellow at the Zurich University Centre for Ethics (ZUCE). His research interests span conceptualizations of sovereignty, urban violence and development programming, and the history of political and legal theory. Recent publications include *Morgenthau, Law and Realism* (Cambridge University Press, 2010) and (with Moncef Kartas) "Ethos of Exploitation: Insecurity and Predation in Madagascar," in *Small Arms Survey 2011: States of Security* (Cambridge University Press, 2011).

Michael Khambatta worked for the International Committee of the Red Cross from 1999 to 2009, serving as the Deputy Head of the ICRC Regional Delegation in Washington, DC (covering the US and Canada) from 2007 to 2009. His previous post was at the headquarters, where he was Deputy Head of Operations for the Middle East and North Africa, covering Lebanon, Syria, Jordan, Iran, and Kuwait. His field experience includes Sarajevo, where he was Deputy Head of Delegation; Bukavu (Democratic Republic of the Congo), Peshawar, and Jalalabad, where he ran offices; as well as Kabul and Kigali, where he acted as a field delegate. Mr. Khambatta has a Master's degree from the Fletcher School of Law and Diplomacy at Tufts University, Medford, Massachusetts.

Robert Muggah is currently a Fellow at the Instituto de Relações Internacionais, Pontifícia Universidade Católica do Rio, where he directs several projects, including one on humanitarian action in situations other than war (HASOW) with the International Development Research Centre, and another on civilian rosters for peace support operations with the Brazilian, British, and Canadian governments. Dr. Muggah also works closely with the Organization for Economic Co-operation and Development, the United Nations, and the World Bank in Latin America, the Caribbean, Africa, the Middle East, South and Southeast Asia, and the South Pacific. He is also a principal of the SecDev Group (Canada) and a Research Fellow at the Graduate Institute's Centre on Conflict, Development and Peacebuilding (CCDP) (Geneva). Between 2000 and 2010, Dr. Muggah was Research Director of the Small Arms Survey and lectured at the Graduate Institute of International and Development Studies in Geneva. He is the editor and author of *The Global Burden of Armed Violence* (Cambridge University Press, 2011), *States of Fragility* (Routledge, forthcoming), *Security and Post-Conflict Reconstruction* (Routledge, 2009), *Relocation Failures in Sri Lanka* (Zed Books, 2008), *No Refuge: The Crisis of Refugee Militarization in Africa* (Zed Books, 2006), and the *Small Arms Survey* (Cambridge University Press, 2001-11). He received his D.Phil. from the University of Oxford and M.Phil. from the Institute of Development Studies, University of Sussex. His work is also published in numerous peer-reviewed and policy-relevant journals, academic volumes, and the international media.

Valerie Oosterveld is an Assistant Professor in the Faculty of Law at the University of Western Ontario, where she teaches international criminal law, international human rights law, and public international law. Before joining the faculty in 2005, she served for many years in the Legal Affairs Bureau of Foreign Affairs and International Trade Canada. She provided legal advice on international criminal accountability for genocide, crimes against humanity, and war crimes, especially with respect to the International Criminal Court, the International Criminal Tribunals for the former Yugoslavia and Rwanda, the Special Court for Sierra Leone, and other transitional justice mechanisms such as truth and reconciliation commissions. She served as a member of the Canadian delegation to the International Criminal Court negotiations and subsequent Assembly of States Parties, and was involved in the creation of the Special Court for Sierra Leone. She earned her J.S.D. and LL.M. at Columbia University Law School, LL.B. at the University of Toronto, and B.Soc.Sc. at the University of Ottawa. Her research and writing focus on gender issues within international criminal justice.

Taylor Owen is a Banting Post Doctoral Fellow at the Liu Institute for Global Issues and he teaches at the Graduate School of Journalism at the University of British Columbia (UBC). He is the Senior Editor of the Canada International Council's opencanada.org. His doctorate is from the University of Oxford where he was Trudeau Scholar. He has been a lecturer at the Trudeau Center for Peace and Conflict Studies at the University of Toronto, Research Fellow at the Center for Global Governance at the LSE, Fellow in the Genocide Studies Program at Yale University, and an Action Canada Fellow. Taylor has an MA from UBC, and has worked as a researcher at the International Peace Research Institute, Oslo, and the International Development Research Center. He is also the Research Director for the Munk Debates. He writes widely on international affairs, security, politics, and the changing nature of media.

Emily Paddon is a Lecturer and Trudeau Scholar in International Relations at the University of Oxford. Her research focuses on the United Nations, intervention, and civilian protection. She has conducted extensive field research in Central Africa, including projects for the Canadian Department of Foreign Affairs and International Trade, the Australian Government, and the Danish Refugee Council. In addition, she has worked for the International Crisis Group, Oxford Analytica, the Watson Institute for International Relations, and Goldman Sachs. She is a former Action Canada and Sauve Scholar, and a recipient of the Department of National Defence's Security and Defence Doctoral Fellowship.

Benjamin Perrin is an Assistant Professor at the University of British Columbia, Faculty of Law and a Faculty Associate at the Liu Institute for Global Issues. A member of the Law Society of British Columbia, Professor Perrin served as a law clerk to the Honourable Madam Justice Marie Deschamps of the Supreme Court of Canada, and was senior policy advisor to the Minister of Citizenship and Immigration (Canada). He was the Assistant Director of the Special Court for Sierra Leone legal clinic, which assists the Trial and Appeals Chambers, and completed an internship in Chambers at the International Criminal Tribunal for the former Yugoslavia at The Hague. He is the author of *Invisible Chains: Canada's Underground World of Human Trafficking* (Viking Canada, 2010) and co-editor of *Human Trafficking: Exploring the International Nature, Concerns, and Complexities* (CRC Press, 2012).

Pablo Policzer is an Associate Professor in Political Science and holder of the Canada Research Chair in Latin American Politics at the University of Calgary. He obtained his PhD in political science from the Massachusetts Institute of Technology, and his BA (Honours) in political science from the University of British Columbia, where he also held an I.W. Killam Post-doctoral Fellowship. His book *The Rise and Fall of Repression in Chile* (published by the University of Notre Dame Press) was named a 2009 Outstanding Academic Title by *Choice Magazine,* and won the 2010 Canadian Political Science Association award for best book in comparative politics.

René Provost holds an LL.B. from the Université de Montréal, an LL.M. from the University of California at Berkeley, and a D.Phil. from the University of Oxford. He served as law clerk to the Honourable Madam Justice Claire L'Heureux-Dubé at the Supreme Court of Canada in 1988-89, and taught international law at Lehigh University in Pennsylvania in 1991. He joined the McGill University Faculty of Law in 1994, first as a Boulton Fellow (1994-95), then as Assistant Professor (1995-2001) and Associate Professor (from 2001). He was the Associate Dean (Academic) of the Faculty of Law from 2001 to 2003. In 2005 he became the founding director of the McGill Centre for Human Rights and Legal Pluralism. He is the author of *International Human Rights and Humanitarian Law* (Cambridge University Press, 2002) and the editor of *State Responsibility in International Law* (Ashgate-Dartmouth, 2002) and *Confronting Genocide* (Springer-Verlag, 2011).

Sophie Rondeau holds an LL.B. from the Université de Montréal and an LL.M. (honours) from the Université du Québec à Montréal. Her Master's thesis addresses the notion of individual reparations in the context of violations of international humanitarian law. A member of the Quebec Bar, she served as a law clerk to the Appeals Unit of the Office of the Prosecutor of the International Criminal Tribunal for the former Yugoslavia, and was co-ordinator of the Rights and Democracy Network from 2008 until 2010. She has been involved with international humanitarian law dissemination and training, promotion of humanitarian values, and emblem protection for the Canadian Red Cross Society since 2005, where she currently serves as legal advisor for the National Office.

Fred Schreier is presently a senior consultant with the Geneva Centre for the Democratic Control of Armed Forces (DCAF). He is a graduate in international relations of the Institut Universitaire de Hautes Études Internationales, Geneva, and in strategic studies of the Fletcher School of Law and Diplomacy at Tufts University, Medford, Massachusetts. A retired colonel, he has served in various command and general staff positions, as well as in different functions within the Swiss Ministry of Defense in his role as a senior civil servant.

Gurvinder Singh works for the Canadian Red Cross as the Advisor for Violence Prevention. He has a Bachelor's degree from Simon Fraser University and a Master's degree from Royal Roads University. Over the last eleven years, he has had roles in Canada and internationally, which have included the development of national programs for the prevention of violence against children ages five to nine in Canada, Sri Lanka, and Guyana. He is currently advising projects in countries in Africa, Asia, and South America. Gurvinder has also co-authored the International Red Cross and Red Crescent Movement's first-ever global strategy on violence prevention.

Sandesh Sivakumaran is a lecturer at the School of Law and member of the Human Rights Law Centre, University of Nottingham. He has acted as an expert for the United Nations Office for the Coordination of Humanitarian Affairs, served as international law advisor to the Appeals Chamber of the Special Court for Sierra Leone, and advised on international law aspects of peace processes. Sandesh is a member of the International Law Association Committee on International Human Rights Law and a member of the Bar of the State of New York. He previously worked at the International Court of Justice and the International Criminal Tribunal for the former Yugoslavia. For his research, Sandesh has been awarded the 2009 Giorgio La Pira Prize and the 2010 Antonio Cassese Prize. He is the author of *The Law of Non-International Armed Conflict*, which is due to be published by Oxford University Press in 2012.

Jonathan Somer is a Legal Advisor and Programme Coordinator on Children and non-State Actors with Geneva Call. Previously, he worked with the Organization for Security and Cooperation in Europe on mission in Bosnia-Herzegovina and Macedonia. He has also worked as an international law consultant with the Humanitarian Policy and Conflict Research Program of Harvard University, and with the International Law Department of the Danish Ministry of Foreign Affairs. In 2007, he was awarded the

Henry Dunant Prize for research on insurgent courts and the equality of belligerents in non-international armed conflicts. He holds a BA from the University of Western Ontario, an LL.B. from the University of British Colombia, and an LL.M. from the University Centre for International Humanitarian Law, Geneva.

Jamie Williamson, a British citizen, serves as the Legal Advisor for the Washington, DC, Delegation of the International Committee of the Red Cross. In this capacity, he is responsible for legal support to the ICRC activities in the US and Canada, with particular focus on Guantanamo and the conflict in Afghanistan. From 2005 until assuming his present functions, Mr. Williamson was the ICRC Regional Legal Advisor based in Pretoria, South Africa, and assisted governments and international organizations in the implementation of international humanitarian law in Southern and Eastern Africa and the Indian Ocean. Mr. Williamson also has extensive experience in the field of international criminal justice, having previously served with the UN ad hoc international criminal tribunals in Tanzania and the Netherlands, and the Special Court for Sierra Leone. He worked on the initial landmark cases, including the first judgment on genocide. From 2002, Mr. Williamson headed the Chambers legal support section of the International Criminal Tribunal for Rwanda Appeals Chamber based in The Hague. He has published numerous papers on repression of war crimes, the regulation of private security companies in armed conflict, command responsibility, and international justice.

Valerie Yankey-Wayne is a PhD candidate at the Centre for Military and Strategic Studies at the University of Calgary. She has an M.Phil. in International Relations from the University of Cambridge, and is a Research Associate with the Armed Groups Project at the University of Calgary, as well as a member of the United Nations Expert Reference Group, reviewing International Standards on Small Arms Control. She previously served as a researcher and policy analyst with the United Nations Institute for Disarmament Research. She was also a member of the international expert panel that reviewed the draft *ECOWAS Convention on Small Arms and Light Weapons, Their Ammunition and Other Related Materials.* Valerie serves on advisory positions with a number of government and non-governmental organizations. She has provided advice and technical support to Ghana's disarmament delegation on all disarmament issues, including small arms and light weapons, Mine Action, and cluster munitions, and was part of Ghana's delegation to the UN General Assembly First Committee on Disarmament and International Security in 2008. Valerie has worked extensively on conflict management, security sector governance, and arms control programs with governments, regional bodies, and civil society groups in Africa, the Middle East, Latin America, and Europe.

Index

Notes: ICTY stands for "International Criminal Tribunal for the former Yugoslavia"; IDPs, for "internally displaced persons"; IFRC, for "International Federation of Red Cross and Red Crescent Societies"; IHL, for "international humanitarian law"; IHRL, for "international human rights law"; MSF, for "Médecins Sans Frontières"; NSAGs, for "non-state armed groups"; PMSCs, for "private military/private security companies"; PSCs, for "private security companies"

extent of, 350-51; gang membership and violence as symptom, 351-52, 353, 354; impact of community, 353(f), 354-55; impact of family/relationship, 353(f), 354; impact on children's future, 352-53; influence of society and culture, 353(f), 355-56; link with poverty, 354, 355; link with urbanization, 351; sexual exploitation, 250-51, 355; sexual violence in refugee/IDP camps, 9, 248-54; *"Street Children" Case* (Guatemala), 303-4; urban violence as global challenge, 10, 249, 290. *See also* child soldiers

violence in cities. *See* urban violence, endemic

Viva Rio NGO, 337

von Pilar, Ulrike, 247

Warner, Elisabeth Decrey, 4, 73-86

Warsaw Pact, 106

Weber, Max, 299

Weiss, Thomas, 318-19

Whole-of-Government, 267, 273

Williamson, Jamie, 7-8, 168-80

women and humanitarian space: attacks on aid workers, impact, 9, 246, 254-56; attacks on recipients of aid, 253; in Darfur refugee and IDP camps, 249-50, 259; gender-based and sexual violence in humanitarian space, 9, 248-54, 259, 260n14, 260n21; narrowing of humanitarian space, impact, 246, 248, 250, 253, 255, 256; sexual exploitation by aid workers/UN personnel, 250-52, 262n47; testimony of women victims about sexual violence, 9, 257-58, 264n86; underreporting of sexual exploitation and abuse, 252; victims of gender-based violence and sexual violence during war, 9; women a large percentage of refugee or IDP population, 247-48

World Food Programme, 133

World Health Organization, 349, 350, 356-57

World Report on Violence against Children (WHO), 350-51

World Report on Violence and Health (WHO), 349-50

Yankey-Wayne, Valerie, 5, 102-20

Printed and bound in Canada by Friesens

Set in Futura Condensed and Warnock Pro by Artegraphica Design

Copy editor: Francis Chow

Proofreader: Helen Godolphin

Indexer: Patricia Buchanan